Sister Sunshine

The Martha Carson Story

*To Emily
Season's Greetings
Doris & Walt Trott
'2004'*

Sister Sunshine
The Martha Carson Story

by

Walt Trott

BOOKS
Nashville

Copyright © 1998, 2000 by Walt Trott

All rights reserved.
No part of this book may be reproduced, stored in a retrieval system, or transmitted by any means, electronic, mechanical, photocopying, recording, or otherwise, without written permission from the author.
Inquiries should be addressed to 1stBooks, or Nova/Nashville, P.O. Box 477, Madison TN 37116-0477.

ISBN: 1-58820-711-0

Library of Congress

1stBooks – rev. 12/11/00

Acknowledgements

We are indebted to the many artists, associates, friends and family of Martha Carson, who have so generously given of their time and thoughts to this project through the years. Invaluable sources of information have included the Ben West Public Library of Nashville, Country Music Foundation, WSM's *Grand Ole Opry*, Renfro Valley Barn Dance, WSB-Atlanta, University of Georgia, AFM Nashville Association of Musicians, the publications *Billboard, Nashville Musician, Country Music People, Country Music News, Entertainment Express, Music City News, Cash Box, Nashville Banner, The Tennessean,* weekly *Variety,* and Broadcast Music, Inc. (BMI), Acuff/Rose, Cox Communications, the record labels Bear Family, Capitol, RCA, Sims, Scripture, Dot, Gusto, and especially Martha Carson, Minnie Garcia, Don Chapel, Gertrude Ramsey, Andre Cosse, Rene Cosse, Kenneth Woodruff, Lana Kolb, Bill Carlisle, Harold Bradley, Scott Turner, Chet Atkins, James Roberts, Kitty Wilson, Faron Young, Ken Nelson, Dee Kilpatrick, Floyd Cramer, Joe Edwards, George McCormick, Buddy Harman, Kitty Wells, Vic Willis, Connie Smith, Skeeter Davis, Mac Wiseman, Arnold Rogers, Lightnin' Chance, Bob Saxton, Eddie Stubbs, John Bell, Charlie Lamb, Bill Gaither, Helen Hopgood, Larry Black, Jean Shepard, Grandpa Jones, Doris Trott, Johnny Wright, Marlene Sloan, Hal Smith, Phyllis Hill, Kathy Shepard, Win Trott, Charlie Dick, Steve Eng, Ruth White, Charles Wolfe, Randall Frank, John Glasscock, Rob Hoyer and Chris Rennie. Cover photo courtesy of RCA Records, and other portraits or pictures courtesy of Martha Carson, Harold Bradley, Arnold Rogers, James Roberts, Patricia Presley and the private collection of Walt Trott.

Dedicated to the Sunshine Sisters --

& Gertrude, their inspirational mom.

Bibliography

Eric Blom's "Everyman's Dictionary of Music" (St. Martin's Press, New York City, 1973); Larry Fotine's "Contemporary Musicians' Handbook & Dictionary" (PolyTone Press, Sepulveda, Calif., 1978), Joseph A. Tunzi's "Elvis Sessions II" (JAT Publications, Chicago, 1996), "Motion Picture Film Daily" (Brulatour, Hollywood, 1938), Joel Whitburn's "Pop Memories, 1890-1954" (Record Research, Inc., Menomonee Falls, Wisc., 1986), Whitburn's "Top Country Singles" (Record Research, 1989), "The Encyclopedia of Country Music" (Oxford University Press, N.Y., 1998), Irwin Stambler-Grelun Landon's "Encyclopedia of Folk, Country & Western Music" (St. Martin's Press, 1969), Bill Malone's "The Smithsonian Collection of Classic Country Music" (Smithsonian, Washington, D.C., 1981), Neal Umphred's "Goldmine's Price Guide to Collectible Record Albums" (Krause, Iola, Wisc., 1989), Jerry Osborne's "Country Music Buyers-Sellers Reference Book & Price Guide" (Osborne Enterprises Ltd., Tempe, Ariz., 1984) and particularly, Webster's New World Dictionary.

Foreword

During the late 1940s, I was featured on WSB Atlanta's *Barn Dance,* where one of the most popular acts was Martha and James Carson. Known as the "Barn Dance Sweethearts," they delighted audiences with their gospel duets.

The Carsons became my personal friends, as well.

After I played KWKH Shreveport, I accepted an offer from Lowell Blanchard to perform on WNOX radio in Knoxville. Next thing I knew, Martha and James were sharing the stage with me again on WNOX's *Mid-Day Merry-Go-Round.* It was also about this time that the couple broke up - and James left the troupe.

Radio performances had created a demand for personal appearances, so we teamed up to do numerous shows within nightly driving distance of Knoxville. Martha, now doing a solo, was often backed by her sister and brother-in-law.

With her marriage over, I knew the deeply religious Martha was going through an especially trying time in her life. Some unknowing fans were less than charitable to this lovely lady, blaming her for the divorce. This further distressed her.

When she sank about as low as she could spiritually, Martha found solace in song, admittedly with a lot of influence from our Maker. This happened in 1951, while we were on tour and driving in my car.

Out of the blue, Martha Carson was inspired to compose her greatest success, "Satisfied." I believe she jotted the lyrics down on a piece of paper picked up off the car's backseat floorboard.

That unique song lifted her spirits more than anything else could have. Of course, we loved Martha and were happy she was able to turn herself around, where she was now "Satisfied" with her new life and able to soar to new heights professionally.

Martha has a great sense of humor and I remember our having a lot of laughs along the way.

She passed some of her good luck on to The Carlisles, as well, sharing her pickin' talents with us on some successful singles. I also sang backup on her million-selling "Satisfied."

I don't know of any other female artist who can entertain a crowd and lift their spirits as much as Martha Carson. Not only is she an exciting, upbeat performer, she's a real champion and the greatest truly Christian lady I've ever known.

I am grateful for all my years of friendship with this dedicated artist, who wrote and lives by her classic gospel theme "I'm Gonna Walk and Talk With My Lord."

Bless her, she's still doing that. Amen.

- Bill Carlisle

Author's Introduction

Meet Martha Carson...

A Cinderella who found that the slipper didn't fit, Martha Carson stunned the music world by saying goodbye to the *American dream*.

Martha Carson's late 1951 recording of her self-penned "Satisfied" was an overnight sensation - and a ticket to stardom. The lady's husky vocals and unique performing style made her records instantly recognizable to fans - an important asset to a singer. Among those boasting such a recognition factor on the secular scene were Jimmie Rodgers, Bob Wills, Ernest Tubb and Hank Williams. Other Carson peers who emerged with personal identifiable sounds were Hank Snow, Webb Pierce, Ray Price and Kitty Wells.

Indeed *Martha Carson* stood on top of the world professionally, a pioneer in her own gospel technique, very much in-demand by booking agents for concert and national TV appearances. Her songwriting provided diverse hits for other non-gospel artists, most notably R&B's Clyde McPhatter, pop idol Johnnie Ray and country star Faron Young, while her exciting syncopated alto vocals and dynamic stage presence had a stylistic influence on such later classic entertainers as Elvis Presley, Brenda Lee, Sleepy LaBeef, Barbara Mandrell and Connie Smith.

As an artist, Martha Carson deserves a revival because she *has* influenced so many important performers and even the genre of rock 'n roll. Several seasons back, she was on a package show in Florida, where legendary headliner George Jones sidled up to her and said, "I thought I'd tell you, Martha. I've copied your phrasing in some of my songs..."

By the mid-1950s, Carson was a titian-haired, statuesque beauty on a major record label and a popular star of the *Grand Ole Opry*. Professionally, she had everything going for her. Yet, she chucked it all for motherhood. Some say she allowed herself to be guided in the wrong direction. Whatever the facts, she never fulfilled the commercial promise shown as a recording artist.

Martha Carson's story traces a woman's journey through life, professionally marred by a dominating desire to be a wife and mother. That wouldn't seem sad at all, if her choice had been appreciated by those she loved and turned to for a similar warmth and understanding.

Arguably the lady's taste in men was less than ideal.

The first mate appears to have been a philanderer, while her second husband sometimes treated her indifferently. As a result, Martha Carson was deeply repressed by the mental and emotional abuse suffered at the hands of the men in her life. Through her faith in God, she survived all obstacles.

During the 1940s, when radio was king, she and her duet partner-husband were celebrated as WSB-Atlanta's "Barn Dance Sweethearts." Their gospel successes impressed Tex Ritter, prompting Capitol Records to sign them, paving the way for what should-have-been an enviable future. However, once the strain of an unhappy private life became too much of a burden to bear, Martha divorced James legally and professionally.

Then, with a realization *she* was being blamed by fans for the breakup of the "perfect marriage," Martha sank deeper into depths of depression. Ironically, it was that very sadness which inspired her to write a song she called "Satisfied," that provided the wings to lift her spiritually to the very *top of the mountain*. The song made her a major artist and encouraged the *Opry* to invite her, its first female gospel star, to join the regular roster of performers in the spring of '52.

An abiding faith continues to sustain this Kentucky lady through peaks and valleys of a tumultuous life. Martha Carson has made her own pact with God. She speaks with him daily and promises to forever sing his praise; but, in turn, she takes no part in the formality of churchgoing. An indomitable spirit, she has an ongoing thing against both musical and religious hypocrisy.

Despite setbacks in her life, Martha Carson confides that today she's truly "Satisfied."

If it were possible for the wonderful, inspiring music she has made to be heard from the pages of this book, then without a doubt, it would be a best seller!

- Walt Trott

CHAPTER 1

'We're <u>Satisfied</u> with Martha...'

"Don Chapel was the night clerk and, like Mom, was hell-bent on making it as a singer and songwriter. He was still struggling but had family connections: one of his sisters, Martha, was a singer and had at least made it to the *minor leagues* of country music; another sister, Jean, was a talented writer and a published one to boot."

This appears in "Tammy Wynette - A Daughter Recalls Her Mother's Tragic Life and Death," a biographical book by Jackie Byrd Daly (with a writing assist from author Tom Carter).

Sadly, it seems to sum up what new generations of people are writing and saying about Martha Carson, who not only achieved success in the duet James & Martha Carson during the 1940s as a Capitol Records act, but went on as a solo artist to write and record a million-selling gospel song "Satisfied." She headlined on both the WSB-Atlanta *Barn Dance* and the WNOX-Knoxville's *Mid-Day Merry-Go-Round,* and on the strength of such achievements, Capitol's gospel star was the first female solo singer signed to WSM's *Grand Ole Opry.*

Her importance as an influential entertainer and ground-breaking artist cannot be overstated, despite revisionists who attempt to take "Quantum Leaps" and alter historical fact. Sadly, many of today's writers and researchers are lazy, relying only on the printed word found in trade publications like *Cash Box* or *Billboad.* Trade journals pretty much ignored "Hillbilly, Race and Gospel" records, occasionally tossing them a bone with a Top 10 listing, or rather whatever number their weekly space available allowed, be it five or eight lines.

"You mean Martha Carson never charted?," asks an incredulous Jim Ed Brown, in a recent interview with this writer.

"Why, she was a *really great entertainer.* I can't believe she didn't make the charts!"

Brown, whose career commenced much later than Martha's, also sold millions of records, including the three-million-selling 1959 classic "Three Bells," which made country, pop - and R&B charts.

The likes of Elvis Presley, George Jones, Kitty Wells, Tex Ritter, Johnnie Ray, Stuart Hamblen, Skeeter Davis, Faron Young, Brenda Lee, Johnnie & Jack, Barbara Mandrell, Tommy Sands, Connie Smith and Clyde McPhatter would be equally surprised to learn Martha Carson never made it as a *star!...*or beyond the "minor leagues."

Even Tammy Wynette, Martha's former sister-in-law, told of a time when her *Mamaw* and *Papaw* drove many miles from their near-Mississippi farmstead to see Martha Carson's show in Alabama -- *and* about how inspiring this beautiful lady was to an impressionable 9-year-old, who could only dream of one day being a singer on stage at the *Grand Ole Opry.*

More recently, April 2000 publicity blurbs in England's slick *Country Music People* fan magazine, and the American Federation of Musicians' union trade paper *The Nashville Musician* proclaimed: *"Gospel great Martha Carson will be guest of honor during dedication ceremonies Sept. 9 (2000) in her old hometown Neon, Ky., to witness a stretch of highway named after the lady, who created the hits 'Satisfied,' 'I'm Gonna Walk and Talk With My Lord' and 'I Can't Stand Up Alone'..."*

This was not news to the septuagenarian, who had learned several years ago of the planned project. It was only the final step, getting the signs up. Forgive us Alan Jackson (who cited *Muric Row* in his song), but *Lord don't the wheels move slow on Legislative Row.*

Actually on Thursday, Sept. 26, 1996, the officials in Neon initially made her aware of their proposal, by inviting Martha and her family to participate in a *"Martha Carson Day."* The fiery-haired guest of honor rode high as Grand Marshal in a parade that launched the festivities, cruising across town in a bright red convertible car.

"Martha Carson Comes Home!" read the banner! How fitting that in the diamond anniversary year of her birth, the gospel singer was being remembered by her home state, with the announcement that a portion of Bluegrass highway would be named for her. It was a memorable occasion - and her beloved mom was there to share the honor.

Occurring to the entertainer was the fact that it had taken only hours to drive the distance from her home in Nashville to attend the Neon ceremony, "but Lordy, it was a long journey from Neon to Nashville, originally!" On the circuitous route she'd traveled, it took 15 years from the first professional gig until she starred on the *Grand Ole Opry*, the top of the mountain for a country girl in her day.

On behalf of the Kentucky House of Representatives, Rep. Paul Mason extended best wishes to one of the State's Favorite Daughters. The Commonwealth of Kentucky's important-looking document, was co-signed Sept. 4, 1996, by Mason and Speaker of the House Jody Richards.

The parchment declared it was awarded, "In recognition of her distinguished career in Country and Gospel music. Martha Carson left Letcher County at the age of 17, to pursue her dream. With her exceptional voice, Ms. Carson was one of the first women appearing on the *Renfro Valley Barn (Dance)* show and at the *Grand Ole Opry*. Martha Carson can be credited with helping Elvis Presley become the 'King.' After 58 years in the music business, Ms. Carson continues to follow her lifelong career by writing and performing. The entire membership extends its very best wishes and expresses the hope for continued good fortune."

Not bad for a gal born in the backwoods of coal-mining country. But there were even more accolades to come:

U.S. Vice President Al Gore, Jr., wired her, noting specifically, "I am pleased to have this opportunity to extend my personal greetings as you are honored with the dedication of a federal highway in your name...I would like to add my congratulations to those of your family and friends at this special time. Certainly, you are more than deserving of this tremendous honor. Your contributions to the music industry are truly remarkable. I am especially pleased to congratulate a fellow Tennessee resident. I am confident that you will enjoy continued success in the future."

Adopted home state Rep. Bob Clement (D-Tenn.) called Martha Carson "a national treasure" insisting, "I could not let this day pass without letting you know how I feel: Martha, what can I say about someone who has had such an impact on the lives of others, including me and the entire Clement family. Through the years, you have been a shining example to many thousands of young men and women, who have had a fire in their hearts to express what they felt with music. Your country and gospel roots have been a blessing to everyone who hears your songs or watches you perform...how appropriate to have a federal highway named in your honor!

"I would also like to say *thank you* for the highway of life you have traveled from Neon to Nashville, and beyond," continued Clement. "Along the way, you have made us laugh, cry and evaluate the things in life which are important through your music. My prayer today is that everyone who travels 'your' highway will find the strength, hope and love you have found on your journey. May you continue to receive God's blessings, and congratulations again on the dedication taking place today in your hometown."

Martha smiles. "My son René was a little late coming in from Knoxville. He arrived just as the parade kicked off. He said, 'If I knew it was this big and that it would be so crowded, I'd have left yesterday to get up here. I had to park in the next town to get close enough!'"

Visibly touched, she points out, "Everyone of my family came in for the event. My sister Minnie and brother Conley came up on stage and performed with me and the Opry's Joe Edwards, who was in my band. My producer, Scotty Turner, played guitar and sang -- and we all just had a beautiful time."

The Little League even had T-shirts made up, citing *"Martha Carson Comes Home!"* Her fan club's T-shirt pictured a color shot of Martha on the back, and the emblazoned logo: *"We're **Satisfied** with Martha Carson"!*

Club members, who drove in for the occasion, presented her with a big bouquet of roses. In summation, she added, "I never had my heart overflow so much for anything. It was the most touching tribute."

The gospel queen's 95-year-old widowed mother was elated. "Momma sat down and played the piano...going up there was like therapy for her. She was visiting her sister's daughter's place. And you know that l'il ol' cowpath leading up to our place in Goose Creek hasn't changed a lick in 40 years!"

Martha reminisces further. "I remember when I was about 9 or 10 and I'd go sit under an old apple tree, and I began writing songs. Of course, I felt they were so inferior, that I just threw them in a waste can."

But had Irene Amburgey changed so much? In her travels she had gained a lot of different names, some legal and some *nom de plumes* (stage names), ranging from Sunshine Sister to Hoot Owl Holler Girl (Marthie) to Mrs. James Roberts and Martha Carson, and finally, Mrs. Xavier Cossé. Still, through many trials and tribulations, she maintained the strength to follow a long-ago dream to play music, thanks to her faith.

On the day after Martha arrived back in *Music City USA* from her "Old Kentucky Home," she was scheduled to host the Saturday night WSM *Midnight Jamboree* (Sept. 28, 1996), her old radio stomping ground. The entertainer was pleased to have *Doodle Ooo Doo Doo* Del Reeves as her very special guest. Del and Martha were friends, having first met when he was struggling to get his career off the ground (before "Girl On the Billboard") and she was the headliner. Of course, the *Midnight Jamboree* is not known in the trade for great guest fees.

"Still, it's a delightful show to play - and when you get on stage and feel the love coming up from the crowd, it just energizes you," notes an enthusiastic Carson. "To know that the people love you, that's the biggest payday in the world to me."

Another important gig for Carson was a reunion show at the Ryman Auditorium, featuring a star-studded line-up of yesteryear acts, including Freddie Hart, Lonzo (a new version, Ken Lattimore) & Oscar (Oscar Sullivan), Bashful Brother Oswald (Pete Kirby), Speck Rhodes and Leona Williams, plus veteran announcer T. Tommy Cutrer and Scott Miller's 14-piece orchestra. Belting out her signature song "Satisfied," Martha was clearly the showstopper.

Of course, the downtown Ryman was once home to the *Grand Ole Opry* - and brought back a lot of memories of the effervescent star's glory days: "They've got more Martha Carson sweat in that wood than they could ever scrub out with a barrel of lye water. It's really nice now; they've done a beautiful job, but I loved it just the way it was. I remember we girls had to change costumes in the *privvy* because there weren't enough dresssing rooms - and there was no air-conditioning! It was also drafty in the winter; but, there was such a warmth with the people back then that just doesn't exist in the place out at Opryland."

``It's a wonderful feeling in that building,'' agrees Porter Wagoner, an Opry cast member since Feb. 23, 1957. ``The sound is great, and people are so close to the stage, it's like entertaining at your home.''

The century-old Ryman, a former church, and the Lower Broad neighborhood deteriorated in the 1970s and the Opry left for the suburbs, but refurbishment of the building has helped bring about a revival of the area, and it was reopened as a concert hall.

As recently as April 2000, Martha was headlining almost weekly in the Old Embers club, located in the touristy Printers Alley, and on July 30, 2000, guested again with Reeves on the *Midnight Jamboree,* earning yet another standing ovation..

Reputedly passive in her relationships with the men in her life, Martha is anything *but* when it comes to performing. Carson is a creative, free spirit musically, facts not lost on those who enjoy her most successful songs, including standbys like "Old Blind Barnabus," "Let the Light Shine On Me" and "Lazarus."

Faron Young enjoyed an early Top Five *Billboard* hit on her composition "I Can't Wait (For the Sun To Go Down)" for Capitol Records. He told the author, "Martha Carson was a class artist. She was also a beautiful woman, inside and out, like a big sister to me. I think she was terribly underrated in this business, but I know for a fact that several of the very biggest (stars) were influenced by her performing style. I was."

"Back when I was the new kid on Capitol, she was their bright hope with 'Satisfied.' Then, shortly after she signed to the Opry, I was given a two-week trial run at WSM myself. Of course, she had headlined on the (WNOX) *Mid-Day Merry-Go-Round* and I had already been on (KWKH's) *Louisiana Hayride*, but Capitol wanted us on the Opry - and I was still in the Army."

Even while in uniform, Young returned on leave to perform in Nashville, and can be seen in a number of the filmed Al Gannaway *Classic Country* shows, sharing the stage with friend Martha (also her sister Mattie O'Neil and hubby Salty Holmes).

Prior to departing for boot camp at Fort Jackson, S.C., on Nov. 25, 1952, Faron went into the studio (Oct. 12) to record some songs, including his first two hits: "Goin' Steady," which he wrote and first charted Jan. 10, 1953, continuing through May, hitting #2 spot; and Carson's "I Can't Wait," which charted June 6, peaking at #5 a few weeks later. (It was actually Young's ninth recording for Capitol.)

Young - who apparently due to ill health, took his own life (dying from a self-inflicted gunshot wound Dec. 10, 1996) - had enjoyed a distinguished career, charting *Billboard* country and pop nearly 100 times during four decades, including #1 million sellers "Hello Walls" (1961) and "It's Four in the Morning" (1971).

Ever candid, he attempted to explain the pioneer's inability to attain the prefix "super" in front of her "star" stature: "The problem was with Capitol, not Martha. She knew how to perform! The *sum'bitches* just didn't know how to promote her; I think mainly because there were really no country/gospel artists back then. Oh sure, (Red) Foley and Stuart Hamblen were singing gospel songs occasionally, but they also had country hits that the label could get a handle on. As far as I know, Martha would only do the *holy roller* songs, and there were no radio stations or gospel charts for her sort of music. She was just really *different.*

"We did a package touring show together (as headliners), which featured a couple of new guys, Ferlin Husky and Elvis Presley, and these two were watching Martha Carson on stage, tearin' 'em up out there! She was something else! I think the only thing Ferlin had going for him at the time were a couple of duets with Jeannie Shepard -- recitations on his part -- and Elvis...why he didn't even have a damn chart record. But these two fellows soon became our most dynamic entertainers."

Not so coincidentally, Faron, Martha and Ferlin were all Capitol recording artists, while newcomer Elvis was then cutting his platters at the fledgling Sun Studios in Memphis for Sam Phillips. Later, both Elvis and Martha recorded for RCA.

During Faron's and Martha's latter bookings with the phenomenal Presley, the newcomer's "Baby, Let's Play House" broke out big for Sun. Faron joshed, "When we went to Amarillo (Texas), and he was really gettin' hot with the fans, he was driving an old Cadillac limousine, while I had a brand new Caddie. We'd park the cars out back of the venue, but when the teen girls came prowling around, they assumed the new car was Elvis's. So for souvenirs, they'd swipe things off my damn car! By the time I got back to Nashville, it cost $2,700 to put the car back into the shape it was, before I went out with Elvis. I'll never forget that."

Young confided that he considered Carson the next real superstar: "She could move you or lift you emotionally. Then when she got married, her husband, X. Cossé, tried to make a glamour puss out of her. He got her out of those gingham dresses, put her into sexy gowns, all at cross purposes with the woman's persona, and then he started booking her into plush New York nightclubs. Poor Martha didn't know whether to sh-- or get off the pot!"

[Ironically, Elvis Presley and Tammy Wynette went into the Country Music Hall of Fame in 1998, followed by Faron Young in 2000, all sad to say, posthumously.]

Another country star whose opinion Martha values is the Opry's Connie Smith, who joined the prestigious show in 1971, hot-on-the-heels of such spectacular hits as "Once a Day," "Cincinnati, Ohio" and "I Never Once Stopped Loving You."

The petite blonde singing star (now Mrs. Marty Stuart) notes, "I've mentioned her so much on stage. I remember especially seeing her at the Pan Theatre in Boston, Ohio, and when she sang up there with the red hair and curls hanging down, with that voice of her's, with all its power and the pep she has; she's just so dynamic on stage! It was truly inspiring. If she had marched off stage then and bid us all to come along, I would have followed her like she was the Pied Piper."

Walt Trott

CHAPTER 2

Musical roots. .

*"Songs such as 'The Old Rugged Cross'...were too depressing for me.
I always wanted to play happy music."*
- Martha Carson

Martha Carson admits she's not a fan of all contemporary Christian music.

She's not surprised, however, that Christian genre artists like CeCe Winans, Sandy Patti, Carman, Steven Curtis Chapman, Michael W. Smith and Amy Grant can now outsell most country acts: "It doesn't surprise me in one sense, because they have another vehicle to work with we never had - music videos. I think videos and the exposure they offer are a real shot-in-the-arm to an artist today."

When her career was getting off the ground, country gospel was regarded as a minority music, though she did much to spread its popularity.

How did Martha Carson's music and performing style evolve?

Hymnology, of course, dates back to the days of that Catholic maverick Martin Luther (1483-1546) and his fellow Germans. Historically, Luther was the leader of the Protestant Reformation and founder of the Lutheran church. He objected to the Catholic doctrine of salvation by merit and sale of indulgences; thus, in 1517 in Wittenberg, Germany, he planted the seeds of Lutheranism. Martin Luther made major contributions to Protestant theology and inspired salvation by faith alone through grace.

Some two centuries later, America's first Sunday school was reportedly founded in Savannah, Ga. (1736). Evangelist John

Wesley (1703-1791), founder of Methodism, was then-minister of Christ Church there. He allegedly also wrote a book of hymns while in Savannah, which was the first hymnal used by the Church of England. Ironically, Savannah is the home of America's first black Baptist congregation, which gathered in 1788.

The toe-tapping, soul-searching sounds that appeal to Martha Carson are derived from the same sort of "Hallelujah" music that so enthralled the black race. Religious or not, many people enjoy the stirring musical style also known as *spirituals*.

According to Eric Blom's "Everyman's Dictionary of Music" (New American Library, St. Martin's Press, New York, 1973), these are "negro song(s) of the Southern states of the USA, with religious words and folk song tunes. One of the chief influences from which jazz and *swing* have sprung."

A similar view of spiritual music comes from Larry Fotine's "Contemporary Musicians Handbook & Dictionary" (PolyTone Press, Sepulveda, Calif., 1978): "A type of syncopated religious song especially developed by black Americans in the Southern U.S. Basically the melodies tend to be quite simple, but the rhythmic syncopations may at time become so complex that it is treated as a secular song with 'pop' characteristics."

Unquestionably, blacks have influenced popular and country music. One of country's most formidable instruments is the banjo, believed to be of African origin, a favored instrument of Negro slaves. Still, as far back as 1835, white evangelist William Walker published a book of hymns titled "Southern Harmony." The publisher wrote many of the songs included in numerous editions of his book, among these the melody for the classic "Amazing Grace." Its lyrics were mainly derived from 18th century hymnist John Newton, a former English sailor-turned-minister.

Black church leaders initially rejected *gospel* singing in their houses of worship. Like white counterparts, the black hierarchy had permitted hymnals as part of the religious service.

The positive, pulsating upbeat spirituals, however, were indeed frowned upon - for a long while.

It was through the efforts and talents of such pioneers as Thomas A. Dorsey, one of America's greatest composers, that spirituals became acceptable in church. (He was born July 1, 1899 in Villa Rica, Ga.) "Down through the ages, gospel was good news," noted Dorsey, who wrote such classics as "Take My Hand, Precious Lord" and "(There'll Be) Peace in the Valley." Dorsey, who lived in Chicago, pointed out that Pilgrim Baptist Church in the Windy City formed the first black gospel choir.

"I've been thrown out of some of the best churches...many, many people have been helped and saved by gospel," said Dorsey, who originally wrote about 300 blues songs, including some for Ma Rainey. "Then the voice of God whispered to me, 'You need to change a little.'"

One of Dorsey's most enduring spirituals, "Take My Hand, Precious Lord," had a very painful inspiration for the preacher. It began with a trip he made to St. Louis for a religious revival meet. On the day after he arrived, Reverend Dorsey received a Western Union telegram informing him that his wife had died: "Come Home!"

He recalled, "Some fellows volunteered to drive me to Chicago, and when I got home, I had the body moved. I had a bouncing boy baby. But that night, the baby died, too. That was double trouble. I felt like going back on God, feeling He had mistreated me. About a week later, after burying my wife and baby in the same casket, I was sitting with the late Theodore Fry...and just like water dripping from the crevice of a rock, the words dropped into the music, 'Take My Hand, Precious Lord, Lead Me Home.'"

"I am tired, I am weak, I am worn/Thru the storm, thru the night, lead me on to the light/Take my hand, precious Lord, lead me home..." (c) 1938, Thomas A. Dorsey. (Hill & Range Songs/Unichappell Music, Inc./RightSong Music, Publisher.)

[Not so surprisingly, the Nashville Songwriters Association International, in recognition of his musical influence on country songwriters, installed The Reverend Dorsey in NSAI's Hall of Fame in 1979. He died Jan. 25 1993, at age 93.]

Situated in Chicago, too, was the South Side Greater Salem Baptist Church, where beloved vocalist Mahalia Jackson became the featured singer at age 16. She later gave recitals in Carnegie Hall in New York City and toured abroad, performing her last concert overseas in Munich.

Born in New Orleans in 1911, Jackson at her peak boasted deep, rich contralto vocals with a spell-binding quality that thrilled listeners. As one of the nation's greatest spiritual singers, she rejected offers to perform blues or jazz, proclaiming "anybody singing the blues is in a deep pit yelling for help. And, I'm not simply in that kind of position."

Her 1948 record release of "I Will Move On Up a Little Higher," which she also wrote, sold more than a million copies and charted pop. Jackson's spiritual "Didn't It Rain" appeared on the national *Your Hit Parade* TV show in 1954. Following Mahalia Jackson's last media interview, conducted with this writer (then-*European Stars & Stripes* daily newspaper entertainment editor), the lady was hospitalized in Munich, before being air-evacuated back to the U.S., where she died Jan. 27, 1972.

Another classic composer was W. C. Handy, known as "Father of the Blues," who before switching to singing spirituals, wrote such standards as "Memphis Blues," "Beale Street Blues" and "St. Louis Blues," the latter one of America's most recorded compositions.

He was born William Christopher Handy on Nov. 16, 1873, in Florence, Ala., son of a preacher. After years as a bandleader (playing cornet and piano), W.C. dedicated his days to teaching music and performing religious songs. Handy died totally blind in 1958, the year that Nat (King) Cole portrayed him in a movie biography "St. Louis Blues," which premiered April 9.

Handy's "St. Louis Blues" proved that black blues and country go hand-in-hand soulfully, as several country-oriented groups have recorded this perennial favorite, notably Bob Wills and his Texas Playboys, Milton Brown and his Brownies and the Callahan Brothers. For his contributions, W. C. Handy was inducted into the Nashville Songwriters Association International's Hall of Fame in 1983, the same year the "Coal Miner's Daughter," Loretta Lynn, was voted in.

Yet another 20th century songwriter Albert E. Brumley confided that he was so inspired by Guy Massey's 1924 country classic "The Prisoner's Song," country's first multi-million seller, that he eventually created his legendary gospel tune "I'll Fly Away." According to Brumley, "I was pickin' cotton on my father's farm and was humming the old ballad (as performed by Vernon Dalhart, Massey's cousin) that went *'If I had the wings of an angel, over these prison walls I would fly,'* when it occurred to me I could use that plot for a gospel song."

In 1932, Oklahoma-born Brumley finally got his country-inspired spiritual published and it became a runaway best seller. (Martha Carson's 1964 version of the spirited composition on Scripture Records, is a *must have* for any true fan of gospel.) Other gospel songs the white composer of Powell, Mo., created include "Turn Your Radio On," "He Set Me Free" and "Jesus Hold My Hand." Songs such as these still evoke the spirit of the good old *brush arbor* days, and no doubt account for Brumley being named to the NSAI Hall of Fame as one of the original 21 songwriter inductees in 1970.

The full-volume, open-throated, upbeat style developed by Martha Carson is a sound anchored in the Appalachian tradition, free flowing from the literal fundamentalism that crystalized among Southern rural religious sects. She helped replace the sedate spiritual singing of her parents generation with a style emphasizing the deliberate, driving rhythms of the archaic ring shouts, with instrumental accompaniment.

Still, more traditional gospel numbers are all some spectators care to hear. For instance, 91-year-old George Beverly Shea managed to enthrall 45,000 people, while performing at a Billy Graham Crusade in Nashville's Adelphia Stadium, June 1, 2000.

Shea simply sang his signature song "How Great Thou Art," a 19th century Swedish folk melody to which English lyrics were added by The Reverend Stuart K. Hines. Incidentally, George Beverly Shea, who surely ranks as one of the all-time vocal gospel greats, shared a 1965 best gospel Grammy Award with the then-Music City-based Anita Kerr Singers, for their collaborative RCA album "Southland Favorites."

Yet another 1970 NSAI inductee - and Country Music Hall of Famer - Merle Travis (1917-1983), rewrote "I Am a Pilgrim," a song he learned from Kentuckian Mose Rager, who, in turn, had learned it from a now-anonymous black singer. Its gospel flavor played no small part in its appeal to country fans as Travis' distinct vocals and pickin' style made it a popular 1946 Capitol recording. (Martha Carson does it full justice on her 1965 RCA Camden LP "Martha Carson Sings.")

Historians have noted the tremendous influence blacks have had on country music, including the fact that the banjo was supposedly brought to the Western hemisphere by African slaves. Reportedly, the instrument owed its existence to Arab traders in Africa. It became a favorite accompaniment among mountain folk, and today is a staple of bluegrass bands. (The guitar, derived by the Spanish and Portuguese from the African Moors, came along later.)

The traditional folk favorite "John Henry," obstensibly about a black laborer, is probably one of the most recorded songs by white country acts. Bluegrass favorites, the Lilly Brothers, Burt and Everett (distant cousins to Connie Smith), recorded a version in 1957, now enshrined in the Smithsonian Collection of *Classic Country Music*.

(For several decades "John Henry" was a mainstay among *Grand Ole Opry* groups, performing and enlivening the famed Saturday night show.)

Spiritual songs feature a simple melodic style, with occasional use of modes or of a pentatonic scale. Its rhythms are frequently syncopated and its harmonies are similar to, and possibly modeled on those of the mission hymns of white communities. In Appalachia, traditional Scottish, Irish and English dance music survived, accompanied by folk fiddling.

Still, the religious songs of the African-Americans are recognized as the first indigenous music, attracting much attention and its fame spread by means of traveling choral groups from educational establishments.

Martha Carson recalls as a youngster going to hear her parents' family gospel quartet perform at religious gatherings.

"They traveled to all the singing conventions and sang songs such as 'The Old Rugged Cross,' which were too depressing for me. I always wanted to play happy music."

Religious songs have long been an important part of a country singer's repertoire. Most country radio broadcasts of yesteryear closed with a sacred song. Such songs were the influences felt by many of the future stars, particularly those raised in rural settings like Martha and her siblings.

Many acts started out singing gospel songs, among them the Oak Ridge Boys, Louvin Brothers, Statler Brothers and Amy Grant before going secular. Some like Jimmie Davis, Molly O'Day, Barbara Fairchild and Paul Overstreet started singing country then switched to the gospel they love. Still others, notably Tennessee Ernie Ford, Wilma Lee Cooper, Connie Smith and Roy Drusky, managed to alternate popular and sacred songs in their repertoire, attesting to strong feelings of faith.

Martha Carson has recorded her share of the great gospel standards. Her 1964 Scripture album includes nothing but gospel evergreens, including "He'll Understand and Say Well Done," "Just a Closer Walk With Thee" and "Lonesome Valley."

Among individual gospel recordings that have proven lucrative for country artists are Jimmie Rodgers' "The Wonderful City," the Carter Family's "Can the Circle Be Unbroken," Roy Acuff's "The Great Speckled Bird," Cowboy Copas' "Purple Robe" and "From the Manger to the Cross," Maddox Bros. & Rose's "Gathering Flowers For the Master's Bouquet," Molly O'Day's "30 Pieces of Silver," Leon Payne's "Gentle Hands," Don Reno & Red Smiley's "I'm Using My

Bible For a Roadmap," Foley's other gospel clicks "Steal Away," "Just a Closer Walk With Thee" and "Our Lady of Fatima."

Who can forget Elton Britt and Rosalie Allen's "Beyond the Sunset," Jimmy Wakely and Margaret Whiting's "Let's Go to Church Next Sunday Morning," Eddy Arnold's "May The Good Lord Bless and Keep You," Hank Williams' "I Saw the Light," Stuart Hamblen's "It Is No Secret," Rex Allen's "Crying in the Chapel," Tennessee Ernie Ford's "His Hands," the Bailes Brothers' and later Kitty Wells' versions of "Dust On the Bible," Louvin Brothers' "The Family Who Prays," Wilma Lee Cooper's "Legend of the Dogwood Tree," Ferlin Husky's "Wings of a Dove," Claude Gray's "Family Bible," Kris Kristofferson's "Why Me, Lord" and Marilyn Sellars' or Cristy Lane's renditions of "One Day At a Time?"

Some of the greater gospel or spiritual songs that have proven especially popular in recordings include "Supper Time" by Ira Stamphill, "Precious Memories" by J. B. F. Wright, "Turn Your Radio On" by Brumley, "Wait a Little Longer, Please Jesus" by Hazel Houser, "Where Could I Go" by James Coats, "Wings of a Dove" by Bob Ferguson, "Dust On the Bible" by Johnnie and Walter Bailes, "These Things Shall Pass" and "It Is No Secret" both by Stuart Hamblen, "I Saw the Light" by Hank Williams, "The Great Speckled Bird" by the Reverend Guy Smith, "The Precious Jewel" credited to Roy Acuff, "Beyond the Sunset" by Virgil Brock and Blanche Kerr Brock, and "Amazing Grace" by John Newton and William Walker.

In his lifetime, Elvis Presley's only Grammy Awards were for inspirational albums.

Another major musical influence on gospel was the *Camp meetings* of the early 19th century, fostering a form of folk spirituals that fed the soul of the farming community. According to George Pullen Jackson's "White Spirituals in the Southern Uplands," the campground meetings kicked off in July 1800 in Logan County, Ky. (west of Martha's home county). Actually, such spirituals were deemed unacceptable by supposedly more sophisticated members of society, particularly those of the Presbyterian, Methodist, Baptist and Catholic persuasion.

Minstrel music (which arguably helped inspire greater interest in mountain and country music played by poor whites) was initially a not altogether healthy slapdash of song and dance that spoofed the black condition in the 19th century. Occasionally the performers would even satirize serious plays or books, such as abolitionist Harriet Beecher Stowe's classic "Uncle Tom's Cabin," performed by black-face minstels as an anti-black parody titled "Uncle Dad's Cabin," subtitled "Life Among the Happy," taking in account Stowe's sub-title "Life Among the Lowly."

Complete with a combination Irish and Negro jig, the following song would attempt to entertain theatergoers: *"Oh, white folks, we'll have you know/Dis am not de version of Mrs. Stowe/Wid her de Darks am all unlucky/But we am de boys from Ol' Kentucky!"*

It was the more sentimental source of minstrel sounds that reflected America's ongoing love of ballads with pretty melodies and strong verses. As minstrel music developed deeper catalogs, the trend for political satire and racial lampoons waned, shifting to songs boasting a broader range. Probably the most celebrated minstrel composer was Stephen Foster (1826-1864), whose songs like "Oh, Suzanna!," "My Old Kentucky Home," "Camptown Races" and "The Old Folks at Home (Swanee River)" became cultural classics. Other durable 19th century minstrel numbers were "Polly Wolly Doodle" and "Dixie."

In singing about God, Martha Carson insists she prefers upbeat songs because it gives the hope for a better life. Her message therefore has been a familiar and consistently positive one.

Coming from a region where life was always hard, often fruitless and its economy cruelly unpredictable, the suggestion of a better way ahead sounded a responsive chord for many people.

Carson's struggles and musical promise helped bring Southern country gospel into worldwide prominence. It was steadiness in the midst of change. Religion remains the hallmark of her life, though she claims membership in no church. In her heyday, she helped define the country gospel style with her evangelical compositions and lively performances.

A lot of successful black acts started out singing gospel music, including the Dominoes, the Drifters, Aretha Franklin and Sam Cooke. The latter, the son of a Baptist minister, kicked off his vocal career performing gospel with the Soul Stirrers.

Several years later (1957), he launched a solo career, creating much dissension among his fans. Still, he went on to achieve great success with such classic cuts as "You Send Me," "Chain Gang" and "Twistin' the Night Away," before being fatally shot by a woman on Dec. 11, 1964, at age 29.

The Dominoes' lead singer Clyde McPhatter started with that unit at age 17 in 1950, after having literally grown up in the church singing gospel songs. It was the only style he knew how to vocalize, and added much intensity to his performance.

One of the Dominoes' hits, "Have Mercy, Baby" became one of the top selling R&B singles of 1952. The song's *Baby* was interchangeable with the name *Lord.* The next year, McPhatter departed Billy Ward's Dominoes for the Drifters, where his vocals helped make hits of such classics as "Money, Honey," "Such a Night" and "Honey Love" before being drafted by Uncle Sam in 1954.

The North Carolina native was discharged two years later and went solo, recording such successes as "A Lover's Question" and "Lover, Please." McPhatter became one of R&B's most distinctive and influential artists, prior to his death June 13, 1972, from a heart attack at age 39. Of course, Martha Carson's "I Can't Stand Up Alone" had the good fortune of being recorded by McPhatter as the flip side of his million selling "A Lover's Question."

Despite formation of various gospel organizations since Martha Carson's heyday, her accomplishments go mainly unsung. It was more than 25 years ago that the Dove Awards were introduced by the Gospel Music Association, near *Music Row*.

There's also a newer organization, the Christian Country Music Association. While neither association has saluted her trail-blazing efforts, Carson's contributions have definitely made an impact, paving the way for others to follow.

Bill Gaither, who has garnered numerous awards with his gospel-oriented Gaither group, told this writer, "Music is a tool I use for a very ulterior motive. I want to say that Christ can make sense in a world that doesn't always make sense."

In spite of suggestions by others to try secular music, Gaither resists such efforts: "I love my wife (Gloria), too, so I suppose I could write love ballads for her, but we have chosen something we believe in very deeply. Something that is more meaningful to those who hear it."

The musical evangelist whose wife performs in the act, added, "We have songs that, at times, provides a release for us; tunes like 'I Feel That Something Good is About to Happen,' that are sort of upbeat."

Bill Gaither's awards include Songwriter of the Year. The vocal group has received a number of Dove Awards from the Gospel Music Association, the Society of Evangelical Songs by American Composers International awards and the coveted Grammy. His songs have been recorded by Lawrence Welk, Pat Boone, Tennessee Ernie Ford and Elvis Presley.

"As a kid, we (Bill and his brother Danny) sang secular songs, but there came a time in our lives that it became meaningless to me," explained Gaither. "I wanted to say something that had meaning for me. I think a real creator, a real artist has to write those things that he really feels from the gut. Hank Williams, when he wrote 'I'm So Lonesome I Could Cry,' didn't just sit down to do that song to make money. I think he was a poor lonesome soul, who was writing from his guts."

Gaither added his thoughts on gospel, "I've often said, I think the only really authentic gospel music is the black music that emerged back in the slave days from the cottonfields. When a man sang 'There's Got To Be a Better Place,' it was an honest, real expression of the soul."

During a winter 1992 interview, then-*Music Row* kingpin Jimmy Bowen, while at Liberty Records, predicted, "I see contemporary Christian music exploding over the next five years as country music did starting about six years ago.

"Nashville is truly the center for country music and for contemporary Christian music. We are minority music specialists here, country music is a minority music and contemporary Christian music is a minority music in the grand scheme of sales."

What made Bowen so certain that Christian sounds would gain popularity? (And they have.)

"The key is to read the pulse of the country to know *what* people are living. Music is a mirror of the times, so therefore, if you know what people are living, what's going on out there, you should know how to find music that relates to their life at the moment.

"Usually, there are dramatic extremes that exist at the same time. If you look at rap music, a lot of the rock music, it has the inner city lyrics of rape and murder, and the tough life that's in the inner cities. There are millions of Americans who *don't* live that lifestyle."

Liberty, which became the country name for Capitol (Carson's original label), was changed back to Capitol Records after Bowen departed, due to ill health. It must be remembered, however, that Bowen was at the helm when Garth Brooks' phenomenal success started a resurgence in country music sales that was unparalleled previously.

Echoing Bowen's belief in a surge for Christian music, Gaylord Entertainment (which owns the *Grand Ole Opry*, Opryland Music Group's Acuff-Rose catalog, Opryland theme park, General Jackson and Music City Queen showboats, Opryland Hotel, Wildhorse Saloon, Ryman Auditorium, KOA Campgrounds and Country Music Television International's cable network system) invested in Z Music Television, a gospel cable network and bought up Word Records & Music.

Prior to divesting itself of two North American cable networks - The Nashville Network (TNN) and Country Music Television (CMT) - for some $1.55 billion in Westinghouse/CBS stock, why did Gaylord feel a 1996 need to pay $110 million to purchase Word from Nashville-based Thomas Nelson Publishers (the world's major Bible sales company)?

E. W. (Bud) Wendell, then CEO and president of Gaylord Entertainment, summed it up, regarding Word's music: "The lyrics speak to faith and we believe the audience for this type of message is huge."

Walt Trott

CHAPTER 3

The Roaring 20s...

*"Look for the silver lining,
and you will find the sunny side of life."*

— **Jerome Kern**

Wake up, Irene! As fate decreed, the gospel-loving Martha Carson was born in a time when American youth were beginning to shed the shackles bound by Puritan principles so predominant in our cultural Christian homes.

By the new decade of the '20s, America was rearranging its house.

Women had the right to vote, thanks to Tennessee's ratification of the 19th Amendment delivered to the Secretary of State, Aug. 26, 1920. Prior to that, the 18th Amendment to the U.S. Constitution, making consumption of booze against the law, was enacted as a national Prohibition Act on Jan. 16, 1920.

While such social significances weren't yet reflected in the songs of the day, there was still a feeling of postwar exhaustion in the nation - and changing attitudes created a generation gap of no small proportions. The postwar recession itself was not especially severe, though specific areas of the country suffered more than others. A temporary downturn, in fact, saw the Farm Index plummet from 205 to 116 from 1920 to 1921.

As Irene Ethel Amburgey arrived on the scene in 1921, the Era of Wonderful Nonsense was beginning. It was a time when the Gross National Product soared from $74 billion in 1921, to $104.4 billion -- before that infamous *Black Tuesday,* Oct. 29, 1929, when the stock market crashed, eventually to an estimated tune of $50 billion (through 1931). Obviously, the '20s prosperity didn't make itself felt in the Amburgey's rural climes of Kentucky.

By 1921, the soon-to-boom Standard Oil stations totaled only 12 in New Jersey, while chain stores were already proliferating, with the A&P grocery stores numbering close to 5,000 sites, and Woolworth's Five & Dime stores numbering nearly 1,200.

("Before we went to WLAP-Lexington, I took a job in the dime store in Neon," says Martha, recalling the next decade's Great Depression. "Minnie was housekeeping - and cooking - for some folks, who had a store in Neon. We'd put all our wages into one pot for the family.")

Radio, which had its practical start in 1920, when KDKA-Pittsburgh announced returns of the Harding-Cox Presidential elections, was also showing promise with radio sales in 1921, grossing some $2 million -- then an impressive sum. The postal department in 1921, sent up its first transcontinental day and night mail delivery, thanks to a daredevil pilot appropriately named Jack Knight.

Youthful insignias of the decade, as depicted in John Held Jr. cartoons, carried by the magazines *College Humor* and *Life* were bobbed hair, cloche hats, knee-length hems for female "flappers," while their male beaus boasted slicked hair, puffy pants, raccoon coats and hip flasks - - though definitely not in the hills of Letcher County (where feed, cornmeal and flour were conveniently bagged in large, colorful sacks -- material that could be sewn into shirts or dresses for youngsters in hard-pressed families).

During the 1920s, the automobile created a major revolution, both in transforming the national economy and how it affected a whole way of life (and romance). In response, one of the Harding administration's first moves in 1921, was to promote the Federal Highway Act, which brought the federal government into road building. No minor job considering that of the near-three million miles of rural highways in 1921, most were merely fit for horse and buggy.

Equally fanning the coals of Flaming Youth were best-selling author F. Scott Fitzgerald ("This Side of Paradise" and

"Tales of the Jazz Age") and Hollywood, which could claim nearly 40 million admissions by 1921, thanks to such silent star box office draws as Charlie Chaplin, Lillian Gish, Douglas Fairbanks and Mary Pickford, the seemingly perennial moppet. Fan magazines carried stories about their goings-on for an eager readership.

When "Little Mary" made 'em cry at the cinema, the public responded by carrying their newly-produced "Kleenex Kerchiefs," first marketed in 1921 (and by 1924, Kleenex tissues were found in nearly every American home - and car).

No doubt, too, theatergoers began mimicking the actions of such *vamps* as Gloria Swanson and great lovers like John Gilbert. The Fox Trot and Charleston became the nation's new dance vogues, while "speakeasies," underground clubs, became a big lure for partygoers seeking the now banned beer, wine and liquor flow.

(Not necessarily in the Bible Belt, where home-made booze - known to revenuers as "moonshine," due to being mainly "manufactured" after hours - was the primary source for those who chose to imbibe. And did the Amburgey or Quillen clan get caught up in the distillation of *white lightnin'?* Martha chuckled, insisting, "Lordy no! If they even looked at it, they thought they'd go straight to Hell!")

Meanwhile, more women were joining the smokers' brigade and many began shedding their restrictive undergarments to enjoy the freedom required for the new dance steps. In fact in 1921, the first Miss America contest in Atlantic City was conducted, shocking the conservative public upon seeing contestants garbed only in bathing suits that showed a bit of skin.

Sports heroes like Babe Ruth and Jack Dempsey even went *Hollywood,* appearing in exploitation flicks that cashed in on their tremendous fan popularity. Thus, sport and film stars became America's royalty, revered by an adoring public.

Musically, ragtime was out, as jazz began finding its niche, thanks to robust bandleader Paul Whiteman, whose big hits included tell-tale titles "Whispering," "Wang-Wang Blues" and "Make Believe," charting the week baby Irene/Martha was born.

The *Jazz Age* would celebrate such names as Ben Selvin, Al Jolson, Ted Lewis, Isham Jones, King Oliver, Nat Shilkret, Ruth Etting, Rudy Vallee, Marion Harris, Louis Armstrong, Ben Bernie, Red Nichols, Bessie Smith and a big-eared newcomer named Bing Crosby.

Country, not yet defined, was mainly the music everyday folk performed at home or in festive neighborly gatherings. In fact, it wasn't until July 1, 1922, that the first commercial country-style recording was made in New York City, when Texas fiddler A.C. (Eck) Robertson played "Sallie Gooden" for Victor Records. Alarmed at the national turn of events, a Southern Baptist publication's editor observed: *"The situation causes grave concern on the part of all who have the ideals at heart of purity and home life - and the stability of our American civilization."*

On another front, the Ku Klux Klan resurfaced with a vengeance, its numbers rising to four million by 1924. Many of America's old values were being tossed out the window with the publishing of new sexual theories by Sigmund Freud.

Meanwhile in Appalachia, coal miners' families still marched to church on Sunday and regularly read from the Bible in their homes to reinforce the religious *word*. It was much the same in other small communities throughout the country, whether the corn fields in Iowa, the cotton belt of the Deep South or the wheat-covered plains of middle America.

"I never want to go to a church that has all that formality - the robes, the building project, etc.," says Martha Carson. "If I can't go to church and come out happy then I don't feel it's what God wants. In my Bible, it talked about Gabriel making a joyful noise unto Him. Whenever you leave church depressed like that, it's more like coming away from a funeral. I don't want them taking my happiness away from me."

Among the Amburgeys, music was a way of life. Theirs being a musical clan that produced some talented entertainers, three of whom were responsible for writing such nationally-recognized hit songs as "Satisfied," "When the Grass Grows Over Me," "Lonely Again," "To Get To You," "Lay Some Happiness On Me," "Triangle," "I Can't Stand Up Alone" and "I'm Gonna Walk and Talk With My Lord."

"When Mommy remarried, she got into an even more extreme religion and they made her feel like it was a sin to go into a theater to see me," muses Martha.

At the very moment of Martha's birth, the top tune in the nation was Jerome Kern's "Look For the Silver Lining," as recorded by Marion Harris, though popularized initially by incandescent Broadway star Marilyn Miller in the hit 1920 Flo Ziegfeld musical "Sally" (after the song was rescued from a flop called "Zip Goes a Million").

The daughter of vaudevillians, Miller was literally *born in a trunk,* Sept. 1, 1898, in Evansville, Ind. Showman Lee Shubert made the blonde teen-ager a star in "The Passing Show of 1914," and she soon became a Ziegfeld favorite in such *Great White Way* attractions as "The Ziegfeld Follies of 1918," "Rosalie" and "Smiles." [She died in 1936, as Martha and her sisters were about to get their own show on the road.]

Harris, *albeit* less spectacularly, also appeared in several New York shows, but gained greater fame as a recording artist, first for Victor and then Columbia, scoring the biggest hits on "After You've Gone," several years before Sophie Tucker made it her signature song, "I Ain't Got Nobody," "A Good Man Is Hard to Find," "Jazz Baby," "St. Louis Blues," "Who's Sorry Now?," "Tea For Two," "The Man I Love" and "I'm Just Wild About Harry," a Eubie Blake classic from one of the first popular all-black Broadway shows "Shuffle Along" (1921). [Harris died April 23, 1944 in a hotel fire at age 48.]

"Look For the Silver Lining" is a perfect theme for Martha Carson. Even in what qualifies as her more depressing days, she held onto a thread of optimism that kept her from being totally dismayed, and eventually let her triumph over all.

"Satisfied" is the most perfect example of this feeling that she carries within her and which has made her the survivor that she is. She says the song was inspired by a less-than-doting fan from Morristown, Tenn. Other Carson compositions also attest to her enduring faith and positive outlook.

Her lyrics to "Ask, You Shall Receive," copyright 1953 by Acuff/Rose, boasts, *"Have faith, have faith in Jesus/Reach out and take His hand/You will find a friend in Jesus/He's the one who understands/Yes, He'll bear all your burdens/He knows all your cares/He won't leave you nor forsake you/If you'll go to Him in prayer...And ask, you shall receive/Seek and you shall find/Knock, knock, knock, it shall be opened/I read these words devine...Ask, you shall receive."*

Give a listen to Martha's "Count Your Blessings," copyright 1954 by Acuff/Rose Publishing, *"Well, I was once downhearted/And I felt so alone/I could see others' blessings/But none of my own/Then I heard a sweet voice saying/'My child, rejoice, count your blessings today'/Then I started counting o'er and o'er/When I got through, I still had more/I got so many blessings/I just can't count them...For I can walk and talk, every day/I can sing and shout, all the way."*

What makes the Amburgeys so different?

For starters, the kids had a very special mom, Gertrude Amburgey, who instilled in her offspring a love of music and concurrently an abiding faith in God. While they may have disagreed on religious affiliations, parents and children always believed in a supreme being and in the Heavenly fold.

What was life like in the Great Smoky Mountain region when Martha was growing up? Of course, the Civil War had resulted in a definite change of attitude on the part of Southern whites, but not necessarily a change of heart -- not for generations to come.

While prancing through the tall rhododendrun-covered Smokies, she heard the melodies of her forefathers, which expressed their sorrows and joys, the heartaches and laughter of mountain life. It was a way of life set to the sounds of a fiddle and guitar.

Martha became steeped in the traditional folk songs heard in her girlhood, a rich heritage of music. Yet, she also liked tuning the family radio in to hear the sounds emanating from other musical formats.

"I can remember listening to Guy Lombardo's New Year's Eve music, and the Benny Goodman Sextet had some good, happy sounds. But people in our church thought it was sinful. You know, years later, I was doing this showcase for RCA and Benny Goodman was also on it. Well, he came over to me and asked for my autograph for his daughter, who he said just loved my record. God! I thought I would die!"

Walt Trott

CHAPTER 4

Mama Sang Alto...

"I was scrawny lookin', but my Granny loved me like I was gold."

— **Martha Carson**

"I remember once asking, 'Mommy, did you find me in a briar patch?' I had over-heard my mother and Aunt Nora talk about finding some kid in a briar patch," recalls Martha Carson. "Mommy would smile and say, 'No, you're mine!'"

From the start, music was a vital part of Martha's whole being.

"I began singing when I was about 6 years old," she explains. "At 10, I learned to play on an old-fashioned peddle organ; then four years later, I got my first guitar. I had to trade my pet calf - which I dearly loved - for the guitar, but it was worth it."

Her mother was a very strong influence.

"We always sung hymns at home," recalled Gertrude Amburgey (a sprightly 95, at the time of the interview). "My family sang in the Church of Christ. They had us - the Quillen Quartet - on every Sunday evening for the congregation there in Goose Creek. There was my dad Richard Quillen, who sang lead; me, playing keyboards and singing alto; my husband, singing bass; and brother Herbert, our tenor. We had some of the most beautiful songs. On one, in particular, 'Don't Forget to Pray,' the bass singer would take the lead all the way through it. We sang it in conventions and they had fits over us."

The Amburgeys usually took their children along when they performed at the various sings and conventions.

"My own daddy was a music teacher," continued Gertrude. "He had taught all of us what we knew, and we learned to play by notes. Later, I paid $5 on an old piano and until then had played a pedal organ. But that was mine! I could play it and play it right."

Gertrude said the Church of Christ, of which she was a member, didn't condone instrumental music: "We never had a stringed instrument in my house. My six learned about music from hearing us. As for the instruments they played, they picked that up themselves."

Her husband, who played banjo, kept his out of sight in their bedroom.

Gertrude stressed that Martha learned to play by ear: "She can beat the *fire* out of that guitar, and I can't. But I played music all right, wherever they had it, if I do say so myself."

Among the songs Gertrude sang and enjoyed were such standards as "Precious Memories," "Standing On the Promises" and "Shall We Gather At the River."

Gertrude Quillen was born July 31, 1901, in Neon, Ky., into a middle-class family of 10 children. Her father Richard, an architect and schoolteacher, was married to the former Carrie Vinters of Portland, Tenn. Besides Gertrude, their children were Bertha, Nora, Mildred, Georgia and Gladys, while their sons were Herbert, Conley, Victor and James.

Martha's paternal grandparents were Alfred Amburgey, a farmer, and his wife, Elizabeth, whom Gertrude's children addressed as "Grandma Betty." Martha's dad, Robert Humphrey Amburgey, was born May 11, 1888, in Hindman, Ky., one of nine children. His brothers were Lawrence, Wiley, John and Riley, while their siblings were Vina, Diana, Minnie and Marguerite.

Robert Amburgey, who originally hailed from Knott County, Ky. (north of Letcher) was a carpenter by trade. Located less than 10 miles from the Virginia state line in Letcher County, the Amburgey homestead, in the scenic Pine Mountain region of eastern Kentucky, was situated about equal distance from West Virginia or Tennessee.

Martha *nee* Irene Ethel Amburgey was born in McRoberts, Ky., on Thursday, May 19, 1921, to Gertrude and Robert. Besides Irene, the other Amburgey children were: Bertha May, born Sept. 17, 1918, in Burdine, Ky.; Opal Jean, March 6, 1923, in the Goose Creek community; Glenn, May 18, 1929; Lloyd, Aug. 2, 1931; and Conley, Nov. 7, 1936, all the boys born in Neon, Ky. Irene's birth had occurred at the family home. Her mother called her Irene, while, oddly enough, her father always called her Ethel.

As a matter of record, just east of Letcher lies mountainous Pike County, Ky., which borders on Mingo County, W. Va., site of the celebrated Hatfield-McCoy feud fought after the Civil War. East of this region is Bluefield, W. Va. (home of WHIS radio, which we'll hit on later).

According to Gertrude, "Really, none of my kids ever gave us any real trouble. The girls were always very talented and musical. Now Glenn cannot read a note of music, but he can play. Conley's a real good singer, and Lloyd (Don Chapel), of course, has written some fine songs.

"I could write, but mostly I was too busy waiting on the kids. As for the girls, I taught them the things they *ought* to know. For instance, they learned how to cook before they left home. Back then, kids *wanted* to learn how to do things."

Music and entertaining came naturally to the Amburgey sisters.

"I always believed I was the ugly duckling, because I wasn't outstanding like my sisters were," Martha confides. "They always caught everybody's eye. I was tall and gawky, while my older and younger sister(s) got a lot of attention. I felt like I wasn't one of them.

"Yes, I was scrawny lookin', but my Granny loved me like I was gold. I always loved to get out and dig in the dirt," continues Carson. "To this day, I ain't living if I don't have a garden. When I was a little girl, my mother would take me to the garden with her. Minnie was the housekeeper, while we were outside. She'd cook and wash dishes - and she loved it. She sure didn't like to get out in the garden."

Martha says her father was a *bratticeman* for the coal company, meaning he designed and constructed wooden support framework inside the mines. Additionally, he also raised stock such as chickens, cows and pigs to help enrich the family larder.

"We were awfully poor, I guess; but, we always had plenty to eat. Daddy built the frames in the mines so they could get the coal cars through…not one of the mines he built frames for ever caved in."

Bertha (now known as Minnie) adds, "Loretta Lynn ain't got a thing on us! We were coal miner's daughters before she ever was born."

Mostly, miners with the Elkhorn Coal Company got paid in *scrip*. This was fine to pay the miner's bill at the company store, theirs located in Hemphill, about two miles from the Amburgey home. Goods were priced higher than in civilian stores. In Neon, when the miner could shop with scrip, he had to deal with it being discounted 20 cents or more on a dollar.

Martha has emphasized her parents' differing backgrounds: "Daddy was a Baptist. But he went to church with my mother to keep peace in the family. My mother and grandfather thought anybody who had a beer was going to Hell! They were very straitlaced about that. Poppy was raised with wine on the table and he liked to go have himself a beer every once in a while. But, believe me, he caught hell for it.

"Another time he got smart and went out and gathered up all this fruit…," Martha pauses and chuckles aloud at the recollection. "He had a big ol' churn and from workin' up that churn, the fruit turned to this beautiful color of rosie pink. I proceeded to sip that and I got drunker than a pissant! Mommy saw that and the churn went flying out the window.

"But Lordy that was good stuff. It was so sweet and I didn't know it was gonna mess my head up. Minnie (Bertha) thought I was going to die. She said, *'If you're gonna die, you can have all my dolls and my other toys.'* Soon as I started improving, sobering up, that is, she took them all back."

Martha recalls that the family often raised little baby chicks (creatures with a high mortality rate): "We even had a baby chick graveyard. They'd get that sickness and die. Their bellies would split open. We used alcohol and would get a needle and thread to sew their little bellies up, and save match boxes, which we used for coffins.

"I remember one time Aunt Nora said, after a calf had died, 'It's a shame that baby calf's out there and no one's said anything over it.' We went out and sang 'Precious Memories' over that dead calf. Things like that stick out in your memory."

Minnie says while growing up that their closest relatives were Quillens: "The Amburgeys lived down in Hindman. We'd get to visit them a couple of times a year. But it was all just Quillens living where we were."

Martha's memory bank is as full as a corn crib in October. "My daddy built our house. It was natural wood (painted white). There were four rooms: a front room, a kitchen and two bedrooms with front and back porches. Out back there was an outhouse. He built rock walls around the yard. We had a little creek running by and were pretty close to the Virginia state line.

"I saw a lot of rabbits and squirrels, but don't recall seeing any deer. No, my Daddy wasn't a hunter, he didn't even have a gun that I knew of. There were a lot of pretty hickory nut trees and different streams and rivers up our way," she continues. "Sometimes we would go to the stream with soap and a washboard to wash our clothes, so that we wouldn't have to draw water up from the well and drag it on in the house...

"Where our house was situated in the hollow, we knew whenever somebody passed a certain gate, they was comin' to see us. Us kids loved when company came. As far as chores were concerned, Mommy would milk the cows when we were small. And I remember standing on a chair to wash dishes. We had to draw our water from a well in the back of the house. We all took a bath in a galvanized tub every Saturday night, whether we needed it or not," adds Martha, grinning.

Their Great Uncle Timothy (Johnson) lived up at the head of the hollow (a valley).

Martha explains, "He was married to Aunt Cosby, my Grandfather Quillen's sister. He had this old mule that was slower than the *Seven Year Itch.* Well, we used to carry jars of milk in the saddlebags, taking it into Neon to peddle - milk and butter. I told Mama, 'Let me walk to town with Uncle Timothy. I could take radishes in town and sell 'em.' I started out selling them for a dime a bunch. I'd wash a radish until it squeaked, it was so clean and pretty. I'd get into Neon, walk up their steps, knock on the door and sell 'em, along with onions and lettuce. Mommy gave me a little handkerchief to tie the money up in...she said to get enough and I could buy a new pair of shoes.

"While in town, I saw the prettiest pair of white patent leather shoes! I just had to have them. They cost about $2.98, and I only had about 90 cents, so I put them on *lay-away,* paying so much each week.

"Well, it took me two months to get 'em paid off and by then my feet had grown into another size. Anyhow, I got 'em and wore 'em, and I wouldn't complain about the tightness because they were so pretty. Eventually, I got blisters the size of quarters on both heels. I never dreamed my feet would grow so fast!"

Irene was 8 years old when the nation plunged into the Great Depression, Oct. 29, 1929, in New York City, as the Wall Street stock market crashed witnessing a $14 million price slump nationwide.

Though beyond her understanding at the time, America's economy was so unsound that 90 per cent of the national wealth was in the hands of only 13 per cent of the American people. Huge segments of society, including coal miners, farmers and factory workers, could barely eke out enough income to keep their families from starving to death.

Hollow reasssurances from newly-elected President Herbert Hoover, insisting, "The fundamental business of the country, that is, production and distribution of commodities, is on a sound and prosperous basis," and multi-millionaire John D. Rockefeller's follow-up, "My son and I have for some days been purchasing sound common stocks," rang flat on ears of people like entertainer Eddie Cantor, who shrugged off Rockefeller's assessment, "Sure, who else had any money left?"

Indeed, the banks would close temporarily and even under the subsequent guidance of a new President, Franklin D. Roosevelt, it would take a decade for the country to recover.

Meanwhile, some 40 million people found poverty a way of life. Foreclosed farmers migrated westward seeking work in the fields, evicted sharecroppers moved northward seeking salvation in city soup-lines, while able-bodied men rode the rails looking for labor, sleeping in "hobo jungles," risking their lives.

One of the harder-hit 1930s Kentucky miners explained their pitiful plight, "We had been eating wild greens since January this year. Violet tops, wild onions, forget-me-nots, wild lettuce and such weeds as cows eat. Our families are in bad shape: children need milk, women need nourishment food, shoes and dresses - that we cannot get."

Martha recalls, too, that when the mines closed down for a time, it did put many local families in dire straits. Finding jobs for so many people was a problem for Uncle Sam. Unintimidated, Robert Amburgey worked hard to keep his own family going, often with an occasional assist from others.

"One thing about Daddy is *he tried,*" Martha emphasizes. "He even sold Raleigh products, which ranged from shampoo to cough syrup and house cleaning materials, you name it - Raleigh had it. Now if Grandpa (Quillen) didn't have a white shirt job, he wouldn't do anything! He would never get out in the dirt with Granny. I think he thought he was too good to sell Raleigh products or work on the county road. But, put my Daddy on a rock in the middle of an ocean and he'd find something to do to make a living."

Martha reflects further on her beloved father.

"Once Roosevelt came in, he started the WPA (Works Projects Agency) and Daddy got work on the county road making a dollar a day. We'd use that to buy lard, soda, salt and sugar - and the pinto beans, Lord, oh mercy!, we can't forget them pinto beans! But we raised our own potatoes.

"Daddy wasn't much of a meat eater. He loved eggs, biscuits and sweets. We'd have those biscuits, eggs and gravy no matter what. It seemed like they were rationing flour for a time, which meant you had a five pound bag to last till the next handout. But, that didn't go far with a big family. If we ran out of flour, we'd just make cornmeal gravy. We'd use a borrowed horse to ride to the mills to make our cornmeal."

Of course, meal was made from corn and as Martha points out, "it was hard to get the kernals off that; once we did, we'd put it into a feed-sack, place it on the old mare's back and take it to the mill. There they'd grind it up and it would become cornmeal. It made the best cornbread you ever tasted!

"We'd have butter and milk from the old cows. When Daddy rolled out of bed to go to the mines, he had to have his bowl of butter. And to get that, you'd have to churn two hours before that butter would form. But, we learned a trick - by warming the milk...you'd save up that cream till it clabbers. There'd be buttermilk on the bottom and butter on top. Me and Minnie would cheat by sitting that churn down in a pan of hot water, with that warmth all around it.

"Oh yes, baked biscuits were another big favorite. But Mother had asthma so bad, she couldn't hardly deal with that flour! The last few years I lived at home, I'd make the biscuits for her."

Martha reminisces, too, about her parents' musical influence on the family.

"Mommy's musical tastes were real reserved, but she played organ and piano. She could hardly stand the 'hillbilly' music we loved. She always wanted us to play hymns like 'The Old Rugged Cross,' but they were too depressing for me. I wanted to play happy music. And she'd say to me, 'There you go with that ol' jiggin' stuff again. People will call you *Holy Rollers!'* Daddy though could play a mean five-string banjo.

"Mommy would get so mad at him when he sang songs like, *'I've got a girl in Cumberland Gap, She's got a baby that calls me Pap...'* He'd cut a little step or two after that, and by then she was ready to kill him. I think she was embarrassed at his behavior."

Although the Amburgeys were far from well off, Gertrude agreed the 1930s didn't mean destitution for them: "We had a garden and we had every kind of good thing to eat in the world, right out of that garden. When work was slack at the mine, my husband managed one of the company's stores. He was a good provider and he'd find something to do."

Martha remembers getting cabbage from her Granny's garden: "It was the best stuff I ever put in my mouth. Granny also had an apple orchard and was always telling the kids in the family to take some apples."

On a dour note, she stresses that "Once my Granny passed away, my granddaddy proved selfish. We could *smell* the apples, but that was as close as we got. He didn't offer us any...In fact, he called us the black Amburgeys, I suppose as in Black Sheep."

Some of the neighbors, however, agreed that the girl was addled-brain for making a *bad bargain* involving her pet calf.

"Oh Lord, we had the biggest love affair going you ever heard of. My Granny gave her to me. I called her *Brownie.* I'd brush her up and keep her clean as could be. Well, there was this fellow named Willard Hawkins who had an ol' guitar...It broke my heart, but I wanted that guitar so bad, I swapped Brownie for the guitar - and got $5 to boot! With that, I got this player piano. And still, I could see Brownie every day, as she was in a pasture right on my way to school."

Walt Trott

CHAPTER 5

The Sun Shines Bright...

*"We're the Sunshine Sisters,
Dropped in to say hello
We hope you'll like our program
of songs from long ago
If you like our program
Send in your requests
We are the Sunshine Sisters
We'll try to do our best."*

(By Bertha, Irene and Opal Amburgey, 1938.)

"You know, we sang this song whenever we got together. We could sing together and know every song we ever sung back then. It was the strangest thing," notes middle sister Irene, who sang baritone, while sister Bertha sang tenor and younger sister Opal Jean sang lead.

As Martha explains it now, there had been more than half a century elapsing since the trio first performed their former theme song. Exuberance and passion marked their performances. These Kentucky songbirds entertained listeners for miles around from a little radio station (WHIS) based in Bluefield, W. Va., during those waning days of the Great Depression.

"We'd do some Delmore Brothers' songs," says Martha. "We did songs like 'Fire On the Mountain,' 'Cindy,' 'Bile Them Cabbages Down' and 'Black Mountain Rag.' I remember that our first sponsored show was on WHIS, where the Chicago House Furniture Company sponsored us."

The musically-inclined Amburgeys had encouraged their children's interest in performing. Bertha also influenced her younger sisters: "We all started about the same time really. We'd listen to the *Grand Ole Opry* on Saturday nights and started singing around the house. That kinda made us think about getting into entertaining. All three of us felt the same way.

"My youngest sister learned to play five-string banjo like my dad. He was her first inspiration. Martha wanted to play tenor guitar like Rabon Delmore. What influenced us more than anything, I suppose, were the songs the Delmores sang. But Big Howdy Forrester was my idol! I thought nobody in the world could play a fiddle like Howdy. We listened to the Opry on a Philco battery-powered radio. Every time it would fade out, we would just about die!"

Radio provided needed entertainment for families - free - in those hard-luck times. Another form of escapism from life's daily dramas were motion pictures. Among the top screen talents during the sisters' formative 1930s era were Marie Dressler, Will Rogers, Shirley Temple and Joe E. Brown. While Neon even boasted a movie theater, the Amburgey sisters didn't have much time to enjoy such stars.

"I think I saw one cowboy film in my lifetime there," cites Martha, thinking that was about 1935. "It was Gene Autry. They played the same movie for a week or two. Mainly, all we had for outside entertainment was what we heard on that radio. We'd listen to *Lum 'n' Abner, Amos and Andy, Kate Smith* or *Ma Perkins*. Sometimes we'd get music coming in from New Orleans. Lordy, I loved that Dixieland music! What a time we had trying to listen to the Opry though...we'd get more static than anything else on that radio.

"Some of the other Opry acts we heard included Sam & Kirk McGee, Uncle Dave Macon and his son Dorris, the Crook Brothers, the Possum Hunters, the Fruit Jar Drinkers, Jack Shook and his Mountaineers, Alcyon Bate, Sarie & Sally, and Robert Lunn - *the talking blues man* - he was great. He would play his guitar and sing the news."

Incidentally, rural comic sisters Sarie & Sally (from Chattanooga) preceded Minnie Pearl as gossipy country hens by a decade. In 1932, WSM increased its power from 5,000 to 50,000 watts, making it easier for folks in outlying areas, even in mountain country, like the Amburgeys, to tune in to the historic weekend Nashville program.

"I remember when our three girls won a Lexington (WLAP) radio station contest," Gertrude said, reminiscing about that 1937 occurrence. "I think first prize was only $10. I made the dresses for my daughters to perform in."

Regarding her seamstress mom, Martha adds, "Mommy made our first stage clothes on the Singer sewing machine from old costumes. The dresses were black taffeta...and believe me, taffeta's cold material. When the wind would be crackling around our legs, we liked to had froze our *kiesters* off!"

Gertrude explained that when the station manager invited the contest-winning vocal trio to stay and perform at the station on a regular basis, the Amburgeys were initially reluctant. After all, Bertha was still only 18, Irene barely 16 and little Opal was just 14.

"Finally, we went with them to see the manager and saw that they got settled in a place that was safe. Times were a lot different back then," stressed Gertrude. "Now, you can't trust nobody out of your sight with your girls. But they didn't have it any too easy as it was. They had to get up and perform at 5 o'clock in the morning."

Rural life kept its populace extremely busy through the week.

"Mommy and me had a rip-roaring garden going," notes Martha. "In the summer, my mother canned vegetables for the winter time. When we got old enough, we girls helped Mommy *can*."

One day while her mother's sister Nora was pregnant, tragedy struck. Nora's husband, Talmadge Pratt, was killed by a car while walking along the side of the road. The young widow was left with three children to care for.

"Aunt Nora asked Mommy to let me go and stay with her to help out and she would pay $3 a week," continues Martha. "I begged Mommy to let me go. I wanted that money. Well, she let me do it...So I had to get the kids up, fix their breakfast and get them off to school. I remember using lye water to scrub the baseboards clean. I'd walk up one hollow to milk three cows. I'd slop the hogs, feed the chickens.

"It was odd because whenever the chickens would pick in the troughs for food, the hogs would get 'em and eat 'em. When I saw the feathers I knew the hogs were eating the chickens. Aunt Nora had me throw some corn down and pick up one of the fat broiler sized chickens she killed and skinned. She said take this out and give it to 'em and see how many more they kill. Well, I put red-hot pepper all over them chicken skins, and the hogs didn't much more get it in their mouth, and they squealed and peed...

"Them young'uns of Aunt Nora's were something else. If I didn't have supper ready when they got in from school, they'd be nasty. I was doctor, cook, farmhand and dishwasher - and I don't know what else. Time I got the kids fed, done the dishes, it was time for me to go to bed. That was a pretty full week for $3."

Another time when she and Aunt Nora were looking through a new Spiegal catalog, Martha recalled, "She thought I ought to get clothes, but what I wanted was a guitar! It was a Spiegal Special for $15 and it had initials you could put on it. I thought that was the greatest thing."

Once teen-aged Martha bought her brand new guitar, it was Uncle Timothy's son who helped her learn how to play: "(Cousin) Luther (Johnson) tuned it for me, then taught me the chords C, D and G. I learned to play by watching how he moved his fingers. Then mostly, I learned myself, from out of the book."

Since their brothers were late arrivals in the Amburgey family, the girls were called upon to perform a variety of duties, some that would usually go to the boys in a family.

"I remember that we had to chop (kindling) wood and do whatever would normally be a boy's job," says Martha. "By the time we girls left home, them boys were like babies. When I was a child, we had rough winters. It seemed like a lot more snow back then than they get now. I can still see that old potbellied coal heater in the middle of the room, and we'd have to get our lessons done by the light of coal-oil lamps. None of us out there had electricity until Minnie and I were pretty good-sized girls."

Bertha volunteers her view, "Back then we had no electric or conveniences like refrigerators, so I knew what I was doing when I went to the church (which had lights). Martha said, *'If you're going, I'm going too!'* Why, I remember the time when we older girls were baptized out in a creek behind the Church of Christ! I was 14 and Martha was 11."

When electricity was finally installed in the Amburgey house, it was a red-letter day. "We got it about two years before we girls left home," tells Martha. "We got our first Philco electric radio and boy, we were in high cotton. Before that, the only way we could hear the Opry - with all that static - was on a battery-operated radio."

The Amburgey girls didn't especially enjoy those Depression era school days.

Martha grimaces. "We walked about eight miles round-trip to attend a one-room school house! Snow or no snow, I never saw any school buses around. I only got one whipping in school in my life and that was because of a fight on the way home from school. There was the Bentley family, the *fightingest* bunch I ever seen. Mabel Bentley was especially hateful. She used to hit my sister Minnie with her geography book, so one day I lit into her - and she complained at school about being hit. Our teacher, Miss Holbrook, heard our stories, then whipped the both of us! I told her not to, but she did - and after that, I never liked her.

"Years later, just after 'Satisfied' hit, she came to one of my shows and sent a note to *tell Martha her schoolteacher was there.* Well, I did invite her backstage and when we got to talking, I told her it wasn't right that she whipped me. It wasn't right then and it isn't right now. She left in a hurry."

After graduating from eighth grade, Martha changed direction, walking along the banks of the river to Fleming High

School in nearby Neon. "I didn't really want to go because the only clothes I had were whatever Mommy could make from hand-me-downs. That's what I wore! After my sophomore year, I dropped out! I think Minnie made it to her senior year, but poor little Jean didn't make it to high school because we got her to grow up too fast.

"But, who knows, school might have ruined us if we kept going," beams Martha. "You don't learn the things we did in books. Learn 'em the hard way and then you'll remember' em."

Minnie insists that the yesteryear picture wasn't always as rosy as Martha or their mother paints it, especially where their father was concerned: "When my Daddy was younger - and believe me I still remember clearly; I'll never forget it - he would be abusive to my mother! It happened whenever he started drinking, and he was pretty bad about drinking then. Me and Martha used to hate to see our daddy come home when he had been drinking. Jean never saw much of that, for she was still busy playing with dolls, whenever we were going through all this.

"He got over it, quit drinking, and went back into the church and straightened his life out," volunteers Minnie. "But, that's where I am different than my mother or Martha. If a man didn't listen to what I said, I'd be throwing things. I tried to tell Martha, you need to speak up and say how you feel about things. Don't let 'em run over you like they do."

Like sister Nora, Gertrude indeed had her share of heartaches. Two days before her 1962 birthday, tragedy struck. On that Sunday, July 29, her husband Robert and their grandson Daniel were killed in a car crash. A second grandson, David, survived, to be raised by his grandmother.

Gertrude buried her husband and grandson on her birthday. "He was killed in a wreck while taking two of his grandsons to church," Martha offers, adding the ironic postscript, "A preacher's son had been out partying and hit their car!"

Another time after Gertrude's kids were grown, she had a rude awakening: "We woke up one morning with the house on fire! It was a big house and we were in the front - and didn't know the fire had started in the other part of the house. You know we got out of there in a hurry! We went over to the car wash (facility) with the police and watched our house burn...fortunately, it was insured."

Ever young, Gertrude raised a second family: "I had two grandsons, Opal's son Kenneth and my older boy's son (David). But I loved being a mother to them. I got a lot of satisfaction getting them off to school and seeing them come home with A's on their report cards. None of them, my kids or theirs, were ever a drag around my neck like some mothers say."

Walt Trott

CHAPTER 6

All-Girl String Band...

"Back home they thought we were really something being heard on the radio. That kept us going."

"Wanting it and getting it, are two different things." Martha wasn't the only one in her family who learned how to get what she wanted, despite definite lack of capital.

"(Opal) Jean got able to horse-trade around and found herself a five-string banjo," says Martha. "Jean was always very musically inclined. Poppy played five-string and Jean would watch his fingers, then watch herself play that way in the mirror until she had it down pat."

Martha next talks about Minnie's resourceful quest for a fiddle.

"She traded eight dressed hens in lieu of $8 for a fiddle. They were big as a small turkey. Then at Whitesburg, Ky., she played 'Cackling Hen' as her first song and won a fiddlin' contest. So the hens got her the fiddle plus $15 (prize money)."

Inspired by the Quillen Quartet, "We girls taught ourselves how to sing our own brand of harmony." Some standards they started out vocalizing included "In the Garden," "He Whispered Sweet Peace to Me" and "Amazing Grace."

Bertha, Opal and Irene Amburgey overcame their initial shyness to perform publicly, in the hometown area, by singing for political campaigners, church socials and occasional community gatherings.

According to Irene, "We would ride around in the back of an old truck, playing and singing all day long for $10, which we had to split up three ways."

When Irene was sweet 16, the sisters won an amateur contest sponsored by WLAP-Lexington radio: "The railroad engineer, who made the run from Hazard to Neon, came to tell us they were interested in an all-girl band. First prize was $15. We spent it on one week's room rent and groceries so we could stay over - eggs were only 11-cents a dozen. We ate a lot of eggs...It was our first radio job."

All the trio received thereafter were expenses for appearing on the station, but the sisters penned glowing letters back home: "We wanted mommy and poppy to think we had succeeded! At night, we'd cry our hearts out from homesickness - and just knowing we were failures. But, we had a pact not to tell, or they would have come and taken us home. Back home they thought we were really something being heard on the radio. That kept us going."

Becoming overnight sensations, however, wasn't meant-to-be for this sparkling trio. Briefly, they performed for WHAS-Louisville, where the headliner agreed to groom the girls as an act: "Cousin Emmy (Cynthia May Carver) put us in her apartment and holed us up there about a week. Then she said we were too young and told us to go back home. Emmy said she would send for us later, but she hasn't sent for us yet! She kept our instruments, too."

According to Minnie, "I think she was a little bit jealous of us because Jean could play rings around her on the banjo. She didn't like that. Jean picked oldtimey like my dad. The next thing we knew, she said she couldn't use us anymore. She told us something like they couldn't afford to pay any more performers at the station...Cousin Emmy said she would release our instruments if our Daddy would pay back our board, something to do with paying where we were living. We chalked it up to professional jealousy."

Carver was herself a Kentucky native, having been born in 1903, near Lamb, in the southern part of the state. The youngest of eight children born into a sharecropper family, she was raised in a log cabin. Radio was her forté and she was regarded as a headliner at such stations as WHB-Kansas City, KMOX-St. Louis and WWVA-Wheeling in the reigning days of radio.

"A few years later, we met her again," taunts Minnie. "But she acted as though she didn't know us." (Cousin Emmy Carver died in Sherman Oaks, Calif., in 1980.)

Martha shares another memory from WHAS: "Jean was fascinated by a bass fiddle that one of the other gals played. She asked about it and wanted to play it, but the girl told her *never* to touch that instrument! Well, Jean did learn how to play it - and she could play circles around that gal, believe me. She also learned how to play mandolin. She was really so talented."

Jean was more charitable with another young artist who expressed interest in her banjo later at WHIS-Bluefield (W.Va.). The newcomer, also from Kentucky (McVeigh), was named LaVerne Williamson. But country fans know her better as Molly O'Day, who learned to pick well enough from Jean to later beat Earl Scruggs in a Renfro Valley banjo pickin' contest with her drop thumb banjo style.

Of course, Scruggs, now a member of the Country Music Hall of Fame, then stood in awe of O'Day's playing, but later became the most famous of all bluegrass banjo players.

Molly O'Day, whose mournful mountain singing had a major impact on modern country music, was born July 9, 1923, in the eastern Kentucky hill country that spawned such other greats as Carson, Loretta Lynn, Tom T. Hall and Ricky Skaggs. Some historians have (arguably) called O'Day "The Female Hank Williams."

One youthful hopeful she inspired to gain more than regional success was Mac Wiseman, who performed nearly a year as featured vocalist and bass player with O'Day's Cumberland Mountain Folks band. He has the highest praise for her talent, and recalled making recordings with her group for Columbia Records in Chicago during December 1946, his first session.

"She was the first artist to record Hank Williams' compositions though, including 'Six More Miles To the Graveyard' and 'The Singing Waterfall,'" notes Wiseman, who like O'Day boasts a unique vocal style. Before adopting her lasting stage name, Molly used the *nom de plumes* Mountain

Fern and Dixie Lee. O'Day, who wed gospel artist Lynn Davis, later dedicated herself to the Church of God (until her death on Dec. 4, 1987).

On WHIS, she was still a struggling entertainer, not unlike the Sunshine Sisters.

Martha, chronicling the sisters early career, says, "We got going in radio at WLAP, remaining there about eight months, then we moved to WHIS-Bluefield, staying close to six months."

Vividly, she still remembers the day they received word to audition for radio.

"We could see down the way a man coming to tell us about it. My daddy hocked some of his tools and took us over himself in that little old rattletrap he drove, which had a bad muffler and barely made it. On the way, we stopped and bought peanut butter and crackers to eat. Well, Jean stuffed herself on peanut butter and crackers, until the exhaust got to her…when it came time for the audition, Jean was scared if she tried to sing, she'd become ill. And she looked deathly ill. So there was our lead singer, with sweat popping out on her forehead! Beneath that blonde hair, she looked green, but she got through it somehow.…"

The Amburgey trio worked with some formidable talents, but Martha acknowledges the pay was nothing: "I remember we ate an awful lot of Jello."

Before leaving Lexington, the statuesque, copper-haired Irene had blossomed into a beauty, who naturally attracted attention from the opposite sex. But, before she had time for any other romances, an ex-swabbie sailed into her life.

"They were all good-lookin' girls," James Roberts readily asserts.

"Before James, I didn't give a darn one way or the other about boys," Martha recalls. "One other time, this fellow sat at my table and began puttin' all this mush on me. I was on radio then and he sent me a love letter with a self-addressed, stamped envelope for me to write him back; but instead, I took the stamp off to write a letter to my mother."

It was April 1939, drolls sister Minnie, "When Martha met James...in Lexington. He came to the radio station looking for a job. Of course, she and Jean couldn't have left home in the first place without me to look after them. So, my family wasn't any too happy hearing about Martha and James..."

Martha remembers their first meeting: "James was just out of the Navy and I thought he was good-looking and a nice person. Then he struck up this acquaintance with me. He kinda swept me off my feet really, because I'd never been shown that much attention before."

From the start, unbeknownst to her parents, Irene and James became an item around the station.

"James had a medical discharge from the Navy, because he had something wrong with his back," Martha shrugs. "I don't know exactly what it was, but he got this little pension. On the radio, all he did was sing old Jimmie Rodgers songs and yodel. Anyway, he started coming over and hanging around our place."

James Roberts had enlisted in November 1937. He attended "boot camp" at the Great Lakes Naval Training Center in Waukegan, Ill., before being assigned to the *USS Mississippi.*

"I was 'striking' for Gunner's Mate, you know, training on those 14-inch or 16-inch guns. They had six big guns forward, and a pointer and trainer on each one. They towed this big target about the size of a house, way off some place...I got through every bit of that and made perfect scores (4.0).

"Then I had to go down in the powder room of the ship and work there a few days," he explains. "They had these big dummy kegs that weighed about 100 pounds. I was going to be a smart aleck and show these guys how to load those things. As a kid, I did a lot of heavy lifting. We farm boys over in Madison County would get together and box a lot in the barn. And we had these flat rocks...we'd see which one of us could lift 'em way up over our head. So I was pretty strong.

"You know, I hadn't really been in the Navy too long, so I really wasn't too sea-worthy or hadn't yet developed my 'sea-legs.' Well, we came into a lot of turbulence and were on the side of the ship that was taking 15- to 20-foot waves.

"When I reached for that powder keg to put it over my head and onto a conveyor belt (which would carry it up to the breech of the gun turret), the ship dropped right out from under me! As I started to set my foot down, there was no deck there, so I went off balance...I tried to hold on to that powder keg and the backward force of it snapped my spine! It was such a slap, it pulled the ligaments loose on the inside of the spinal cord.

Roberts adds, "They operated on me at the Naval Hospital in San Diego, and I've never felt such pain before or since! I went down from 180 pounds to 140 in no time. They kept me there 13 or 14 months. I was just thinking about it the other day, and if it hadn't been for that head surgeon there, I might have been paralyzed or crippled for life."

James confides that he never thought he'd live to be over 40. But he was 81 at the time of this interview, and appearing quite robust: "You know I've had pain in my back all my life. I don't believe it's ever quit, but I try not to think about it, and I just keep right on going."

James William Roberts was born Feb. 10, 1918, near Richmond, Ky., to Anna Frances (Risk) and Phillip (Doc) Roberts. Doc Roberts was born April 26, 1897, also in Madison County, Ky.

Overall, Doc Roberts recorded some 80 songs himself, and played fiddle on as many more for other acts. He started off playing for neighboring dances, then as his fiddlin' style, which included a smooth, long bow technique, caught on, he began competing in fiddle contests and playing a bit farther afield.

Doc introduced his 10-year-old son to the art of recording, as he encouraged young James to sing tenor harmony, accompanying fiddler Asa Martin, who sang lead, while Doc picked instrumental mandolin lead and played fiddle. (Another son, Thomas, played guitar, but only around the town.)

"I don't know if you know this, but fiddlers are particular about their instruments. My Daddy wouldn't let me touch that fiddle of his. I've got it now, and I've had it repaired and put together twice.

"I never will forget he had one of those old crank-up machines (record players), where you put a record (cylinder) on it. He used to buy them masters they made back in the 1920s at Richmond, Ind. He bought those of the artists like Gene Austin ('My Blue Heaven') and Vernon Dalhart ('The Prisoner's Song'). He'd stand me up and have me sing along with them, until I learned their songs. I was 7 years old.

"We had an organ and I'd listen to him sing while my mother played that organ. We had a hymn book she played from...One day he brought home a stringed instrument that looked like a potato bug, and it had a round back on it. And it had *Neopolitan Opera-something or other,* printed on it.

"I remember him laying on that bed, with his head propped up on the headboard, playing that instrument. I can still see and hear him pickin' that mandolin - and I thought that was the prettiest music I ever heard."

Thankfully for James, Doc wasn't as particular about that mandolin as he was about his fiddle. "So, I got that mandolin, unstrapped it and pulled it out one day and I went to sit on the steps in the back of the house, trying to play. I'll always remember that first tune I learned to pick out, 'Wreck of the Old '97.' I'd heard it on the other side of Vernon Dalhart's 'Prisoner's Song.' Well, I picked those notes out by myself and I thought that was a big accomplishment."

And indeed it was for one so young.

James says he grew up in "a big, long house made out of poplar logs, 12-to-14 inches wide, and situated on the other side of Richmond (Ky.) in Madison County. We had two upstairs, with a set of stairs leading up to each, one in the back, where I picked out my first tune on the mandolin."

He was one of 11 children born into the Roberts clan. "Nine lived to maturity. My youngest sister Rosella was the first to die of cancer. She lived in Cincinnati. In all, we've lost five to cancer. The other kids were Curaleen, me, Anna Mae, Tom, Doris, Clevie, Donald and Kenneth, the oldest."

His brother, Phillip Jr. died early on. James is the last surviving sibling.

His favorite sister, Margaret Lucille, died when she was 4 years old.

"They thought she just had croup. But after she died they found out she had diptheria, then they quarantined the entire family. My older sister, my father and I had it, too. I never did go to bed with it. I walked around in the rain and did my work, too. It's a wonder it didn't kill me. But, my little sister died of it.

"I can see that doctor standing there by her bed while she suffered. He told mother to go get hot water and some clean sheets. He was gonna perform a procedure (tracheotomy) to open up her neck and insert a tube so she could breathe. She was choking, as I saw him laying out his (surgical) tools. When my mother came back with the hot water she'd heated, he turned to her and said, 'It's too late. There's no use. She's gone!'"

James eyes brim with tears at the retelling of this tragedy.

"When I went out to the Roberts' family graveyard, I looked through the fence and saw this tombstone with the words inscribed: 'Budded On Earth, To Bloom In Heaven,' That's how I came to write that song. I always thought that marker belonged to my little sister, but later, after I'd written the song, I went to the cemetery and they had cleared away the growth and I saw it was actually my cousin's. But I had written it in memory of my sister."

Fiddlin' Doc Roberts' first recordings were in fall 1925, with Dennis Taylor's Kentucky Boys, for Gennett in Richmond, Ind. Taylor was then a sort-of talent scout for Gennett.

According to son James, however, Doc had a two-year contract with Dennis: "But he wasn't pleased, not getting his name on the records. Dennis just didn't suit him, so he let the contract expire before recording again."

The later recordings (made between 1928 and 1934), were issued under titles like Doc Roberts Trio or sometimes Martin &

Roberts, and distributed to various record stores, though their biggest sales came from being featured in Sears & Roebuck or Montgomery-Ward catalogs.

His records were often under four or five different names and issued on that many different labels. Among numbers performed were such favorites-of-the-day as "My Dixie Home," "Little Box of Pine" and "Knoxville Girl," but few originals.

Doc Roberts was especially noted for his lively version of "Shortnin' Bread." The adolescent Roberts also recorded some solo vocals for Gennett Records. This time, Martin was the unofficial A&R man for Gennett.

"In 1927, I started playing chords on mandolin. Then in August 1928, while school was out, me and Asa (Martin) recorded four numbers. I was 10." (Reportedly these were: "East Bound Train," "Lilly Dale," "Friends of Long Ago" and "Old New Hampshire Village.")

In those youthful days, James' voice was not yet baritone. He would blush when he heard fans inquire of Asa Martin about who the girl was singing on their records.

For a time, the Roberts clan moved to a farm in Iowa, in an area later popularized by the 1990s novel "Bridges of Madison County." It was where Doc and his boy would work on radio.

"In 1932, I went out to where my daddy was in Council Bluffs (Iowa). At 14 years old, I got on a train and went out there alone. This guy, Mr. Savage, who owned *Georgie Porgie* breakfast food wanted daddy to advertise his product, as he had heard his records. Mr. Savage's little son's picture was on the cereal package...

"Well, when I arrived, I didn't know where to go, so I asked a taxi-cab driver if he knew anything about them, and he said, *'Yeah I do, and I know where they are right now.'* They were having a party, and he drove me there."

Roberts continues, "That was the first time I can remember we were on the radio. (During that period) I recall we were on the grain exchange station WAAW-Omaha, at WOC-Davenport and also over on WHO-Des Moines."

James recalls, too, a youthful escapade: "It was the only time in my life I ever saw a stripper, Sally Rand! It involved me and Bucky Yates, who finally wound up working with Curly Fox. Me and Bucky rode a trolley train from Council Bluffs over to a theater in Omaha. Out there, they mixed lime rickey and pure grain alcohol. You bought your bottle of alcohol first and you'd go someplace where you'd sit down inside and they'd serve you mix, a bottle of lime rickey.

"In Council Bluffs, Bucky gave me the pint of alcohol and told me to hide it somewhere. So I put it in my belt on the front of my britches. We got on that trolley and you know what it did? That pint bottle slipped down the leg of my britches and slid out, and went right down the aisle! I had to run it down! Boy, was I embarrassed!

"We went to the show and after we left there, they had a riot and tore that place up! I'll tell you this: I was never an alcoholic, but I was never opposed to taking a drink if somebody wanted a drink or to have a bottle of beer. I'm just not a fanatic."

Doc Roberts also worked a short stint with Asa Martin at WHAS-Louisville.

"Daddy never worked regular. My dad run the county poor farm in Richmond for a long time. He didn't want to go too far away from home to make a living. But he liked playing those dances. When they recorded him, he couldn't figure out why he couldn't play a 15-minute fiddle tune in the studio, like he did at the dances."

In 1932, Doc Roberts landed at the then-new station WLAP in Lexington, explains James: "It had moved here from Louisville. I remember Ted Grizzard was the program director, announcer and everything at the station except maybe engineer. And who knows, he might have done that! I know he stayed there until he died. They had live shows, anything you could think of, including preachers, church choirs, 'colored' bands with horns, strings and things, and a *Man On the Street,* who was Ted Grizzard."

James says Doc's Trio was on Monday, Wednesday and Friday: "There was my father, me, Arthur Rose - he went to New York and recorded with us one time - and another fellow, Ownie Muse, who filled in. He did some twin fiddlin' with my father, which was becoming popular.

"(On WLAP) there was also the Lee County Boys, who also had a fiddler. They were from Irvine and Flemingburg (Ky.) and I remember the leader worked near (Lexington) at a narcotics farm. They also did country, but more of a pop-country."

Others on WLAP who came to mind for him were Matt Adams and his Kentucky String Ticklers; and the Fiddlin' Linvilles, consisting of Charlie Linville and his wife, who played twin fiddles.

In 1934, James did some superb solo vocals with the Roberts trio for ARC (American Record Company), most notably "Stringbean Mama" and "Duval County Blues," which also included his yodels.

James Roberts remembers several shows taking place at Lexington's Woodland Auditorium during their WLAP stint. One memorable fiddlin' contest was co-conducted there by Doc Roberts and fellow pioneer Clayton McMichen, late of the WSM *Grand Ole Opry's* Skillet Lickers band. Georgia born, McMichen was two years younger than Doc. He also wrote "Peach Pickin' Time in Georgia" (recorded by Blue Yodeler Jimmie Rodgers) and later formed his popular Georgia Wildcats, which also played Dixieland jazz.

At a fiddlin' contest in Cincinnati, James relates seeing McMichen beaten by Natchee (Lester V. Storer) the Indian (who teamed with singer Cowboy Copas for a time).

During the Woodland Auditorium contests, James adds, there was a talented family headed up by "Short-Buckle" Roark, who played banjo, along with his sons and young daughter. He believes the family hailed from Richmond (Ky.).

"They'd play Jimmie Davis' 'Bear-Cat Mama,' which was real hot, and then the little girl would hit the floor and do her buck dancin' and her daddy'd take his hat and fan her feet...They'd beat us all every time in these contests by a mile. The audience just loved 'em. I think the old man made some records for some company at one time."

Another act, two sisters from Ravenna (Ky.), sang duets on WLAP.

"I had the measles and my daddy thought I was gonna die, because they wouldn't break out on me," says James, recalling he was about 17. "So when I didn't show up at the station, this one sister - she and I were gettin' kind of too friendly, you know - came on over, and jumped on my bed and began huggin' and kissin' me. Then when she left, I really broke out with the measles! Next thing I heard, she had 'em, too!"

During an engagement at Woodland Auditorium, James met Uncle Dave Macon, the Opry's first star attraction: "He walked out on stage and said, *'I thought I'd never get here. I came on a Greyhound and it stopped at every telephone pole!'* He got a good laugh."

After his Naval hospital stay, James got Asa Martin to use him, first on his WLAP *Morning Round-Up* program. With maturity, James' voice dropped a few octaves, and his father's training had turned him into a skillful mandolin picker.

"I heard Asa was on that station. He had a whole lot of people working for him, but he didn't pay any of them," says Roberts, who joshes that later he heard WLAP had a nickname all over the state: *We Let Anybody Play!*

By now, Doc Roberts was down on Martin, because he didn't feel he was trustworthy. James, however, needed the work. He began by doing an occasional ballad, pickin', singing and yodeling on the early morning show.

Before long, however, he was smitten by the teen-aged, red-haired beauty of Irene Amburgey. Not only did she play guitar, but she was also able to play the oldtime pump organ, which she learned from her mother. An insecure, lonely girl, Irene welcomed James' advances, while thwarting those from guys like Martin.

"My sisters didn't care too much for him. At that time, I couldn't figure out why. Later, I did. I think he had eyes for my younger sister. Every time she'd have a date, he'd almost die. He would talk to me and say she's *too young* to see guys. He was very derogatory and negative about her. All the while, I thought it wasn't any of his business. I believe now he wanted all three of us!"

Jean, who James called by the nickname "Paddlefoot," was only 16 at the time. But back then in hill country, a lot of girls were brides by that tender age.

One job Asa had given James was collecting the "gate" for dances the radio troupe put on out in High Bridge, Ky.

"They had round and square dancing inside this big round wire cage that had a platform in there. They'd play 45 minutes, then take a 15-minute break, during which they turned the nickelodeon on for dancing. Then they'd clear the place out (and start over).

"We sold tickets to get in, charging 'em by the car. Then we'd charge them to get back in again. We did that all day long. I don't know if it was legal or not, but Asa told me to do it - and I was working for him. We didn't know how much Asa made, but every night Martha and her sisters *owed him* $8 or $10.

"Every time they had to buy a pair of panties, he charged it up to them. If they wanted anything, he'd give them money to buy it, then write it down in a book. He had them indebted to him - and I didn't like that!"

Asa Martin, born in Winchester, Ky., June 28, 1900, played guitar and musical saw. He had three sons, but after his first wife Eliza divorced him, he married Geneva. Apparently, he had a roving eye when it came to the ladies.

"I remember doing a tour with Asa, Stringbean (David Akeman), Little Georgia Hale and the all-girl band down where the sisters are from in Letcher County, playing those coal-mining camps. We packed them places full and came back without a penny for us. Asa put it all in the bank. That's when Martha and me left. I told her, *you can put up with this if you want to, but I'm leaving!"*

Pressured by his persistent courtship, Martha had succumbed and agreed to become *Mrs. Roberts*, making her the first of the Sunshine Sisters to marry.

"At first, we were too young to marry without my parents consent," she says, so they delayed, but then decided to drive across the state line into Indiana, where there was no waiting period. "It was June 1939, when we were married (in Jeffersonville)."

James Roberts recalls their wedding: "I didn't have enough money to even buy a marriage license. My uncle, who lived on Lincoln Avenue (in Lexington), took us to get married. He rode us to Jeffersonville (near Louisville, on the Indiana state line)."

Nonetheless, like the Shulamite of the Bible, Irene Amburgey was undefiled. Yes, she confides simply, James was her first lover: "I went to bed on my wedding night with bra, panties and nightgown all on. I was so dumb. When he tried to push my legs apart, I thought he was the dirtiest man around! When James and I checked out of the hotel, I felt dirty! You know, I ain't never been married right."

[Ironically, as Martha Carson, then in love with Xavier Cossé, it was back to Indiana - this time Evansville - to tie the proverbial knot.]

Besides the ever-lasting emotional upheaval of her wedding night, there were other problems. The couple lacked money to subsist on while working at WLAP. The ex-sailor's small pension didn't stretch very far.

Martha reiterates: "The station didn't pay us anything...We sisters were part of *Asa Martin's All-Girl Band,* so he paid our rent. But every time he gave us any money, he wrote it down in that book. We were nearly a year with him - and when we left, he said *we owed him money."*

Asa's all girl band also included his then-girlfriend Betsy, a tall bass fiddler, and Georgia Hale, whose accordion was bigger than her, according to James. During their Lexington radio stint,

Martha says the station manager also tried to make a play for Minnie, which didn't set too well with the Amburgeys: "He was a married man, so my sisters went on home. Since I was married, I went to live with James' people. At the time, my father-in-law (Doc) had a little ol' farmhouse in Richmond, where he did some farming. He raised tobacco and corn, stuff like that. Doc and his wife had nine children, as I recall, and I lived there with them for several months."

James concurs, adding: "Martha told her momma and daddy what was going on, so they came to get the other girls. Her mother's brother, name of (Herbert) Quillen, brought them in a pick-up truck. Well, Asa hid them girls, so they couldn't find 'em. One of the sisters was under age (Jean), so the police arrested Asa and took him to the police station. I sat in town in the police station office and Asa don't know how close he come to getting killed. The uncle said something to Asa...

"So Asa told Martha's uncle to go back up in the mountains and crawl in one of those rat holes (mines) up there! He (Quillen) turned white as a sheet! Then I saw the uncle reach for his gun and I thought, *phew! Asa was a dead man!*

"Well, he told 'em where the girls were and the police told Asa to get out of Lexington, that they didn't need his kind there. That's when he went to Ashland (Ky. to station WCMI, also run by WLAP owner Gilmore Nunn)."

Asa Martin, incidentally, was 79 when he died, on Aug. 15, 1979. Asa's former partner Doc Roberts died a year earlier on Aug. 4, 1978, at age 81.

Minnie has recalled her over-amorous suitor at WLAP was not only married, but had several kids: "His wife lived out in the country with the children and he was living in the city with a bass fiddle player. One time he said to me, 'You're gonna be my girl,' and kept on insinuating that. When he put his hands on me, I shoved him and told him straight up, *'Don't ever put your hands on me!'*

"He'd say, 'You're so pretty. I'll put you in Hollywood, if you listen to me.' Well, that rascal tried the same thing with young Jean. She was nothing but a living doll and *did* look like a movie star. You know they even made a screen test on her in Chicago."

In retrospect, James Roberts says there are only two men he worked with that you couldn't believe a word they said: "Asa Martin was one of them. The other? I'll tell you. He was Joe Isbell, who came down to Atlanta from Cincinnati. First thing we knew, he told us so many different stories, we came to doubtin' whatever he was saying."

CHAPTER 7

Bluefield and beyond...

"I had plenty of confidence while singing in the acts. It was just having to do something by myself that scared me half to death."

- **Martha Carson**

"James wanted to sing duets with me, so I taught him the sacred songs (using shape-notes like those seen in the gospel songbooks of publishers like Stamps-Baxter or Vaughan). But, we never did duets at WLAP," Martha says, reflecting on the long-ago beginning of an acclaimed vocal partnership. "After moving to WHIS, we did some duets, but our main act was still the Sunshine Sisters (string trio)."

The late Ira Louvin once told a writer that he and his brother were influenced by the talented combination of James and Martha Carson. Bluegrass Hall of Honor recipient Mac Wiseman, who worked with the duo at WSB in the late 1940s, called them the best gospel duet he ever heard, singling out performances on "The Sweetest Gift (A Mother's Smile)" and "Budded On Earth."

During their formative years, the Amburgey girls were taught by their grandfather to utilize shaped notes. Shaped notes or *fasola* derive from a system of ear training once used in Britain and Colonial America, starting in the late 17th and early 18th centuries, a concept based on the syllables *fa so la*.

Actually developed from naming of the degrees of the musical scale (known as *solmization*) by Italian Guido d'Arezzo during the 11th century, it was used as a teaching aid, i.e., *do, re, me, fa, so, la, ti, do*.

One of America's oldest musical traditions, shape notation presents notes as a series of shapes (circle, square, triangle, etc.)

corresponding to the aforementioned musical diatonic scale. Easily learned, the system makes it possible for a group to get together and quickly master harmony singing in four parts, much as the Quillen Quartet and later the Jordanaires did.

Author, composer and music historian Arnold Rogers discusses the process of country songwriting as he sees it: "I do a lot of lead sheets and it opens your eyes to a lot of things. You can see in a matter of a couple of hours that blues and gospel have always been close in pattern. Black gospel and black blues are almost the same. It's true of country and gospel, too. Buddy Killen once said, 'Bill Anderson only rewrote the Protestant hymnal' for his songs."

(Anderson, with such successes as "City Lights," "Still," "Think I'll Go Somewhere and Cry Myself to Sleep" and "Tips of My Fingers," is one of country's premier songwriters. His magical pen helped create a new star in Connie Smith, thanks to "Once a Day," "Then and Only Then," "Nobody But a Fool," "Cincinnati, Ohio" and "I Never Once Stopped Loving You," and aided a comeback for veteran Lefty Frizzell via "Saginaw, Michigan," among others.)

"Songwriting is just mathematics," continued Rogers. "Country songwriter Harlan Howard ('Pick Me Up On Your Way Down,' 'Heartaches By the Number') is heavy on quarter-notes and Anderson is, too. In fact, they're awfully close to each other in writing styles.

"Don Gibson ('Sweet Dreams,' 'I Can't Stop Loving You') pretty much used the scale in composing. Fred Rose ('Be Honest With Me,' 'Texarkana Baby') did too. But Rose had a dotted half that identified much of his music. In his 'Blue Eyes Crying in the Rain,' *blue* had three beats while *eyes* had one beat and *crying in the rain* had one beat.

"Jim Anglin ('As Long As I Live,' 'Ashes of Love') always had this little eighth note he slipped into his songs almost like a signature. For instance in the ('One By One') line *as sure as there's a Heaven,* Anglin would use one note on *Heaven* where anyone else would make it two syllables.

"A Kris Kristofferson song ('Help Me Make It Through the Night,' 'Jody and the Kid') had its own little meter built into the song. He really was a magnificent writer. Neither John Loudermilk ('Abilene,' 'Talk Back Trembling Lips') nor Boudleaux Bryant ('Hey Joe,' 'Bye, Bye Love') used the scale much. They used more of a variety than just three notes..."

After WLAP, the reunited Sunshine Sisters next stop was West Virginia.

As before, in the trio at WHIS-Bluefield, Martha sang bass, but when she did occasional duets with her mandolin-pickin' husband, she sang tenor.

"Yes, James sang lead and I sang tenor," acknowledges Martha, whose accompanying guitar also blended well with his mandolin. "I never sang lead with any of them until I had to stand on my own two feet to survive. I had plenty of confidence while singing in *the acts.* It was just having to do something *by myself* that scared me half to death."

Roberts remembers it was fall 1939, when they went to WHIS. He also recalls that Martha suffered a miscarriage, which led some doctors to believe she might never conceive again. Mostly, Martha blocks this from her memory.

"We went to see this horror movie, I think it was 'Hunchback of Notre Dame,' and it scared the *bejeebers* out of me," she offers, when pressed about the interruption of the undeveloped fetus.

At WHIS, one of the station's mainstays was Joe Woods, who called his group the Pioneer Gang. Besides the daily programs, the musicians performed at dances and shows, a lot of them in the coal camps that regularly tuned in WHIS. The Sunshine Sisters had their own 15-minute gospel program, and sang commercials for Chicago House Furniture.

According to Roberts, "We did make a little money there, for a change."

For a time in Bluefield, Minnie said she dated a fellow who played fiddle: "I think he was about three years younger than me.

Sometimes when we were booked on shows together, we'd play twin fiddles."

Minnie, who always looked as youthful as her siblings, recalls, "While we were at Bluefield, James and Martha started singing together on the air. When they started singing together, people responded to them. You had to hand it to James, he could sing. They sang so well together, they could almost convert you."

John Lair, however, was more interested in an all-girl string band.

"John may have heard us on radio, either at WLAP or even WHIS, which reached out pretty far for a little station," Martha surmises, recalling Lair contacted them in late 1939 to perform on his *Renfro Valley Barn Dance* program.

Her first husband, however, insists: "I had already got those girls an audition with John Lair before we went over to West Virginia. We had met in Richmond, before Bluefield, and I arranged that."

Roberts continues, "John needed somebody to work for the Coon Creek Girls. Rosie was fixin' to have a baby and Lily May was the only one left. When he contacted the girls, however, I was under the assumption we were going to do whatever we were doing at Bluefield. But, I still didn't do anything except park cars."

Indeed, the Sunshine Sisters were invited to temporarily replace Lily May Ledford's "sisters" as part of the popular Coon Creek Girls on Lair's show. It was the first step into the big time for the Amburgey sisters, who now had an opportunity to be heard nationally during the NBC network portion of the *Barn Dance*.

A true pioneer, John Lair had initially organized one of the more popular musical groups - The Cumberland Ridge Runners - in Chicago on WLS's *Barn Dance* in 1929, then went on to found two unique country radio programs: *The Renfro Valley Barn Dance,* which aired on both WLW-Cincinnati and WHAS-Louisville; and the WSB-Atlanta *Barn Dance* a wee bit later.

Important acts Lair helped promote via the shows were Red Foley, Whitey (Duke of Paducah) Ford, Lulu Belle & Scotty, Karl & Harty, Linda Parker, Clayton McMichen, Homer & Jethro, Girls of the Golden West (Dolly & Millie Good) and the Coon Creek Girls.

Lair promoted vocalist-fiddler-banjoist Lily May on WLS after she won a fiddler's contest in Kentucky. She came by her fiddlin' honestly enough, having learned that instrument - and banjo - from her daddy, Daw Ledford, father of 14 children.

Lily May was born March 17, 1917 in Powell County, Ky. Several other Ledford siblings also learned to play instruments. In fact, her first band included sister Rose on guitar; brother Coy on fiddle; and a neighbor boy Morgan Skidmore, pickin' guitar and sharing vocals with Lily May. Lair auditioned her band in 1935 for WLS, but not sufficiently impressed to hire them, though he did take Lily May under his wing from then on.

Later, the original Coon Creek Girls became a sort of flagship act for the fledgling *Renfro Barn Dance Show,* first broadcast direct from WLW-Cincinatti, Oct. 9, 1937. Besides Lily May, the Coon Creek Girls then included Ohio fiddler Evelyn Lange (as Daisy, performing bass fiddle); Esther Koehler (as Violet, a mandolin picker) from Wisconsin; and Lily May's real-life sister, Rosie Ledford (on guitar).

During March 1938, Lair herded the all-girl band into Chicago's ARC Studios, under the guidance of Uncle Art Satherley, to make their only-known recordings - sharing studio time (and providing musical backing) with another Lair act, Aunt Idy.

Ledford's Coon Creek Girls achieved a nationally high honor in the form of an invitation from Franklin and Eleanor Roosevelt, then President and First Lady, to perform for them at the White House (June 8, 1939). They appeared as part of "A Program of American Music," which also boasted black contralto Marian Anderson and other important, uniquely American performers. In the very elite audience being entertained were England's King George VI, his wife Queen

Elizabeth, Canadian Governor General W. L. Mackenzie King, Vice President and Mrs. John Nance Garner and the late President Woodrow Wilson's widow Edith Wilson.

Some of the fine folk-styled songs performed so well by the Coon Creek Girls were "You're a Flower That's Blooming," "Pretty Polly" and "Little Birdie."

After Violet and Daisy departed (to form another act, also briefly called the Coon Creek Girls, in the Southwest), Lily engaged her younger sister Minnie, billed as "Black-Eyed Susan," to perform. Violet (Esther Koehler), incidentally, married Lily's brother Custer Ledford.

Years later, Opal/Jean Chapel treasured a warm message she received from Lily May, which read *"To the Entertainer's Entertainer, who would give her last dime to help someone else - and probably has."* Lily May (Pennington) lived to see her son J.P. Pennington succeed nationally as composer (he wrote Alabama's "The Closer You Get" and "Take Me Down") and as lead singer of yet another pop-country group, Exile ("Kiss You All Over," "Give Me One More Chance"), before she died in 1985.

Today, the *Renfro Valley Barn Dance* - a network broadcast for over 12 years - is over 60, and still going strong. Lair's song about his childhood home, "Take Me Back To Renfro Valley," written for his WLS protegé Linda Parker, served as the theme. (Unfortunately, "The Little Sunbonnet Girl" died in her early 20s, following an appendectomy surgery in August 1935.) A stanza of the song:

> *"Take me back to Renfro Valley*
> *When I'm free from earthly care*
> *Lay me down by Dad and Mother*
> *Let me sleep forever there*
> *When it's springtime in the mountains*
> *And the dogwood blossoms blow*
> *I'll be back in Renfro Valley*
> *As in days of long ago..."*

"Renfro Valley became the first community in the nation to originate and broadcast a radio program put on by the actual residents of that community," Lair noted, before his death Nov. 12, 1985, at Central Baptist Hospital in Lexington, Ky. (At 91, Lair had lived 33 years longer than his younger friend and one-time partner, Red Foley, who died Sept. 19, 1968, at 58).

John Lee Lair was born July 1, 1894, the son of Thomas Burke Lair and the former Isabelle Coffey. He grew up in the mountainous terrain surrounding Kentucky's scenic Renfro Valley.

Following his father's death, the family was forced to sell their farmstead to settle the estate. The world, meanwhile, was on the brink of disaster when John elected to serve his country in World War I. Upon discharge, however, he returned to more familiar ground.

To make a living, John taught school in Mt. Vernon, worked for a weekly newspaper in Corbin, and then operated a print shop in Louisville. It was after he became an insurance adjustor, working in New York and Chicago, that he was able to renew his interest in music.

Although John had no special musical skill, he formed the Cumberland Ridge Runners, which proclaimed "Old-Time Fiddlin'" and Kentucky Mountain Songs" its specialty. The Runners landed a spot on WLS' *Barn Dance* in Chicago. The station, initially owned by Sears & Roebuck - hence its WLS ("World's Largest Store") call letters - historically had a slight link to Nashville's WSM.

Accordingly, the Chicago station had engaged George D. Hay in 1924, to announce and help organize a weekend broadcast, showcasing country performers, christening the show the *Barn Dance.* Late the next year (October 1925), Hay was hired by National Life & Accident Insurance as program manager for its new station WSM ("We Shield Millions"), where he created a similar format, likewise dubbed the *Barn Dance.*

(Its first performer was an elderly fiddler, Uncle Jimmy Thompson, followed soon by Dr. Humphrey Bate and his contingent, which included teen-aged daughter Alcyon Bate on piano. By the time WSM made a name change to the *Grand Ole Opry*, string bands were the craze and the show's star was Uncle Dave Macon, "The Dixie Dew Drop.")

Incidentally, another Cumberland Ridge Runners' bit on WLS teamed Clyde (Red) Julian Foley with Myrtle Lee Cooper (later Lulu Belle). Lair had Red and Myrtle sing duets and do comedy skits together, before she partnered professionally and maritally with *Skyland Scotty* Wiseman.

Lulu Belle & Scotty scored national hits such as "Does The Chewing Gum Lose Its Flavor (On the Bed Post Over Night)," "Remember Me" and "Have I Told You Lately That I Love You," the latter two he wrote.

When Foley first burst onto the Chicago scene, Bradley Kincaid was the station's star, billed as the "Kentucky Mountain Boy With the Houn' Dog Guitar." Kincaid set some sort of record at WLS singing "Barbara Allen" every Saturday night for four straight years. (Both he and Foley were alumni of Berea, Ky., High School, though the former was 15 years Foley's senior.)

Chicago radio also boosted budding careers of Gene Autry, Arkie the Arkansas Woodchopper, Jenny Lou Carson (and sisters billed as The Little Maids), the Maple City Four, Grace Wilson, Eddie Dean, the DeZurik Sisters (Mary Jane & Carolyn), Smiley Burnette, Louise Massey, Rex Allen, George Gobel, Pat Buttram, the Hoosier Hotshots, Patsy Montana and the Prairie Ramblers, among others.

Lair loved music, and early on humorously performed on the jug bass with his Cumberland crew on WLS. He was a songwriter, as well, and co-authored "Banjo Pickin' Gal" with Lily May Ledford, regarded as one of her better efforts. Among other tunes Lair wrote are "Lonesome Lulu Lee," "Keep Fiddlin' On (Uncle Doodie)" and the gospel-sounding "Only One Step More."

His goal had long been to build a country venue in the heart of the Bluegrass State, to fulfill the musical wants of Kentuckians, while possibly luring music lovers from other states.

"My dream was, in a way, to move backward, across the years almost to the very beginning," stated Lair. "But I knew it would take a lot of money to do all this. I had none and no apparent prospects of ever getting hold of more than enough for a comfortable living, so that was the answer to all that. But a boy will dream…"

Thus, in financial partnership with brothers Red and Vern (Cotton) Foley and Whitey Ford, Lair was able to build the *Renfro Valley Barn Dance* site, consisting of a huge show barn, 12 log cabins and a lodge near Mt. Vernon. During construction, the show emanated from WLW-Cincinnati (starting Oct. 9, 1937).

Finally, on Saturday night, Nov. 4, 1939, Lair introduced the first broadcast from Renfro Valley. With a jerry-rigged hookup of telephone lines (connected through an open window), the maiden on-site show was fed to Ohio for broadcast.

On that first show, Lair promised a free photo emanating from the *Renfro Valley Barn Dance* for each request received. Reportedly, there were 253,000 requests! Highlights of that premiere program included the Coon Creek Girls playing "Cacklin' Hen," Red Foley plaintively performing "Old Shep," Pleaz Mobley nostalgically singing "Barbara Allen," Aunt Idy (Margaret Lillie), and the Norwood Hoedowners.

The Amburgey sisters worked the *Barn Dance* until Lair invited them to do a similar show he was busily coordinating for his Atlanta business contacts, at the start of the new decade.

Meanwhile, the *Renfro Valley Barn Dance* did a booming business. Within a short time, Lair bought out Ford and the Foleys, gaining majority ownership, but then sealed a pact with Keyes Advertising in Chicago, retaining 51 per cent to their 49 per cent.

Sunday Mornin' Gatherin', a gospel-influenced show Lair started, was inaugurated in 1943, and carried by clear channel WHAS-Louisville for many years (and picked up by CBS for 15 years). Finally, in 1945, Lair launched *The Bugle* newspaper, to help publicize the program.

In the early 1950s, Lair was able to license his own radio station - WRVK - call letters translating to "Welcome to Renfro Valley, Ky." In 1956, the first televised show, *The Renfro Valley Folks,* was filmed for Pillsbury as a 12-part series.

There was even a 1970s movie, "John Lair's Renfro Valley Barn Dance," filmed in Eastman Color and directed by William Johnson, under Lair's supervision.

"It had no plot or story line, but it did spotlight the different styles of the Renfro Valley fiddlers," recalled Pete Stamper, who still entertains on the program. "Word went out to Sleepy Marlin, Lily May (Ledford), Buddy Durham and all ex-Renfro Valley folks to come back home and join Ralph Marcum and B. Lucas for this special occasion. Their 'battle of the bows' was a highlight of the movie."

Incidentally, from 1968, and for about 10 years, a former fiddler Hal Smith owned the Renfro Valley operation. For a time, he even engaged Mac Wiseman to manage the Renfro Valley Bluegrass Festivals. Smith confided, however, that commuting, as he was doing between Renfro and Nashville, was no way to run a business. Finally, he sold the works, opting to remain in Nashville with his session-guitarist wife Velma Williams-Smith (she's heard on such hits as "Bluebird Island" and "Detroit City" and vocally on Western-style singer Jimmy Wakely's 1949 Top 10 hit "Someday You'll Call My Name").

Still, John Lair's dream continued. In 1979, 22 years after Lily May retired her act, Lair even put together a contemporary band of females, calling them *The New Coon Creek Girls.* According to original member Vicki Simmons, Lily May gave her blessing to the newly-formed act, and today the musical "descendants" officially own the title - and perform on the vintage program. (They also have CDs marketed, including the acclaimed Sonny Osborne-produced "Ain't Love a Good Thing" on Pinecastle Records, boasting a great, poignant number called "Casting Stones.")

The recent *Barn Dance* still boasted the talents of Old Joe Clark's son Terry Clark, and a host of newcomers, while guest stars ranged from Ricky Van Shelton to Connie Smith and her fellow Opry star, the late comic Jerry Clower.

There's no stopping progress. Indeed, the complex grew. Recent co-owners Ralph Gabbard, Glenn Pennington and Warren Rosenthal added a 1,500-seat, air-conditioned auditorium as the new barn. The old barn housed the show's historic artifacts, serving as a museum. In the Fire House, an animated John Lair figure recounted the story of Renfro Valley for visitors.

In tribute to all the mountain people he loved, Lair wrote "Only One Step More." Its message (here in part) inspired the common man of that era:

> *"I have known a life of sorrow*
> *I have borne a heavy load*
> *And my weary feet have stumbled*
> *On the rough and rocky road*
> *Soon my burden will be lifted*
> *Soon my trials will be o'er*
> *Soon my journey will be ended*
> *For it's only one step more..."*

Roberts remembers that Lair also had a show on WLW-Cincinnati called *The Possum Hunt,* which commemorated his beloved country living: "They had corn shuckin' and quiltin' and certain things to do (on it)...we left before it ended. I didn't work the Renfro Valley (show) at all."

Some of the acts Lair had were Granny Harper, Charlie Hobbes, the Range Riders: Roland Gaines, Guy Blakeman and Jerry Burns (who married Little Ella); comic Gene Cobb; and the comedy act Cy and Fannie with their live burro L'il Abner:

"This burro would put a jump-rope in his teeth, while one held the other end of the rope and the other did the jumpin'."

"You know, I bought my first car from Bill Russell, the comedian on the Renfro Valley show," adds Roberts, nostalgically.

He remembers, too, how entertaining an act was put on by Aunt (pronounced A'int) Idy and Little Clifford: "He weighed 300 pounds and she was a little bitty woman. Margaret Lillie was the first Aunt Idy, but when she left John Lair got Ricca Hughes to act as Aunt Idy. But for a while, whenever we did a show, someone showed up to attach the box office, claiming it wasn't the right Idy (advertised)."

Granny Harper, however, was James' buddy because she told it like it was: "She said Asa Martin was the biggest liar she ever heard in her life. She said he told her he had running water and lights in his barn. *'Well, I went back there one time and looked it over good, and the only running water he had was when in rained in through the holes in his roof, and he had lights when the lightnin' struck and you could see light throughout the barn!'*"

Martha also remembers Granny Harper with delight: "She was a pistol! Played that fiddle like no one else, sang a little and did a little buck dance, too. I remember that we did five or six shows a day on those fair dates and she kept right up with us young'uns. I can see her sitting on that accordion case now, when Little Clifford (who was John Lair's 300-pound nephew) yelled over at her, *'Aw hush up, Granny. No one wants to hear you!'* And without hesitating, she'd shoot right back at him, *'Little Clifford! I slept away more sense than you ever had!'*

"Those fair dates were something else. We'd be driving in the car and then stop to go in somewhere and eat, makeup smeared, face a mess, from sleeping in the car. I can imagine what those waitresses thought."

At Renfro, there wasn't much work musically for James, so he made some money parking cars to help support him and his bride.

"John paid me $2 a day for whatever I did," James corroborates. "I got $3 for parking cars on Saturday night. John Lair paid each of the girls' $25. If I went on the road, I usually got $15...and we made $2 or $3 a piece on personal appearances."

Fair-and-square Lair made a momentous trek to Atlanta along about October 1940, concerning a business proposition he was being offered. The station engaging him was then owned by the *Atlanta Journal* newspaper. WSB's *Barn Dance* went on the air Nov. 16, 1940.

"Before I knew it," Martha Carson affirms, "I became a staff member at WSB, remaining there nine years, a rather lengthy run, thanks to Mr. John Lair."

Walt Trott

Walt Trott

CHAPTER 8

Barn Dance Sweethearts...

"We cover the South, like the dew covers Dixie,"
Atlanta Journal motto.

John Lair was the first real showman Martha Carson had yet met, a barnyard version of famed Broadway producer Florenz Ziegfeld, who knew the intrinsic value of combining beauty and talent on stage.

Lair's eye for both was apparent when he engaged such distaff talents as Linda Parker, Lulu Belle, Lily May Ledford, Molly O'Day and, of course, the Amburgey sisters, for his shows. Obviously, he had enough faith to take them from a small town station to featured status on major network affiliates, in a time when radio ruled.

At first, at the *Renfro Valley Barn Dance,* the Amburgeys were merely filling in for the Coon Creek Girls, performing in relative anonymity. According to Minnie, "Lily May was having problems with her girls. One got sick, another got married and quit, and another was having a baby. Well, we fit in perfect and with Lily May there nobody knew the other girls were gone, really."

Still, they did get a chance to glow in the musical spotlight, particularly after they made the move to Atlanta, a city that thrived on country music. Actually, Georgia's capital had been the scene of the first radio broadcast programming old-time country music, March 16, 1922, right there on station WSB. The Jenkins Family became 1922 favorites of the WSB radio audience, as did Fiddlin' John Carson. A popular WSB country program of the 1930s was the *Crossroads Follies,* but there was no Saturday night frolic yet. (Ironically, more recently WSB has programmed primarily soft rock via B98.5 FM.)

Atlanta also was the site of numerous early recording projects for pioneer performers like Fiddlin' John Carson (1923, "Little Old Log Cabin in the Lane"/"The Old Hen Cackled And the Rooster's Goin' to Crow"), Smith Sacred Singers (1926, "Where We'll Never Grow Old"), Tarleton & Darby (1927, "Columbus Stockade Blues"/"Birmingham Jail"), Gid Tanner & His Skillet-Lickers (1929, "Soldier's Joy"), J.E. Mainer's Mountaineers (1935, "Maple On the Hill"), Blue Sky Boys (1940, "East Bound Train") and later Kitty Wells (1949, "Death At the Bar"), among so many others. It was a prime distribution center for major labels like RCA Victor.

In December 1939, Cox Enterprises of Ohio, a communications conglomerate, purchased WSB, a 50,000 watt station. Cox owned the city's daily *Atlanta Journal,* originally founded in 1883. (Cox also bought the competing *Constitution,* founded in 1868, and later combined their news operation as the *Journal & Constitution.*)

Impressed by Lair's work in Chicago and Cincinnati, Cox had contracted him to help establish a program showcasing artists from that region to boost its listening audience. Lair felt strongly about using the Amburgey sisters, whom he renamed the Hoot Owl Holler Girls. He invited them to launch their group with "Aunt Hattie," in Atlanta.

Thus it was fall 1940, when Lair started getting things up and running.

"John had sent us down and when we got there, we saw our picture plastered on the front page of the *Atlanta Journal!* They were welcoming Aunt Hattie - who was sort of our mother figure - and the Hoot Owl Holler Girls," emphasizes Martha. "It was also the first time we saw our new names: Minnie (Bertha), Marthie (me) and Mattie (Opal). Since the *Journal* owned WSB, Lordy, they had something in there almost every day about the *Barn Dance* people."

Minnie confides: "I never did like the name Bertha, but I was named after my aunt. My daddy wanted Martha to be called

Ethel, but at least mama got the Irene first. Opal was the only one that escaped being named after someone in the family."

"Aunt Hattie" was actually a lady named Ricca Hughes, who was in her 60s and a veteran comic, who initially replaced Margaret Lillie as Aunt Idy at Renfro Valley.

"John Lair was great at promoting these women," notes Minnie. "Granny Harper, who was humpbacked real bad, could play that fiddle like you wouldn't believe! She was close to 80 - and a star on the *Renfro Valley* show. Aunt Ida was another'n."

"I remember that Aunt Hattie bought a brand new automobile and I did most of the driving for them on personal appearances...," says James. "John Lair made a deal to start the *Barn Dance* in Atlanta (with J. Leonard Rensch, manager of WSB). John brought in Aunt Hattie and the Hoot Owl Holler Girls, Dwight Bratcher, the Sunshine Boys, Doug and Marvin, but they kept on Harpo Kidwell, who had been on their early morning show, Glenn and Jean Hughes (from Cincinnati), and Hank Penny and his Radio Cowboys. I think that's all they kept."

Harrison (Chick) Kimball managed the Atlanta *Barn Dance*, since its official kick-off, Saturday, Nov. 16, 1940. From the git-go, 10 or 12 acts performed on the weekend show, among others Penny, Pete Cassell, Swanee River Boys, comedian-fiddle player Chick Stripling, utilizing a *Renfro Valley Barn Dance* format.

"In those first years, Hank Penny was our host," adds Martha. "He had a young fiddler named Boudleaux Bryant, who later wrote all those great Jimmy Dickens and Everly Brothers songs. Hank was a seasoned entertainer, the best I'd ever seen."

Especially adept on banjo, handsome Herbert Clayton Penny hailed from Birmingham. He was known for his theme song "Won't You Ride in My Little Red Wagon," originally penned by fellow Alabaman Rex Griffith (who also wrote "The Last Letter." He died in New Orleans in 1958).

After leaving WSB, Penny went to Hollywood, where he worked with Spade Cooley's western swing troupe, and was wed to blonde pop singer Sue Thompson ("Norman," "Sad Movies") from 1953-'63. Hank had several hit records himself, most notably "Steel Guitar Stomp," "Get Yourself a Red Head," both 1946, and "Bloodshot Eyes," 1950, all peaking at #4 on *Billboard* country charts. (Penny died from heart failure, April 17, 1992, at age 73.)

Bryant, a Shellman, Ga. native, was born Feb. 13, 1920. He boasted a classical music background, having studied as a youth, hoping to be a concert violinist. Bryant actually played a season with the Atlanta Philharmonic Orchestra before going country (which he enjoyed playing).

Now a Country Music Hall of Famer (with songwriting partner-wife Felice Bryant), he's responsible for composing such classics as "Hey, Joe," "Bye, Bye Love," "Wake Up Little Susie," "Blue Boy" and "Rocky Top." (He died in 1987, at age 67.)

Another key WSB alumnae is Joseph (Cotton) Carrier, a gifted emcee and accomplished picker, who joined the crew a short time after the Amburgeys arrived. Carrier found himself a wife at the *Barn Dance* - petite singer Jane Logan, who played accordion.

"Jane had a little solo stint she did, and she also done little novelty things, as I recall," offers Martha. "She and Cotton got courtin' and then they got married and had a big family, maybe three or four kids." (She was even briefly a Hoot Owl Holler Girl.)

After arriving in Atlanta, James was discouraged to learn that the station had a policy implemented that barred married couples from working together. That sort of put the *kibosh* on plans to team vocally with his wife, for awhile. Yet, his situation took an upturn in Atlanta.

"We didn't get our duets started up until six months after we got to Atlanta…But before long, I was doing personal appearances with Hank Penny and with Pappy Slatts, who was on WAGA, another station in town. So, I was making as much as Martha."

Meanwhile, the Hoot Owl Holler Girls went over big with WSB audiences. They made a handsome trio together: Marthie being red-haired, Minnie a brunette and Mattie's angelic face was complemented by blonde locks.

Minnie recalls, "Martha used to say to me, 'Move up front where people can see you.' I'd say, 'Leave me alone. I'm happy right back here.' I never did push myself. I preferred to stay in the background all the time. But, I loved to watch them advance - Martha and Jean - because performing is what they wanted most.

"Truthfully, more than anything else, when I finished high school, I wanted most of all to meet a good man, who would make a good husband and father, live in a white house with a white picket fence and wear a red-checked apron. I had it in mind to be a good cook, mother, wife and housekeeper. I never was interested in fame, other than to help make my younger sisters happy."

The trio's sweet harmony earned them even more money as sponsors requested their vocals to help sell such products as *Wildwoot Cream Oil ("Charlie")* hair tonic. Their popularity, of course, also created a demand for the act to play personal appearances within listening radius.

"I remember that we did the morning *Farm & Home Hour* at 5:30 a.m., which was like the middle of the night when you wouldn't get in from a show the night before until 2 or 3 a.m.," says Martha, growing weary, just at the recollection.

At one point, a new Hoot Owl Holler Aunt materialized. Ricca Hughes departed, probably due to a contract dispute, and was quietly replaced by Edna Wilson, who had earlier scored on WSM's *Grand Ole Opry* in a comedy duo called Sarie and Sally. (Incidentally, Sarie's real-life husband was a noted Cajun chef.)

Once, while doing the show in the Women's Club Auditorium, Martha denotes she invited James to join her: "I didn't have permission to do it, but I called him up on stage to do a song with me. Well, the audience went wild - and we got an encore!"

James recalls their first duet on WSB differently: "Aunt Hattie called out to me one time, accusing me of making eyes at one of her 'nieces.' She said, 'Can you sing at all?' I said, 'Why sure I can sing." And she said, 'Then how about singing us a song?' I replied, 'If you let me sing with your pretty niece Marthie…'

"Well the very first song we ever did on WSB together was (the original Carter Family's theme) 'Keep On the Sunny Side.' In the next day or so, they got about 70 or 80 cards and letters wanting us to sing that song again. So they soon changed their policy."

According to James, one 15-minute show they appeared on was even titled the *Sunny Side of Life* program, which aired shortly before noon. He said they also sang on the morning *Barnyard Jamboree* and the 30-minute *Georgia Jubilee* shows.

Whenever Hank Penny would call on James, he'd introduced him as "James Carson," rather than Roberts. One wag had it that Penny confused Kentucky's Fiddlin' Doc Roberts to Georgia's own Fiddlin' John Carson, a legendary artist who was arguably the first country musician to earn a million-selling instrumental record, via his 1924 hits "You Will Never Miss Your Mother Until She is Gone" coupled with "Fare You Well, Ol' Joe Clark."

Thus, unwittingly, Penny christened the future star duet *James & Martha Carson.* (In his final days, John was seen operating an elevator in the newspaper building. Carson reportedly was a big fan of the duo, who latched onto his surname, until his death on Dec. 11, 1949, at age 81. He had often performed himself with a woman, his daughter Rosa Lee, who was actually billed as "Moonshine Kate.")

After WSB abandoned its "no couples" edict (which also pleased Cotton Carrier and Jane Logan), Hank Penny found himself more and more introducing James & Martha Carson, who soon became known by the well-earned sobriquet "The Barn Dance Sweethearts."

Their popularity was such that within the year, Martha and James were a featured act. Minnie muses, "That kind of hurt us, me and Jean. It appeared that he was taking her away from us and our act."

Mattie, meanwhile, was blossoming into a blonde beauty with her wholesome good looks and shapely figure. The winsome teen-ager found herself the center of attention among the young swains on the Atlanta scene.

Minnie was doing her utmost to protect and chaperone her kid sister from the wily wolves about town. Even far from home and on her own, Minnie had an irrational fear of being labeled "boy crazy," so she seldom dated. One evening, however, Jean encouraged her to come along and watch another act, Pop Eckler & His Young'uns, in performance. Eckler, who later had the country hit "Money, Marbles and Chalk," was a headliner on competing Atlanta station WAGA.

Jean admired another young musician in the group, while Minnie started feeling vibes from Charles (Ducky) Woodruff, an Eckler bandsman, who was only six months older than she. Like the song said, her *dreams were getting better all the time...*

One night while accompanying Jean to an Eckler gig, Ducky tried to engage Minnie in conversation, but she proved too aloof: "When I seen him coming towards me, I took off for the car. I figured ain't nobody gonna tell me I'm chasing after guys. He always called me *'the demure little miss'* after that.

"The next time I did talk to him," continues Minnie, this time smiling. "One thing that made me start liking him was his honesty. We all went together one night down at The Varsity, which was *the* hot spot in town. I heard him tell another guy, 'Leon, you would put me in this spot. I'm broke!' Well, that didn't bother me none. I said, 'Hey, c'mon and eat. I've got some money.' We didn't think anything of that then in show business."

Oddly enough, she adds, goodnaturedly, "I learned that's how Charlie got his nickname. Every time the bill came around, he had a way of *ducking it.* Charlie and I dated three or four months. We were married March 16, 1941. But, I'll tell you, I couldn't have found any better man living. We were married some 40 years, when he got sick with cancer (Charles, 64, died in March 1982)."

Harking back to the sister act, Minnie maintains the trio lasted little more than a year together at WSB: "Martha started doing double duty; that is, she sang with us and started singing with James, as well. After they got so good together - and received so much audience response - she started spending more time (performing) with him."

Minnie and Charlie departed Atlanta in late 1941, when Pop Eckler busted up his band: "My husband didn't have anything to do there, so we moved to Cincinnati, just before Pearl Harbor was bombed, and had our first child (Sandra) in March (1942, also her parents first grandchild)."

On Sunday morning, Dec. 7, 1941, that "date that will live in infamy," as declared by President Franklin D. Roosevelt, the Japanese bombed Pearl Harbor, Hawaii, plunging the U.S. - and the world - into war against the Axis forces: Japan, Germany and Italy.

America had just pulled itself out of the Great Depression - and now it faced an even more perilous threat - from outsiders. The sneak attack on Pearl Harbor, however, united Americans - and their allies - as nothing else seemed to be able to do before.

It also wrought changes on the music scene as many young male performers were drafted into military service. Small flags popped up in residence windows, with stars indicating the number of family members serving their country.

War-time songs proliferated, including such hits as "Remember Pearl Harbor," "Don't Sit Under the Apple Tree (With Anyone Else But Me)," "Praise the Lord and Pass the Ammunition," "There's a Star-Spangled Banner Waving Somewhere" and "He Wears a Pair of Silver Wings," for which audiences clamored.

In recognition of Martha and James' growing popularity, WSB - which was located on the top floor of the Biltmore Hotel on Peach Tree Street - rightly assigned the couple the Saturday 2 p.m. *Georgia Jubilee.* When Minnie left, Martha kept the Hoot Owl Holler Girls going briefly by engaging another musician, Jane Logan, to join her and Mattie.

Martha points out, "Meanwhile, we got another daily show at 11:45 until noon, *James & Martha Carson,* sponsored by the Vick Chemical Company. We'd get in about four gospel songs during that 15-minute segment, along with commercials. I don't know if it means anything now, but the Vick Company offered us a lifetime contract way back then."

All of this was in addition to the *Dixie Farm & Home Hour,* the weekend *Barn Dance* and numerous personal appearances throughout the region. The war time gasoline and rubber rationing prompted the artists to be a bit creative in obtaining tires and gasoline to get to and from p.a. dates.

"We'd do the best we could with what rations we had (starting in July 1942, the government restricted drivers to three gallons of gasoline a week), but between us all, we'd get enough to go back and forth to those little ol' gigs at night," beams Martha.

When the crowds outgrew the 500-seat Women's Club Auditorium, the WSB *Barn Dance* moved into the larger downtown Erlanger Theater, she acknowledges.

"It would hold perhaps twice that many. The Erlanger was a former movie palace, which had prettier, more theatrical-looking curtains and such."

For the Saturday night show, the cast would sit on hay bales to lend a little rural atmosphere. Usually, James wore dress trousers and tieless sometimes-checkered shirts. Martha wore country-style gingham dresses that looked appropriate with her shoulder-length wavy auburn hair. Speaking of tresses, Martha insists, "I have problem hair; that is, it's fine as baby hair. Believe me I struggled with it. I had to roll it at night and style it myself every day."

After "Mattie" left the act, she visited with Minnie (who thereafter was known by her stage name) and Charlie in New

Richmond, Ohio, a town that sits almost on the Ohio-Kentucky line. Charlie's younger brother Bruce soon turned her head and it wasn't long before Jean, now 19, and Bruce were a twosome, as well -- and soon to be a threesome.

"Unfortunately, theirs would prove to be a short union," laments Minnie. "There wasn't really anything to it." (Nonetheless, Jean and Bruce's son Kenneth, born in 1943, would be a lasting legacy of their liaison.)

Although the *Barn Dance* wasn't scripted, merely performed spontaneously *a la* the *Grand Ole Opry,* the show resorted to remote broadcasts, which involved a portion being taped live and played back accordingly.

"You know that was also the first experience I ever had hearing how my voice sounded when I talked," Martha explains. "They were doing the show at 8 o'clock to be played back at 10 p.m. Well, afterwards we were riding in the car to a showdate and I heard myself on the radio. I thought *'O'migosh! That's me! I'll never talk again!'* Well, about the only competition I figured I had talking in that husky voice was Ma Kettle (Marjorie Main)."

Mac Wiseman recalls when he arrived in '49, WSB's show was "Out at (Atlanta's) East Point, and they were taking it on the road to other auditoriums, and (would) remote it back. I had been at Bristol with the Foggy Mountain Boys, when Bill Carlisle got me on WSB. For a fellow who didn't have any records, they treated me well. I remember I liked Atlanta, and it was pretty there in the spring."

Although there in Atlanta, Martha's talents were helping to generate a greater family income, she didn't personally benefit much from her box office luster.

"When we first moved there, James and I had an apartment, which we kept for a couple of years. Finally, even James had to admit, we were doing really well. We were working for a good salary, and the two of us had a pretty good income. So, we bought a home."

In retrospect, Martha spent years of her life under financial dictates of others, first her parents, then sister Minnie, Asa, and finally the two men she married. It was hard for her in Atlanta, knowing that the money was flowing in, but not benefitting her too much.

"I couldn't even write a check. James kept the checkbook. I remember some of us would go out to eat between shows - to get a hamburger, coffee or something - and if James wasn't along and I didn't have money, I'd have to hit someone up to lend me enough to pay my check. There was no need of that, as we had a good, healthy joint bank account!"

Musically speaking, their teaming during the 1940s represented a milestone in the evolution of instrumental duos. Earlier, the mandolin-guitar-vocal pairings had been male partners, who became extremely popular, starting in the 1930s, among whom were the Delmores, Karl & Harty, Mac & Bob, Bill and Charlie Monroe, the Shelton Brothers and the Atlanta-based Blue Sky Boys (Bill and Earl Bolick).

Suddenly, here was a male-female duo, whose harmonic vocals and breakneck tempos not only captured the imagination of many thousands, but seemingly anticipated the raw bluegrass sound that's so much in vogue today.

"Actually, we were mostly singing the hymnal or old traditional tunes done up with our own arrangements, songs like 'I'll Fly Away' or 'He Will Set Your Fields On Fire.'" insisted Martha (who notes, too, that as writers she and James were signed to Acuff-Rose Publishing, on April 7, 1949).

"Some of the newer numbers we performed, as I recall, were 'I Ain't Got Time,' which Buford Abner (of the Swanee River Boys) wrote; 'There's An Open Door Waiting,' by James; and one written by Hank Williams, 'Sing, Sing, Sing,' which I believe Fred Rose gave to us."

Early on, James Roberts also recalls being given a list of songs that were *verboten* (forbidden) at WSB.

"Yeah, I remember one time they handed me a list of songs that you *could not* perform on their station, including 'Pretty

Quadroon' and 'Sweet Kittie Wells' (both of which dealt with black women)."

CHAPTER 9

Silent Partner...

A Christian is a man who feels
Repentance on a Sunday
For what he did on Saturday
And is going to do on Monday.
— **Thomas Russell Ybarra's** "The Christian"

"I had read the Bible since I was a little girl, but I couldn't really understand what I was reading," confides Martha Carson. "While I was performing in Atlanta, however, a controversy developed. Some were questioning our religious affiliation - and I needed answers."

With their popularity as the *Barn Dance Sweethearts,* the couple became a major influence on radio listeners. Before long, they learned fans were even naming children after them, while still others saw in them a way to fatten their coffers.

Despite the fact that he had guided Martha and James to WSB success, John Lair never claimed any management or agent affiliation with them.

"Once in awhile, John came down, but he never did that. I suppose he might have got a percentage off the show, however, since he helped to get it going," admits James.

Martha and James Carson had literally burst onto the scene as the first couple whose gospel songs became classic statements of evangelical Protestantism. Before long, the husband-and-wife team were being contacted by nearly every religious affiliation, many of whom were camping out on the doorstep of their suburban Lakewood Park home, seeking their membership.

WSB's number one act became fascinated with a radio evangelist called Brother Merck, of the Missionary Baptist Church. "I was impressed by the happiness and love of God he was preaching," notes Martha. "We both worked for him sincerely - and even left the radio station for awhile. We played a string of tent revival meetings where poor farm people would come out to see us. He had a radio show, too. He invited us over to his house, and I saw that he and his wife had cookie jars and piggy banks full of money...I even taught Sunday school, calling up religious feelings from my heart, and James almost became a preacher. That's how strongly we felt about this church."

James Roberts says it also marked the first time he was "saved," and he credits the Reverend Merck.

One Friday night, however, the revivalists took up what they called "a love offering for James and Martha Carson," then the deacons slipped out behind the tent and counted up some $500 in cash donations.

To Martha's disdain they then decided to take up another *love offering* Monday night: "It bothered me to see humble, poor people coming out with five or six barefooted young'uns and giving us their money. They would even bring chickens or hams for us. I told them, *you keep that food for your family.*

"Brother Merck said it was OK for them to donate money, because 'God layed it on their hearts to give.' I could see with him, it was money, money, money. That broke my heart. So, I told him, *'God is not laying it on my heart to come and take their money. We're going back to the station (WSB).'"*

"People were throwing all these things at me from the Bible that I didn't understand. I thought, *Lord, let me learn, let me understand this word.*"

As a result, Martha bought a Bible dictionary, thinking it would be a good way to study the Good Book. What she learned was enlightening indeed: "I found that 90 per cent of those who criticized us, wanted us because we would increase their audience (and therefore their 'take' from parishoners). When Brother Merck said, 'You don't *need* to sing in those worldly places,' I asked him, *'How did you hear me?'* Well, of course, he'd heard me on the show. I told him, 'In my Bible, it says don't hide your talent under a bushel basket...If I just come out here to your church, I don't think I'm letting my light shine very far.'"

Indeed their light shone brightly throughout the decade.

According to a Feb. 5, 1949 news item in *Billboard,* the trade weekly, *"Martha and James Carson return to WSB Atlanta after a nine-month absence,"* which indicated the couple had left the show the previous summer to work with Brother Merck. In an ironic postscript to their association with the evangelist, Martha frowns, adding, "A few years later, I heard he fell in love with a young choir singer and left his wife and little boy for her."

A current review of James and Martha Carson's 1940s performances reveals why their style so strongly influenced other musical teams and earned them an affectionate place in the hearts of fans. There's a quality of timeliness in their duets that will appeal to music lovers who weren't even alive during their heyday.

Beautifully blended vocals, combined with their vigorous musical dexterity and strong stage presence, should have rivaled the national success of Lulu Belle & Scotty. Unfortunately, James and Martha didn't get to record until the postwar era, which seriously hampered much-needed exposure offered by platter success.

Some contemporary critics have even likened the music to bluegrass.

"I told 'em my music ain't bluegrass. My pickin' and Bill Monroe's was never alike. I played my mandolin like daddy played his fiddle. Bill never played like that...and I was always sincere in what I did."

It was inevitable that the Carson duo would be offered a record pact.

"After we got popular and before we got our contract with Capitol, two people signed us to record contracts, but never did record us. John Lair was one of them. He had bought a lot of old equipment from the King Record company in Cincinnati, and he was gonna record people from Renfro Valley. In fact, he wanted to move the equipment down to Renfro Valley. Trouble was, the equipment wore out and John never got it off the ground, and didn't have the power to do it. I went to see him about it once and when he found out I was there, he took off. I followed him until he got on a train, and never could catch up to him."

RCA, which had a strong presence in Georgia's capital city, had hired James Carson to play mandolin on a session for the Jones Sisters (Judy and Julie) in the old Fox Theater building, but did not consider recording the *Barn Dance Sweethearts.*

Why? James grins and replies, "Chet Atkins could tell you...he asked Steve Sholes (RCA's country chief) about recording James and Martha Carson, and Steve said, 'That's nothing but a hopped-up Blue Sky Boys act,' referring to a brother team (Bill and Earl Bolick) then on RCA."

(Incidentally, unhappy with the Bolicks, Sholes soon replaced them with Johnnie & Jack, a duo that boasted a more innovative beat, highlighted by a Latin-flavored shuffle, best exemplified on their 1951 breakthrough hit "Poison Love.")

Back in late 1946, however, the Kansas City-based independent White Church Records label contacted the couple to record several sides (in Atlanta).

"Deb (Delbert) Dyer had been at Renfro Valley, but not when I was there," recalls Roberts. "John Lair may have told him about us. Anyway, we did something we never should have, we went and recorded six or eight numbers for him. The deal we had was to buy so many records from White Church to sell at our shows."

Once a session was scheduled, possibly at WGST-Atlanta's studio, the husband-and-wife team actually chose the following eight songs: "The Sweetest Gift (A Mother's Smile)," "He Will Set Your Fields On Fire," "Got a Little Light," "There's an Open Door Waiting," "I Ain't Got Time," "When He Heard My Plea," "Man of Galilee" and "Budded On Earth (To Bloom in Heaven)," the latter three penned by James.

The couple used their legal surname - James and Martha Roberts - on releases from the White Church recordings. [The gospel disc company also had a secular label called Red Barn, but the Roberts' agreement was only for gospel tunes.]

"A lot of critics hear those tracks and say our records on White Church were better than those on Capitol, though we re-recorded all those at Capitol," says Roberts, running his fingers through his steel-gray hair, still parted in the middle.

"I believe that we were the first to record a number of songs we popularized, including 'The Sweetest Gift' and 'Budded On Earth,' which Roy Acuff also recorded," Martha states matter-of-factly.

Recording "The Sweetest Gift" (written by J. B. Coates) held a bittersweet touch of irony for Martha, who yearned to be a mother herself. The Carsons' version of that poignant number *was* the first recording of the song. A short time later, the Bailey Brothers (Danny and Charlie, a WROL-Knoxville duo from Klondike, Tenn.) also cut it.

Martha says she first heard it as sung by the Blue Sky Boys (on Atlanta's WGST); however, that RCA duo didn't get around to recording it until 1949. (More recent cuts include those by the bluegrass cult favorites Seldom Scene, Emmylou Harris, Linda Ronstadt and the Judds.)

The Carsons' reputation as a major attraction in the Southeast spread rapidly. Famed cowboy star Tex Ritter knew about their *Barn Dance* popularity and suggested that his Los Angeles-based label, Capitol Records, give the team a listen. Ritter, incidentally, was Capitol's first country artist signed after the label was founded in 1942, by singer-songwriter Johnny Mercer, music store owner Glenn Wallich, and Broadway and Hollywood producer-publisher B. G. (Buddy) DeSylva.

During a business trip to Atlanta with Ritter, Capitol's then-A&R chief Lee Gillette heard Martha and James on the radio, and decided to record them. A musicians' strike, however, stalled any studio effort (the union's year-long recording ban went in effect Jan. 1, 1948) until 1949.

Gillette had the duet signed to a seven-year contract, however, and later assigned Walter (Dee) Kilpatrick to handle production chores there in Atlanta. Dee said he would usually conduct sessions in such radio station studios as WSB, WAGA and WGST.

"I think Dee was then living somewhere in North Carolina and he used to drive in for our recording sessions," recalls Martha. "I think we did four or five Capitol sessions altogether."

Actually, Martha and James did five sessions, the first on Thursday, March 31, 1949, when the couple recorded two previously-cut songs (for White Church), "Ain't Got Time" and "Budded On Earth." Four other tracks recorded were "(I'll) Shout and Sing," "When God Dips His Pen of Love in My Heart," "Living in the Promised Land" and an old-time temperance tune, "Don't Sell Him Another Drink."

The latter number, dating back to the 1870s, was somewhat off course for the duo; but then as now, preachers were regularly warning the multitudes against alcohol as another evil tool of the Devil, leading to degradation and mortal sins.

On "Shout and Sing," where his mandolin playing was praised, Roberts says he got off track from his usual performance after he thought the duo had made a flub on a run-through: "I just wanted to play straight intro, interlude and start interluding around...I wasn't interested in selling my mandolin playing at all then; I was just trying to concentrate on what we were doing: *singing.* So I thought we'd messed up...but the guy in the control room kept making signs and so I just took off on that mandolin, doing a little *obligato*...we usually made two or three tapes. I didn't learn until later they chose the one I had played the last chorus, sounding more like I was jammin'."

It should be noted that in separate interviews with Martha, Dee Kilpatrick and James, there are disagreements over *where* the actual sessions occurred. Kilpatrick tends to feel the first few were at WSB itself, while she insists the first recordings were made in a studio located in the downtown Emory Hotel.

James, however, agrees the first Capitol session was at WSB: "The next ones we did at WGST, because they didn't like the (WSB) studio, as it didn't have an echo chamber."

Mac Wiseman, who was in a car with Bill Carlisle, musicians Sandy Sandusky and Georgie Tanner, and anxious to head out with the Carsons (for a package show) on the road that day, recalls: "It was their first session for Capitol, and we had to wait on 'em as they were a little late. But Martha may be right, because it seems to me it was at the hotel. I know the recording session was all they talked about enroute to the show - and I listened, as I was interested in how Capitol conducted theirs."

Nonetheless, Martha and James' second session, was scheduled on Monday, Aug. 22, 1949. Of four songs recorded, two were unreleased: "Where Could I Go" and "When Mother Read the Bible." Capitol released the others, "Looking For a City" and "King Jesus Spoke to Me," which for the first time featured backup vocals from a group called the Carroll Family.

"We were looking for a congregational sound," explains Kilpatrick, who at the time of the sessions had an office on Cortland Avenue in Atlanta, as branch manager for Capitol. "I remember that on Martha I used this echo effect they had done earlier in Chicago - and it worked well. There was also the Carroll's teen-aged son (Ronnie), who sang a high part in falsetto on 'Looking For a City.' You know, he later became a promotion man for Mercury Records."

Martha recalls the contributions of the Carroll Family, too: "I really wasn't too pleased with the added voices, as I felt it sort of drowned me out and distorted my true harmony. They were a gospel group from Georgia, and this one old gal sang flat as a billy goat's butt. The hand-clapping was dubbed in later by Ken (Nelson) on the coast. But, I guess the crowd sound on the record made it a big seller. So with 'Looking For a City,' we had our first hit. I learned a long time ago, if the people say it's right, then it's OK."

In their performances, however, there were usually no backup singers, and James handled any patter or introduction of songs. She says, "We played all over on personal appearances, including high school auditoriums, gymnasiums, civic clubs and movie theaters where they would combine our live shows with screenings of current films.

"When the deal was together, James did all the talking. I was the silent partner. Actually, I was scared to open my mouth, afraid it might upset him...Then when other radio stations started playing our records, we began getting calls from states where we hadn't performed earlier."

Martha continues, "We started doing shows up in Kentucky, down in Florida, and outlying places like Virginia, West Virginia and North and South Carolina."

In addition to her entertainment chores, Martha found her svelte figure put her in line for other jobs: "I guess I began to blossom out in Atlanta. I started getting more compliments and I was also asked to model clothes and furs. Despite James' attitude, I must have been a little attractive. But, all he could say about modeling was 'You'll not do anything of the kind! That's a whore's job!' (Apparently, with James, money talked, for she took the assignment.)"

Indeed Martha suffered an inferiority complex, an obsessive behavioral condition her husband possibly helped prolong: "I didn't even drive a car because James always said I didn't have sense enough. And I believed him. I guess that I believed almost anything he said, because I had always felt so inferior."

The artist insists, however, that she always felt equal to the best once on stage: "That's the only place I didn't have feelings of inferiority. I'm not being conceited or boastful or anything, but I take my cue from the crowd. I just love people for the most part, and there's a thing that I have that goes out to them and it comes right back to me. I can tell that their response is genuine. That gives me confidence."

She wishes such insight would have worked for her off stage.

"James disarmed you. To meet him, you would think here's one of the nicest guys in the world. What I first thought I'd seen in him, besides his good looks, just wasn't there in the long run. He had like a Jekyll and Hyde personality."

Despite trouble in paradise, the *ideal couple's* third Capitol session with Kilpatrick occurred on Sunday, Dec. 4, 1949. The four released songs were: "When I Reach That City On the Hill," "Crossing Over Jordan," "Heaven's Jubilee" and "Filled With Glory Devine."

By then, fans were requesting souvenirs of the popular pair on the road, so a picture songbook had been printed up to sell at shows. It proved to be a real money maker and had to be reprinted more than once.

While the *Barn Dance Sweethearts* were going great guns as stars of the WSB shows and on the recording scene, their behind-the-curtain drama would have done justice to any *Our Gal Sunday* soap opera saga then on the airwaves.

"Financially, we were getting by much better than we did in Lexington, Bluefield or Renfro. Now we had a home and a car paid for, and we were very much in-demand, but it wasn't enough for him," cites Martha.

What confounded her first, she emphasizes, was the fact that James was forsaking his faith. She says he told her he was going to the library, but she learned he began hanging out in bars. Before long, his alleged dalliances with other women, she says, became legion among the show people, none of whom wanted to hurt Martha by informing.

She says he dated waitresses or other women who probably were flattered by the attention of a local celebrity. As his prowling increased and became more apparent to Martha, she prayed that he would get some sense and not jeopardize their marriage and career.

"After Minnie left, the *Barn Dance* head wanted me to audition girls to take her place, which I did. There was this raw-boned girl from Kentucky, who was a pretty fair singer. She didn't know anything about stage presence, however, so I was told to take her under my wing and teach her - which I also did."

Before long, Martha says James took a fancy to the newcomer, Mildred Frederick, whom he recalls as being from near Corbin. Martha insists he decided she'd do some performances with them as a trio.

James denies this: "There was a trio we used, but it was the Carroll Family."

One Saturday while looking for James, Martha says his car wasn't at the theater, "so I called Mildred to see if she knew where he was. Her room-mate answered instead and said, 'Martha, come over here, there's something I want to talk to you about.'

"Well, she sure gave me an ear full, she told me that James was picking Mildred up after we did our *Georgia Jubilee* program and they would go out on their little courtin' trips."

That conversation confirmed what Martha had already suspected. She says he had told her when he was going out that he was going to a movie or another stage show, "but he took her up to Stone Mountain. I confronted James about it, and he was very bold. He told me, *'She can give me what you can't. She can have children.'*"

James' hateful words were hurtful to Martha.

"Whenever we drove together to our shows, he'd be holding her hand in the front seat, while I was sitting in the back. This went on for several months, and was most repulsive. We'd be standing up on stage, singing about the Lord, and all the while knowing that he was sinning."

Martha closes her eyes and frowns, as though seeing it all again.

"It was more than hypocritical. I kept thinking about all those fans who praised us and were naming their babies after James and Martha, or their children, who were naming their little pets after us, I thought, 'If they only know the garbage that was going on! Then how would they feel about their *Barn Dance Sweethearts*'?"

Martha emphasizes she kept up a brave front for family and fans, though she did put an end to their joint bank account: "Initially, he took my salary and deposited it in an account with his. He'd give me $2 and say *go shopping* - and I'd have to take a streetcar! He was a skinflint! When I started drawing my own paycheck, James didn't like that at all!

"I stayed with him, just because of the fans. A few times he was even physically abusive to me. Of course, he was verbally abusive all the time after that. I offered him a divorce. Once I said to him and her, *'I'll be glad to step aside and you two can form your own duet - or do whatever it is you want to do.'*

"James said flat out, 'I don't want no damned divorce!' He apparently saw no sense in losing the money we made. I told him I didn't care to continue in this kind of a mockery of marriage either.

"Later, I learned that all of our co-workers and friends knew about James' philandering long before I did, and 100 per cent of them sided with me. They thought he was the worst kind of S.O.B. WSB's manager was also very supportive."

James retaliates that the manager was *more* than supportive. Chick Kimball was a tall, heavy-set fellow, long past middle-age. As James and Martha's boss, he had legitimate concerns about the discord that was creating a lack of harmony between the on-stage songbirds.

Naturally, hubby's good ol' boy male ego was ruptured by any thought that Martha might turn to another man. James even suspected Martha was having a rendezvous during a few days' visit with her parents in Ohio.

"I went up to Cincinnati because I think she had been up there with somebody else," he states, adding, "That was the beginning of our problems...and it really became a stormy marriage."

Martha rejects her ex's charges as *absurd* and a cover for his own behavior.

With the marriage in near-shambles, she found herself in a precarious position at WSB: "Suddenly I was being hit on by others who knew what James was doing. I was told I was a fool for being so true to him. I said it wasn't my way to stray from our marriage vows.

"James heard about some of this and started accusing me of flirting and leading them on! I never even thought about that. Living together in that sort of situation was not a degree above Hell!

"It was during this time that I lost my voice. The doctor told me it was from stress and that if I didn't change my home life, I would suffer a nervous breakdown. This meant I had to take that time off...Looking back now, I could never live like that again. Back then, I subscribed to the thinking that when you made your bed, you had to lay in it.

"Right at the time we were thought of as the ideal couple, his baby sister became pregnant out-of-wedlock and so his mother (Anna) called me. Well, I always felt so much pity for that woman because I felt James' father mistreated her. Here was another woman abused and unloved, who called me to see if her daughter could come down to Atlanta and stay with us awhile.

"Despite my disgust with James, I couldn't deny his mother, who said that she had nowhere else to turn. Well, he wasn't too happy about it, but his sister came to live with us. We eventually got her a job with the telephone company and helped her get back on her feet. I guess we kept her with us about a year, but I'll tell you this, she hated her brother's guts by the time she moved on."

She says James was less cooperative when Martha learned her own mother was ill and she invited Gertrude to Atlanta for a visit.

"We'd went to Cincinnati to visit my parents when we learned the doctor had only given her a few months to live," recalls Martha. "I begged her to ride back with me, but she wouldn't. She was suffering from an ingrown goiter which caused an enlarged heart. She had spells of passing out, and her eyes would nearly bulge out. They said her condition was too dangerous for surgery. It was decided to fly in radioactive iodine for treatment. Before we left, I gave her money enough to come to Atlanta."

It was during their marriage's most volatile period that Gertrude came to visit.

"Mommy had to have medication on the hour, and was really suffering from asthma. James was really acting up," continues Martha. "So, I was half crazy. They said any excitement could be fatal for her. He came in one night at about 3 a.m. and I was so afraid she would hear him. He went into the bathroom to wash off that smell from the other woman, and then came into the kitchen where I was and he told me to *get my tail into bed* with him!

"I stood up to him - all in a whisper, mind you - and said, *'If you upset my mother, I'll take this butcher knife and shove it right through your guts! I know where you've been, what you've been doing - and I mean it!'* Of course, that's the last thing I would ever do."

Martha was a loving nurse to her mother. She remembers her mom telling her, "You're saving my life. Your daddy's sister wanted me to miscarry and not have you, but I wanted you - and now you're saving my life."

Later, Martha learned her mother was aware of the trouble between Martha and James: "She developed almost a hatred of him. While she was staying with me, he ignored her like dirt. He resented the fact that I was trying to help her get better."

Walt Trott

CHAPTER 10

Think About It Tomorrow...

*"Tell me Lord,
What's the matter with the people today?
...Well, I've got some good people,
But some bad ones that teach,
They don't even practice
the things that they preach..."*
- © **Martha Carson**, "Tell Me, Lord,"
Acuff-Rose 1954

"Except for the fact that I love gardening and growing flowers like my mother does, I think Minnie and our brother Don (Lloyd) take more after Mommie," declares Martha. "I believe that I'm more like my father. I have my mother's hair coloring, but I'm tall and willowy like he was, and also determined that if I want to do something bad enough, I can do it."

Martha felt that Minnie influenced their parents to relocate: "They left Kentucky after Minnie married and moved to Ohio. She was sort of Mommy's pet, and she got them to move up there. The place they bought was an older house, but real homey. It was located about 20 miles out of Cincinnati on the road to Columbus. They loved it."

While at WSB, Martha saw another side to her father: "He was a trusting soul and as a result, got in a lot of financial difficulties. My daddy and I always felt that everybody else is just as honest as we are. I've been used more than an old road map, so I know it doesn't work that way all the time.

"Dad was a carpenter involved in the building of a sub-division of homes. A preacher was also in this project. After Daddy saw the furnaces they were putting into these new homes, he said he sure would like one of those new furnaces for his older home. Well, the preacher told him he could have one, for cost, and that he would deduct $25 out of his weekly paycheck to pay for it. Of course, Daddy trusted the preacher to do the right thing.

"Well, a couple of years later, I got a call from Mommy who was crying that the furnace company had come out and put a *For Sale* sign in their yard because the preacher hadn't been making the payments. So I had to go and withdraw a couple of thousand dollars to save the old home place.

"Then later, I learned my Dad had put the house up as security on a loan and the same thing occurred. This time I had to withdraw about $1,500 to save the house since they were literally in the same fix again. I talked to WSB's manager of the *Barn Dance* and told him about the problem. He suggested that the folks deed the place to me, so there was no chance that my father could use it as collateral for any more loans.

"I talked with my parents about it, telling them I didn't make the kind of money where I could be paying out thousands of dollars every few months. Well, I told them by deeding the place over to me, no one could take advantage of them again or put a garnishment on the house. I also said I would pay the taxes and house insurance payments and that they could live there as long as either of them lived. They agreed to that, and I made those payments for about 12 years."

After James and Martha landed their own recording pact with Capitol, she says, "I wanted to get the trio (Minnie, Marthie & Mattie) on the label, but James said no - and was real bitter about it, insisting, 'I'll get on my knees and pray it never happens.'"

Meanwhile, in Cincinnati, a call came in for Minnie and Mattie from Cowboy Copas and Fiddlin' Red Herring: "They wanted us to help them get a show going and start up a barn dance (at WLW). Jean and I went down and we did good for awhile working as the Sunshine Sisters. There wasn't any real traveling to it, just a morning show that we did for about a year."

Hank Penny, former announcer-host at WSB Atlanta, was the next to relocate to Cincinnati, where he performed on WLW's *Midwestern Hayride*. In '44, he moved again, this time to the West Coast.

"Then Jean left us and went back to John Lair's *Renfro Valley* show. You know, she was real witty on stage, and, in fact, has done many shows in clubs just by herself. Jean was a good entertainer, and just cut out for that."

A while later, Minnie was also called by Lair to perform once more at Renfro: "Merely to help out, as he put it. It was about a three hour drive for me. Next thing I knew, Charlie and I started doing a duet for them."

Sadness set in for the Woodruffs, however, when Wilbur (Curley) Woodruff was reported killed in action on Okinawa during April 1945, while battling as a fire team leader with the First Marine Division -- *only weeks before Victory was declared* throughout the world.

Aside from their marital situation, James and Martha had another concern during their WSB tenure. Martha says a fellow from Virginia was making records with Lucille and Johnny Masters, a couple from Jacksonville, Fla., cutting songs fans identified with Martha and James. In fact, his label was calling the Martha and James soundalikes, the *Dixie Sweethearts.*

"Well, James and I rode up to where he lived and confronted him about this with an intent of suing him if they didn't stop. We had to ask around a lot to locate this guy. But, what we found was a little ol' crippled man and we didn't have the heart to hurt him. He did say, however, that he would take them off the market."

The *Dixie Sweethearts* were good singers, who went on to recruit their son Owen and started performing as the Masters Family, a formidable gospel group (who would later record with James singing lead!).

In the Feb. 18, 1950 *Billboard,* a news item appeared proclaiming: *"James and Martha Carson recently moved from WSB Atlanta to WNOX Knoxville."* It was certainly not a move for more money, says Martha, "We took a little drop in pay. But, on the other hand, we didn't have that early morning show to do, thank the Lord."

James says they left WSB because Kimball, "The man who run the show down there went nuts! He was an old man, about 60, who got up there in a hotel in Atlanta and was acting crazy. The police went up there and said he had whiskey bottles all lined up around the room, after running up hundreds of dollars in liquor bills. He was finally told to get out of Atlanta, and I think he ended up working for ol' J. L. Frank (the noted promoter)...I think the *Barn Dance* itself ended in 1952."

Martha recalls it was the Program Director's lack of respect and feeling for their music, which really hastened the show's demise: "I think his name was Johnny Outler or something like that. Anyway, he expressed the sentiments that if any hillbilly could make more money than he did, it was time to throw it all out the window."

At the time, James and Martha moved to Knoxville, the WNOX shows consisted of the *Mid-Day Merry-Go-Round* and the Saturday night *Tennessee Barn Dance,* where they continued to call the Carsons the "Barn Dance Sweethearts."

Before leaving Atlanta, they had sold their Lakeside Park home and James bought a trailer, which was home during their brief Knoxville time together. Like the Atlanta station, WNOX was owned by a daily newspaper, the *Knoxville News-Sentinel* (an independent established in 1886). Unlike the *Atlanta Journal,* the *News-Sentinel* didn't allot much space to its radio artists, although attractive redhead Martha once made the cover of the publication's weekend color entertainment guide.

Among acts headlining the WNOX shows upon their arrival were good pal Bill Carlisle, Carl Story & the Ramblin' Mountaineers, Don Gibson, Red Rector, George (Speedy) Krise, Jamup & Honey, Fred Smith, the Louvin Brothers and Molly O'Day and Lynn Davis. At the time, the *Tennessee Barn Dance* was also part of CBS' *Saturday Night Country Style* programming, a national presentation.

Martha had hoped the change might bring about a miracle in their marriage: "The only change was from bad to worse. I had thought maybe James would get his faith in God back. I know now I had lost my love for him *before* I left Atlanta. I think I felt sorry for James by then because I believed he was sending his soul to Hell!

"I thought perhaps if he got out of the Atlanta area, where he had all these bar gals and was used to visiting and drinking, it might be quieter and he'd settle down. I hoped he might clean up his life if he became a believer again.

"Long before we left Atlanta, I had already gone to the twin bedroom (set-up)," confides Martha. "I had known of too many of his women friends. You see, by then I felt like he was a stranger, more than a husband. It got to the point where I would not let him see me take my dress off to put my nightgown on. I felt dirty if he were to see my body."

Unaware of their marital discord, WNOX audiences responded enthusiastically to Martha and James' brand of entertainment. Promoter Charlie Lamb, a Knoxville native, recalls Martha and James from those days: "When I first knew James Carson, he was a real quiet, thin guy, olive-complected, never seemed to have much to say. Martha was a real lady. And I knew she and her sister were fabulous songwriters."

Martha had made it a point not to let the real heartbreak she felt inside show.

"I went out there on stage and played that same stagnant role. It was a hurting thing to have to do," explains Martha, whose eyes were brimming with tears at the recollection. "I loved those songs we sang and I believed in them sincerely. I felt like a hypocrite myself; you know, being called the *Barn Dance Sweethearts* when there's really no sweethearts living there at all."

In Knoxville, the couple agreed to do yet another Capitol session, again in Atlanta with Kilpatrick at the helm, slated Sunday, June 18, 1950.

Of six sides recorded, one - "I Feel Like Shouting" - remains unreleased.

The other numbers recorded were: "Got a Little Light (And I'm Gonna Let It Shine)," James' "Man of Galilee," "He Will Set Your Fields On Fire" (all of which had previously been cut by them for White Church Records), "We Shall Rise and Shine" and Albert Brumley's classic "I'll Fly Away."

Martha says goodnaturedly, Kilpatrick - who later became manager of the *Grand Ole Opry* - tended to try one's patience with the number of retakes he demanded.

Still, not nearly as trying as James...

"We lived about 20 minutes outside Knoxville in this trailer park, which had no fenced-in area for my little Pekingese dog. So I'd let it outside in the yard for a short while before we had to leave for the station. On this one day, we started off and then I remembered Ching-a-Ling. I told James I had to go back as I forgot to put her in the trailer.

"Well, James started griping and then made this terrible, terrible, filthy character assassination to me concerning the little dog. That did it for me, right there! I didn't talk back to him, but I thought to myself right then, 'This is the last time you'll ever have an opportunity, Mister, to say something that nasty to me again!' I went and put the dog back in the trailer and didn't insinuate what I was planning to do.

"But after we got through with the *Mid-Day Merry-Go-Round,* I told Bill Carlisle and Lowell Blanchard that I wasn't going back to the trailer with James. Instead, I was going home to my mother and daddy's, and that I was leaving the show. I went to the Greyhound bus station and bought me a ticket home."

Martha stayed off the show three months, during which she says she worked on her parents' property, cleaning and making renovations here and there, anything to take her mind off a failed marriage. She also instructed them if James called to say she wasn't there and they didn't know where she went!

"I left the horrible job of going back to the trailer, to get things I wanted, up to my Daddy, God bless his soul," laments Martha, then brightening at the happy remembrance of being reunited with Ching-a-Ling. "Finally, one day Lowell and Bill called saying the show needed me. 'Martha, this girl James brought in from Atlanta is terrible, and she's just not going over at all.' Well, I told them I missed my job, and said I'd come back; but I made it quite clear that I was not coming back to live with James."

When Martha debarked from the plane, however, she says she was stunned to see her estranged mate waiting to meet her: "What are you doing here?," she inquired icily, as he grabbed her luggage, carried it out and tossed it into the car.

"I'm here *to work,*" she added, with emphasis, " but I'm not coming back to you!"

Martha indicates James proceeded to imply he was *willing* enough to take her back in the act, but, in turn, she ought to help his pregnant friend through her ordeal.

"Remember that little dark-skinned gal that worked across from WNOX? Well, I've been dating her since you've been gone, and she's gonna have my baby. I want you to give her whatever she needs."

Stunned by his arrogance, Martha says she shot back: *"Whoa! I didn't screw her! That's your monkey there! You give her whatever she needs."*

Martha had James drop her off at a hotel, then soon settled in by renting an apartment within walking distance of the show. Still, singing songs of faith, she couldn't shake the feeling of hypocrisy which engulfed her daily.

"It didn't seem to bother him none," she suggests. "In fact, he was telling me that there was no God, and if he had a child, he would teach it that there was no such thing as sin, right or wrong, or Heaven and Hell!"

James thought back to that period. "Yes, Betty Logan sang with me two or three months while Martha was gone...I had called Martha in Cincinnati, but her mother and daddy didn't know where she was at. One day backstage, Lowell Blanchard told me somebody wanted to talk to me on the phone, and it was Martha. He had done told me before he wanted Martha back, so here she was asking if I would sing with her again. I think she said she was in Chicago - maybe she was fronting Pee Wee King's band for J. L. Frank and his new promoter! Anyway, I said I would sing with her, but that was all."

The re-teaming of James and Martha Carson was fraught with tension.

Martha says she found it both frustrating and nerve-wracking to continue living a lie.

"I'll tell you, I longed for that little facet in my life, where somebody loved me. I guess that's just normal, but I used to wonder *is there no happiness at all for me?* I deserved a Tony for acting on stage, but I never did get one."

Meantime, sleep came harder for Martha, who obviously needed rest to face up to the tasks at hand. She remembers imploring Bill Carlisle for some pills or something to help her sleep.

"Before long, Bill began worrying that I was taking them too much and he mentioned it to Lowell Blanchard. Lowell came and talked to me and said, 'Martha, I want you to go see this doctor, an Osteopathic physician my wife goes to.' I agreed, but I found out it was actually a psychiatrist. Poor Lowell didn't want to tell me that."

The doctor told Martha it was time to give up hoping to save her marriage.

"He told me, a leopard never changes its spots and if I went back to James, he would only treat me twice as bad. 'Throw away the sleeping pills, and if you start thinking about the situation, say aloud, *To Hell with it, I'll think about it tomorrow,* and eventually you'll know you can.'"

CHAPTER 11

A Solo Flight...

*"What picks me up when I'm down
And sets me on higher ground,
Inspiration, Inspiration from Above..."*
- © **1953, Martha Carson,**
"Inspiration From Above,"
Acuff-Rose Publications

Martha poured her rage and humiliation into the one thing she knew best - work. Still, harassment from her estranged husband, she says, continued even during their on-stage pairings.

Numbly, she adds, "We were sitting there on a bale of hay facing the audience, and tauntingly, he'd say to me out, of the side of his mouth, *'I know everyone tells you you're pretty, but you ought to see who I was with last night. She looks like she stepped out of a picture book.'* Then he'd tell me nasty things, like about sex that they had."

Feeling that three years of unhappiness was enough, Martha retained Knoxville attorney Ray Jenkins (who gained some celebrity participating in the Army-McCarthy Hearings) for a 1950 divorce from James. Wanting to be fair, she asked only a 50-50 split of their possessions, and even paid her own legal fees.

"I got the divorce papers from your attorney!" she says James snapped at her one night, "But, I'll see you in Hell before I sign 'em!"

Martha relayed James' message to Jenkins, who warned that if he didn't sign the papers within a reasonable time, he'd personally serve them to him on stage at the *Barn Dance!*

"I told that to James and that's how I got him to sign," says Martha, who nonetheless consented to bookings as a duo, usually traveling to area shows with Bill Carlisle. "I remember sitting in the backseat of Bill's car with him, he'd tell me about all the things he'd done the night before. Oh, he was drinking pretty heavy back then. I had to be subject to all this and then get out there and do a show, going on stage with this monkey. It was rough."

One final incident proved too much for mild-mannered Martha, who then vowed to break up the popular gospel music team.

"We were doing a p.a. in a little bitty auditorium that probably didn't seat more than 75 people. A little child - out in the country like that, they're not used to staying up past 8 o'clock - was sitting right on the front row. James was talking between songs, and I knew the people couldn't hear what was going on, as this youngster was just screaming.

"Well, I recalled that I had some sticks of gum in my purse, which was sitting on a piano bench where I set it, about 10 or 12 steps from center stage. Politely I said, 'Excuse me just a minute,' dashing over to get the gum, then I handed it down to the little kid, hoping to do James a favor as he was fighting all that noise. As soon as I gave it to the child, it turned off the crying just like you turn off a water faucet.

"It had done the trick! But James put his hand on his hip, and right into the microphone, says to me, *'Now can you think of anything else you can do to detract from me?'* I thought to myself, 'Damn you, I will!' Looking out at the audience, I decided to lay it on him now, but do it discreetly. So I said to the audience, *'Will you all excuse me just a minute? My guitar's sick and I'll be right back.'* I just walked off and left him hanging out there with his little mandolin.

"Boy! Did that hit a nerve. He came walking off stage, drew his fist back and said, 'I ought to knock your goddamned head off!' I said, 'Go ahead, because it will be your last opportunity.' I knew in the morning, I was gonna see Lowell Blanchard - and I told him that. James spat at me, 'I'll see you wash dishes for a living!' I said, 'You know what! I won't even have to take lessons, I already know how to do that.'"

Of course, Bill Carlisle witnessed the temper tantrum and duly reported the threats to Blanchard the next morning before either Martha or James arrived.

"When I came in, Lowell took me aside and said to me, 'Bill told me about what happened last night, and I don't expect you to try to work with this guy anymore. In fact, I'm giving James his notice this morning.'"

James stresses that the chewing gum incident was only one of a number of times Martha did something to distract from the show: "We had 30 or 40 minutes to entertain, and I was Master of Ceremonies. But, she'd do something to disturb me every time. I remember telling her three or four times not to do it. I can still see her stepping down into the audience walking up the aisle and passing out chewing gum here and there...my face must have gotten beet red!

"When I came off stage, sure I told her, *'This is the last time you're gonna embarrass me on stage!'* The next morning after the chewing gum incident, I got up early to go see Lowell Blanchard. When I got down there, her and Lowell came walking down the steps together. She'd got there before I did! So I said, *'Well, I see I don't have to turn in my notice, you done took care of it!'*

"Lowell said, 'I don't want you to go...' But I said, 'I guess she's already told you I'm leaving! If you want me to work out a notice, I'll do it. But, if you want to pay me off now, I'll take it! But, I'm definitely leaving.' They paid, I think, every two weeks. I believe, however, he cut me my check that day.

"I was going to Florida and lay on the beach. But I got as far as Atlanta, and Cotton Carrier told me that Stoney Cooper had called looking for a mandolin player to record with, and would I be interested. Well, I got to thinking, I really didn't want to go to Florida, because I'd waste a lot of time and money laying around. Initially, I just wanted to go down and relax and get my mind off my problems.

"Cotton was working for a record company then," continues Roberts. "So, he got on the phone and talked to Stoney. Then

Stoney told me to come and play with them Saturday night (on the *Wheeling Jamboree)* and I went up to West Virginia. While I was there, the station (WWVA) changed its policy and hired a staff band. I was one of six to get hired."

(Carrier, who had emceed and helped direct the *Barn Dance,* later pioneered country music shows on Atlanta television with Boots Woodall and the Wranglers. He played both guitar and fiddle, and also wrote such compositions as the gospel-flavored "I Have But One Goal." At age 75, he died of heart failure on July 18, 1994, a decade after being inducted into the Atlanta Country Music Hall of Fame.)

Meanwhile, Martha had appreciated Lowell Blanchard's supportive attitude during her confrontation with James, but she also felt beaten as an artist. "I told him, 'Lowell, I might as well give my notice, too, because I've never done anything by myself. I started out singing harmony with my sisters in a trio, then I did harmony with my husband in a duet. I've never sung solo before...I don't know anything to do by myself.' He said, 'Martha, I think you've got more talent than you realize. I want you to stay on and give yourself a chance.'

"God love him! If he hadn't said those words, there wouldn't be no Martha Carson. I did say I'd try; but, that was the hardest thing I ever did in my life. Nobody knows. To stand up there and sing by yourself, when you have never done it before, it's like starting all over. My knees liked to knock together, until I was afraid the audience could see 'em. I was so nervous and I had no confidence at all."

Martha said reaction to her solo stint was mixed: "After all, this was the audience that had seen me as half of the *Barn Dance Sweethearts,* and they probably wondered *what's she trying to do up there without him?*

"I continued for a short while like that, suffering through, trying to do those solos. Then I called my sister Jean and her husband Salty Holmes in Chicago and invited them over to help out on stage, and work with me and Bill on the road."

She recalls that some of their bookings left a lot to be desired and included a number of low-pay, one-room schoolhouses: "We'd put sheets on a wire to separate us from the audience - and it was our makeshift dressing room. There were a number of bigger boys trying to lift the sheet to peek at us. We waited to get dressed when Bill (Carlisle) was standing watch on the other side of the sheets.

"I remember one such show up in Kentucky after I'd finished my set, and I was on the way back to the car carrying my makeup kit with my costume draped across my arm, when one of those boys said to me, *'Boy, I'd sure like to f--- you!'* I was stunned and just kept on walking. The next day I said to Lowell Blanchard, 'If you ever want to get me off the *Mid-Day Merry-Go-'Round,* don't fire me, just book me back at that place in Kentucky!'"

On the subject of scary moments, she proceeds, "I've had a few frightening things occur when I was in Knoxville. After divorcing James, I had a little apartment, which was located right downtown on the riverbank. I could walk down Gay Street to WNOX, and could walk back to my little ol' apartment in a short time.

"Sometimes I would stop downtown and maybe go in the dime-store or a dress shop to look around. I loved to dress nice by then. On this one occasion, I had on a white linen suit with green accessories, including a scarf around my neck, and I thought I looked pretty good. As I was walking home, I spotted a couple of hard-looking guys standing where I had to go by. While passing, I heard one say, *'I'd just love to get that kerchief from around your neck and choke you to death with it!'* I pretended to ignore him and just kept right on walking - fast - on to my apartment. Believe me, that was scary!"

By fall of 1950, two of the hottest songs in the nation were Hank Snow's self-penned "I'm Movin' On," which eventually stayed in the number one slot 21 weeks, starting Aug. 19, and the Red Foley-Ernest Tubb novelty duet "Goodnight Irene," which first charted Aug. 12 and later succeeded Snow's song at the top (for two weeks). Meanwhile, on the pop side, the Weavers' folk rendition of "Goodnight, Irene" was number one 13 weeks and a multi-million seller to be reckoned with, featuring a flipside hit (that peaked at #2) "Tzena, Tzena, Tzena."

Being the professionals they are - and under contract, Martha and James were cajoled by Capitol into recording yet another duet session in Atlanta, on Monday, Oct. 23, 1950. Five tracks were recorded: "Shining City," "Lay Your Burdens At His Feet," "I Ain't Gonna Sin No More," "Salvation Has Been Brought Down" and Hank Williams' "Sing, Sing, Sing." It was their last studio effort together.

"I'm the one who got them back together," recalls Dee Kilpatrick. "I picked Martha up in Knoxville and had to bring her back there. We worked day and night, and I got some of the best sides I ever got in my life from them. You know Martha could really play that guitar. The only fault was she would play so hard that it tended to drown out her vocals. I had to watch that...

"They weren't together then, of course. At this last session, James was hot," continued Kilpatrick. "I used to not let him hit hot licks on that mandolin because we were doing gospel songs. But, I let him go at it this time, and I had never realized that he was such a good picker. If you know anything at all about my history, you know I dug duets. And James and Martha Carson melded as good as any duet I ever heard."

Dee, an ex-Marine, was two years younger than James. He hailed from North Carolina, where he grew up listening to - and loving - sacred sounds: "Gospel music was kind of in my blood."

After producing for Capitol, Kilpatrick went to Mercury Records. Among artists he worked with in the studio were Tex Ritter, Hank Thompson, Carl Story, Jimmy Dean, Sue Thompson, Johnny Horton, Benny Martin, the Stanley Brothers and the Statesmen Quartet.

According to Kilpatrick it was at the October 1950 James and Martha Carson session that he first met Acuff/Rose publisher-producer Fred Rose, who had brought the Hank Williams song to them.

"I saw him and I kidded him, saying, *I thought I was producing this session.* He smiled and said, 'You are, but these are my writers.' Fred had a lot of faith in Martha. She was a barrel of fun back then...Always had something to say. Martha was not only a great talent, she *knew* talent. She was then starting to work with her sister and that fellow she had married, Salty, who not only played a great harmonica, but was a fine showman."

Billboard's April 28, 1951 edition duly announced: *"James and Martha Carson have split. She is working with Bill Carlisle at WNOX Knoxville."*

William Tolliver Carlisle, 91, is a legendary performer, still active on the *Grand Ole Opry,* which he first joined in 1954. Like the Amburgeys, he's a Kentucky native from a large family of musically-inclined pickers, who assembled on radio for *The Carlisle Family Hour.*

Elder brother Cliff Carlisle (born March 6, 1904) was the first to launch a music career, initially performing with Wilbur Ball and Fred Kirby. Soon, he took young Bill (born Dec. 19, 1908) under his wing, entertaining throughout the region. Incidentally, Cliff Carlisle pioneered in playing the dobro steel guitar. During the late 1930s, he recorded for Decca, even utilizing his kid brother on the sessions, some in New York City, with his band The Buckle Busters.

Actually, earlier a Brunswick Records scout (W. R. Calloway) had heard young Bill singing "Rattlesnake Daddy" on the family radio show in Louisville and signed him to record the number, which was also the first song he had written.

"Why, I thought this music business is a piece of cake. But I didn't make much money," he chuckled. "We didn't know we was supposed to get paid...But if you was a recording artist back then, you were really something.

"You see when I was growing up, our family would get together for a good old-fashioned sing-a-long every Sunday," explains Bill Carlisle (who graciously wrote the *Foreword* for this book). "We had quite a chorus with Mom, Dad and my four brothers, two sisters and me. Those were great days back in Wakefield, Ky., and I'm sure they had a lot to do with my becoming a musician and entertainer."

While in high school, Bill entered a jumping contest, setting a school record of five feet, one inch. Later, he would close his shows jumping - and won wide acclaim as "Jumpin' Bill Carlisle."

According to the late Clifford Raymond Carlisle, their "family farm" was a tobacco sharecropper's tenancy, consisting of a poorly-constructed log cabin: "Many a winter the snow would come through the cracks."

After two decades of performing and recording together, Bill and Cliff cut "Rainbow At Midnight" for King Records, while on WLW-Cincinnati. It became a Top 10 record in 1946, preceding hit renditions by both Ernest Tubb & The Texas Troubadours, and Texas Jim Robertson & The Panhandle Punchers.

Cliff's early years' traveling and performing on the Keith vaudeville circuit taught him a lot about comedy material, which adapted well to hit songs such as "Is Zat You, Myrtle?" Reportedly, Cliff had also accompanied "Father of Country Music" Jimmie Rodgers instrumentally on some of his recordings.

As a writer (and performer), Bill says he's always fared best commercially with novelty numbers: "But I write the pretty songs, too."

Somewhat earlier than the Amburgey girls, the Carlisle boys first regular radio exposure was also on WLAP-Louisville (albeit in 1931). They later landed spots on stations farther afield in Knoxville and Charlotte, N.C.

One of Cliff's finest Decca recordings, the traditional tune "Black Jack David," was cut in New York City in July 1939. It's a song he learned from T. Texas Tyler and was derived from the

British ballad "The Gypsy Laddie." It also features Bill on guitar.

Cliff, who initially went into semi-retirement in 1947, resided in Lexington, Ky., and died April 2, 1983. "His health wasn't too good for quite a long while," notes Bill. Once Cliff left the act, Bill began performing on WSB Atlanta, where he met Martha and James Carson. Both acts eventually moved to Knoxville to appear on WNOX's *Mid-Day Merry-Go-Round*.

"When I went to work on the *Mid-Day Merry-Go-Round*, I did *Hot-Shot Elmer*, a rube act and I'd go barefooted," explains Carlisle. "Archie Campbell and I also did some comedy wrestling matches together."

Martha Carson insists, "Bill Carlisle is one of the funniest human beings ever on this Earth."

James Roberts recalls whenever they'd go into a restaurant, Bill had a habit of emptying the toothpick holder and putting the contents in his pocket. "When I asked him why, he answered, 'My daddy runs a lumber company and I'm trying to run the price up.'"

Bill, who wrote many of his successful songs, has enjoyed several Top Five records in the novelty vein, including "Knothole," "T'ain't Nice to Talk Like That" and in 1966 for Hickory Records, "What Kinda Deal is This?," which hit the charts 20 years after his first Top Five.

"Too Old to Cut the Mustard," according to Bill, was the biggest money-maker: "I remember I first did that while at Knoxville, guesting on the *Grand Ole Opry* (1951) for Red Foley's portion, the *Prince Albert Show*. Foley and Tubb also recorded a version (for Decca) that was quite successful (#5)."

Strangely enough, the song was also selected by Mitch Miller as a duet for the unlikely pairing of lush pop singer Rosemary Clooney and legendary screen siren Marlene Dietrich. On the Columbia soundtrack, the band was led by Stan Freeman, and when released in 1952, became a #12 *Billboard* pop success.

"I was just a country boy then. I wasn't at all smart. I was paid $50 flat rate for recording that song myself - and that's all I ever got!," snaps Carlisle, adding, "But, they all did it and it made a lot of money. Acuff/Rose bought it. They were the finest people you could ever wish to work with. It made you feel good to know that if you had 10-cents coming, you'd get it."

It was Bill Carlisle, incidentally, who wrote the tender ballad "Gone Home," one of Bill's pals Grandpa Jones' more poignant recordings. Still, novelties are what fans associate Bill Carlisle with, for the most part. For much of his career, Bill did his crowd-pleasing high-jump at the conclusion of shows. Due to recent replacement of both hips, he has discontinued the spectacular leap.

Ever the showman, however, he began arriving on stage with aid of a walker, but delighted Opry fans, upon leaving the stage, by slinging the walker (which he no longer needs) over his shoulder, earning a standing ovation each time.

Since the untimely death of daughter Shelia, 45, from a stroke on Dec. 31, 1991, Bill's act has included longtime friend George Riddle (ex-George Jones' bandleader), as well as son Bill Carlisle Jr.

Like the Carlisle brothers, the Amburgey sisters recorded for Sydney Nathan's King Records in Cincinnati. The girls had one single released in November 1951, "You Can't Live With 'Em (And You Can't Live Without 'Em)," a saucy number written by Minnie, and featuring "Tennessee Memories" on the flipside. All others went unreleased.

"I've still got a notebook full of songs. I sat down and wrote 'em for emotional release…," reflects Minnie, "Not to present to somebody else."

Performing with sister Jean again, Martha found herself relaxing and starting to *get it together* on stage after her split with James. Jean and Salty, who were wed in August 1949, blended beautifully, adding needed sparkle and energy to Martha's gosple set.

Tall and rugged, Holmes was a man with impressive credits himself. Floyd Lee (Salty) Holmes was born March 6, 1909, in Glasgow, Ky. (Ironically, he and Jean shared their birth day, though he was 14 years her senior). He played guitar, harmonica and the "jug." With yodeler Patsy Montana, the Prairie Ramblers had recorded the million-selling hit "I Want To Be a Cowboy's Sweetheart," on Aug. 16, 1935, in New York City (released by Vocalion Records). They sang their song again in Gene Autry's musical Western film "Colorado Sunset," released in 1939.

Montana's self-penned, Western-styled number "borrowed" its upbeat melody from Stuart Hamblen's 1934 Decca Records' success "Texas Plains," but Patsy offered the talented composer no credit nor royalties.

Still, "I Want To Be a Cowboy's Sweetheart" became a 1936 Top 10 *Billboard* pop record, standing historically as the first country hit by a female artist. (It was also her 1996 ticket - albeit posthumously - into the Country Music Hall of Fame.)

Prairie Ramblers were a hit before "...Cowboy's Sweetheart." The boys first included Montana in their recordings for Victor in December 1933, utilizing her vocals on "Waltz of the Hills" and "Montana Plains," yet another reworking by her on Hamblen's "Texas Plains."

Originally, Floyd Holmes ran away from home at 15, to join a theatrical stock company (Chester Davis') as an errand boy. After a few seasons in stock, Holmes became a guitarist (who played harmonica) in the Kentucky Ramblers, along with Charles (Chick) Hurt (mandolin), Shelby (Tex) Atchison (fiddle) and Jack Taylor (bass), all of whom claimed to have been born in log cabins in Kentucky. In 1930, the foursome worked their first regular radio program over WOC-Davenport, Iowa. By 1932, they were performing on WLS-Chicago.

The troupe's Prairie Ramblers tag, adopted by Taylor, fit in well with *Prairie Farmer,* the periodical which bought WLS from Sears & Roebuck. It also neatly complemented Patsy Montana's cowgirl image during their WLS appearances.

Taking a break from WLS, the Ramblers accepted a 26-week stint on WOR-New York in 1934, and while there made some fine recordings, one which had Holmes blowing into a jug, in addition to his harmonica flourishes. (Noted songwriter Bob Miller was included, playing piano, and he later played on the historic Patsy Montana-Prairie Ramblers " . . . Cowboy's Sweetheart" cut. Clarinetist Willie Thawl was also an added attraction, and he later played on Hank Williams' records.)

Among the Prairie Ramblers songs audiences requested most were "Shady Grove" and the talking "Go Easy Blues." The Chicago group also recorded as the pop-oriented Sweet Violet Boys, a name derived from their biggest hit single. Their top three *Billboard* pop tunes were: "Sweet Violets" (#12, 1936), "Sweet Violets No. 2" (#16, 1936) and "I Haven't Got a Pot to Cook In" (#15, 1937), all for Vocalion.

Some of the Violet group's lesser known titles included "Hurry, Johnny, Hurry," "Jim's Windy Mule," "What Would You Give in Exchange For Your Mother-in-Law" (no doubt a take-off on the Monroe Brothers' similarly-titled gospel tune "What Would You Give in Exchange For Your Soul") and "There's a Man That Comes to Our House Every Single Day (Poppa Comes Home and the Man Goes Away)."

Yes, occasionally, the boys would record what were considered risqué songs (for that era), sometimes recruiting Chicago-based singer-songwriter Jenny Lou Carson for backup vocals. She later wrote such country classics as "You Two-Timed Me One Time Too Often," "Jealous Heart" and "Let Me Go, Lover." Her sister Eva Overstake became the bride of Red Foley and later reportedly committed suicide.

Talk about family branches: Eva and Red were parents to Shirley, who married pop singer Pat Boone, whose daughter Debbie Boone recorded the successful cuts "You Light Up My Life" and "Are You On the Road to Loving Me Again." Debbie, in turn, married Gabriel Ferrer, son of Oscar winner Jose Ferrer and singer Rosemary Clooney, who is aunt to current screen heartthrob George Clooney. George's dad Nick Clooney hosts movie screening on the American Movie Classics cable show; while his other sister Betty was once a singer and recorded with Rosemary a Top 40 pop song in 1954, appropriately titled "Sisters." Earlier, Eva and (Lucille) Jenny Lou sang as WLS' Little Maids, a trio, with their elder sister Evelyn Overstake, herself a solo recording artist. Remember, too, Red also recorded with his daughter Betty Foley...Whew!

For the record, the Prairie Ramblers recorded during the late 1930s until June 1941 for ARC, the American Recording Company. Original band members Holmes and Atchison had been replaced by the time the Ramblers made their final studio session during December 1947 for Mercury Records. Wade Ray, who later did shows with Martha, also served a stint as a Prairie Rambler.

"Salty" obtained his nickname, thanks to his classic rendition of the song "Salty Dog," a blues variation of which Red Foley took into the Country Top 10, "Salty Dog Rag" in 1952.

According to the Film Daily Motion Picture Yearbook (1938), Salty Holmes' solo film credits up to then, included "Banjo On My Knee" starring Barbara Stanwyck, Joel McCrea and Walter Brennan (the same year he won the first of three supporting actor Oscars), released Dec. 1, 1936; and "Arizona Days," starring Tex Ritter and Eleanor Stewart, released Feb. 2, 1937. Reportedly, Holmes made three more Westerns, appearing with Ritter and Charles (Durango Kid) Starrett, through 1941.

Under this billing, *Salty Holmes & Mattie O'Neil* were a welcome duo on WLS' *National Barn Dance*, WLW-TV Cincinnati's *Midwestern Hayride* and WNOX's *Mid-Day Merry-Go-Round*, and they recorded together for MGM, King and London Records. The couple first met in Atlanta in 1946, but it was three years before they made it legal.

"They had an entertaining act. Salty did the talking harmonica and she played five-string banjo and, of course, could sing up a storm," proclaims Martha, who was fond of Salty.

Among his many writing credits, Holmes penned the popular "Mama Blues," recorded by the Alvino Rey Orchestra. Rey, a noted electric guitarist set out on his own after years with Horace Heidt's band, in 1940. (He had a fondness for upbeat novelty numbers and the Rey band is best known for the hits "Deep in the Heart of Texas," "Strip Polka" and "Cement Mixer Put-Ti, Put-Ti.")

A drinker, Salty was just not cut out to be a family man. He and Mattie/Jean were divorced several years after the birth of their daughter Lana (1951), who sometimes performed on stage with her parents as a toddler, and today writes songs. (Salty Holmes died New Year's, Jan. 1, 1970, in Indianapolis. Fifteen months earlier, Red Foley also died in Indiana, following a show date in Fort Wayne.)

"I named Lana. Jean always reminded me of (movie star) Lana Turner," says Martha. "In her younger days, Jean was so pretty. Anyway, the baby was named Lana Rondell Holmes."

While working with Salty, Mattie, Bill and fiddler Sandy Sandusky, Martha was uncertain as to whether or not she could ever score any major success as a solo artist: "James always made me feel like I was the least important part of the duet, even though I taught him all those early songs."

Through the grapevine, she heard that James had moved on to Wheeling, where he joined Wilma Lee & Stoney Cooper and their Clinch Mountain Clan. The husband-and-wife team were then headliners on WWVA's *Wheeling Jamboree*.

On Dec. 18, 1950, in fact, James did a Nashville studio session with the duo, actually singing a *trio* with Wilma Lee & Stoney on "Faded Love" and "Mother's Prayers." Other cuts the unit recorded were "Ghost Train" and "The Golden Rocket," featuring James on mandolin. (The latter tune had already been recorded by Hank Snow a bit earlier, and was destined to become his second #1 RCA release.)

In Wheeling, James Roberts was not only staff bandsman, but had formed the Country Harmony Boys with Will Carver: "We were known as Will and Jim, but Paul Meyers who run that show then, took that name away from us, Country Harmony Boys, and I was the one who came up with that name.

"He was a strange guy. I remember him telling me to keep all the girls away from the Jamboree (backstage). I asked him, *'Why are you gettin' on me about them girls? They might have been comin' here to see Hawkshaw (Hawkins).'* But I think Paul was just jealous that they weren't coming to see him."

One woman who attended the show regularly eventually became James' second wife, Pearl Arman. "She worked there at a dollar store. She was originally from Powhatan Point, Ohio."

Martha, meanwhile, was coming of age as a single. She started dating - and one gallant gentleman proved to her that she indeed had sense enough to learn to drive an automobile. Her sister, Salty, Bill and Lowell were very supportive of Martha, encouraging her to start living again and, literally, *"look for the silver lining."* Still, Martha insists she wasn't ready for any really serious romantic entanglement.

Dee Kilpatrick, mindful of her recording contract, was determined to get Martha back in the studio again as a duet. He invited her to record with WROL-Knoxville star Archie Campbell.

"I always believed he was a skirt chaser and just wanted to get close to me," confides Martha. "He made me sort of sick because I felt that he thought he was hot stuff. Much later, when we were both performing in package shows, I overheard him boasting about some female conquests, so I asked him point blank if he wasn't married. He said, *'Oh, my wife knows I'm a cocksman.'* I realized then that I had judged him right earlier on."

(Earlier, Campbell had been a member of the *Mid-Day Merry-Go-Round* cast, but when Martha first knew him, he was a star with WROL-Knoxville's competing *Cas Walker Show*, sponsored by Walker's supermarkets. On WROL, Campbell helped pioneer Knoxville's first country TV show *Country Playhouse*. Born Nov. 7, 1914, he became known best after 1969, thanks to the long-running *Hee Haw* TV series, and even hosted his own *Yesteryear in Nashville* show on TNN. Campbell died Aug. 29, 1987.)

It was also in 1950 that Martha first met face-to-face Ken Nelson of Capitol Records, a man she would come to respect highly: "He came to Knoxville at Dee's suggestion to talk me into recording with Archie. But, I was determined not to record a duet with him or any other man."

CHAPTER 12

'I'm Satisfied...'

'I knew it was an inspiration from God...'

"Without the *Merry-Go-Round,* I don't think the *Grand Ole Opry* would have been as rich with talent as it was in the 1950s. It was sort of a stepping stone to the Opry, like Off Broadway is to Broadway (theater). A lot of the greats - Roy Acuff, Bill Carlisle, Chet Atkins, Kitty Wells, Johnnie & Jack, Homer & Jethro, Don Gibson and the Louvin Brothers - all played Knoxville first."

Martha Carson adds that she felt blessed to have been part of the early 1950s *Mid-Day Merry-Go-Round* and to have worked with producer Lowell Blanchard. Blanchard, who had done some singing and songwriting himself, had a knack for spotting talent in others. He was emcee of the historic one-hour, noon-day program, and had a friendly rivalry going with grocer Cas Walker, an entrepreneur, who recognized the value in sponsoring country music shows.

Some of the acts Walker offered a helping hand to were Carl Story, Archie Campbell, Flatt & Scruggs, the Bailey Brothers (Danny & Charlie), the Osborne Brothers (Sonny & Bobby), Carl Smith and a 10-year-old named Dolly Parton.

After leaving Wheeling, James Roberts also worked with Cas Walker at radio station WROL, and later at Knoxville television stations he was affiliated with, Channels 6 and 10: "Cas was on almost every station there was in town. Cousin Emmy was on the first TV show I did (fall 1953). I didn't sing much gospel then. I'd dropped that and sang and yodeled secular songs. You know, after I had my tonsils taken out, I couldn't yodel a lick...about 1960, I left Cas Walker."

Martha gave the edge to Blanchard.

"Lowell was such a talented man," she says. "He should have been a major network announcer. And he had some offers, but he turned them down."

During Martha Carson's WNOX tenure, the radio station was located downtown on Gay Street. After *Mid-Day Merry-Go-Round* was launched in 1935, its popularity was such that within months the show was being performed, with star act Roy Acuff & His Crackerjacks in the 1,500-seat Market Hall.

It's interesting that by comparison to WSM-Nashville, both WNOX and WROL programmed a lot more country music. Apart from the famed Opry, little country music was heard on WSM during the 1940s, as the station was busily building its schedule to suit NBC, seeking to become a national contender.

East Tennesseans were more interested in music that emanated from the surrounding hill country, and thus created a demand for "hillbilly" music and newly-emerging bluegrass sounds. (Earlier, they had run Pee Wee King and his cowboy songs and garb off to Nashville, where the Western style was more welcome.)

According to Chet Atkins, a native of Luttrell (near Knoxville), "There were more than 150 half-hour programs a week at WNOX, mostly country."

During 1951, Capitol Records released two James & Martha Carson records, the first which paired "Shining City" with "Sing, Sing, Sing" was issued May 14, while the duo's final single "Salvation Has Been Brought Down," with "Got a Little Light" on the flipside, hit the record stores Sept. 17.

Steadfastly, Martha was continuing to perform sacred songs that audiences could best identify her with, though her style was still developing. The entertainer remembers the day that changed her life.

"Bill warned us not to waste time talking to the audience members after the show. We were scheduled to go to Bryson City, N. C., that day after the *Mid-Day Merry-Go-Round,* and Bill wanted us to get an early start. He pulled the car right up in front - and I'm the last one to get out there. Of course, somebody had stopped me for an autograph and I obliged. Time I got out there, they done got all their equipment loaded into the car and they all had their heads together..."

Martha recalls how they had hushed up when she approached, so in the car she proceeded to chide them for talking about her. Bill told Jean, *"Tell her what we were talkin' about,"* but Jean remained mum. Bill then turned to her husband and repeated, "Tell her what we were talkin' about, Salty."

Ol' Stoneface was equally non-compliant.

"Well, if you all ain't a-gonna tell her, I'm gonna tell her," continued Carlisle, pointing out that a woman from Morristown, Tenn., went to the WNOX management and told Mr. Westergaard that if they ever booked a show in Morristown and Martha Carson was on it, no one would attend, because *if there was anything to that woman, she would have left when that man (James) did!*

"I was stunned!," exclaims Martha, who worried that her hanging on there with an unhappy marriage for the past few years had all been in vain. Now she was being reviled by fans, who apparently blamed her for the breakup of the so-called *Barn Dance Sweethearts*.

"I began crying when we left Knoxville and I cried uncontrollably all the way up the (Smoky) mountains...then all of a sudden, it was like a whole new world opened up for me, and I knew it was an inspiration from God, as the thought came to my mind, *'I'm satisfied, and You are satisfied'* (so who else matters?) - and that's how the song was born. It came to me that quickly and I had to write the words down.

"All I could find, however, was a blank check of Bill's lying on the floor below where I was sitting. It had dried mud and shoe prints all over it, but I dusted it off, turned it lengthwise and wrote 'Satisfied' on it. The melody had also come to me at the same time. It was like a miracle...one that proved to be my salvation."

Martha remembers she sang it on stage that night in North Carolina: "The people just loved it. I think it was because the words were so sincere and had come straight from my heart. To this day, that song is my refuge."

With the song came a more definitive Martha Carson performance. As a solo artist, she developed the needed assurance and self-confidence that seemed to dry up after her split with James.

"I didn't live until I got rid of him. Neither one of us did much movement on stage. It all just came to me when I did 'Satisfied.' I was truly reborn. That song just brought a joy out of me that I'd never experienced before...It done something to the audience, too, and for the first time in my life, I felt I was being loved for me!"

She continued to tour and entertain with Carlisle, her sister and Salty, but with a brand new vigor that succeeded in sparking a new commitment from her old fans, while winning new converts to her spirited musical evangelism.

For those rural folk who had never heard gospel - or country, for that matter - sung at full-throttle, the effect was hypnotizing! The lady was joyful, deliciously audacious, and, most definitely, something different to behold.

"It's not enough to merely open your mouth and sing the tune and words," as Kitty Wells later observed, "Martha Carson understands and *intimately feels* the message in her song, and therefore she delivers that message with a sincerity and honest conviction that only comes from within."

Kitty had performed at WNOX earlier and was another vocalist Lowell Blanchard predicted big things for down the road. Her own vocal style was miles from that of Martha's bombastic, no-holds-barred belting, but lent itself well to the "heart" songs and "sincerity" she spoke of, and which would become her forté at Decca.

Ironically, both began vocalizing with family: Kitty with cousin Bessie Choate as the Deason Sisters, and Martha, of course, with her own siblings as the Sunshine Sisters. Both were 16 when making their radio debuts. Kitty *nee* Ellen Muriel Deason bowed on WSIX-Nashville in 1936; while, a few hours away on WLAP-Lexington - albeit in 1937 - could be heard the sweet sound of the Amburgey girls. Each had made her first recordings in Atlanta.

Another coincidence was that each paired up with males during the 1940s: Kitty with singer-husband Johnny Wright on such stations as WCHS-Charleston, W. Va., WNOX-Knoxville and KWKH-Shreveport, La.; and Martha with James at WSB and WNOX. Yet, both attained their greatest national standing solo in 1952, Martha first with "Satisfied" and Kitty that same summer via "It Wasn't God Who Made Honky Tonk Angels." Martha and Kitty were both 30 or more when they had their first solo success. It was in '52 that they met in Nashville, as new members of the Opry family.

Oddly enough, "Satisfied" almost went to another artist.

"Right after I wrote and started singing 'Satisfied,' there was a guy in Knoxville who had just signed with RCA Victor," explains Martha. "He liked my song and I wanted him to record it because Dee (Kilpatrick) had told me I couldn't sing a note - solo! Well, I believed him, so I tried to get this guy to do it, but he only did a couple of sessions and RCA dropped him."

Martha had an opportunity to work with veteran showman Cliff Carlisle, before moving to Nashville. He stepped in briefly after Bill called for him, notes Martha: "When Jean was expecting Lana, her feet were so swollen, she couldn't go on some of the show dates. So Cliff came in for a few shows. He was just a laid-back ol' country boy, a bit more reserved than Bill, but just as easy to work with. He was also a portrait painter, very talented. I always respected the Carlisle Brothers - and them boys sold quite a few records in their time.

"But Bill was the showman, that's for sure. And a genuinely funny man. I remember one place we played somewhere up in the mountains in North Carolina. We got there just as it was beginning to get dark. Someone had been digging a well and they left this seemingly bottomless pit open. Bill saw it and made a point of warning each of us, 'You'all be sure to watch out for this hole here, because when we come out tonight, it'll be dark.'

"So who comes out with a guitar in one hand, a p.a. set in the other, and a costume bag under his arm, and then disappears down the hole! Bill! We helped pull him out and he raises his britches and his legs are all bloody, but he just stood there, dyin' laughing.

"I usually had to play *straight man* to his comedy antics. One time he used to bring this three-legged rooster along in the car. He said it had two legs and a landing gear. Next, he had a pet skunk he used with his rube character Hotshot Elmer. They'd always ride in the backseat with me. When it came to the skunk, I said, 'Come on, Bill! I don't want to ride with a polecat!' But Bill said he was de-skunked.

"Well, I remember one night coming back to Knoxville and the ol' skunk had to go potty #2. Bill had him fixed up in an orange crate with the top on it. He'd padded it with paper and leaves and such. Well, this critter would reach his claws out thru the cracks and just tear up my nylons. Then, when he had to go potty, I was just fuming at him!

"I said, 'Bill, I just can't stand this. There's no way I can stand it!' Bill just died laughing, and at that time he used to chew on cigars. He very seldom ever puffed it, but he'd keep at it until it stunk you out of the car. So, between the cigar and the smelly skunk, I was ready to be sick.

"Bill threw his head back, laughing, and looking at me. But, then he stopped the car on the shoulder of the road, took the crate out, cleaned it and put fresh leaves and paper in there, so we could get the skunk back home. He smiles at me and says, 'That's better, ain't it?' Another time I was on stage, singing one of my gospel numbers and he let the skunk loose and it came walking out on stage. I told him, *'That's the last straw, Bill! I don't want to do duets again with another polecat!'"*

She quickly recalled another time when they had driven up into the Smoky Mountains, stopped to rest and it was pitch black outside, when a big black bear wandered out of the woods: "Well, Bill saw him and honked that horn, and that bear blowed pee all over our windshield! And Bill just turned the windshield wipers on and took off!"

When "Wild Bill" started recording again, he invited Martha to a session in Nashville during late 1951. He and his recent partner, brother Cliff, had scored a Top Five single for King Records (in Cincinnati) in 1946, with their rendition of "Rainbow At Midnight" (nearly a year before the Ernest Tubb or Texas Jim Robertson versions).

The Carlisles had yet another King triumph in "Tramp On the Street" (#14, 1948), a song that garnered lots of jukebox play. This time around, however, Bill was slated to record for a relatively-new label, Mercury Records, most notably his satirical "Too Old To Cut the Mustard."

"Too old to cut the mustard was a line Bill used as Hotshot Elmer, which also included *Aw! he makes me sick!* and *He done got too old*...it was a little ol' smart-alecky thing, and Bill wanted me to do it. I told him, I'd play on it, but I wouldn't sing. So I called my sister Minnie to come down from Cincinnati and taught it to her. She sang a lot higher than I did. I didn't see no harm in doing a little ol' fun song, but I was concerned that others might think it was hypocritical for a gospel singer to do."

Incidentally, the song charted *Billboard* just before Christmas and in early 1952 became a Top 10 record - a sleeper - and the first of a new streak of Top 10 novelty tunes for Carlisle and company, and his ticket to the *Grand Ole Opry.*

Worth mentioning, too, is a late September 1951 impromptu session Bill and Martha did at Champs Studio in Johnson City, Tenn., when they recorded the duet "Lookin' This Way"(1031-B), a song Bill had written. It also marked the first solo recording by Martha, who cut the gospel number "I Want To Rest" (1031-A), which ended up as the A side for the occasion.

"Lookin' This Way" was a rouser by the pair, sure to keep listeners from dozing off at their shows. They recorded the songs for an independent: Rich'R Tone Records. Created by local businessman Jim Stanton in late 1945, the Rich'R Tone label has the distinction of having cut the first records ever done on the

Stanley Brothers and Wilma Lee & Stoney Cooper. Others Stanton recorded included Jimmy Skinner, the Bailey Brothers and later Vernon Oxford. Stanton did it all himself, primarily pressing vinyl for jukebox distribution and play.

"You know, I'd almost forgotten about those sides we did," reflects Martha, when reminded. "But, once you tell me the titles, I can remember us doing them."

Nothing much came of the 1951 Rich'R Tone tracks.

While in Nashville, however, Carlisle took Martha to Fred Rose's home on Rainbow Trail in Nashville's suburban Green Hills, where Bill asked Fred to listen to "Satisfied." She recalls, "Reluctantly, I sang it for him. Just me and an acoustic guitar. He seemed to like it…Anyway, he wanted me to put it with Acuff-Rose, which I did."

Fred Rose, blown away by both her song and solo performance, asked, "Gal, who are you recording for?" Martha replied, "I'm not recording for anyone right now, but I'm still under contract to Capitol." She added that her producer Dee Kilpatrick didn't think she'd sell solo, "They're trying to team me with Archie Campbell."

Fred next got on the phone to Capitol in Hollywood. The publisher-songwriter inquired as to whether they planned to record Martha solo, and if not, he wanted the opportunity to produce her and the song. (Reportedly, Rose had a studio in his home.) Martha wasn't really aware of Capitol's reaction: "I didn't know what they were saying on the other end of the line."

Of Fred, who first admired her as a duet act, she says, "What a precious man he was. But you know, Fred had this thing with his eye…you couldn't hardly tell who he was looking at…"

Once back home in Knoxville, Martha didn't give much thought to the encounter with Rose, though she *was* pleased that such a renowned composer as Fred Rose had admired her song, especially one written on the spur of the moment.

Fred Rose songs were classics, among them "Blue Eyes Crying in the Rain," "We Live in Two Different Worlds," "Roly Poly" and "Pins and Needles (In My Heart)."

For the uninitiated, Fred Rose was born Aug. 24, 1897, in Evansville, Ind. (the town in which Martha would wed her second husband), one of two children of Andrew and Annie (West) Rose. He spent his youth living with relatives in St. Louis, where he dropped out of grammar school and began playing for tips in waterfront bars.

The 18-year-old subsequently hopped a freight train to the Windy City, where he began as a songwriter. His first successes (pop songs) occurred via Tin Pan Alley promotion, including "Sweet Mama" (#5, 1921) for Marion Harris; "Red Hot Mama" (#4, 1924), a *hotcha* ballad that became Sophie Tucker's signature song; "Honest and Truly" (#4, 1925) by Henry Burr; and "Deed I Do" (#2, 1927) by torchy thrush Ruth Etting.

For a time, singer-pianist Rose recorded and performed on radio as Freddie Rose, at one time entertaining regularly on WSM-Nashville (1933-'34). In 1935, however, Rose met cowboy singer Ray Whitley, who a year later would begin appearing in low-budget Western movies. The two collaborated on such songs as "I Hang My Head and Cry" and "Lonely River."

Rose's association with the first of Hollywood's singing cowboys, Gene Autry, however, resulted in mega hits like "Tweedle O'Twill," "At Mail Call Today," "Tears On My Pillow" and "Be Honest With Me (Dear)," a 1941 best song Oscar nominee.

Rumor has it that Rose also had a hand in such pre-Hollywood Autry cuts as "That Silver-Haired Daddy of Mine," a multi-million seller credited to Autry and Jimmie Long (Gene's former boss), and even later "Back in the Saddle," Autry's radio theme song.

Unconcerned with ego, when Rose believed in a writer's talent potential, he would edit or polish the lyrics into a more craftsmanlike form, often without credit for his input. Among those he took under his wing were Whitley, Jenny Lou Carson, Mel Foree, Zeb Turner and Hank Williams.

For the latter, he co-wrote such classics as "Mansion On the Hill," "Kaw-Liga," "Settin' the Woods On Fire," "Take These Chains From My Heart" and the sadly prophetic "I'll Never Get Out of This World Alive."

According to Chet Atkins, "I believe Fred fixed up just about every song Hank wrote. Fred is the one who made Hank's songs acceptable to the pop market, because Hank was a real country boy; he didn't write pop lyrics. Fred would recognize a line that would perhaps hinder a song, and he'd doctor it and patch it and make it acceptable. There is a lot of Fred Rose in most Hank Williams' songs."

On Oct. 13, 1942, in a partnership officially with Mildred Acuff, Rose established Acuff-Rose, the first major music publishing firm based in Nashville. Of course, the man behind the investment was Mildred's husband, Roy, soon-to-be King of Country Music.

It wasn't long before Roy Acuff took the helm himself, and his near-sighted partner brought in his brilliant, but previously-estranged son Wesley Rose, all of whom helped Nashville evolve into *Music City USA*.

Incidentally, as a lark, Rose recorded "Tender-Hearted Sue" on the Okeh label using the stage name *The Ramblin' Rogue*. But the tunesmith was pleasantly surprised when "...Sue" became a Top Five single on *Billboard's* 1945 country chart.

For these contributions - and more - Fred Rose was one of the first three elected into the Country Music Hall of Fame (the others, Hank Williams, his protege, and Jimmie Rodgers "Father of Country Music") in 1961.

Among other Rose classics (either penned as Rose or his *nom de plume* Floyd Jenkins) are "Guess I've Been Asleep For All These Years," "The Last Mile," "Fire Ball Mail," "I'll Reap My Harvest in Heaven," "Low and Lonely," "No One Will Ever Know," "Waltz of the Wind," "Texarkana Baby," "Afraid," "Deep Water," "Crazy Heart," "It's a Sin" and both "I Gave My Wedding Dress Away" and "I Hope My Divorce is Never Granted," for a singer he admired, Kitty Wells.

Earlier, he had offered a helping hand to singers Molly O'Day (who worked with the Sunshine Sisters in Bluefield), Rosalie Allen (a yodeler, who enjoyed brief success with such RCA Top 10's as "Guitar Polka," "Beyond the Sunset" and "Quicksilver," the latter two duets with Elton Britt) and gospel-oriented Martha Carson.

[Twenty-three months after Hank Williams' premature death at age 29, his mentor Fred Rose, frail and ill, died on Dec. 1, 1954 at 57.]

"I think he was probably the greatest songwriter country music ever had, and I am happy that I knew him, if only for a few years," attests Carson. "He wanted me to put all my songs in his publishing house - and I'm so glad I did back then."

Walt Trott

CHAPTER 13

New Beginning...

"Martha's recording boasts a joyous, uplifting beat that marks it as the first real rockabilly anthem, complete with a message of faith."

"I went back to the *Mid-Day Merry-Go-Round* in Knoxville," says Martha. "We were home three or four days when a letter from Capitol came and I figured it was more hokum about doing a duet with Archie, so I just stuffed it in the desk drawer and didn't open it.

"One day, I got back from the radio station and the telephone was ringing in my little apartment - and it was Fred Rose. He said, 'Girl, didn't you get a piece of mail from Capitol?' I said *I sure did, but I assumed it was the same old stuff about singing with a partner, so I put it away, unopened.*

"Fred said, 'Well, get that out and open it! It's a top royalty priority solo contract. We want you in here next week to record.' So I got it out, signed it and mailed it on back. It was a five-year contract for me as a solo artist (through 1956)."

Carson's historic cut was recorded at the Castle Studio in the Tulane Hotel in downtown Nashville on Nov. 5, 1951, with producer Ken Nelson and the following backup musicians: Chet Atkins, lead guitar; Harold Bradley, rhythm guitar; Ernie Newton, bass; Marvin Hughes, piano; and Bill Carlisle, Jean/Mattie & Salty Holmes providing harmony vocals. Martha also accompanied her upbeat vocals on acoustic guitar, playing rhythm.

"When I went into record, Dee wasn't there. Whenever Dee was in charge of recording, perhaps you'd get it right the first time, but he'd still make you do it 25 times or more! I guess that was to make you think he knew something that you didn't know.

He'd say, *'Do this or do that...or, while you're up there, let's do another take.'*

"I didn't know Ken then. He was just a very quiet, nice gentleman, who was there in the control room. I did the first take on 'Satisfied,' and I'm waiting to catch hell from the control room like before, but nobody's saying anything. In fact, it was deathly quiet to me. I thought, well maybe it was just too bad for anyone to comment. That quiet scared me to death, nobody saying nothing, not *it's great, it stinks,* nothing!

"To break the silence, I said, *'Let's do another one while we're all set up here.'* I finish again and it's still quiet...To me, it's a miserable quiet. Finally, I said on my microphone, 'Mr. Nelson, If I'm doing something wrong, please feel free to make suggestions. I'll be glad to hear what you have to say.' After my previous experience, I'm just lost without being hammered on by Dee or James.

"Then his mic comes back on and Ken says, 'Martha, you're doing just fine. If I start telling you how to do it, I'll wind up with a Ken Nelson session. I came here to get a Martha Carson session. If I leave you alone, that's what I'll come out with. You're doing just great.' That was the extent of the conversation. We did three takes on 'Satisfied,' and I believe a total of four songs for that first solo session. Fred was there and I imagine he had told Ken about all the songs. He had told Dee about it."

She got to pick the songs for the two-day session, also including "Crying Holy Unto the Lord," "Old Blind Barnabus" and "Hide Me Rock of Ages," Nov. 5; and "Fear Not," "I Wanna Rest," "You Sure Do Need Him Now" and "Weighed in the Balance," Nov. 6.

"I feel like the musicians all loved doing it, because it was different for them from the usual country numbers they always did." Martha was especially pleased about Chet's superb pickin' on lead guitar. Of course, Ernie Newton's walkin' bass added much to Martha's reaffirmation of life songs, as did Bradley's rhythm stylings and Marvin Hughes' keyboard wizardry. All of these musicians would play a major role in the next decade, creating the innovative *Nashville Sound* that kept the country music business from going belly up with the influx of rock and roll.

"Hide Thee Rock Of Ages" was the song selected as the flip for "Satisfied," her first solo single from Capitol, released Dec. 10, 1951. By the time Capitol released her follow-up single - "You Sure Do Need Him Now," backed with "Weighed in the Balance" - on Feb. 18, 1952, "Satisfied" was a hot seller and one of the most-requested songs on the airwaves.

"When I first heard 'Satisfied' on the radio, I could have died. I thought if only I could go back in the studio and redo it! But, the listeners must have liked it when they heard it, because enough of them went out and bought it. I remember that Acuff-Rose took out ads for me and my song in all the trades."

Unlike Foley's previous country-gospel successes, Martha's recording boasts a joyous, uplifting beat that marks it as the first real rockabilly anthem, complete with a message of faith.

"One day we got a call from WDOK in Birmingham (Ala.), wanting me to come down and do a show. Of course, I was still living in Knoxville, and Lowell Blanchard said they'd pay me $300, but I'd have to split with Bill (Carlisle), 'He'll go with you. Your record is #1 there, Martha!'

"Well, we were booked in the National Guard Armory and they had to have a police guard to get me in and out of the building! It was my first booking since the song took off. We drove up to the building. They said they had turned three bus loads away. I almost had a coronary!

"I was given a Key to the City and they made me an Honorary Member of the Chamber of Commerce. The Governor of Alabama had declared it *Martha Carson Day!* It was the first time a spiritual song had ever hit the trades and they said there wasn't a pool hall in the state of Alabama that didn't have 'Satisfied' on the juke box!

"Later, it tickled me when I learned from an inter-office memo - Capitol would send me these all the time - that they had to take Les Paul & Mary Ford's 'Hold That Tiger' (actually titled 'Tiger Rag') off to press 'Satisfied' as they got so many requests for it," adds Martha.

After Jack Stapp heard Carson's record on the radio, he contacted her in late 1951 to guest star on the *Grand Ole Opry*. A Nashville native, Stapp had worked as a production executive at the CBS radio network in New York during the 1930s. Upon returning to Nashville, he began at WSM as an assistant to Harry Stone and later became the Opry's program director (and founder of today's enormously successful Tree/Sony Music, a major song publishing house). Stapp briefly fronted his own Opry band (he died in December 1980).

WSM, of course, were the call letters for the station which kicked off in 1925, and stood for the motto "We Serve Millions." (Until its 1983 sale to Gaylord, WSM was owned by the National Life & Accident Insurance group.)

Martha was still on the *Merry-Go-Round* and *Tennessee Barn Dance* in Knoxville when invited by Stapp: "But to be asked on the Opry was a thrill of a lifetime for me! And can you believe this? I got sick with a cold! I told Bill, 'I won't be able to sing a lick with this dern cold!' Well, he knew a pharmacist and went and got me a load of penacillin tablets to take. I didn't know I was allergic to it!

"So I wound up in the hospital. Still, I was determined to keep my date at the Opry, and I couldn't even put my feet on the floor. The next day, I told a nurse to get my doctor because I had to check out and go sing on the Opry...

"She said, 'You are not well enough and you're not eating anything. The doctor says if you try to leave without his consent, he cannot take responsibility for what happens to you!'

"So, I called Jean and Salty to come and get me out. It's true, I was still weak as water. They drove me to the airport, however, and Ken Nelson met me in Nashville. When I went on that stage, I was so sick. Actually, I can hardly remember that performance. Roy Acuff brought me on. I did it and it must have went over big, because they asked me to stay over - and I did."

Martha's still a bit fuzzy on the dates of her first appearance, but officially she joined the Opry cast, April 12, 1952. She was the first solo songstress signed as a regular, a few months before Kitty Wells was added to the roster. *Billboard* duly noted in its April 15 edition: "Martha Carson has joined the *Grand Ole Opry.*"

"I went back over to Knoxville to tell them - and to say goodbye. It was hard to break with all the old friends, especially those who had been so supportive of me when I was down…they had seen me come from nowhere and move on up, and I know they were all sincerely happy for me. And, for the most part, when I moved to Nashville, the reception was equally warm."

Gordon Stoker of the Jordanaires recalls Carson as a joy to work with: "We would sing with her almost every time she'd perform on the *Grand Ole Opry,* and Lord, I don't remember how many records we did with her and Ken (Nelson)."

It was in Knoxville, however, that Martha became a licensed driver for the first time: "I had dated a man who drove a new Buick. He agreed to teach me to drive. Once I learned enough, Bill took me to the highway patrol office for my driver's test. Well, after I got my license, I bought me a Pontiac Catalina right off the show room floor! It was the prettiest thing: Robin's egg blue and cream-colored, with leather seats. That car was a beauty!

"That's how I moved me and Ching-a-Ling to town. At first, I stayed at the Andrew Jackson Hotel, walking down the street to do my bit at the Ryman Auditorium every weekend…

Since 1943, the 3,000-seat Ryman was home to the Opry. Built in 1889, as the Union Gospel Tabernacle, it was rechristened in 1904, posthumously after its founder, ex-steamboat skipper Tom Ryman. Rarely was a seat empty come Saturday night, during the Opry's more than 30-year reign in this 19th century building, now listed on the National Registry of Historic Places.

"In those days the Ryman was drafty in winter and slightly overheated in summer. We didn't have any air-conditioning, and you can picture us performers strutting our stuff in 100-degree weather. But I would rather sweat buckets, performing on that old stage anytime. There's just something so special about that theater.

"As for rivalry among the acts, I didn't notice any to speak of...Minnie Pearl was like an old Mother Hen, always giving me advice on what NOT to do! She said, 'Don't ever go to bed with Jack Stapp or Jim Denny.' I said, 'Minnie, I don't have no intention or any time for such things.'"

The Ryman didn't boast much in the way of backstage facilities; most notable to Martha was a lack of dressing rooms: "We all knew our boundaries. Whoever was scheduled earlier on the program, had to get dressed first; so the other gals made themselves scarce so you could get into your stage clothes and be ready when you were announced.

"I started designing my own dresses before I joined the Opry...I created the dress with the pinafore that had a little apron on it. Kitty Wells, Jean Shepard and even Minnie and the Carter sisters copied my style. Before that on the Opry, women like Texas Daisey and Texas Ruby mainly wore cowgirl costumes.

"When I initially drew the pictures of how I wanted the dresses sewn, I thought it would look more graceful for the artist to have longer skirts, especially because the stage was elevated. I think it cheapens a woman to go on in those short-short skirts. You know those mini-dresses like Wilma Lee Cooper wears today on the Opry that don't do a blasted thing for her!"

In 1960, Wanda Jackson had a Top 40 rockabilly success with "Let's Have a Party," after having established herself a few seasons earlier via a country duet "You Can't Have My Love" (with Billy Gray). Hot-on-the-heels of her hit, she guest-starred on the Opry, and came ready to go on in a form-fitting, low-cut cocktail dress with spaghetti straps.

Conservative cast member Ernest Tubb took one look at the artist and had her don a jacket before going out on stage. This so angered Jackson that she never again appeared at the Ryman, but went on to become the darling of Las Vegas. (Her other major chartings include two she wrote, "Right Or Wrong" and "In the Middle of a Heartache," both decidedly country cuts.)

Carson describes her early Ryman costumes: "My dresses had yards and yards of material in the skirts - and petticoats underneath. One night on the Opry, I was fit to be tied! They had made me one of those little ol' crinoline petticoats to wear under the dress, and the waistband fastened with a hook-and-eye. And, you know me, when I sing, I can't stand still; If you cut my legs off, I can't hit a note!

"Well, when I put that dress on, I added a black velvet cummerbund and I laced that sucker up tight. Little did I know what was gonna happen, once I got moving on stage. The house was full that night and I was determined to give them my best shot.

"While I was performing, however, I felt my petticoat come unsnapped! Then I felt it start to creeping down my hips…I spread my legs trying to catch it and stop its progress. I thought, 'Oh my God, what's gonna happen here!' The skirt surrounding the petticoat must have had six yards of material all around - it was a real full skirt.

"Now I knew I couldn't spread my legs too far apart or I'd look ridiculous out there. Next, I mashed down on the guitar, pushing it up against my tummy - and that's the only way I kept the petticoat from falling down in front of that audience.

"I was thinking, 'My God, if I lose my petticoat, I'll just die!,' while backing off stage, pressing hard on my stomach with the guitar…that guitar kept me from shame. Believe me, once off stage, I ran straight to the dressing room to fix that dude."

Her backup band remained unaware of the boss lady's dilemma.

"Lightnin' Chance played bass for me Ernie Newton-style, that is, with a drum head attached to his bass fiddle, which gave the effect that I had a drummer, as well. Marvin Hughes usually played piano, my sister and brother-in-law provided backup vocals, and Chet Atkins played lead guitar for me.

"In fact, Chet backed up nearly everyone at the Opry...although he played most of my spots on the Opry and also on my records, he never went on the road with me. You know, if it wasn't for Chet and (his wife) Leona, I don't know what I'd have done during those first days at the Opry."

Atkins had met his singer-wife Leona Johnson at WLW-Cincinnati, where she performed with her twin Lois (who married mandolin picker Kenneth "Jethro" Burns of Homer & Jethro fame) on the *Boone County Jamboree,* which evolved into the *Midwestern Hayride.* A few years earlier, Atkins started professionally as a fiddler out of Knoxville, touring with Bill Carlisle.

"Chet was a better fiddler than he was a guitar picker back then," chuckles Johnny Wright (husband of Kitty Wells), who hired Atkins to work with his Tennessee Hillbillies at WPTF Raleigh on the *Carolina Barn Dance,* after he'd left WLW. "But it didn't take (Chet) long to learn to master the guitar. I think he started out playing *Merle Travis style,* but, of course, he soon developed his own unique pickin' methods."

Leona and Chet, who wed in 1946, named their only baby - daughter Merle - after Dad's music hero (fellow Hall of Famer Travis).

"I think Leona felt sorry for me, living in a two-by-four hotel room," continues Martha. "I stayed in the hotel until I could afford to get my furniture moved over from Knoxville. She would call me and say, 'Martha, why don't you come over here and eat dinner with us?' That would happen four or five times a week.

"Chet, who was three years younger than me, had worked the road a lot earlier with the Carter sisters. Lordie, I remember the day Leona called sternly to say, *'One of the Carter girls just gave me the news that you are having an affair with my husband!'* - but then she burst out laughing.

"She sent Chet over later to pick me up and bring me home again to dinner! Leona knew me well enough to know I'd never get involved with him. I reckon June just got a little jealous of me."

Chet's name came up much later in a more serious romantic allegation, suggesting he had fathered a son by his secretary, who happened to be Mrs. Tommy Jackson, then wife of the renowned studio fiddler. (Jackson, who died Dec. 9, 1979, backed musical royalty like Hank Williams, Kitty Wells, Webb Pierce and Jim Reeves, playing on such cuts as "I'm So Lonesome I Could Cry," "Yonder Comes a Sucker" and "Back Street Affair.").

"I never knew Mrs. Jackson, but I do know Chet called X saying Tommy was going to kill him, and X told him to take out a Peace Bond (restraining order) on Tommy to keep him away (from Chet)," Martha muses. "That's so strange because I remember when both Chet and Tommy, along with steel player Jerry Byrd, played on an Amber Sisters session we did for Capitol, where everybody got along great."

Walt Trott

CHAPTER 14

Pop Goes the Gospel...

> '*Country music is the music of the people...a spontaneous musical outburst of events in their daily lives - their joys and hopes and fears...music of the heart.*'
>
> **Frank G. Clement**, Governor of Tennessee, 1956.

It's an axiom of history that to know *where we are going*, it's necessary to know *where we've been.* After all, this provides us direction and inspiration. Country's roots are in the rural (hillbilly) and bluecollar (honky tonk) South and derived from the traditional folk music of the British Isles. The line separating oldtime Appalachian mountain fiddle songs and Irish laments is a fine one indeed. It was the Irish miners who brought over the fiddles that became mainstays of the mountain string bands.

In Bavaria (Southern Germany), we hear the strains of *oompah* bands and folk drinking tunes, all too reminiscent of America's country music. Probably the biggest boons to the expansion of country-style music were the singing cowboy westerns, radio shows, jukeboxes - and World War II.

Singers and songwriters like Gene Autry, Jimmie Davis, Patsy Montana, Lulu Belle & Scotty, Ernest Tubb, Roy Acuff, Floyd Tillman, Cindy Walker, Fred Rose, Jenny Lou Carson, Roy Rogers, Tex Ritter, Bob Wills and Al Dexter were helping to spread the sounds of country and western music even farther afield.

The GIs from the south mingled with those from the north, an occurrence which played no small part in enlightening the uninitiated. Such factors sounded the death knell for regional sounds as boundaries broke down creating new trends in country thereby expanding its audience. (This writer, for one, first appreciated R&B music, while living in a Marine Corps' barracks at Camp Geiger, N.C.)

Most music historians agree that country music's *golden years* ranged from World War II through the pre-rock 1950s. There came then a rich lode of talent, including the likes of Autry, Tubb, Ritter, Wills, Dexter, Acuff, Foley, Eddy Arnold, Jimmy Wakely, Pee Wee King & Redd Stewart, Hank Thompson, George Morgan, Hank Snow, Lefty Frizzell, Webb Pierce, Kitty Wells, Ray Price, Carl Smith, Jean Shepard, Ferlin Husky, Faron Young, et al.

Earlier, we cited Rep. Bob Clement, who praised Martha Carson as "a national treasure." From a political family in Tennessee, his father was Frank G. Clement, noted statesman and Democratic party chief in the Volunteer State.

While visiting New York City in 1956, as principal speaker for the *Radio & Television Executives Society* luncheon at the Hotel Roosevelt Grill, then-Tennessee Governor Clement offered his own sentiments on the growing popularity of country music.

"Country music is the music of the people. It's the spontaneous musical outburst of the events in their daily lives - their joys and hopes and fears...this was and still is the music of the heart; of love and hatred; of jealousy and generosity; of sympathy and sincerity, and all the myriad emotions that make Man what he is. And it speaks of God and faith; it sings of courage and home, and a fundamental decency.

"You people on Madison Avenue and others across the country, sometimes make a big *to do* about not being able to understand the popularity of country music or the phenomenal success of a show like the *Grand Ole Opry*.

"Country music has been with us always - as long as people have sung at their work, danced away their leisure hours, plucked a guitar or sawed on a fiddle," continued Clement. "It is one of the resources of a people, of an intelligent, neighbor-loving, God-fearing people, steeped in folk tradition and folk culture. I love country music, because when I hear it, I hear America singing."

As the late Tennessean noted so succinctly, country music is heavily rooted in the conservative, working class South - and was once nearly exclusively male. The prevailing chauvinistic creed of the time was "Woman's place is in the home."

Martha Carson was the *first* modern-day country roots-female to appeal to a national audience, *first* to perform on nationwide television, *first* booked into New York's plush nightclubs and the *first* solo female singing star invited to join the historic WSM *Grand Ole Opry* roster on a regular basis - in the spring of '52.

If the music honchos had known what to do with a new gospel artist, Martha might have been the first country female to score #1 on the chart with "Satisfied," which, despite its huge sales and popularity languished somewhere in chart limbo (in an era when the trades reported only the Top 10, as space allowed).

That achievement was left for Kitty Wells, who indeed scored #1 on the *Billboard* country chart with her assertive answer song "It Wasn't God Who Made Honky Tonk Angels," garnering a bid to join the Opry family during fall 1952. (Her recording represented a spunky retort to Hank Thompson's "Wild Side of Life," the country song of the year.)

It's a shame that a lot of yesteryear's hit country tunes go unrecognized as such today, because the trades back then failed to list more than 10, and in some instances in *Billboard,* only five or eight were listed, depending on space left over, after all the ads were printed.

A couple other releases that come to mind in 1951, successes on radio and in record stores, were Carl Smith's breakthrough song "I Overlooked An Orchid," and Johnnie & Jack's classic "Ashes of Love," which didn't surface on *Billboard's* abbreviated charts.

For a short while on the Opry, Carson and Wells had it all to themselves. Soon other talented young artists like Jean Shepard and Goldie Hill joined their ranks at the Ryman. [It should be noted, however, that Minnie Pearl was the first female to break through the Opry's male bastion in 1940. Still, Pearl was a non-singing, spinsterish comic, who for some seasons served mainly as the foil of fellow Opry comedian Rod Brasfield.]

Another female artist who appeared on the Opry regularly from 1953, was pianist Del Wood, whose credits include the 1951 pop-country crossover instrumental "Down Yonder," which also sold a million singles. Non-Opry members, the Davis Sisters garnered national attention, too, with a million-seller, "I Forgot More Than You'll Ever Know (About Him)," charting #1 country several weeks in 1953, and #18 pop.

Vocalists Carson and Wells' accomplishments, however, demonstrated that women could be the equal of male stars, opening floodgates for the Patsy Clines and Loretta Lynns to follow in the next decade.

Historically, Martha Carson was the first country-style female to perform with an aggressive fervor that later characterized such male dervishes as Elvis Presley, Little Richard and Jerry Lee Lewis. Actually, women - and men - were quite static in their musical performance until Martha came along. With her unflagging exuberance, she would respond to an audience by reaching out and grabbing them emotionally.

Gospel queen Carson boasts a lot of country soul. That's a bit deeper than heart, though she has plenty of that, too; possessing a gleeful feel for music that inspires the common folk to want to shout "Halleluiah!"…"Amen!"

Another who matched Martha's passionate performance was sister Opal Jean.

"She's also the only one who could ever write for me. Jean had an open door to my heart and she could write it out just like the inspiration had been given directly to me. I suppose it's because she knew what was close to my heart."

The young Martha used other artists as inspirational starting points. But she soon learned it's not enough to have a voice. By composing your own songs, your chances are enhanced. Fortunately, she had long ago been inspired to write, simply because she had something to say - which goes along with a need to entertain others.

Aggressive messages of faith are her hallmark. Martha Carson writes about issues most Christians care about. Whenever she performs, however, literally she wants the joint to jump. On stage, therefore, she's combined non-stop energy and pure gospel, with a winning way.

Almost the same time as Martha Carson was shining through, Johnnie Ray was bursting forth as the hottest pop singer in the nation. His breakthrough record, "Cry," quickly sold more than two million copies, becoming the #1 song on the *Hit Parade* on Dec. 29, 1951, remaining in that illustrious spot 11 weeks, and was #1 on *Billboard's* R&B chart, as well. Amazingly, the single's B side, "The Little White Cloud That Cried," soon soared to #2 on the *Billboard* 1952 pop charts and to #6 on R&B's list.

The Okeh recording artist was unique to audiences in that he was extremely passionate in his presentation, writhing and breaking out in tears, while vocalizing, and expressing previously-inhibited or repressed feelings of raw emotion. More than anyone else, he exemplified the strong and magical hold an artist could *hammer-lock* onto a youthful audience; a futuristic preview, if you will, of what would occur several years hence with the arrival of Elvis Presley.

Regarding his own rather-frenetic performing style, Ray mused that when a man ought to express emotions, "he suppresses himself, because he doesn't think that it's manly...I just show people the emotion they're afraid to show."

Ray's success was especially notable because he suffered from severe hearing loss and had to wear a hearing aid since his youth. (Born on a farm in Dallas, Oregon, Jan. 10, 1925, he was 12, when his playmates tossed him up in a blanket, but failed to catch him coming down, causing damage to his head - and hearing - as he hit the ground.)

Following the phenomenal success of "Cry" and its flip hit, Columbia Records almost immediately released two follow-up songs, producing yet another momentous million seller for Ray, with the number six-ranked "Please Mr. Sun," and yet another Top 10 flipside "Here Am I, Broken Hearted." Other Ray Top 10'ers were: "Walkin' My Baby Back Home," "Somebody Stole My Gal," "Just Walkin' in the Rain" (#2) and "You Don't Owe Me a Thing" (1957).

Ray was also teamed in 1952 with screen thrush Doris Day for a trio of tunes: "A Full-Time Job" (a cover on Eddy Arnold's #1 country hit), "Ma Says, Pa Says" (a South African-style song) and "Candy Lips."

The following year, Johnnie Ray scored with Carson's "I'm Gonna Walk and Talk With My Lord," which became a Top 20 pop success for him, Jan. 17, 1953. Ironically, that same year, he went before the Hollywood cameras for the first time, portraying a man-of-the-cloth for the big-budget family musical "There's No Business Like Show Business," which co-starred Marilyn Monroe, Donald O'Connor, Mitzi Gaynor, Dan Dailey and Ethel Merman, a 1954 20th Century-Fox box office champion.

"It was one of the greatest thrills I think I ever had, when he recorded two (also 'Satisfied') of my songs," acknowledges Carson. "I also got the pleasure of meeting him and seeing him perform. He told his audience that anytime he ever had to put his hand in the bag to top 'Cry,' he always pulled out a piece of material written by a lady who was in the audience, by the name of *Martha Carson!* He wowed them singing 'I'm Gonna Walk and Talk With My Lord,' then he had to come back until he was drenched with sweat, for an encore. He was such a great entertainer!"

In 1958, surgery restored much of the star's hearing, prompting Ray to josh about hearing his voice for the first time, that it was "like the first atom bomb exploding in pieces everywhere; 31 is a heck of an age to have your voice change."

Married briefly (1952-1954) to Marilyn Morrison, a non-performer, he was rumored to have had liaisons with the married New York show business columnist Dorothy Kilgallen, a dozen years his senior. Still, his career was plagued by arrests allegedly for making homosexual advances to undercover lawmen acting as decoys.

In reference to his problematic lifestyle, he said, "Friends are so vital to me...I must have friends...and when I had some trouble - you know? - I found out who my friends were. I had maybe this many," showing 10 fingers, "and none in show business." (On Feb. 24, 1990, Johnnie Ray died in Los Angeles at age 65.)

In retrospect, it could be said that Ray and the lady whose music he so admired were inspirations for a musical phenomenon that would diminish sales in both pop music and that emanating from Nashville. Indeed, their feverish performing style helped give birth to the similarly enthusiastic rock and roll entertainers to come.

It was in Memphis that an upstart record company began the trend, making tracks on redneck boys, who began fusing the sentimental strains of country to raw, raucous "race" music (or *Rhythm & Blues* stylings) of the early 1950s, into a combustible blend.

Among these new white faces at Sun Records were Elvis Presley, Bill Black, Scotty Moore, Carl Perkins, Jerry Lee Lewis and Johnny Cash. In effect, these innovators helped to create *rock 'n' roll,* an infant music form that nearly destroyed country, gospel and pop music as we knew it.

Ironically, Elvis, the man who almost single-handedly killed off the other genres, and who later became "King of Rock 'n' Roll," was a big fan of Martha's. On Sept. 10, 1954, while still a relative unknown and then under the aegis of producer Sam Phillips, the newcomer chose to record Carson's composition "Satisfied."

During that same recording session, he cut "Tomorrow Night" and "I'll Never Let You Go (Little Darlin')," both of which were released. Unfortunately, "Satisfied" was not released. According to author Joseph A. Tunzi in his "Elvis Sessions II" (JAT Productions Publication, Chicago, 1996) the actual Presley cut on her song has not yet been located for posterity's sake.

"I was told that Elvis was so unhappy with his performance on 'Satisfied' that he said he wanted the tape of 'Satisfied' destroyed, supposedly because he felt he didn't do it as well as Martha Carson did," explains Carson, with a wry grin. "But Lord, wouldn't it be great if they found a copy - and then I could go in and do a duet with him on it!"

Carson's "I'm Gonna Walk and Talk With My Lord" was also featured in a 1958 20th Century-Fox film "Sing, Boy, Sing," as sung by Tommy Sands, then 22. The crooner was best known for his #2 *Billboard* single "Teen-Age Crush," featured in the Kraft TV Playhouse musical drama "The Singin' Idol" (1957), a part obtained for Sands by then-manager Colonel Tom Parker. (Oddly enough, "Teen-Age Crush" also charted as a Top 10 on the R&B chart for three weeks.)

Sands, who hails from Shreveport, La., is the son of Chicago band pianist Benny Sands. Tommy was briefly wed to Nancy Sinatra (1960-65), and later married non-professional Sheila Wallace (in 1973). It was no secret that Parker landed Sands the "Singin' Idol" project, after nixing it for another client, Elvis Presley.

Incidentally, in the TV show, Sands portrayed a Presley-like character. Sands' own recording career eventually hit a snag after his last two Top 20 tunes: "Goin' Steady" and "Sing, Boy, Sing." The latter song was utilized as the title of writer Claude Binyon's big screen expansion of the original Kraft teleplay, fashioned by author Paul Monash.

Produced and directed by Henry Ephron (father of writer-filmmaker Nora), "Sing, Boy, Sing" was also reminiscent of the first Talkie (in 1927), Al Jolson's "The Jazz Singer," instead with a religion switch from Jewish to Christian (and remade twice, with Danny Thomas in 1952, and Neil Diamond in 1980.)

During "Sing, Boy, Sing's" opening credits, character actor John McIntire as a revivalist preacher, conducts a born-again congregation musically, with his prepubescent grandson accompanying him on their rousing rendition of "I'm Gonna Walk and Talk With My Lord."

Defying granddad's desire that he become an evangelist himself when grown, Sands sets out to follow his heart's desire, becoming a rock and roller. Meanwhile, his greedy manager (Edmond O'Brien) cuts him off from contact with his family, refusing even to tell him McIntire is dying.

After bolting for home, Sands becomes so overwhelmed by grief upon his grandparent's passing, that he decides to abandon the "sinful" rock world. He takes to preaching the gospel, but his wise aunt (Josephine Hutchinson) sees his heart isn't in it and convinces him to use his God-given talent to better advantage: "Sing, Boy, Sing."

Sands gets to reprise Martha Carson's great gospel number and ends up happily in the arms of hometown sweetheart Lili Gentle (nowadays known as producer of Faith Hill's award-winning music video "Breathe," and as wife of movie mogul Dick Zanuck).

The film also features a fine supporting performance by Nick Adams and a cameo spotlighting Nashville DJ Biff Collie. Sands appeared in several films, most notably "Mardi Gras," "Babes in Toyland," "Love in a Goldfish Bowl" and "The Longest Day," before dropping out of the national limelight. For a time, he was also involved in a tourist travel program in Hawaii.

More recently, a sixty-ish Sands has been in touch with Carson's current manager Scotty Turner, supposedly regarding a possible biographical screen venture for the sacred singer.

Back when he was being compared to Presley, Sands stated some obvious differences in style, less-than-subtly adding, "I stand still when I sing. I like rock 'n' roll, but I don't want to be classified…(however) what happened to Elvis should happen to me."

Walt Trott

CHAPTER 15

Star Trappings...

*"Oh, I heard a voice from Heaven, saying 'Come unto me,
And I will make you happy, If you'll just abide with me.'
Oh, I'm a gonna walk and talk with my Lord..."*
- © **1952**, Acuff/Rose, Inc.

Now that she wore her official badge of approval from the *Grand Ole Opry* and "Satisfied" was still burning up the airwaves, Martha soon felt the need to enhance her stage presence.

She smiles at the memory of that first flush of solo stardom. The first duo she chose, Kitty and Smiley Wilson, marked the beginning of a life-long friendship for the trio. With seemingly little effort, Kitty and Smiley Wilson maintained the beat, but were with Martha professionally on a regular basis only about two years.

Mary Kathleen (Kitty) Wilson was born in Rome, Ga., Dec. 11, 1927. She was a singer-songwriter, who played standup bass. One of her earliest jobs was with a regional group calling themselves Moonlight Ramblers. Her guitarist-husband-to-be Hamilton (Smiley) Wilson was born Aug. 23, 1922. An Alabama native, he performed in the late 1930s with a band called the Rogers County Cowboys.

In October 1942, he married Kitty (not yet 15), then had to take time out to serve Uncle Sam as a Marine in World War II. He returned to join Kitty in the Circle 3 Ranch Gang in 1945. The couple recorded a modest hit, "Red Silk Stockings and Green Perfume," in 1947. They were also in the 1949 low-budget film "Square Dance Jubilee."

The Wilsons' daughter, Rita Faye, also tried her hand as a child performer, with a degree of success. When she grew up, she married musician Earl Richards (Sinks) and became a homemaker. Kitty, incidentally, wrote the songs "We Lived It Up," recorded by Jimmy Dickens, and "I Know," cut by Hank Snow.

"Kitty could slap that bass. Smiley played good rhythm guitar and he was just an excellent emcee," Martha raves, "The fans really loved our shows."

A month after joining the Opry, Ken Nelson suggested it was time Martha scheduled another studio session for Capitol, and told her to pick the songs. When inspired to write "I'm Gonna Walk and Talk With My Lord," she sensed it was something special, just as "Satisfied" had been a bit earlier: *"Oh, I heard a voice from Heaven, saying 'Come unto me, And I will make you happy, If you'll just abide with me.' Oh, I'm a gonna walk and talk with my Lord, I'm a gonna walk, walk and talk with my Lord. He's the Lily of the Valley, He is bright as the morning star..."*

Of course, that was at the top of the list she submitted to Capitol. Another she composed that she hoped to record was more morose, touching on loss of loved ones. Titled "Beyond the Shadows," it started out, *"Don't weep when loved ones, in death beds are slumbering/Don't grieve over them when they go away/Don't cry for them, they're just passing through thru the valley/We'll see them beyond the shadows someday,"* and the chorus proclaims, *"We're told beyond the shadows, eternal light there'll be/From pain and disappointment forever, we'll be free/Lift up your head and look for tomorrow, beyond the shadows, sweet Heaven we'll see..."*

Martha called Minnie and Mattie, too, wondering if they would like to join her in the studio, subject to Ken Nelson's approval, of course. The producer had fond memories of the Dinning Sisters, who had done so well for the label five years earlier, so he acquiesced rather easily to her request.

Besides Martha's two solo offerings recorded May 19, 1952, the assemblage also made tracks on two secular songs that showcased the critically-acclaimed vocals of Martha, Minnie and

Mattie, billed as the Amber Sisters (short, of course, for Amburgey). The numbers were "Lonesome Road Blues" and "When I Want Lovin', Baby (I Want You)," co-authored by Mattie and Salty Holmes.

In the fall of 1951, Syd Nathan had first recorded the trio Minnie, Marthie & Mattie for his King Records label, with the solid input of Salty Holmes on harmonica. Three of the songs were: "You Can Dish It Out (But You Can't Take It)," an uptempo, clever creation by Mattie (which was never released); "You Can't Live With 'Em," another putdown, written by Minnie; and the plaintive ballad "Tennessee Memories," Martha's contribution. The latter two, reportedly, were coupled as a single.

Mattie's banjo pickin' on the session is a listener's delight.

"She's the only woman I know who played that five-string banjo like that without using a pick, only her fingers," Martha notes, with unmistakable pride.

Mattie also sang beautiful lead on all three songs, supported by impeccable sisterly harmonies and superb instumental input from each. No less a light than Tommy Jackson added some fine fiddle playing to that of Minnie's, Atkins was on guitar, and the legendary steel guitarist Jerry Byrd also played some guitar licks. "He is very genuinely acoustic," insists Martha. "No one can play like Jerry."

As this writer listened to those tracks which are nearly 50 years old, the drive, the same feel, the freshness, is, miraculously, still there. None of the girls' records, however, were promoted properly by King or Capitol.

Had Martha remained a little longer between husbands, the trio might have made a hit on Capitol. The label released their first effort Nov. 17, 1952; by then, the women had recorded four more songs during another shared session with Capitol for Martha, on Oct. 9, 1952.

The tracks laid down on that studio visit were "I've Waited Too Long," "Useless," both written by Bill Carlisle, "Cherokee Eyes" and "One More Time," the latter two penned by Mattie.

The Carlisle songs would comprise the Amber Sisters single released March 9, 1953; and the songs by Mattie were coupled onto a single released July 20, 1953.

One last Capitol sesssion for the sisters would be arranged, again during a Martha Carson solo stint on Sept. 18, 1953, this time featuring Martha's composition "So Tired Of Your Runnin' Around," speaking from experience, no doubt; and "Look What Followed Me Home, Tonight," a song co-written by Porter Wagoner, Billy Walker and Si Siman. That pairing of tunes would surface on a single released Dec. 14, 1953, some two months after being recorded. (Incidentally, Billy Walker wouldn't have his first Top 10 until summer 1954, "Thank You For Calling"; while Wagoner would wait until fall 1954, before hitting with his Top 10 debut, "Company's Comin'.")

"Fred was at all my Capitol sessions...he was very much there to guide me, and I have no doubt that he was a genius. I'll never forget the time, now...what was the song I was singing? Well, anyway, it had some S'es and I never could handle that letter very good. Whenever I sang something with an S, I'd lisp. Ol' Fred said, *'Martha, you're hissing a little bit.'* But he was mainly there for moral support, because he knew that I felt inferior."

The man who had instilled that psychologically-damaging thought in the artist wouldn't go away gracefully: "When James first went to work in Wheeling (with Wilma Lee & Stoney Cooper), he would telephone me at least once a month. I guess he had called WSM and got my number, before I'd thought to tell them not to give it out. He even asked if I wanted him to be my chauffeur!

"James boasted one time, 'I took the boss's girlfriend away from him - and she's pregnant.' I replied, 'Maybe then you ought to marry her.' But he insisted that he didn't want to marry again. A couple of months later, however, he told me that he had helped to get her an abortion, but that she was pregnant again. Well, again, I told him to marry her...I heard he did marry her right after that, but I never knew if they had the baby or not."

Indeed James and Pearl, who died of cancer in December 1987, were parents to a son Phillip (named after his paternal grandfather) and daughter Anna Marie. As of press time, neither had made James a grandfather. A year after Pearl's death, he wed widow Sally Griffith Fitzpatrick of Lexington, his third wife: "I knew her a good while. We went to church together."

In 1952, Martha's new-found fame and divorceè status was a signal for both bachelors and straying husbands to try and put the make on the glamorous redhead: "When I first came to the Opry, it almost made me sick how they came on to me, mainly because I'd *been there* and had such a bad experience with James. And I really didn't have my mind set on being attracted to any man just then. A lot of the guys would come up and try to butter-me-up, saying all those pretty-sounding things; but, I felt all they had on their mind was getting me back somewhere to go to bed. So I let 'em know real quick - *that dog ain't gonna hunt, baby, be gone!"*

In retrospect, Carson says, "Now when I look back, I think it was complimentary that any of them had designs on me. But, I was just so wary then, after my bad marriage."

During those early days at the Ryman, she could rely on the chaperoning of Leona and Chet, and even her prime publisher and mentor Fred Rose, despite the fact that he had been married three times (divorced twice) and had conducted a (mostly-)secret liaison with songwriter Jenny Lou Carson (a charmer from the Chicago area).

"Fred was always more like a father figure to me, very protective. He also counseled and advised me professionally; like when I did those shows at the Astor Room in New York, he and (son) Wesley came up and were in the audience every night."

Martha utters a rather indignant "No," when asked if Fred ever made a pass at her: "But, I'm sure he really did love that little gal, Jenny Lou Carson." Although rumor had it that Rose made improvements to the creations of Carson (who wrote such standards as "Jealous Heart," "Let Me Go, Lover" and "Don't

Rob Another Man's Castle"), Redd Stewart ("Tennessee Waltz") and Hank Williams, Martha was adamant in her insistence that he didn't "doctor" her compositions.

"I never wrote with anybody. Generally, when I had an inspiration come to me, the words and music all seemed to come at one time, so I didn't need anyone. If it's a Martha Carson inspiration from the Good Lord, just get outa my way and leave me alone. I just need to get somewhere and close the door. I don't even want anybody to talk to me.

"I've learned when inspiration's workin', write it down right away. It won't come back a second time...if I think I'm going to have a problem remembering it all, I recall my little shape notes. I don't actually write it down according to lines or spaces, and I don't really know how to put the time down; that's all in my head."

As noted earlier, shortly after becoming an Opry regular, Martha was invited to perform in New York City on a trial booking of the WSM cast members, to see how well they would go over in the Big Apple. In effect, this made her the Opry's first female singer to play within the beacon of the *Great White Way*.

Tennessee Gov. Gordon Browning flew up New York to sing the "Tennessee Waltz," thus officially opening the country music programming on that occasion.

Although the others failed to catch fire and were sent back to Nashville sooner than anticipated, Martha fulfilled all her scheduled dates and proved to be a major attraction for eight weeks. Word had spread about this vibrant hillbilly performer who sang sacred or "religioso" with a beat, and soon it became trendy among Broadway's elite and visiting Hollywood celebrities to catch the Astor's new copper-haired headliner in action. Among such VIPs were Jane Russell and her then-football hero hubby Bob Waterfield.

Initially, Carson had regarded Dee Kilpatrick as a sort of nemesis, due to the fact that he had told her she couldn't make it as a solo artist and was insistant that she record with another male partner. She told him if he didn't feel she was capable enough alone and refused to sing duets again, "then release me from my contract!" But the Capitol official stated flatly, "No! I won't do that!"

Following her success with "Satisfied" and being signed to the Opry, "Dee became my biggest champion. In fact, he even followed me up to the Astor and everytime I looked out, he was in the front row. I think he enjoyed eating his words."

Jim Denny, who was then heading up WSM's Artists Service Bureau, which booked most Opry acts, liked to tell this one on the new star: "After she joined the *Grand Ole Opry* in April 1952, she was immediately booked with several other acts into the Astor Roof in New York City. The stage of the Astor was electrically controlled to move out onto the dance floor. Martha was introduced to sing one night; she rounded the curve to step on the platform only to slip on the dance floor and fall. Several members of the audience helped her to her feet and when she collected herself somewhat, she said into the microphone, 'I've always wanted to make a hit on Broadway, but I didn't know it would hurt that badly.'"

Even today, Martha recalls that slip as her most embarrassing moment on stage.

From the start, Martha Carson was a hit with the Ryman crowd. Her pulsating performances helped heat up the drafty auditorium in the colder months, and since neither she nor most of the fans had grown up with air-conditioning, the added warmth she generated, didn't seem to bother the summer attendees either. (The Ryman was home to the Opry until 1974.)

One of her many fans was apparently too shy to say so, but his mother told on him: "One Saturday night (May 10, 1952), Hank brought his mother, Lillian Williams (Stone), with him to the Ryman, at about 10 o'clock. She said, *'I want to tell you, Martha, how much Hank likes you. He said to me, 'Mama, I love the way that girl sings.'* Well, I liked his singing and writing, too, so that meant a whole lot to me." (That next day was Mother's Day, no doubt the reason Lillian was in town.)

By then, Williams was riding the crest of a wave of popularity propelled by such hits as "Lovesick Blues," "Mansion On the Hill," "Honky Tonkin'," "I Can't Help It (If I'm Still in Love With You)" and "Honky Tonk Blues." Unhappy over his failed marriage to Audrey, he was drinking again, and putting lots of hard times feeling into his country blues.

"I think that Hank died of a broken heart," theorizes Martha. "I remember one week day he came in to check his mail and there were several Opry people there. He just sat down and we could all see he was really drunk and was dozing off. They snickered at him and were watching to see if the cigarette between his fingers would burn down and scorch his flesh. I walked over and took the cigarette from his hand and put it out. He never woke up, but he was so pitiful to me. And I thought that was so mean of those looking on."

By late summer, Hank would be fired from the Opry by the powers-that-be, allegedly for missing several show dates due to being "stoned" - and it was Jim Denny who carried the word to Williams on Aug. 2, 1952. After returning to his mother's home in Montgomery, Ala., she castigated him for being sacked from "the greatest country music show on earth." (Less than five months later, he would be dead.)

Backstage at the Opry, Martha had another visitor, bandleader Lynn Davis: "He walked in and was talking to me about Lee Moore and Juanita, who used to be on WHIS (Bluefield) with us. He don't carry much of a humble stick. He was married to a real sweet girl (Molly O'Day), though...but what a good riddance it was when he left. I still feel the same way."

Davis, like Carson, by then performed mainly gospel with his Cumberland Mountain Folks, featuring O'Day, who was the first name artist to perform then-unknown Hank Williams' compositions, notably "The Singing Waterfall," "When God Comes and Gathers His Jewels" and "Six More Miles to the Graveyard" at a Chicago studio session, Dec. 16, 1946 (with the afore-mentioned Mac Wiseman playing bass).

Occasionally, she would be notified backstage that this one or that one was asking to see her from her old Kentucky home place: "Those same people that had made fun of me and laughed because I wanted to play the guitar and sing, were falling all over themselves to say they're my aunt or whatever, to get *backstage.* I thought to myself, *'Why don't you still be ashamed of me?'* I needed you back then, but I don't need you now."

She continued to turn a cold shoulder to those musicians or colleagues, who were hoping to become socially involved with the Opry newcomer; but, of course, she did it with as much finesse as she could muster. Her band members were also protective of the boss lady.

One fellow who did manage to date Martha, while she was on the Opry, says Dee Kilpatrick, was an American Airlines captain: "He was a fine ol' boy, who piloted a DC-6 and wanted in the worst way to marry Martha. She's tall, but he was a half head taller...the gist of it was, I had met him with Martha. He wanted me to tell her she should marry him. We were then good friends, so if I had to bet, I would have bet on him."

Probably what soured Martha on the proposal was that the pilot wanted her to quit singing and be waiting for him with arms open wide when he landed. Her music meant more to her than that. (Odd that she had such a clear head with that fellow.)

Faron Young also joined the Opry cast in 1952, at 20, one of its youngest regulars. He started pickin' and grinnin' early on, back in his home state of Louisiana, where his father operated a dairy farm. While attending Centenary College, one of his favorite pastimes was writing songs, which he'd perform in gigs around his hometown of Shreveport.

At Shreveport's KWKH, home of the *Louisiana Hayride,* Young met some up-and-coming stars, among them Webb Pierce. Faron would take songs to Webb, who would listen patiently, hour upon hour, as the teen-aged writer sang his compositions. Well, Webb did use some of the material, which only encouraged the novice tunesmith to create more. With great patience, the artist would listen to the songs he was being serenaded with by young Faron.

Finally, Webb said calmly, "I've been listening to you sing your songs a long time now, and do you know what? You sing a whole lot better than you write. I think it's time you started singing with my band."

Of course, Young joined Pierce's group, performed on the Hayride - and the rest is country music history, as they say.

Capitol Records, Martha's label, took a chance on the handsome newcomer in 1952, having him cut "Have I Waited Too Long" and "Tattle-Tale Tears" on March 1, as his first release. His chart debut, however, came with the self-penned "Goin' Steady," which zoomed into #2 spot on *Billboard's* list during 1953. (That number had actually been recorded Oct. 12, 1952, after which he received his draft notice.)

"We became good friends when he came to the Opry," recalls Carson. "While talking to him backstage at the Ryman one night, we got to talking about recordings and how we both liked to write. Faron said, *'Why don't you write me a song.'* Soon after that the thought came to me for a song for Faron. Sid Kessel (of Southern Music) was over at Chet's while I was there one night, but they were in another room when I wrote it. I took it out to Chet and Sid, asking if they thought Faron would like it. They did. But, it ended up with all three of our names on it when it got to Faron. I was the only one who had a word or a note in it."

The song, "I Can't Wait (For the Sun To Go Down)," became Young's second Top Five record after it first charted on the anniversary of D-Day -- June 6, 1953. By then, the dark-haired bachelor was an Army non-com himself, who had a two-year hitch still to serve.

Martha said she always looked on Faron like a kid brother: "He was a nice person and always one of my biggest boosters. A lot of people just didn't understand Faron. He talked loud, but I think he liked to shock people. Down deep, he was simply a good ol' country boy at heart. I miss him."

CHAPTER 16

Workin' Girl...

"Martha's the best entertainer I've ever seen, with a tremendous amount of energy. She's also a beautiful lady and my good friend,"
- **Chet Atkins**

"I worked with just about anyone then performing on the Opry," says Martha. "Jim Denny was doing about all of my bookings back then" (and assessing a 15 per cent commission).

Among the Opry attractions then were Acuff, Tubb, Pearl, Lonzo & Oscar, Mother Maybelle & the Carter Sisters, Hank Snow, Little Jimmy Dickens, Bill Monroe, Red Foley, George Morgan, Rod Brasfield, Whitey Ford, Hank Williams, Johnnie & Jack, and soon Carl Smith, Kitty Wells, Faron Young, Ray Price, Webb Pierce and Marty Robbins would be added to the roster. Quite an array of stars.

"Roy Acuff was the first emcee to introduce my appearance on the Opry, and Tubb was just a little ol' teddy bear to work with. We toured a lot together."

Martha says she didn't recall working with Snow. "He was a very popular artist and did a lot of those uptempo train songs. But I could've looked at him all day and never known he was the opposite sex. I think he was wearin' a rug even back then.

"I played a lot of dates with Wally Fowler (founder of the Oak Ridge Quartet) and it seems like me, Little Jimmy and Ferlin did a number of shows together. Ferlin was a good entertainer, but Little Jimmy was one of the very best. I just love that little 'Tater to death!"

Her memories of working the Opry are mostly warm ones: "It was much more of a family atmosphere back then. We were all close. But you had to promise to do so many shows...I remember having to interrupt a tour in Canada just to fly back to keep my commitment to the Opry."

Amazingly, Martha Carson didn't have a personal manager during her first year at the Opry: "But I do well when I handle my own business...that's what happened to me, once I started letting other people make decisions about my career. I think an artist can deal from the heart and usually come out all right, but a manager generally can't."

It had taken a long time to reach national stature and she was making the most of it: "I was into my work so much, I didn't get lonely, because I really enjoyed what I was doing. And, I was still pretty skeptical about men. But, as I said, I was real, real busy. I had put my unit together, so I was involved in payroll, checking with promoters, counting the money, getting itineraries together, performing every night and just handling everything out there."

"Before the interstates, we averaged 100,000 miles a year. That's hard traveling," assesses Martha. "Any direction you went out of Nashville, was crooked as a dog's hind legs. You couldn't make good time on roads like that. It's also very tiring...So you see that didn't leave much courtin' time. On the road, I just hung out with my friends."

Some of the non-Opry acts Martha shared show dates with included Merle Travis, Tex Ritter, Rose Maddox ("She was sort of in her own bag then.") and the Maddox Brothers, Jimmy Wakely, Tex Williams, Johnny Bond, Rosalie and Joe Maphis, and Tennessee Ernie Ford, most of whom had Capitol connections. Ken Nelson, who had taken over as the label's A&R chief for the country artists in 1951, would fly in for Carson's recording stints. He always gave her a free hand.

"You know there weren't very many women out there in our part of the country performing in those days. Today, they talk about it being cramped quarters riding in those cars or sharing dressing rooms. Sometimes it wasn't even quarters, let alone being cramped. I remember doing a long tour for a man who was running for governor of Arkansas.

"I was riding with the Duke of Paducah (Whitey Ford) - and sometimes there weren't any dressing rooms. One place I had to get into my costume behind a meat counter in a store. When there weren't dressing rooms, you'd have to make yourself one by hanging up blankets or sheets to gain some privacy. I remember that ol' Duke would wash his socks and drawers out every night with Rinso (brand) soap powder. Then he'd hang them in the back of his Cadillac, right where I sat.

"I told him, 'Gosh that looks awful!' I asked why didn't he get himself a line and hang 'em outside the car? Why, we'd drive up in these little towns and his drawers would be hanging up in my face...It's a colorful life, with no two days ever being exactly the same."

Benjamin Francis Ford had a colorful career indeed. Born in DeSoto, Mo., May 12, just 20 years before Martha, he was raised in Arkansas. Young "Whitey" served in World War I in the Navy, then in 1922 formed his own Dixieland Jazz Band.

In the late '20s, Ford teamed with vaudevillian Bobby Van as a banjo duo. Afterwards, Ford joined Otto Gray's Oklahoma Cowboys playing the Keith circuit, before moving on to WLS Chicago's *National Barn Dance* and working briefly with Gene Autry.

Ford wrote, directed and hosted an NBC affiliate show *Plantation Party*, which gave his career a real shot-in-the-arm. As noted earlier, he was also one of the original partners in the *Renfro Valley Barn Dance* deal (with Lair, Red and Cotton Foley). In 1942, as the Duke of Paducah, he came to the Opry with his famous punch line: *"I'm goin' back to the wagon, boys, these shoes are killin' me!"* (Whitey Ford, who died June 20, 1986, became a member of the Country Music Hall of Fame four months later.)

In 1952, there were no other country gospel female stars that Martha could run across. Even country females were few and far between. Since they were such a rarity on stage, the audience welcomed troupes that featured female vocalists and, in turn, male stars were happy to oblige the fellows in the crowd.

Usually, the songstress would get one or two songs in the spotlight or help the man in a duet, sometime during the program - whenever it suited the star. Roy Acuff, Pee Wee King and Johnnie & Jack were among those acts then featuring female singers.

Martha Carson was a thoroughbred of another color, however, following her million-selling single and follow-up hits such as "Old Blind Barnabus" and "I'm Gonna Walk and Talk With My Lord." Her rousing presentations prompted many of the superstars slated in the traditional final slot to hedge their bets and insist on not having to follow the redhaired tornado.

"Most of them put up a little noise about where I was to sing, but I never paid 'em no mind. Nearly every package show I was ever on, they asked me to open up after the intermission. I didn't care where I was placed, just so I could do my thing."

One day Jim Denny called her from WSM to inform Martha she was being booked for a tour by promoter A. V. Bamford: "Mr. Bamford had booked me in the Southeast, starting at East Point, Ga., going on down to Jacksonville, Fla., and then to Tampa. When I got to East Point, I'm met by Xavier Cossé, who was then working with Mr. Bamford. Since I had never met him, he came over and introduced himself and told me he'd be on the whole tour. He even asked me to go out with him, but I said no.

"X then asked if I wanted him to make hotel reservations for us in Jacksonville, and I said OK…At that time, Smiley and Kitty Wilson were touring with me. I had them and a lead guitar player (Blackie Bennett). So we were going to spend the night in Atlanta. Kitty and Smiley would stay with her mother in Marietta. X was going on to Jacksonville."

Martha points out that Bennett hailed from Richmond, Va., and was only with her a few months: "Last I heard, he went back to Richmond and got married."

She recalls that when her troupers finally hit Jacksonville, they had a surprise awaiting them: "Once we got in, we went directly to the hotel, but no one had made reservations for us. We drove around two hours, trying to find rooms. When we got to the show that night, X acted mad. He said, 'Where the hell were you?' I explained that we went to the hotel and they said we didn't have reservations, 'They said you hadn't made reservations and all but drove us out of the lobby.' He insisted that he had made the reservations. (It was an impasse.)

"For the next date in Tampa, X was flying in and we were driving. He had made our reservations at the same hotel he was in . . . we took our sweet time and then went on over to the auditorium. Once again, he yelled, *'Where the hell you been?'* I said we'd been at the hotel. X said, 'I had it all set up for you to go to the race track with Bob Martin (a DJ in Tampa), his wife and me.' I told him that I didn't know anything about it, but that I was sorry."

In Tampa, Ray Price was also a headliner. "We had two shows to do, one, I think, at 7 and the other at 9 p.m. Ray Price's woman was in the dressing room with us and she had a big bottle of scotch...X would come down during intermission and she'd fix him a drink. They were also staying at the same hotel.

"Later, Ray's woman came to me and said Ray was leaving as he had to join up with another show. She asked, 'Can I check out of my room and move in with you - and save rent?' I consented only to help her out. I also figured with Ray leaving, she'd have something going with X, since she was feeding him their scotch.

"That night when I finished my part of the show, I returned to the hotel. Lying there on the bed, she asked if I was going out to eat with the others. I asked *who's going?* She said Bob Martin, his wife and X, then added she didn't want to go. X called and said they all wanted some barbecue. So, I agreed and met them all down in the lobby. It seemed Bob had a small coupé, so they asked if we could go in my car. I said fine. After we finished eating, X said he wanted to go to a club, which we did.

"Finally, we got back to our hotel, where he's like on the fourth floor and I'm on the seventh. In the elevator, he says, 'Let's stop at my floor first, I've got something I want to show you. 'Uh huh...if it's what I think it is, you're gonna walk all the way up to my room.' When we got to his room, he opened the door and I just stood there.

"He asked, 'Aren't you coming in?' I told him to go in and get what he wanted to show me and I'd see it out there. He laughed. Well, I said, 'Are you ready for the stairs now?' I made him walk his tail up the steps all the way to my room...Nearly every man that came on the scene, I could see him undress me with his eyes. I knew they had one thing in mind, and that was one thing he wasn't going to get. That was how X and I started off."

Martha said for part of the Florida tour, young singer Autry Inman was on the package show: "Well, X told Autry that he was going to marry me, and that made me so mad, I could have died. And we hadn't even had a real date yet. Well, X started sending me roses and gave me the sweetest treatment, which I hadn't been used to...I began to think he was the kindest, most thoughtful person I'd ever seen in my life."

Following the Bamford-arranged tour, Carson had a number of theater dates to fulfill: "I was in some dinner theater in Kentucky, in costume, sitting in my dressing room when a stagehand knocked on the door and said, 'Miss Carson, you've got a long-distance call.' I walked all around that theater to answer the phone and it was X. It seems he wanted to make a date as soon as I got back to Nashville. I agreed, but in the long run, I didn't keep it. I had changed my mind and stood him up."

While on the road, X caught up to her by telephone again, wondering if she wanted to do a show in Oklahoma City for $1,000. Since she hadn't received any fee that large yet, she said yes, and then learned the other artists would be Hank Thompson, Minnie Pearl and Little Jimmy Dickens.

"These were all gigantic names over mine, because I hadn't been at the Opry that long," confides Martha. "When we drove into town, I saw this big sign in neon lights - you could see it from all over town, all lit up! It proclaimed: *Martha Carson in Person!* I thought to myself, 'God, I'll get knifed in the back before I get out of these city limits.' It really scared the hell out of me, to have all those big names on the show and my name lit up on top!

"That's what you call really setting me up," muses Martha. "X was doing it to impress me. Well, we had a matinee show first and Hank invited the troupe to come over to his house after the performance. So we went. When I came back for the evening show, X was again mad as hell. He said, 'Where were you? I had it all set up for you to go to Vonetta Craven's (who was co-promoter with him on the show). She has a fine, big home.'

"Sure, he had it all set up, but failed to tell me about it. At intermission, he came around to my dressing room to pay me. He threw the money down on the dressing table and said, 'You better count it!' Well, I did and told him, 'You're $5 short.' He plunked the $5 down, and stormed out.

"I had an uncle living in Oklahoma City, who was about X's age, a very nice-looking man. He came over to the auditorium and wanted to take me and show me Oklahoma City, after I came off stage.

"Smiley and Kitty said, 'Why don't you take X along with you? He's crazy about you.' I said I didn't care about him going. Smiley said, 'Martha you ought to be ashamed of yourself. He's really nuts about you.' I said, 'If you want him to go with us, you go tell him.'"

Getting in the car, I sat next to my Uncle Jim (Quillen); I hadn't seen him in years. Then I introduced him to my friends. X said, 'If that's your uncle, how about you riding in the backseat with me?' Then we all went out to one of them clubs. I was staying at one hotel, and X at another. They drove X to his hotel first and then me to mine."

After that gig, Martha and X didn't get to see one another for a few months: "At the time, he was helping with Hank Williams' bookings and I was traveling off in other directions. (Near the end of Hank's life, he was also managing him.)"

A Virgo, Xavier Benedict Cossé was born Sept. 19, 1917. He was a graduate of St. Aloysius College in New Orleans, his birthplace. Like Martha, X had a bad marriage behind him. He had been wed to a model named Sara, who gave birth to two children: a boy, Trent and a girl, Donna. Home for awhile had been New Orleans.

Reportedly, he had studied as a medic for two years (at the Army Medical School) in the Washington, D.C. area, learning the ins and outs of being an X-ray technician. He put his training to good use at Bathesda Naval Hospital in Maryland.

During World War II, Cossé served with a special services unit, managing Army shows in Panama, and was sent overseas to book shows for the USO. Cossé was an entertainment director for the Armed Forces.

He later put his experience to good use, handling bookings for the Steel Pier in Atlantic City, N.J. and also managing the popular Ice Capades' roadshows.

In those postwar years, X had accumulated some money in his pocket and hooked up with Alfred Vincent Bamford, who took him in as a junior partner. Bamford, a short but colorful man, was of Cuban parentage and had immigrated to the U.S. at age 14. He developed a positive reputation of reliability among his clients, always paying them on time. He and wife Maxine also became good friends with Martha.

Bamford had earlier worked with veteran country promoter J. L. Frank, derisively nicknamed "the Flo Ziegfeld of the hillbillies." Frank, it should be noted, helped promote such legends as Gene Autry, Roy Acuff and Pee Wee King (who became his son-in-law), and was the man most responsible for lifting country shows out of one-room schoolhouses and into auditoriums and huge arenas, while devising the all-star "package show" concept.

In turn, his protegé, Bamford, used to line up prosperous tours for country acts, all the way from Florida to Minnesota to Texas, where he owned a major country station, KBER-San Antonio. He little worried, however, about the distances troupes had to cover, in order to keep the dates.

Cossé also worked some with Oscar (The Baron) Davis, a flamboyant disciple of Colonel Tom Parker, both of whom owed allegiance to Frank (who was voted into the Country Hall of Fame 15 years after his death, in 1967).

Having worked with such promoters as Frank, Davis and Parker, WSM's Artists Service's Director Jim Denny learned how to wheel and deal. After he became an investor in both Cedarwood and Driftwood music publishing firms, he wasn't above using his influence with the Opry artists to interest them in cutting a particular song.

The story went that one day Denny sent Red Sovine a tune he throught suited the veteran singer, but after hearing it, Sovine rejected the song. On his next tour, however, Sovine found his show-dates stretched farther apart. In one instance, he had a show slated, with the next a 1,000 miles away, requiring a lengthy drive. According to Sovine, when Denny saw him back at the Opry, he rubbed it in: "I'll bet you'll think twice before turning down a song I send you, next time, huh Red?"

Early in 1953, Jim Denny summoned Martha into his office and told her she needed a manager - and highly recommended X. Cossé: "If Hank Williams hadn't died (New Year's Day 1953), I probably never would have had to hire X as my manager."

Baby Irene... a.k.a. Martha Carson

Gertrude Amburgey with daughters Irene and Bertha.

Amburgey Children...

John Lair

Jean Chapel

The 1940's Sunshine Sisters relax: Bertha, Opal and Irene (Martha).

James & Martha Carson with Joe Isbell perform at WSB-Atlanta in the mid-1940's

Capitol Records' 1953 chartings; Martha wrote #5 and scored #10

At WNOX-Knoxville 1950: James & Martha Carson perform with Bill Carlisle (left), Sandy Sandusky (right) and unseen bass player Hubert Carter. In rear are Lowell Blanchard, Charlie Louvin, Wiley Birchfield, Charles Hagaman, Dave Durham.

Martha at home, early 1950s.

Martha on stage, early 1950s.

A shot from the Opry's first 1950s telecast, featuring (from left) Ray Price, June Carter, Hank Snow, Minnie Pearl, Ernest Tubb, announcer, George D. Hay, Roy Acuff, Carl Smith, Martha Carson and Little Jimmy Dickens.

Martha's sister Jean Chapel with Opry newcomer Jean Shepard (left) in 1955.

Promoting a star-studded concert in Tampa are 1950s stars Ferlin Husky, Martha and Marty Robbins. Directly behind the WALT mic is DJ Bob Martin, and that's X. Cosse on the right.

Fred Rose

Tommy Sands

Martha and husband-manager X. Cosse backstage, 1954.

At home with Martha and Xavier Cosse, mid-1950s.

Mid-50's touring troupe, (from left) Paul Warren, Shot Jackson, Johnny Wright, Kitty Wells, Hank Thompson, Martha, Grady Martin, Tommy Jackson, Ray Price and Lester Wilburn.

Johnnie Ray had a Top 20 hit on Martha's "I'm Gonna Walk and Talk With My Lord," in 1953, the year he played an Army chaplain in 20th Century Fox's musical "There's No Business Like Show Business," with Mitzi Gaynor, Dan Dailey, Ether Merman, Donald O'Connor and Marilyn Monroe. (The box office smash was released in 1954.

SUNDAY - FEB. 6
TWO SHOWS ★ 3:00 p.m. & 8:00 p.m.
AUDITORIUM
MEMPHIS, TENN.

FARON YOUNG
★ "IF YOU AIN'T LOVIN'"
MARTHA CARSON
★ BEAUTIFUL GOSPEL SINGER
FERLIN HUSKEY
THE HUSHPUPPIES
Doyle and Teddy
WILBURN BROTHERS
Plus... MEMPHIS' OWN
ELVIS PRESLEY
SCOTTY and BILL
He'll Sing "HEARTBREAKER" • "MILK COW BOOGIE"
MANY MORE...

A 1955 Memphis poster

Martha Pickin' and singin' on the Opry.

Mattie O'Neal and Salty Holmes, 1952.

Martha and "little brother" Faron Young.

Martha and Rene at play.

Matha's band (from left): Ducky Woodruff, Blackie Bennett, Martha Carson, sister Minnie and George McCormick.

Robert and Gertrude Amburgey shortly before his death.

Martha with first born Rene.

Expecting Andre.

Clyde McPhatter

Don Chapel

Martha in late 1950s New York glamour mode.

Martha's friends A.V. Bamford and Connie Smith

At 1964 DJ convention (from left) Bobby Bare, Gene Davis, Ken Nelson. Martha Carson and Freddie Hart in Nashville.

Martha with young sons Rene and Andre.

Patsy Montana & The Prairie Ramblers (from left): Jack Taylor, Chick Hurt, Salty Homes (later Martha's brother-in-law) and Tex Atchison in Chicago, 1935.

An early 1950s Martha Carson.

Martha endorses Gretsch Guitars.

Martha weathers the storm.

Martha with Rene and Andre.

A full-page ad in trade journal.

Kitty and Smiley Wilson up front on the WLAC-TV set of "Country Junction," with George Morgan, Anita Carter and Whitey Ford.

Tammy's stepdaughter Donna Kaye.

Martha's beloved mom Gertrude at home.

Backstage at the Opry: Spider Wilson, Joe Edwards and Calvin Crawford.

Octogenarian James Roberts today.

Martha with biographer Walt Trott at Fan Fair.

Martha's pride and joy - granddaughter Michelle Renee.

Guitarist Bob Saxton and Martha following a recent performance.

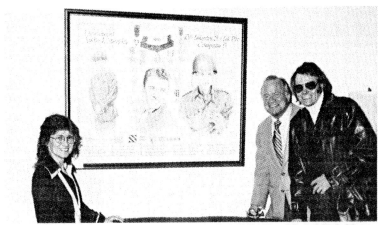

Martha's friend Scotty Turner and ASCAP official Ed Shea (left).

Martha wishes colleague Kitty Wells a Happy 80th Birthday in August 1999.

Martha's grown-up sons: Rene and Andre.

At her last recording session with (from left) Thom Bresh, Michael Behymer, Buddy Harman, Harold Bradley, Billy Linneman (rear) and Jack Daniels. Super musicians all!

CHAPTER 17

One More Time...

"Marthie is a wonderful lady. Every song she writes is based on a scripture or verse from the Bible. So, hearing her sing is just like hearing a good ol' fashioned sermon,"
- **Bill Monroe**

"My songs ain't gonna sound right without a drum," insisted the usually soft-spoken vocalist, as she bared her feelings to tough-talking Vito Pellettieri, the Opry's brusque stage manager.

When it came to Martha Carson, however, Vito could soften a bit, revealing the affection he felt for this shining star. She had a plan and though he was adamant about not permitting big band instruments, like drums or brass, in an Opry band, he was willing to hear her out.

During his 40-year reign at the Opry, Pellettieri organized the programming into 15-minute segments and suggested each segment be offered to paying sponsors. Despite his hard-nosed approach, even to the biggest of stars, he was highly regarded by the cast members.

"Well, (drummer) Buddy Harman agreed to play for me and we had him stand behind the drapes, as drums weren't considered a country instrument," continued Carson, adding he was then a member of Carl Smith's superb Tunesmiths band.

According to Harman, a Nashville native, "Lightnin' Chance used to have this drum-head mounted on the top of his bass fiddle, so he loaned Junior Huskey his bass at the Opry to play, and I stood on the other side of the bass and used two brushes to play the drum head! It was really silly looking - and very humiliating."

It was an unwritten rule there would be no drums or even a snare on the Opry stage: "I played a few times behind the stage curtain and also played behind hay bales when they did TV shows in the '50s."

Although he recalls making his recording debut in 1952, with pianist-vocalist Moon Mullican, at radio station WHIN-Gallatin, Harman said he first began using a full set of drums initially for sessions, while recording with Martha Carson.

"From that time on, I started getting more and more calls to come into the studios," notes the drummer, long one of the Opry's senior staff musicians. More important, financially, that is, he soon became one of the most in-demand drummers, a charter member of the fabled studio A-Team, which helped create the *Nashville Sound* as early as Ferlin Husky's #1 classic "Gone," a Capitol cut released in 1957.

In fact, Buddy Harman is the most-recorded drummer in country music history, logging more than 18,000 sessions. He can be heard on recordings of artists from the Everly Brothers, Patsy Cline, Jim Reeves, Brenda Lee and Marty Robbins to those of Elvis Presley, Anne Murray and Kenny Rogers.

At first, in the eyes of traditionalists like Pellettieri, drums did not seem to conform to the simplistic, but rigid three-chord patterns of country and folk songs. By the late 1950s, however, it was *do or die* time and, in order to satisfy more sophisticated country tastes, a new style began to evolve, which owed its allegiance to the Nashville Sound, championed by label chiefs Owen Bradley and Chet Atkins.

"There weren't all that many of us then, but apparently we had the right bunch of musicians to record," says Harman. "Of course, we didn't know anything about the Nashville Sound back then. We were just doing our job. I had no idea it was going to turn into what it did or to make the musical history it has."

Born Murrey Harman Jr., Dec. 23, 1928, his early inspiration came from his parents who both played in a band. Mom, however, played drums, which her son started on as a teen-ager.

Little Buddy bought his first drum set - Gene Krupa's Slingerland brand - "on time," paying it off with $3 a week earned as a movie usher. While in high school, he formed his own band.

In the Navy, he played in off-duty situations. Following discharge, Harman enrolled in college and later switched to the Roy Knapp School of Percussion in Chicago, where he studied three years.

Harman learned to play a rhythm that would help "fatten the rhythm section up. I tried as much as I could get by with...but a lot of times they would say it's *too busy*...so it was strictly keep a good beat and stay out of the way of the guitar for a long time. It had to be taken in degrees.

"We have opened up more on the drums in the studios here (since), but when I first came in, I didn't know - and I had to pay my dues. There was no precedent for me to learn from, so I just had to figure it out."

Buddy has always been a big fan of Martha Carson's upbeat musical style. (He reunited with her in the studio in 1997.)

The Martha Carson discography was growing. Of course, 'Satisfied" was still selling, but her new show-stopper, "I'm Gonna Walk and Talk With My Lord," came out in July 1952, but that winter it was still in heavy rotation with radio programmers.

Adding to the appeal of Martha's latest gospel success, no doubt, was the fact that ultra-hot Johnnie Ray had a Columbia single on it, too, which shot into *Billboard's* Top 20 pop list early in '53.

Meanwhile, a Capitol release in February, by the Amber Sisters, was prophetically titled - at least for Martha - "I've Waited Too Long," coupled with "One More Time." In May, Capitol released Carson's next single as a soloist, "Ask, You Shall Receive," with "I Feel It In My Soul" on the flipside, all of which spoke volumes to *Monsieur* Cossé.

Now that Martha was paying X to look after her business interests, he assumed a lot of the responsibility she'd shouldered before; but, when it came to picking the pickers who backed her, she gave that her very personal attention.

"I came into the Musicians Union (June 2, 1953) and started working with Martha Carson," says George McCormick, who's still a familiar figure at the Opry, where he alternated with Porter Wagoner and Grandpa Jones, until the latter's debilitating stroke on Jan. 3, 1998, and subsequent death (Feb. 19, 1998).

"I heard she needed a baritone singer, so I went over to the Ryman and auditioned for her in the dressing room. I could sing any part - tenor, baritone or lead - but she needed a baritone at the time. Soon as I finished, she said, 'You're hired!'

"It was the greatest thing, going with Martha Carson at that time. Boy, when she hit that stage, dressed like she did, and with that red hair and guitar...she was phenomenal. Martha could hold the people in the palm of her hand. She was hot! A great performer."

Born June 16, 1933, near Carthage, Tenn., George McCormick was barely in his teens when he started playing guitar at cakewalks. He was 14, when he and two other young area musicians lit out for Nashville. George soon began pickin' with local entertainer Carl Tipton.

"The two boys went back and I stayed with Carl about a year. But, there was no way to make a decent living, so I quit. I went to work for the Werthen Bag Company. Then Big Jeff (Bess and his Radio Cowboys) asked me if I'd like a job. At the time, he had five or six shows on WLAC (Nashville), starting in the early morning. I started out at $25 a week and stayed with him about five years."

During that early summer 1953, Martha's romance was all the buzz backstage at the Opry, as X stepped up his courtship of Martha. "It was plain to see she was so in love with Cossé," adds McCormick.

The day that Martha and X made it official was July 31, her mother's birthday, though merely coincidental. Simply put, it was just the most convenient day in a very busy touring schedule. In fact, manager X was so determined that they fulfill all their engagements, there wasn't even time for a honeymoon. She had to play the Opry on Saturday night - and then hit the road.

"I was his only act at the time, and I was usually booked every day, so it was a profitable business arrangement." Carson, whose average take was about $750 per show, says she once sang in three states during a 12-hour period.

The gospel star's live performances had a spark that few entertainers could equal. While her best show dates were weekends when she could draw the most money, she was also locked-in to so many Saturday nights at the Opry per year. It was a hard-and-fast rule back then that even the biggest acts had to abide by, even though paid little more than union scale for their appearance.

(Today, regular cast members, among them Dolly Parton, Clint Black, Loretta Lynn, Garth Brooks, Holly Dunn and Alan Jackson appear rarely. They leave it up to the older school artists like Jean Shepard, Stonewall Jackson, Jeannie Seely, Del Reeves, Bill Anderson, Jack Greene, Jan Howard, Jimmy Dickens, Wilma Lee Cooper, Bill Carlisle and Porter Wagoner to carry on. It galls the more loyal members to see Dolly or Loretta trot out only when there's a special or major televised birthday gala that assures them of a wider audience.)

The show was also broadcast via WSM's 50,000-watt clear channel station on Friday nights, then called the *Friday Night Frolics* (but now known as the *Friday Night Opry* show).

It was on a Friday, ironically, that the couple high-tailed it on up to Evansville, Ind., where they became Mr. and Mrs. Cossé, before a justice of the peace. Her own family wasn't completely sold on Cossé, and anyway none were invited.

Minnie says Martha was an Opry star when she met and married Cossé: "I heard he was trying to court Hank's former wife, Audrey Williams, but she preferred younger men. So, he turned his attention on Martha...When she married X, I think he had 28-cents to his name. I don't think he even had a decent suit."

Nonetheless, Martha was determined to give marriage a go "one more time." Just before consenting to marry X, a jittery Martha had given Dee Kilpatrick a call: "She asked me to meet her for a drink. I met her at 5:30, and we stayed there 'til about 9:30 or 10 o'clock. *How high is up?* Well, I think she wanted me to tell her it was OK."

Before long, Xavier Cossé was also booking all of Martha Carson's shows.

It's ironic that both Kitty and Smiley encouraged Martha to pay more attention to the handsome, wavy-haired Cossé back in Oklahoma. In the end, it was X's decision to dismiss the dynamic duo.

"Yeah, they would have stayed with me longer," admits Martha. "But X fired 'em! I think he was jealous of me and Kitty, because we got along so well. He couldn't stand it when anyone got too close to me."

(Up until her death, Kitty Wilson, herself a widow, remained Martha's dear friend.)

"It's true," says McCormick. "X wouldn't let Martha out of his sight. He was that jealous of her."

Before long, however, the ambitious Cossé began booking gigs for Martha's friend Bill Carlisle (hot with the #1 "No Help Wanted") and her labelmate Ferlin Husky (who had the #1 duet hit, "A Dear John Letter" and its Top 10 follow-up "Forgive Me, John.").

"Usually X would transact all the business backstage and occasionally at (their then-Trimble Road) home," remembers Martha. "X had a secretary come out there and he'd dictate correspondence to her."

Martha's popularity had grown so much that a fan club was organized with a Georgia lady, Gladys Wadsworth, managing it. (At last check, her fan club was being run by Margaret Helmer of Henryetta, Okla.)

"I love my fans - and the ones that write me, I keep in touch with. Yes, I answer each letter, and in turn, I find they're very loyal to me."

The nucleus of Carson's traveling show represented expert fiddling, great guitar licks and melodic harmony. Filling the void was easy for Minnie, whose baggage included her musician-husband Ducky Woodruff and their precocious 5-year-old performer-son Mike (youngest of their three children).

"Yes, Minnie and Charlie moved to Nashville to work with me." Martha smiles. "I dressed little Mike, like I did the adults on my show - and everybody thought he was a midget. He was so precious and knew all the Hank Williams songs. The only problem I had with Mike is one time we were doing a big package show and naturally had to cut down our time because there were so many acts to go on...

"I think we had like 45 minutes, so I warned Mike, 'When I ask you on stage what are you gonna sing today, you say, 'Kiss Me Big,' OK?' Well, the little guy didn't like that at all. It was a Tennessee Ernie Ford song and it was popular at the time.

"Mike said, 'I want to sing 'I'm So Lonesome I Could Cry.' Of course, he spoke then with a lisp and it *was* cute, but that song went on and on, almost as bad as 'Barbara Allen.' I told him we didn't have time enough for that song today, as we've got a short show.

"Now Mike always went over big. So we knew he'd get an encore. I told him to say his second song would be 'Jambalaya.' Well, when I said to the audience, 'Mike wants to sing 'Kiss Me Big' for you - and I knew he wanted so much to do 'I'm So Lonesome I Could Cry' - he put his hand over his mouth, so it couldn't be picked up by the microphone - at least he knew enough to do that - and said to me, 'Just for that I ought to do three songs!' He was a card."

On Sept. 17, 1953, two days before X's birthday, newlywed Martha marched back into the studio to cut four songs as a soloist: "I've Got a Better Place to Go," written by Floyd Wilson; "Bye and Bye," which Martha arranged; and two she wrote, "Lazarus" and "Singin' On the Other Side." The session also marked the final recording stint for the Amber Sisters.

Minnie feels the sisters could have recorded regularly for Capitol, if not for Cossé: "Ken Nelson wanted us three to sing together, but X wouldn't hear of it. He said it would hurt Martha as a spiritual singer. We completed two sessions and was working on another when X put a halt to it. He simply told Ken, *'no more.'*"

Continuing its general policy of releasing a new Carson single quarterly, on Oct. 26, Capitol issued her "Singin' On the Other Side" (with "I've Got a Better Place to Go" as the B side).

By late 1953, Acuff-Rose Publications prepared a 50-page booklet, "Martha Carson's Spiritual Song Folio, No. 1," for release early in '54. It contained words and lyrics to 20 of her compositions plus a dozen photographs of the shapely 5'7" songstress, some with her husband, sister Minnie, bandmembers and Opry staffers. (It proved to be a best-seller and was reprinted several times in the ensuing years.)

Meanwhile, over in Knoxville, James Roberts was recording again, this time with Cousin Ezra Cline's Lonesome Pine Fiddlers, playing mandolin for a few sessions, with the discs slated for release by RCA Records.

James had written a topical tune "Let's Go Bunny Huggin'," that newcomer Sonny James recorded, and which Roberts says was inspired by the young people's fad dance, the Bunny Hop.

"I got a check once from Central Songs for $400 or $500, but then I moved and never did get another check," grins Roberts. (Sonny James' hit-making career kicked off in 1953, with a rendition of "That's Me Without You," culminating in his #1 country-pop smash "Young Love" a few seasons later.)

Fellow hitmaker Kitty Wells was building a career that already encompassed three Top 10 answer songs, the latest being "I'm Paying For That Back Street Affair" and "Hey, Joe." Yet another female who had made her mark during 1953, was Goldie Hill, who like Kitty, was also a Decca Records artist, hitting #1 with an answer song, "I Let the Stars Get in My Eyes." Only 20, she was being billed as "The Golden Hillbilly" in her press releases.

Seemingly from out of nowhere, a duet called the Davis Sisters hit big with the #1 million-selling Cecil Null ballad "I Forgot More Than You'll Ever Know," which also spun off into a Top 10 reply by Maine's Betty Cody via RCA's "I Found Out More Than You Ever Knew," that same year. Tragically, on Aug. 2, 1953, Betty Jack Davis died in a car crash, which ended the career of the Davis Sisters (who were unrelated actually), though Skeeter Davis would later resume her career as a solo artist.

Meanwhile, Capitol Records introduced 19-year-old Jean Shepard to the country - and pop - charts with the #1 "A Dear John Letter" (the duet with Ferlin Husky), which that same year spawned their Top 10 answer, "Forgive Me, John."

Bonnie Lou, a blonde singing star from Cincinnati's *Midwestern Hayride,* chalked up back-to-back Top 10 singles in 1953, with "Seven Lonely Days" and "Tennessee Wig Walk" on the King label, but soon faded from the scene.

The only one of these artists to join Martha and Kitty on the Opry in 1953, however, was Goldie Hill. Yet another female joining the ranks that year was instrumentalist Del Wood, like Kitty, a Nashville native.

"I'd always had a very peaceful and at rest feeling with the women I met and worked with in the business," Martha points out.

On the other hand, Opry newcomer Webb Pierce was not so friendly to her, according to the vocalist: "One time I was on Webb's segment of the Opry. Well, I had to catch a flight to Atlanta for a midnight, all-night gospel sing, so I asked him if he could put me on the front of his show, which is normally a bad spot, so I could get on my way. He blew up at me, saying, *'My God, I'm the star of this portion! Who do you think you are, the star of the show?'* That really hurt."

(It has only been in recent years that female artists have emceed Opry shows.)

If she thought Pierce was snippy, her own manager-husband's words stung even harder: "If you would sing some of the songs like Kitty Wells does, you'd sell a lot more records!" Martha's reply: *"I don't want to sing those songs. I want to sing my own songs. I just want to be myself, because God didn't make but one of me."*

In a revealing interview with Dixie Deen of *Music City News,* Skeeter Davis spoke touchingly about her effort to play the Opry, following the death of her former singing partner: "Everyone was playing 'I Forgot More...' and every time someone would turn on the Opry, Marty Robbins would be singing it, and Jerry Johnson (Wilma Lee Cooper's sister) did it a lot, too. I didn't think I wanted to sing again, but I had this awful longing and I told the family that I had to sing our song just once on the *Grand Ole Opry* for Betty Jack - and me."

RCA's Steve Sholes learned of Skeeter's desire, so he called Jack Stapp at the Opry to make it happen. Taking Betty Jack's sister Georgia Davis with her, Skeeter made the trek to Nashville to fulfill her wish: "As it began to get near the time to go on, I didn't think I was going to be able to go through with it. Martha Carson was on the Opry that night and she gave me a lot of courage, and 'Georgie' stood with me. You know it was a strange thing. I had never been able to sing lead."

Martha Carson, of course, had been in a similar situation only a few seasons back.

"I always had sung high harmony," continued Davis. "And people back home, who heard me that night, and I, too, when I heard the tape played back, were amazed because I was singing with B.J.'s voice! The audience was so nice, but, of course, I was in tears and couldn't go back for the encore."

On an upbeat note, Martha Carson was the recipient of yet another BMI award, for "I'm Gonna Walk and Talk With My Lord," a 1953 book-end to her "Satisfied" honor - but one that had scored on the pop chart, as well. The Acuff-Rose songwriter registered her output with Broadcast Music, Inc. (BMI), a music publishing license agency, which competed with the older ASCAP (American Society For Composers, Authors &

Publishers, which for years had ignored "hillbilly" and "race" music contributors).

While at the peak of her performing powers, Martha Carson established her own music publishing firm, Marpat, Inc., while in New York, for the first time.

Of course, there was also the Top 10 BMI hit she'd written for Faron Young, "I Can't Wait." So, all in all, 1953 ended as a pretty good year for Xavier's bride and new client, who continued to sing her beloved upbeat gospel numbers.

Carson remained the show's sole country-gospel star: "I felt like I was standing in a field by myself."

Nor was she particularly welcome among certain church groups, who denounced such singing and performing as blasphemous. It always puzzled Martha why the servants of God insisted on offering their congregation such damning sermons, when there are so many happier, positive texts in the Bible to choose among.

Of course, today, many men-of-the-cloth not only have lightened up a lot while preaching from their pulpits, but now even embrace singers - and guitars - as part of their sabbath services.

Nonetheless, sticking with her musical genre during the sometimes frustrating '50s, Martha Carson numbered a lot of fans among fellow cast members, including the venerable "Father of Bluegrass," Bill Monroe, a fellow Kentuckian, to boot.

"Marthie is a wonderful lady. Every song she writes is based on a scripture or verse from the Bible. So, hearing her sing is just like hearing a good ol' fashioned sermon," noted Monroe (who died Sept. 9, 1996, at age 84).

Another veteran entertainer, the late Grandpa Jones, had said nostalgically, "I remember (back at the Ryman) Martha playing her guitar so hard that she always broke strings at every show…God bless her. She is one of the greatest of the greats."

Walt Trott

Walt Trott

CHAPTER 18

On With The Show...

"What Miss Carson does to the uptempo, quasi-religious numbers is a showstopper! . . ."
- **Paul Schlemmer**, *Columbus Dispatch* newspaper critic.

Despite the narrow, twisting network of roadways connecting cities into the 1960s, as more and more super highways surfaced, there appears to be fewer star deaths on the road than those recorded in aviation disasters.

Without benefit of research, deaths that come to mind in car wrecks include Betty Jack Davis, Johnny Horton, Jack Anglin, Ira Louvin and Dottie West, while fatalities recorded in plane crashes seem more numerous, claiming Buddy Holly, Patsy Cline, Cowboy Copas, Hawkshaw Hawkins, Jim Reeves, Ricky Nelson, Jim Crocé, Lynyrd Skynyrd's boys, Reba McEntire's band members, John Denver, and Walter Hyatt, among others.

Nonetheless, accidents on the road, often caused by icy conditions, were scary enough, if not all fatal. With fewer turnpikes and interstate highways, Minnie says there were serious incidents occurring on roads of the 1950s.

"One time, we almost went over the Smoky Mountains backwards," she recalls. "I remember we hit a patch of ice and the car turned around in the road, struck a cliff and started sliding backwards! Our rear back wheels were actually hanging in space!

"If it hadn't also been muddy, the front wheels wouldn't have held to the road. In that car was me, Charlie and our 5-year-old boy (Mike), who was touring with us at the time. He bumped his head against the dashboard. We were so certain we were going over that mountain, we just sat there frozen in time."

"Me and Charlie worked a year or better with Martha," continues Minnie.

She says the actual turning point for her also occurred on the road, this one while enroute through North Carolina for an all-night gospel sing with Wally Fowler in Norfolk, Va.

"Martha's driver wanted to stop for cigarettes and he pulled over without even giving a signal and got hit by a truck. That truck jumped into the air when it hit them and came back down hitting my side of the Cadillac. I had been asleep and woke up and saw nothing but street out there...the whole side of that car, the center post and both doors had just rolled up! Charlie was driving and he later said he was afraid to look around at me because *he just knew* my whole head would be gone!

"Well, I thought, if the good Lord spares me to get back to Nashville, I'll promise him, I'll never do this again! That and the Smoky Mountain incident cured me. I said *I ain't hangin' around for a third time.* We had our three children and a very nice lady watching after them, while we were traveling, but Charlie and I wanted to be with our children - they were our lives - so we had to stop."

George McCormick, Martha's driver during the North Carolina accident, recalls he was feeling "a bit woozy" from lack of sleep about 4 in the morning, so he decided to stop at a roadside market to get coffee and Viceroys (cigarets). He was turning, when a big truck came barreling up over the hill, seemingly from nowhere, and struck their lead Cadillac in the front. It then ricocheted across the road and hit the Cadillac Charlie was driving. McCormick saw the truck's bumper hook onto the Cadillac's door and jerk it right off!

"That was a close one for Minnie. I heard that her head was resting right on the door. If it had turned inward, it would have killed her, but thank God, it went out. In our car, Martha was down on the floor in the backseat scrambling around...all it did was bump my arm.

"We found a *shade-tree mechanic,* who bent the tie-rod out with a 2 by 4 (piece of wood), straightening it out the best he could. He took some plastic and put it over that door and we were on our way into town to make our show.

"X was driving and I warned him that the hood's loose and to not drive too fast. He said, 'Aw, it'll be alright.' Then came a big semi- that passed us and the wind pressure from the truck blew that hood up and it smashed the windshield! We had to stop and buy sun-glasses to keep the remaining glass segments out of our eyes from the wind.

"While we were doing the show, they had a man put a windshield in and patch up the door, so that we could at least drive back to Nashville. It took $2,200 to fix up the cars - and that was in the 1950s. They didn't make any money from that trip. We sure had some times though…"

During that period, Martha explains, they traveled in two Fleetwood Cadillacs: "We'd have three persons in each car, because we had so many instruments, amplifiers, costumes and everything…We traveled thatta way so we could get to the show dates more presentable."

"George McCormick was my chief driver, while I usually rode what they call 'Shotgun.' You know sit by him to make sure he didn't get too sleepy. And I'd just talk his head off. But, just about every time we'd head out for North Carolina, George had a heavy foot and he would be sure to get a speeding ticket.

"I remembered the last time we were there, they'd stopped him and said if you ever get stopped for speeding here again, we're gonna pull your license. Back then, they'd notch your license for speeding. Poor George didn't have any more space for notches.

"This particular time, X had just gotten out of the hospital after hernia surgery. I told him to stay home, because he didn't need to be riding and traveling, but he insisted on going, and then said he could rest in the backseat.

"Before he dozed off, however, he warned George, *'Be sure to keep this car at the exact speed limit! Don't go over it!'* Well, X had taken phenobarbital and was sleeping soundly and, of course, I'm riding shotgun up front.

"It was so foggy out, George and I had the windows open, struggling to see our way over this Great Smoky Mountain. I've got my head hanging out the window to help find the road. When we get to the top of the mountain, it's just beginning to get daylight. We had worked the Opry, before we left Nashville...At the top, you could see a straight line as the sun was peeping out.

"After driving so slow and with X asleep, I said to George, *'Step on it! My Lord, I'm so sleepy, I'm about to die.'* Well, he floored that bugger, but by the time we reached the bottom, there was this *boogerman* (cop) sitting behind a bush. Then his light started flashing! And George panicked, saying, *'Gawd-a-mighty, Martha, what am I gonna do? X is gonna kill me!'*

"I told George, just tell 'em we got a sick man back there and we're trying to get him to a hospital, and that I'd straighten it out with X. He pulled us over, shined that flashlight in George's face and then looked at his well-marked license. George said, 'I know we were goin' fast, officer, but we've got a man in the back who just had surgery, and I think he may have busted his stitches. We're trying to get him to the hospital to be checked out.'

"The cop says, *'Follow me!'* Once the policeman gets in front of us, I'm leaning over X, shaking him and telling him to wake up, 'Daddy, Daddy, wake up, we're taking you to the hospital.' He yelled, 'Like hell you are! I just got out of the hospital!' and he was raving on...

"By the time we get to the hospital, I'd made X see we had to go along with the story. At the hospital, the policeman parked his car to make sure we were on the up and up. So the doctor takes X into the treatment room to look him over, and George and I are waiting. We could hear X saying, *'I'll be all right, Doctor, I'll be just fine.'*

"But the doctor had this rubber glove on, trying to get X to bend over, so he could examine him. We're dying laughing, and I hear X say, 'Hell no!' The doctor follows him right out to the exit door, wearing a rubber glove with his finger pointed in the air. The doctor says, 'Sir, I haven't discharged you yet!' X says, 'Like hell you ain't.'

"We all got in the car and I said, 'George, don't move this car any faster than it takes to keep it running.' But, at least we didn't have to pay anything at the hospital and nobody notched George's driver's license. But that policeman followed us until we drove completely out of town. Boy, X was mad."

McCormick recalls another road story, this one on *Miss Martha:* "Shortly after the Oklahoma Turnpike opened, we were warned while traveling between Tulsa and Oklahoma City, to beware a speed trap. Blackie (Bennett) was driving the other Cadillac and X drove the lead car. They were trying hard to keep the cars right at the legal speed. Martha had been asleep, when this policeman drove past Blackie and pulled up to X and stopped us.

"He led us on into this little ol' sleepy town. Martha was trying to wake up and X was telling her we hadn't been speeding. Well, the policeman got this judge or justice of the peace, whatever, out of bed and he's still in his *long-handles*. We tried to tell him we hadn't been speeding.

"But was he ever nasty! I'm sitting and looking right at this judge, and can't believe I'm seeing what I'm seeing. He looks at me and snaps, 'What do you think about it?' I replied, 'I don't think nothing about it.' He barked, 'Don't think nothing and you won't be in trouble!'

"Boy, Martha was mad by then and, son, when she gets angry, that red-hair would stand up! She spoke up and said, *'Why you sorry Sonofabitch...'* and X tried to shush her, 'Now baby, control yourself.' But he fined us $50 for each car - in those days $100 was a lot of money.

"Martha asked, 'What if we don't have the money?' The judge said, 'That's OK, then you'll all go to jail!" Of course, she had the show dates to keep, so Martha paid up and we went on into Oklahoma City. It happened that she knew the governor, so she got him on the phone...and do you know that governor fired the both of them."

Speaking of temperament, Martha recalls a time that her brother-in-law went to the Nashville union to complain about how X was splitting the take on road shows. Specifically, he alleged that the booker was not properly reimbursing them on overnights. In turn, X had to explain the method of payment utilized.

Of course, X griped at Martha, regarding the embarrassment of having to air their disagreements publicly. After that, X did ante up the hotel fees for the Woodruffs, but Minnie says he never reimbursed them retroactively: "He probably told Martha and George Cooper (musicians' union president) that he did, but he didn't."

It really came to a head with Charlie a bit later, over some "bicycle dates" that were booked for Martha & company. "Bicycle dates" are those bookings where you might do two or three in the same day, within a short distance. For instance, when country troupes would play the coal camps in Kentucky, they might play one small camp of about 100, then down the road a few miles would be another small camp. But, the miners from one camp wouldn't come over to see your show at the other site, so you had to go to them and play individual shows. Sometimes it was done on a percentage basis or a flat fee, dependent on the contract offered by the area booker.

"Well, we had some of those bicycle dates in Carolina," notes Martha. "We'd do one and then load up and go to the other. Minnie's husband started bitchin' about it again, and I said, 'I explained it to you!' But the more I thought on it, I felt like he was questioning *my* honesty, and I don't take that lying down or standing up. I told Charlie, *'Since you trust me so little, it'll be your last date with me!'*

"Now X was the poorest driver, bless his heart. But, on the way back, when we got by Chattanooga, we stopped at a truck stop for coffee. Well, X asked Charlie if he could help drive, because he was tired. I think Charlie was a little lazy, and he wouldn't do it. I was mad, so I got right behind the wheel and drove 'em right up to the door in Nashville, and let 'em out. That was their last date!"

Touring also included guest stints on such shows as the WWVA *Wheeling Jamboree* in West Virginia, the KWKH Shreveport *Louisiana Hayride,* and one of Martha's favorite shows to play on, the *Big D Jamboree,* broadcast by KLRD-Dallas (a CBS affiliate) on Saturday nights at the huge Sportatorium.

When Martha got rid of the Fleetwoods, she immediately purchased a seven-passenger 1955 stretch limousine.

"One of the first trips we did with that car was a Canadian tour. I believe that Martha was sharing the bill with Little Jimmy Dickens and Ferlin Husky," reflects McCormick, who said Dickens was driving one just like it. "There was me, Lightnin' Chance, a singer named Becky Bowman (who had toured earlier with the Carter family), and I don't know who was playing guitar, it might have been Blackie Bennett, in our troupe. Anyway, I was driving.

"Well, we were up in Montana, riding along, and Lightnin' said he could see an occasional deer. It was just about dusk, and Lightnin' said, 'It would be awful if one of those big things jumped out in front of you.' Just about that time, another car coming our way hit a deer and it was left lying in the road. We were going so fast, we couldn't miss it. With that stretch limo, it felt like we were running over a log.

"That knocked the front portion of the Cadillac back into the fan, and tore up the radiator! We had it pulled into town and stayed at a little ol' motel. It was so cold, me and Lightnin' slept *under* the mattress.

"Well, they patched that new car up and X insisted on driving," continues McCormick. "Back in those days it was mostly dirt roads up in Canada. Next thing we knew, X hit a chuck hole and a rock damaged the oil pan. Sure enough, the oil light went on. We said you better stop, but X said, *'No, it'll be all right. We need to get on into town or be late for our show.'*

"We almost made it, but the car stopped. Lightnin' flagged down 'Tater' (Dickens) and they drove us on into Calgary. X had repairmen go and tow the limo in because the motor locked up. Since we had a show the next day, X rented a car. But in renting the Canadian car, the deal was, we had to have a licensed Canadian driver, which cost Martha $100, since the car was going out of the country to Butte, Mont. They got this albino fellow to drive us. Martha and X were going to wait and fly in.

"Tater's in the lead. I'm in the front with the rental driver and Lightnin', Blackie and Becky's in back. It wasn't long before I realized this albino couldn't see too well. I just knew something was gonna happen. Sure enough, a car pulled out in front of us and he hit it smack dab in the back. I ended up on the dashboard. Didn't nobody really get hurt, but we had to have another car before we finally made it to the next show town. But we didn't let that guy back behind the wheel again."

Meantime, Martha had thought everything was arranged and was reassuring herself it would be safe to fly.

Thinking back, she reflects, "You know those dirt Canadian roads then were like hog paths. To make it worse, it had been raining...there were holes you could bury a steer in. I remember we spent most of that whole tour pushing that big ol' Fleetwood out of mud holes. Then those guys would climb back in on those plush carpets until it looked like it had been in a mud bath.

"After the wrecker towed our limo into Calgary, the Cadillac place said it would take months to order the parts to fix the car properly," continues Carson. "I think when they saw plates from the states, they always had *bad news.*

"X decided on the U-Drive-It car for the band to go on ahead, since the next show (Butte) was about 700 miles. He said he'd found a single engine plane we could charter, rest up and then fly over the next morning.

"Well, we went into this restaurant to eat and the next thing we knew they paged us to come to the phone. The U-Drive-It driver had a wreck just 40 miles out of town. So, they had to come back into Calgary for another car. By this time, I was totally upset. I told X that *Someone's* trying to tell me something.

"There's no way I'm taking that small plane 700 miles. Let's go back to that Cadillac place and see their mechanic again. We gave the mechanic $100 extra, under the table, and he got it ready to roll. *I'd been down that road before.*"

Meanwhile, in Butte, McCormick says, everyone was restless, "We waited and Martha was the headliner, but no Martha. Tater went on, and everybody did something, until it was 11 o'clock and people were all tore up. Finally, in they come. They had waited for the car to be fixed, rather than fly in."

The audience was soon as excited as if it were the shank of the evening when they heard such showstoppers as "There's a Higher Power," "Satisfied" and "I'm Gonna Walk and Talk With My Lord." She soon had 'em on their feet, screaming for more, as though there hadn't been any shows earlier.

Perhaps music critic Paul Schlemmer's review of a Carson concert (in Ohio), best describes a typical performance, one he covered for the *Columbus Dispatch* daily newspaper: *"What Miss Carson does to the uptempo, quasi-religious numbers is a showstopper! Blessed with an infectious smile and abundant charm to match her fine voice, she wails away in true Bible-belt style."*

Walt Trott

CHAPTER 19

Capitol Connection…

Her *pickin' partners* ad for Gretsch Guitars, attracted a lot of attention.

The big news at the Opry in 1954, was when Red Folcy left, going back to Springfield, Mo., to host a new broadcast called *The Ozark Jubilee*. Meanwhile, X Cossé began booking more acts that year. He also developed a good working liaison with the Opry's Jim Denny, after a false start on a package show earlier.

Charlie Lamb, a friend of Denny's, who was stringing then for *Cash Box*, the trade weekly, was a sort of runner for the Opry's Artists Services branch. He recalls Martha's troupe arriving for a show, and while she was getting ready in the dressing room, "X came out to the box office, where I was, inquiring about the tickets. He was really a sharp dresser and looked important enough.

"But, I didn't really know him at the time, so I asked 'Who are you?' He said, 'I'm Martha Carson's manager and I just want to see the tickets.' Well, I told him who I was and said, 'You don't need to see the tickets; we have people who handle that.' He said he only wanted to see the 'start number' of the tickets. So I explained it to him that he could get the ticket start number, but nobody was going to touch the box office take, because that was going straight to Nashville and put directly into a bank's night depository.

"When I got back to the Opry, I mentioned our encounter to Denny," continues Charlie. "He said, 'Wait just a minute.' He called X in, but I thought it best to leave. I heard later that Jim had warned X never to interfere with his representatives on the road, 'That's the same as us being out there.' Of course, X and I soon became friends. I had a lot of respect for him, and especially for Martha."

During 1953, Denny had acquired interest in the music publishing firms, Cedarwood, in partnership with Webb Pierce, and Driftwood, in a three-way split with Carl Smith and Troy Martin, with both companies registered at BMI. Yet, a third company, Jim Denny Music, was established with ASCAP.

Xavier Cossé was similarly ambitious, anxious to turn the *Martha Carson* name into gold. She continued as a name act, criss-crossing the U.S. and Canada with the country elite, while recording for Capitol. Having experienced life on the lower rung of the ladder, Martha was grateful to be making a good living, but she wasn't obsessed with having money. The church teaches not to go for the gold on Earth, merely in Heaven.

X, however, seldom missed a trick. Nor had it escaped his attention that the royalties paid on pop recordings, *a la* Johnnie Ray's cut on "I'm Gonna Walk and Talk With My Lord," were considerably greater than those garnered on gospel discs.

Martha's picture was splashed on signs and in the print media plugging her "Pickin' Partners" ad for Gretsch Guitars, which attracted a lot of attention. Her good looks inspired photos and profiles in news feature sections and magazines. X was frustrated by Capitol's failure to promote her obvious *cover girl* image, something James had disavowed.

Understandably, Capitol felt a glamour girl build-up was at odds with her gospel star status. That was more befitting their belters like Kay Starr or Margaret Whiting.

On April 27, 1954, Martha and Ken Nelson reunited in the studio, to record her composition "I Bowed Down" with one she didn't write, "He'll Part the Water." Within a month, these two numbers were out as her new single.

By now, however, Martha's influence may well have reached beyond the boundaries of gospel and country audiences, for out-of-the-blue, Hollywood sexpot Jane Russell was treading on Carson territory. She had admired the redhead's style.

Not previously a recording artist, Russell collaborated with former big band singers Connie Haines, Beryl Davis and Della Russell (no relation), to record several upbeat religious numbers, most notably "Do Lord (Oh, Do Lord, Do Remember Me)."

Released on the Coral label (with musical backing from the Lyn Murray Orchestra), "Do Lord" charted *Billboard* May 8, 1954 as a near-Top 20 pop tune. It had an infectious beat, not unlike Carson's widely-hailed discography of songs. Until then, Russell was most famous for her ample bosum, and as a discovery of the eccentric billionaire Howard Hughes.

The former pilot-engineer starred the ex-model as the sulty half-breed Rio in his censorable 1943 RKO western "The Outlaw," with another handsome newcomer, Jack Buetel as Billy the Kid (and veteran actors Walter Huston and Thomas Mitchell). Reportedly, Hughes was so determined to improve on nature, he designed a special bra to uplift his star's main attributes.

Hughes rented billboards nationally to pictorially display his find's well-endowed measurements, while lying in a hayloft, along with a brazen blurb: *"How'd ya like to tussle with Russell?"* Women's groups and religious orders raised such a ruckus with the Hay's office (which kept reins on movie fare) that Hughes' film was "canned" until 1946. Still, Russell became one of World War II's top pin-up favorites.

Despite her notoriety, Russell went on to respectability as a screen name and became an advocate of homeless children, even serving as founder and President of WAIFS, a national adoption agency. When queried about her religious affiliation, Russell replied, "God is a living doll!" (When Russell quit her recording act, another glamorous screen star Rhonda Fleming briefly joined the others for a few recordings, but the redheaded beauty soon bowed out herself.)

RCA's A&R chief Steve Sholes was well aware of the vogue for uptempo religious music, and began feeling out his assistant Chet Atkins about the availability of his friend Martha Carson. "Chet told me how badly Steve wanted me on RCA...he was already dickering for another Capitol artist, Kay Starr," notes Carson, under air-tight contract to her label in 1954.

Starr, of course, generated a passel of hits for Capitol, ranging from "Hoop Dee Doo" to the revival of "Side By Side." She had a rousing, hand-clapping style, somewhat reminiscent of Carson, except she stuck to secular songs.

Another artist who would switch to and have a big effect on RCA - and the music world - was Elvis Presley. At 19, he made his first record "That's All Right (Mama)" and "Blue Moon of Kentucky" at Sun Records, a small independent studio, on July 5 and 6, 1954.

He was initially being handled by sideman Scotty Moore, who soon turned the task over to promoter Bob Neal, a DJ on Memphis station WMPS. Seeing the potential in Presley, Neal lined up some bookings for the newcomer with major country acts during late 1954 and early '55.

Among those tours Cossé had coordinated for Carson were several with star names Faron Young, Ferlin Husky and Presley, the struggling singer who, to her way of thinking, dressed so flamboyantly in pegged pants, bright colors and sported a faddish duck-tailed haircut.

"I think he only had one record out when I first worked with him," says Carson. "He was so polite and respectful. As I recall, we toured Georgia, Florida and in Tennessee. After he got to know me, and we had a break, he'd say, *'Miss Martha, come on back to the dressing room and we'll sing some of those good ol' spiritual tunes. Let's sing a little of this one and a little of that one,'* I was surprised that he knew the words to my songs. Later, he did record a couple of them.

"Elvis was a dear boy, a really nice person.. The Jordanaires told me later that he said he'd developed his performing style from Martha Carson," continues Carson. "To me, that was a great thrill and compliment to me. I loved the Jordanaires - and another group who sang for me on my early records was the Anita Kerr Singers; Anita was such a joy to me. The Jordanaires did 'Dip Your Fingers in Some Water,' one of my songs."

Helen Hopgood, Bob Neal's widow (he died in 1983), recalls that Elvis would have been the first to admit, "Martha could hold her own with him on stage. She was just a wonderful performer."

On Sept. 25, 1954, Presley made his only Opry appearance, performing on Hank Snow's segment. He was disappointed and hurt by the lackluster reception from the hillbilly audience, and reportedly Denny told him he'd better go back to driving truck in Memphis. [Instead, he joined KWKH-Shreveport's *Louisiana Hayride* cast and went on to become the greatest rock and roller.]

Four days later, on Sept. 29, Martha went in the studio again with Ken Nelson, a collaboration which would mark their last for six years. It included her first Christmas songs, "Peace On Earth (At Christmas Time)" and "Christmas Time Is Coming," both of which she wrote, and two more Carson originals, "It's All Right" and "Counting My Blessings." The Christmas songs became a November single.

Changes were certainly in the air. Cossé was at work behind the scenes, going around Nelson to find a way to boost his wife's stock at Capitol. He contemplated some less-than-subtle musical changes in her style…

When Nelson first moved to the West Coast, Capitol's female pop roster was an impressive one, boasting such powerhouse vocalists as Whiting, Starr, Betty Hutton, Peggy Lee, Ella Mae Morse, Helen O'Connell, Jo Stafford, Martha Tilton, and The Dinning Sisters..

Whiting, blonde vocalist daughter of composer Richard Whiting ("Till We Meet Again," "Too Marvelous," "Louise"), scored her first major pop chart success with her father's song "My Ideal" in 1943. Other hits include "That Old Black Magic," "It Might As Well Be Spring," "There Goes That Song Again," the million seller "Moonlight in Vermont," "Now Is the Hour," the million selling "A Tree in the Meadow," "Far Away Places," "Forever and Ever," "Baby It's Cold Outside" (with Johnny Mercer) and much later "The Wheel of Hurt."

244

Joining voices with cowboy star Jimmy Wakely, they made an impressive mark in recording country. Their string of successes included Floyd Tillman's "Slippin' Around," which was #1 pop three weeks in 1949, and #1 country 17 weeks, followed by the answer song "I'll Never Slip Around Again," #2 country and #8 pop. Actually the flipside to "Slippin' Around" was also a hit for the Whiting/Wakely team: "Wedding Bells," which peaked at #6 country (#30 pop). Other country Top 10s were "Broken Down Merry-Go-Round" (#2), "The Gods Were Angry With Me" (#3), "Let's Go to Church Next Sunday Morning" (#2), "A Bushel and a Peck" (#6), "When You and I Were Young Maggie Blues" (#7) and "I Don't Want to Be Free" (#5). All except the latter were also pop hits.

Starr, an Oklahoman, had a more natural country feel to her vocals, but earned her spurs singing for big bands Joe Venuti, Glenn Miller and Bob Crosby. In the summer of 1950, however, she and Tennessee Ernie Ford had a top five country cut "Ain't Nobody's Business But My Own" for Capitol, followed that fall by the #2 flip "I'll Never Be Free." Both crossed over, but "I'll Never Be Free" soared highest, becoming a #3 pop hit. Starr's interest in country-flavored numbers became quite apparent on some of her pop successes, notably Redd Stewart-Pee Wee King's "Bonaparte's Retreat," "Wheel of Fortune" (a #1 million seller) and "Changing Partners."

Jo Stafford enjoyed experimenting with country-inspired songs. As *Cinderella G. Stump* she provided exaggerated *hillbilly* vocals for Red Ingle & The Natural Seven's #1 cut "Temptation (Tim-tay-shun)" in June 1947, a #2 country charting. Stafford's solo novelty "A Feudin', a Fussin' and a Fightin'," was a #5 country and #7 pop later that year. She followed that hillbilly tune early in 1948, with a female version of "I'm My Own Grandpaw" (Grandmaw, in her case), #21 pop, but it failed to chart country (though Lonzo & Oscar had a #5 country single via their version and Guy Lombardo, of all bands, charted Top 10 with a pop rendition).

A Californian, Stafford had Top 10 cuts on "Ragtime Cowboy Joe," "Goodnight Irene," "Tennessee Waltz" and "Hey, Good Lookin'." Her 1952 two million-selling (#1) ballad "You Belong To Me" was another co-authored by Stewart-King, while her million-seller "Jambalaya" was penned by Hank Williams. Other successes she enjoyed that were country-derived, include Lefty Frizzell's "If You've Got the Money, I've Got the Time," Stuart Hamblen's "It Is No Secret," Williams' "Settin' the Woods On Fire" and Bill Trader's "A Fool Such As I," a Hank Snow smash.

Les Paul and Mary Ford, guitar and vocal duo, were then married and hot sellers for the label. Oddly enough, only one of their cuts, "Mockin' Bird Hill," a million seller, charted country (#7, 1951). This despite the fact that nearly all of their releases boasted a solid country sound, including their other million-selling discs "How High the Moon," "The World is Waiting For the Sunrise" and "Vaya Con Dios." Earlier, unbilled, Mary's vocals helped Jimmy Wakely chart #1 with "One Has My Name" for 11 weeks of its 32 weeks on the (1948-'49) country list.

Mary and her husband, however, had a further Top 10 pop record on "Tennessee Waltz" and recorded successfully such songs as "I Wish I Had Never Seen Sunshine," "I Really Don't Want to Know" and "I'm a Fool to Care."

Capitol's male list was equally strong, including boss man Johnny Mercer, Gordon MacRae, Dean Martin, Mel Torme, Jack Smith, Andy Russell and Nat (King) Cole. Some of the great bands on Capitol during its formative years, included Freddie Slack, Stan Kenton, Benny Goodman, Sam Donohoe and Paul Weston, at a time when bands were all the rage.

Ironically, Capitol's *first* immediate million-seller was by country singer Tex Williams, with his #1 pop novelty number (which actually sold more than two million units) "Smoke! Smoke! Smoke! (That Cigarette)" in 1947. Recordings like Slack's "Cow Cow Boogie," Kenton's "Artistry in Rhythm," "Tampico" and "Shoo-Fly Pie & Apple Pan Dowdy," and the

Pied Pipers' "Dream" were eventually million sellers, as well. Other country and western stars that scored on pop charts included Tex Ritter (Capitol's first country act), Wakely, Ernie Ford, Merle Travis and Hank Thompson.

Some other C&W acts Ken Nelson's credited with bringing to the Capitol roster are Faron Young, Jean Shepard, Ferlin Husky, Tommy Collins, Buck Owens, Wanda Jackson, the Louvin Brothers, Rose Maddox and Sonny James. Nelson himself served 33 years at Capitol, where he personally produced stars ranging from Martha Carson to Merle Haggard.

Nelson's story sounds like the makings of an old Hollywood movie. He was born Jan. 19, 1911 in Caledonia, Minn., and dropped on the doorstep of an orphanage by his mother when less than a year old. Nelson's active musical background commenced at age 11, with a job singing at the White City Amusement Park in Chicago.

Barely into his teens, he sang, accompanying himself on banjo, while apprenticing in the Melrose Brothers Music Publishing firm in the Windy City. During his Melrose days, Ken landed a radio stint in 1925, a banjo solo at a small Chicago station.

Popular singer Gene Austin liked what he heard and engaged Nelson for Austin's publishing house in 1926. Under the wing of Austin (best known for his mega hit "My Blue Heaven"), Ken spent a year in New York City, pickin' and singin' on radio.

Once back in Chicago, Nelson teamed with Lee Gillette as the *Campus Kids.* Radio stations worked included KOYW and WBBM, where sometimes they performed in a trio. Later, at neighboring WJJD-Chicago, Ken worked with hayseed entertainer *Rhubard Red,* who in reality was Les Paul.

Another legendary name Nelson became associated with in Chicago was that of Fred Rose, who was also at KOYW: "The man was a genius. I wrote a song many years ago, published in Chicago by Fred Foster, 'Waiting At the Train For You,' and just couldn't get the lyric right. Well, Fred came in and got it right. Years later, the publisher of 'I Forgot More Than You'll

Ever Know' brought the song to me. It was a hell of a song, but it needed a little change to the melody. So, I'm going to Nashville to record it with Sonny James.

"We started to cut it, but the middle lyric was sort of cockeyed, so I called Fred. It took him two seconds to change that middle part to where it made sense. Well, I told the publisher about it and they asked for a dub. I guess that's how it got into the hands of the Davis Sisters. That was a lousy trick. RCA's Steve Sholes put it out and it made a lot of money. Our record didn't do anything."

Not so, says Skeeter Davis. The publishers asked her and girlfriend Betty Jack Davis to make a *demo* recording in Detroit, because they wanted to pitch the song to Patti Page, who was known for her multi-track recording technique. So the unknown "sister" act cut the demo, but were stunned sometime later to hear it being played regionally as released by the publishers' Fortune label.

Davis thought it might queer a deal they were negotiating with Steve Sholes in New York. But to their further surprise, Sholes liked what he heard and promoted the single via RCA's extensive machinery and the song scored #1 eight weeks on the country charts and crossed over, selling a million records (unfortunately, Betty Jack Davis, killed in a car crash, never knew just how *big* a hit they had).

Nelson's friendship with Rose, of course, led to Martha Carson recording solo. As soon as Rose heard Carson's spirited new composition "Satisfied," he put the pressure on Nelson for Capitol to record it or let him do so for another label.

Back in 1940, Ken Nelson had become musical director and program director at station WJJD. He was P.D. for one of the more popular Midwestern shows, *Suppertime Frolics.* Then World War II started up and Nelson spent two years as a military medic. Upon discharge, he accepted a job again as music director at WJJD.

"Meanwhile, Gillette went to Hollywood, where he'd met Glenn Wallich, who at the time was running a radio shop (music store) and making dubs off the air for various acts," notes Nelson.

Wallich had joined forces with singer-songwriter Johnny Mercer and producer-lyricist B. G. (Buddy) DeSylva in April 1942, to form *Liberty Records,* which, because they didn't then own the rights to that name, had to be changed to *Capitol.* (DeSylva worked some at 20th Century-Fox, before being signed to run Paramount Pictures.)

Several decades later, Capitol country chief Jimmy Bowen, flush with Garth Brooks' astounding success, thumbed his nose at his big city bosses and scuttled country's Capitol name in favor of Liberty. Bowen, when faced with cancer, stepped down in favor of Scott Hendricks during 1996, who changed the label name back to Capitol-Nashville. (What goes around, comes around. When Scott and Garth clashed on an album promotion, Hendricks was replaced by company man Pat Quigley.)

Nelson, in recalling his connection to Capitol, continued, "Lee (Gillette) ended up working with me at WJJD, then Glenn came and hired Lee (as A&R) for his new record company. Lee was doing sessions (in Chicago) and Glenn called, told him to drop whatever he was doing and fly to New York for a recording session there.

"Well, he *couldn't* drop what he was doing, so he called me and said, 'OK, Nelson, take over.' I said, 'Well, what do I do? I don't know what to do!' He said, 'I can't help it, I've got to get to New York -- it's your baby!'

"Well, I did it. I won't mention the artist because the singer was so drunk, we had to hold him up to the mike. I'll never forget it. It was very, very rough. But we got through it somehow."

One act Gillette had recorded and turned over to Nelson in 1946, was Uncle Henry's Kentucky Mountaineers. Nelson began handling all Capitol's Chicago recordings, including the popular Dinning Sisters (Ginger, Lou and Jean), who had a big pop success on "Buttons & Bows," with the Art Van Damme

Quintet. (Actually that 1948 release was a million seller for Capitol, charting 16 weeks and peaking at #5 on *Billboard.)*

When Capitol started, it did like established labels, creating a subsidiary label - Americana - on which to release *race* and *hillbilly* cuts. Tex Williams was one of those assigned to Americana, while oddly enough white Kay Starr was initially signed as a rhythm and blues singer.

James and Martha Carson recorded under the Capitol-Americana banner, helmed by Dee Kilpatrick. By 1950, however, Capitol had abandoned its Americana label.

Simply because Nelson had once *announced* classical music on WJJD, he was considered a prime candidate to represent Capitol's new classical division in Los Angeles in 1948. Upon his arrival, however, he learned Capitol changed its mind, putting him instead in charge of transcriptions. Nelson's buddy Gillette was producing Capitol's country artists.

"I stayed in transcriptions until 1951, when I took over the country department (as A&R chief)," explains Nelson, "Lee went on to pop."

Nelson had a unique formula for finding a sound to ensure success of Capitol's country output: "I'd go into bus stops and saloons to hear what the people were playing and find out what they liked, and who were their favorites." While producing Martha Carson, Nelson says he became the first producer to utilize drums on a country soloist's record: "She was doing spirituals and insisted, 'We've got to get that feeling!' So I went for the drums. Others told me I was crazy, but I decided to go with it anyway."

In order to succeed, Ken Nelson feels an artist has to appeal emotionally to the people. Technically, he says, a great voice doesn't necessarily mean an artist will be a hit singer.

"If you can stir people's feelings with music, voice or lyric, that's the thing that counts," adds Nelson. "Once in awhile, you'll get hold of a record with a fantastic rhythm background that will stir them musically. But, basically, it's the voice and the lyric, not only in country but in anything. We've had artists with beautiful voices, but we can't give them away, because they don't relate emotionally."

Carson was surprised at how creatively satisfying it was recording with Nelson, and particularly relished the artistic freedom he granted. With Kilpatrick, she had experienced a very different set of rules. He was a stickler for conformity and produced her and James according to his code of conduct.

"Oh, I believe you have to coach an artist a little bit," assures Nelson. "But you never intimidate them. Instead, you try to put them at ease. I think that has always worked for me. In fact, it's my philosophy, that you hire an act for what *they* do, not for what *you* do."

Probably the first artist Nelson signed as A&R honcho was cowboy crooner Eddie Dean, whom he knew had a beautiful voice. "But he was just too smooth a singer. You couldn't give his records away. That was sad." (Dean finally had a Top 10 country cut, "I Dreamed of a Hillbilly Heaven" in 1955, on the independent Sage & Sand label. It was later revived by labelmate Tex Ritter, who enjoyed a comeback hit with the number in 1961.)

In his quest for talent, Nelson says sometimes it was hit and miss. During a visit to Shreveport, home of the talent-rich *Louisiana Hayride* in the early 1950s, he signed Faron Young, but passed on Kitty Wells, whose 1949 recordings for RCA had done nothing.

The bespectacled Nelson takes particular pride in the product he produced on Merle Haggard and Buck Owens, noting, "I think down through the years, these two are the most outstanding country artists. Merle is someone I loved to record, but I became so wrapped up in his singing that sometimes I didn't know what was going on. He's a very creative, sensitive man. Buck has a good creative sense and is a fantastic business man.

"What is sad is that I have met artists through the years that I see fall by the wayside financially and every other way. I've had several disappointments because they have not been able to adjust to success. Every artist goes through these periods. I want an artist to become his own man (or woman). Some have the ability to *know* what's good for them."

Nelson can take a bow for the many hits he helped Capitol amass, including Hank Thompson's "Wild Side of Life" (Song of the Year in 1952), Jean Shepard and Ferlin Husky's million-selling cross-over "A Dear John Letter," Stan Freberg's pop smash "St. George & The Dragonette," Sonny James' "Young Love," Gene Vincent's "Be Bop a Lu La," Husky's "Gone" (which helped launch the Nashville Sound era), Buck Owen's "I've Got a Tiger By the Tail," Wanda Jackson's "Right or Wrong," Tex Ritter's Oscar-winning "High Noon" and Carson's "Satisfied."

"What happened with Martha was that one of our producers - I'm not sure if he was head of the (A&R) department at the time - Voyal Gilmore, opted to do pop songs with her. I told him, it won't work."

Nelson theorizes that Gilmore and Cossé had put their heads together regarding a new direction for Martha Carson, which her producer felt just wasn't in the cards.

"It seems to me at the time that Kay Starr went over to RCA, and they wanted a *new Kay Starr* at Capitol. I wanted Martha Carson to record the songs she was more comfortable with. But, they came out (to Hollywood) and did a pop session on her and believe me, it was horrible. I refused to release them because I knew it would harm Martha's career. Well, X said *release the records or release Martha!"*

Mainly, Martha was backed by the Van Alexander Orchestra. He had the pop hit "Hog Dog Joe" (1939) and was in Hollywood, mostly scoring music for TV and films during the early 1950s. (Alexander had cut his teeth as an arranger for the orchestra of Chick Webb, who brought Ella Fitzgerald to national attention with songs such as "A Tisket, A Tasket.")

Ken Nelson knew Martha Carson's strengths.

"You see with Martha Carson, you've got to let her be. I told them, you've got to follow *her,* she don't follow a band. The orchestra has strict tempo. Even Voyal, who cut them, agreed that the recordings didn't work. I had new recordings on Martha, 'Counting My Blessings' and 'I Bow Down' (released in December 1954), and I would have liked to continue to record Martha Carson."

CHAPTER 20

On the right side…

"Another label singer, Betty Hutton, covered it, and they went with her version. As far as I knew, that was the reason for the angry words between my manager and Capitol Records."

- Martha Carson.

At year's end, WSM's Artists Bureau had booked 2,554 outside shows, attracting crowds of more than eight million. Meanwhile, attendance at the home base of the Opry - the Ryman - tallied 232,808 tickets sold in 1954.

A sad statistic for Martha - and the industry - was the death of Fred Rose on Dec. 1, 1954. His musical legacy was a long and lasting one that would earn him earliest induction into the newly-created Country Music Hall of Fame, several years later.

"Right after Fred's funeral, Mitch Miller (Columbia's pop A&R chief) came to me and asked if I'd write a song for Mahalia Jackson. I guess he was producing her then. I said, 'If I can, Mr. Miller, I will.' But she sang the more sad gospel songs and to me religion sparks happiness. Of course, I loved to hear her sing. She sang with such soul. But I was more into someone like Sister Rosetta Tharp, whom I thought was just fantastic. Her sound was so good to me, because she was joyful."

It had been a strange year - 1954 - in that so few artists attained #1 country songs. Hank Snow and Webb Pierce had dominated the top of the charts with Snow's "I Don't Hurt Anymore," 21 weeks; and Pierce's "Slowly," 17 weeks. Pierce's "Even Tho," was #1 two weeks, and his "More and More" (stretching into 1955) was tops 10 weeks. Remaining top spots in '54 went to Jim Reeves' "Bimbo," Hank Thompson's "Wake Up, Irene," Eddy Arnold's "I Really Don't Want to Know,"

Johnnie & Jack's "Oh, Baby Mine," and the Kitty Wells-Red Foley duet "One By One."

Today's chart-toppers are lucky to get two weeks in that position, Three or four weeks is a rarity. In 1955, only seven artists scored in the #1 country spot, with Webb Pierce again leading the pack via "In the Jailhouse Now," for 21 weeks; "I Don't Care," 12 weeks; and "Love, Love, Love" (written by black songwriter Ted Jarrett), 13 weeks, and he again stretched into the next year. Others holding top spot in '55, for shorter stints, were: Carl Smith ("Loose Talk"), Hank Snow ("Let Me Go, Lover"), Faron Young ("Live Fast, Love Hard, Die Young"), Porter Wagoner ("A Satisfied Mind"), Eddy Arnold ("Cattle Call," "That Do Make It Nice") and Tennessee Ernie Ford ("16 Tons").

Incidentally, Ford's "16 Tons," a monster hit for Capitol - #1 on both country and pop charts - was written by Merle Travis.

"Merle Travis once said he wanted to produce me," recalls Martha. "I wonder how that would have turned out...he was such a talented man. I did do his 'I'm a Pilgrim' over at RCA."

It hadn't set well with Martha, "when one of the executives at Capitol said, *'Martha's gonna be our new Kay Starr!'* I didn't much care for that remark."

It was never Martha's intention to be anything other than herself.

"I wasn't cut out to do pop singing. I didn't want to do 'em at Capitol, but I was told to. I did like one I sang pretty well, 'Stay On the Right Side, Sister,' which at least suited my style better. But, another label singer, Betty Hutton, covered it, and they went with her version. As far as I ever knew, that was the reason for the angry words between my manager and Capitol Records."

After the aborted pop-oriented recording sessions at Capitol, Cossé got his wish that the label release Martha early, so he took her straight to RCA, much as Kay Starr had done months earlier. Steve Sholes and Cossé were both pleased at the turn of events.

It's ironic that she also joined about the same time as her youthful admirer and former touring compadré, Elvis Presley.

Earlier, a poster proclaiming a Feb. 6, 1955 show at the Memphis Auditorium, depicted Faron Young (discharged from the Army, Nov. 16, 1954), Martha Carson and Ferlin Husky as its top-billed artists. Relatively new acts, the Wilburn Brothers and "Memphis' own" Elvis Presley, rounded out the bill, with the advertising noting Presley had a new Sun record, "Milk-Cow Blues Boogie" (and "You're a Heartbreaker"), not one of his more successful releases.

According to Carson musician Joe Edwards, who remembers it vividly, as it was only his first week with her band (having joined on a Wednesday): "It was a Sunday that we were in Memphis and what an unforgettable line-up we had. Besides Martha, Faron Young and Ferlin Husky as headliners, there were The Browns (Jim Ed and Maxine), Texas Bill Strength, the Wilburn Brothers, Johnny Cash and Elvis Presley - all on the bill!

"Bob Neal had Presley at that time - and I don't believe he nor Johnny Cash had a hit, at least not on the national charts - but it was only a matter of weeks before Colonel Tom (Parker) got Elvis," Edwards points out.

(Actually, it was Aug. 15, 1955 that Presley signed with Parker. After edging Hank Snow out of the management deal, the Colonel negotiated a pact between Phillips' Sun label and RCA Records, effective Nov. 19, 1955, that would tie Presley to RCA.)

The Wilburns were the first to chart in June 1955, with "I Wanna, Wanna, Wanna" for Decca. In July 1955, Elvis first hit the *Billboard* charts with "Baby, Let's Play House" and it wasn't until November that Cash scored with "Cry, Cry, Cry," both Sun releases.

During the spring of 1955, Carson's crew headlined a 40-day tour that also featured rockabilly newcomer Elvis, notes Edwards: "I remember when we played the 'Gator Bowl in Jacksonville, Fla., and the Colonel hired young girls to come in and scream. It didn't seem to work at first, but he arrived from then on."

A Hoosier, Joe Edwards was born Oct. 5, 1933 in Stanford, Ind., the elder of three children born to Olive (Powell) and Ralph Edwards. At 13, he became one of the original Hoosier Kids on WTOM Bloomington radio. As an 18-year-old, Joe was part of *Uncle Bob* Hardy's troupe on the Channel 4 *Hayloft Frolic,* WTTV-TV, where he worked beside fellow teen Bobby Helms.

Helms, of course, is the man who scored his three biggest hits all in the same year. In March 1957, Helms first charted with "Fraulein," a number one record which charted an amazing 52 weeks, crossing over into the Pop Top 40 lists, as well. In October, his Decca follow-up single "My Special Angel" charted, going on to become another country charttopper and also a Top 10 million-selling pop hit. As if that weren't enough, Helms' scored with a Yuletide success that year, "Jingle Bell Rock," which became another million-seller and an annual favorite for many years.

Born in Bloomington, Bobby was only several weeks older than Joe. Thus they became fast friends in those early years. Besides doing the Channel 4 show, the troupers also performed on Channel 49 in Muncie, Ind.

"Bobby Helms and I sort of grew up together," continued Edwards. "He came off that show just before I did."

From late 1954 until early 1955, Joe says he was one of the musicians backing artists booked by agent Dick Blake in Indianapolis. (Blake also established an office in Nashville.)

"Back then, Blake had a tavern in Indianapolis. Often, he'd rent the Lyric Theater and sponsor a show on Sundays there with Nashville names - and sometimes other non-Nashville stars like Rex Allen. Well, we'd back up those artists who came without a band."

One momentous week, Ernest Tubb's troupe, the Texas Troubadours, came up. Tubb's guitarist Billy Byrd had been told by Martha Carson to be on the lookout for a thumb-style guitar picker.

"Before he left, Billy got my name and number. I didn't think I'd ever get a job with her, but I told him to turn my name in anyway. It was Wednesday, three days later, that we got this call from Nashville. I didn't have a phone at the time, so the local grocer came to the house and gave me the message that *Martha Carson* wanted me to audition.

"I couldn't believe it! But I talked my dad into taking me down to Nashville for the first time. We went to Studio C (then home of WSM) with my machinery...I had made me some speaker boxes hooked up to an amp; And I had two of those jokers.

"Well, Martha took one look at those and threw up her hands. She decided she was gonna use me no matter what. My dad left me there and for the first time in my life, I was truly on my own.

"The first place I stayed was the Clarkston Hotel. By Friday, I found out about Mom Upchurch's place (a musician-friendly boarding house) from Faron Young. That same night I did my first stint on the Opry playing the *Friday Night Frolics* in the WSM studio (back then)." (In 1957, the "Frolics" officially became the *Friday Night Opry,* and henceforth was performed similar to the Saturday show at the Ryman.)

Martha was like a big sister to her bandsmen, especially Joe. She saw great potential in him as a musician, because he was also quite adept on the fiddle. The big plus with George, of course, was his versatile vocal talent.

The Opry welcomed her lively stage presentation. Unlike the other singers, she didn't just come out in front of a band and sing a ballad, she literally rocked the crowd.

Regarding bookings, Jim Denny felt she was a natural to schedule with other acts performing sacred songs. Surprisingly, she preferred her engagements with country-oriented acts, (but did enjoy the All-Night Gospel Sings she did with Wally Fowler, though not one of his biggest fans).

"Oh sure, I played a lot of gospel shows and did them until I got educated real good," explains Carson. "I remember working a package show in Birmingham with the Blackwood Brothers, the Sunshine Boys and the Florida Boys. There was me and my little group and all those religious acts lined up across the stage, while a minister from that particular city came out and opened the all-night *gospel sing* with a prayer.

"Now I don't care what denomination the preacher is, that don't make any difference to me. We're all praying to the same God and I reverence the Lord enough to bow my head in prayer, no matter who's praying.

"But the Blackwoods were standing on one side of me, and the Sunshine Boys on the other side, and some were blaspheming and cussing under their breath, while the prayer was being said, and I thought my skin would break open with chills!

"We were at the Birmingham National Guard Armory and one of those gospel groups, the Lefevres was there, too. One of them thought he was a comedian and waited until I was singing a very serious spiritual song, then came out on stage with a fly-spray can and started shooting. I was mortified! I stopped the show, stood there with my hands on my hips and said, *'When he gets done, we'll continue with the song.'* They booed him, and I went on.

"When I got back and talked to Jim Denny, I said, 'Mr. Denny, don't ever book me on any more of those gospel things, because I made a vow that I wouldn't do them anymore.' I have turned down some big money and some long tours, because I didn't want to perform with those kinds of groups."

Martha said she had read a few months later where the Blackwoods' plane had crashed in Alabama and two of their members were killed (Bill Lyles and R. W. Blackwood, while attempting to land the group's privately-owned, twin-engined Beechcraft).

She recalled that for many years, a lot of those in the genre had looked down on her: "Gospel made fun of me and called me a hillbilly, but I noticed a lot of the quartets recorded my songs. Yes, I'm country and I'm gospel. It's just that most of them don't do the real happy gospel that I really love to specialize in. I've never sat down and tried to figure out what to call my music, but I guess it would be *country gospel."*

In addition to securing her RCA contract, X also got Martha to sign with the General Artists Corporation talent agency in New York City, which handled major names in the music, theater, film and broadcast fields.

That was pretty heady stuff for a girl from Letcher County, Ky. As 1955 hit like a thunderbolt for Martha and company, one of the top songs in the nation was "This Ole House," written by pioneer country artist Stuart Hamblen. Not only did Hamblen take it near the top of the country charts, but it became a Top 20 pop success for him, as well.

As if that weren't enough, screen songstress Rosemary Clooney performed "This Ole House" running it right up to the #1 pop spot, where it roosted three of its 27 weeks run on *Billboard.* Amazingly, the flipside of Clooney's single was "Hey, There," from the Broadway smash "Pajama Game," which also soared into the #1 pop spot for six weeks, making it a highly valuable, four million-selling disc.

Hamblen now had a nice retirement nest, thanks to that almost-gospel-sounding song, which Martha would later record herself. In 1951, Hamblen's unquestionably gospel ballad, "It Is No Secret," was a major seller for the Texas native and a Top 10 country cut to boot. To fatten his wallet further, pop vocalist Jo Stafford (who had just departed Capitol) hit #15 on *Billboard* with her version, which was the B side to her new 1951 Columbia hit "If," a Top 10.

Stuart Hamblen was his own man, not locked into the *Nashville's our country music capital* syndrome. While he did guest on the Opry, he was never a cast-mate. In fact, Hamblen got his start performing as "Cowboy Joe" in 1925, on stations in the Dallas-Fort Worth area. He made his first recordings for Victor in Camden, N.J., in May 1929. By 1930, he was in Los Angeles, where he performed on KFI's *Saturday Night*

Jamboree, before working briefly on KMPC with the *Beverly Hill-Billies* group.

Hamblen shone as a songwriter, almost from the start. His "My Mary," which he'd also cut, was a hit for Jimmie Davis, while "Texas Plains," which he had recorded in 1934 as Decca's first signed artist, was "borrowed" by Patsy Montana to create her historic "I Want To Be a Cowboy's Sweetheart."

Martha Carson admired Hamblen's talent for turning inspirational songs into masterful messages of faith that could appeal to a wide audience. "It Is No Secret" alone was translated into 60 foreign languages and reportedly sold more than 10 million copies of sheet music.

"(Remember Me) I'm the One Who Loves You" was a #2 song for him in 1950, and a Top 10 for Ernest Tubb, and years later a success for both Dean Martin and Willie Nelson. Hank Snow, who recorded Hamblen's inspirational "These Things Shall Pass" in 1951, also had a double-sided Top 10 with Hamblen's compositions "Born To Be Happy" and "Mainliner (The Hawk With Silver Wings)" in 1955.

Another memorable Hamblen gospel song "Open Up Your Heart (And Let the Sun Shine In)" was a Top 10 pop record by his Cowboy Church Sunday School that same year. Hamblen also appeared in Hollywood films and a movie serial.

So imagine Martha's reaction when Steve Sholes told her he wanted a session with her and Stuart Hamblen. Better yet, here's Hamblen's reaction: *"Oh, my God! That's like teaming a jackass with a race horse. Lord, I can't ever keep up with that woman."*

Martha recalled she had said no more duets, but this was so special, she didn't hesitate. Here was an artist who, despite being a 6'2", 200-pound toughie, was right on her wave length: "He was really the thoroughbred. Stuart was very respectful and his wife Suzy was such a sweet lady. We cut a record that featured 'I've Got So Many Million Years' with 'Lord, I Can't Come Now,' which I felt was a good release. But I remember that WSM banned it (the latter number) because of the title. Times do change, don't they? They play anything now."

Recalling "Lord, I Can't Come Now," Martha says, "It was about an old man on his death bed, who told the Lord, he wasn't ready to die now, because he had chores to do, like repairing the roof. It was really well-written, the sort of story song that could've went over well back then, if people heard it. I sung the lead verses and he would chime in with me every now and then."

[In 1963, Carson's colorful duet partner cornered and shot an escaped panther at L.A.'s Jungleland, making headlines. Hamblen died March 8, 1989, at age 80.]

If Martha was surprised at her pairing with that heavyweight, she had a few more surprises at her RCA sessions. One number, "The Battle Hymn of the Republic," featured the celebrated Harlem-born actor and former choral singer Brock Peters, then 28, who had earned praise on stage in "King of the Dark Chamber" and his then-recent film debut "Carmen Jones." (Still ahead for Peters were the movies "Porgy and Bess," "To Kill a Mockingbird" and "The Pawnbroker".)

"Brock was a sweetheart of a person to work with," says Martha, who added that he supplied his beautiful bass voice for their rendition. It had been arranged by Neal Hefti, the Grammy award-winning pop composer-orchestrator (whose credits included the Arthur Godfrey, Kate Smith, Fred Astaire shows, *American Bandstand* and later *Batman* TV shows). "Our record came off pretty good, but it wasn't me really."

Indeed, Martha Carson was in a whole new setting, complete with orchestra and choral group, notably Joe Reisman's Orchestra and Chorus. RCA's chief A&R man Steve Sholes was personally producing her session.

"Chet had helped work out the deal with Steve, when he came to town, but I didn't enjoy working with him (Sholes) at all. I cut all of my RCA stuff in New York. I felt cramped with Steve from the start, he just wasn't a natural for me. He didn't have that certain feel that I could jell with. It seemed to me that what he knew, he learned from a book."

(Steve Sholes, who was born in Washington, D.C., Feb. 12, 1911, had been associated with Victor since his high school days in Camden, N.J. After graduating from Rutgers University, he continued working with RCA. In 1937, he became an A&R man, working with jazz artists. During an Army stint in World War II, he helped produce the last recordings of Fats Waller.

(In 1945, Sholes became manager of both the country and race repertoire. Among artists he signed on the country side were Chet Atkins, Homer & Jethro, Hank Snow, Jim Reeves and Presley. Sholes was recognized in 1967, for his contributions by induction into the Country Hall of Fame. Several months later, he died - April 22, 1968 - while on a business trip in Nashville.)

"Now Brad McEuen produced the best session I ever did for Victor. He knew music and he had a warmth, I could blend with. I just never did make that communication with Steve. You know Steve didn't live in Nashville; he would come in and play all these songs they had selected for me, and insist that I do them.

"The recordings? They'd do it all live. I'm up there in New York, out of my element, working with all these trained musicians, most of whom I didn't know - I did know George Barnes. He was a great jazz guitarist, but that wasn't a style I was best on.

"I'd usually try to arrange all my own songs for a session. But then some arranger up there would get hold of it and then it just didn't have the spirit I needed. It sure makes a big difference who does your arrangements. I am not very proud of anything I ever done for RCA."

On a personal note, Martha was disappointed seeing the end of her sister Mattie's marriage to Salty Holmes: "He was very talented and together they did a great act. It was too bad that Salty let that booze ruin him. He really loved my sister, as much as he could with the problem he had..."

Although professionally, Martha's career seemed to be going great guns, she was privately feeling unfulfilled in marriage. She still longed to be a mother, something that Martha had been told might never happen...

While she didn't necessarily think in terms of a ticking "biological clock," the vocalist was nearing her mid-30s, when indeed having a baby was becoming high priority, and the tune that best fit her situation then, would no doubt be an upcoming Elvis Presley charttopper, *"It's Now or Never!"*

Walt Trott

CHAPTER 21

The Greatest Gift...

"Ain't nobody doing what I do, what I love to do, what I want to do - sing about Him! And that's what I'm gonna do!"

"I had prayed to God so many times to bless me with a baby," says Martha, who had about given up hoping, when one night while alone, she heard a premonition. "It sounded like a sainted woman's voice I heard...she told me, *'Don't worry. You're going to have a baby.'* I had the lamps on and looked all around the room, then while I was looking, I heard every syllable of that statement repeated back to me, *'You're going to have a baby.'* I didn't wonder anymore."

Martha swears she wasn't asleep, but recalls she felt like she was experiencing the burning bush! Indeed, she saw it as a sign from God that her prayer was being answered.

"All the doctors said she'd never be a mother," notes Minnie. "I had went with her to a number of those visits. That woman has had trials and tribulations that would knock out the average person. But she'd say it doesn't bother me, pray, then keep right on going."

Look for the silver lining...

It was almost too much joy for Martha, whose career was at its peak, and now she was being blessed with child. She asked for a year's leave of absence from the *Grand Ole Opry*, which was granted.

That, of course, was also fine with her manager-husband, who was coordinating efforts with RCA to broaden the singer's career horizons. What didn't sit as well with Xavier Cossé, however, was the news that he would be a father again.

"He told me that he didn't marry me to have more kids, and he said, 'Don't expect me to go to the hospital with you when it's time to have that baby. There's nothing that I can do.' I never did insist that he go..."

First things first. Martha and X moved to New York City to be nearer the sort of showbiz action that he hoped to generate on her behalf. For starters, RCA added her name to an array of stars scheduled to perform or more precisely "audition" for some of the industry's movers and shakers at Grossinger's, a plush country club in upstate New York.

Among the other names on the dance card, she recalls, were Jim Reeves, Diahann Carroll, Vaughn Monroe, Pete Fountain and Julius LaRosa (who was then hot news copy, having just been fired on the air by Arthur Godfrey).

"Jim and I were the only two Nashville acts on the bill. We arrived there a couple of hours early and the band wasn't there yet. It was a lovely place. The grounds, which included these old, huge trees, were just beautiful. I knew we weren't playing for the public. It was strictly network television producers and other industry folk.

"I went out walking on the grounds with X and Bunny Millar, who were trying to tell me what songs to sing. They said all the others were doing ballads, blues and standards. Well, I told 'em I needed to be alone, because I had some talking to do with my main producer - and I always love to stay in touch with Him.

"I figured all these other acts are doing their own thing. *Ain't nobody doing what I do, what I love to do, what I want to do - sing about Him! And that's what I'm gonna do!* When they asked me what I was going to sing, I told them, *I've got it! I know what I'm going to do!* And, I went and gave my music to the orchestra. I heard 'em say, 'Oh, I hope it's right.' I said, *'It is!'* They reminded me that most of those producers were of the Jewish faith and they weren't sure how sacred songs (from a gentile) would go over with them."

Unflinching, the singer went to prepare herself for the upcoming show, for which she wore a gingham gown. The songs she'd chosen to sing were: "Satisfied," "Let the Light Shine On Me" and "When The Saints Go Marching In."

["Satisfied," of course, she wrote riding in Carlisle's car, and "Let the Love Shine On Me" was likewise written on the road, this time during a midwestern tour with Little Jimmy Dickens. "When the Saints..." is a lively Dixieland standard, popularized widely by Louis Armstrong's Top 10 record in 1939, and has much the same feel as her originals.]

"Well, each act went on and received a good reception - and I was set to close. I went on and did my spirituals, and before it was over some of those industry types were actually standing up on those white linen-clothed tables, cheering me on, they were so excited. They called me back three times!"

One NBC producer, Bill Balchar, had already completed his season's guest line-up, but insisted on changing it to add Martha Carson to his variety series *Washington Square,* hosted by legendary dancer Ray Bolger (best known for Hollywood's "Wizard of Oz" and Broadway's "Charley's Aunt"). Balchar, who would insist she sing the same songs and wear the same gown, had cried out: *"That woman must be the finale for my next show!"*

Meanwhile, several of the biggest agencies in New York were waiting in the lobby to sign Carson, who wouldn't put the pen to anything before she talked to Sholes.

"I got four TV shows booked from doing that show. It seemed then they had some sort of rule that you couldn't be on one TV network two weeks apart, something like that."

Nonetheless, four days after her RCA showcase, Carson was given exposure on NBC-TV in a rousing finale that showed national audiences the tremendous performing style she used in driving home a gospel song with a modern beat. Country girl that she is, Carson had always heard *if it ain't broke, don't fix it.*

Here she had proved her songs and style could win 'em over, whether in the Catskills, at a coal-mining camp or on the national network. So why was RCA trying to put her in front of a 30-piece orchestra singing songs like "I'm Sitting On Top of the World," "Dixieland Roll" or "Music Drives Me Crazy (Especially Rock & Roll)"?

"That ain't me at all! I'll never understand it. They wanted to make me over, making me wear sexy evening gowns, which is not me," she reflects, rather wistfully.

Early in 1956, her first album was released, "Journey To The Sky." Sure enough, it boasted a glamorized Martha Carson on the cover, wearing "the most gorgeous gown I'd ever seen," designed by Ceil Chapman. Indeed, she looked more like a movie queen than a gospel star. Of course, the critics would agree with Martha that it was over-produced and derided her producer for feeding her such pablum as "The Bible Tells Me So," a favorite of the Sunday school brigade.

One song that stood out, however, was Carson's fiery rendition of Travis' "I'm a Pilgrim," which should have been a single. Instead, their follow-up release was "Laugh a Little More" (backed with "Let the Light Shine On Me"), which did little to help album sales.

"I sure didn't sell many records, and I think it was because they tried to make a new me," says Carson, adding. "I didn't like it up there in New York. Finally, I told X, 'I'm not going to have this baby in New York.' Well, he agreed, so we made plans to return home. It seems like we were up there almost a year."

By now Martha was blooming with expectant motherhood.

"When I was four or five months pregnant, X decided to bring his children to town. I think the little girl was in kindergarten and the boy in grade school at the time. It hurt to know he didn't want my baby, but here I had put him back in touch with his children. He would ask me to fix his little girl's hair, so he could take them out to dinner, but he would never ask me to go along…"

Despite her condition, Martha was still receptive to guest spots.

"I did Red Foley's TV show, when I was pregnant with my first baby. It seems to me, I was really fat, but I remember that they put me in a chair because my tummy was so big. They figured my guitar could hide it better if I was sitting down. I think I also did one of those Opry television shows (the Opry was first televised Sept. 30, 1950, but not on a regular basis) while I was pregnant."

The late Springfield, Mo.-based producer Si Siman remembered additional appearances by Martha on his show, "Time and again, Martha guested on *Jubilee USA* during its six-year lifetime, and every time she rocked the stage of our old studio building to its very foundation. This lady, to my way of thinking, is surely a one-of-a-kind performer...her charm, her explosive and soul-thrilling presentation of a song and the responsiveness she can arouse in an audience go positively unchallenged by any other entertainer in the business today."

She says that her ex-brother-in-law Salty and Red Foley were old friends from their days on the WLS *National Barn Dance*. Martha had always been a big fan of Red Foley's, but she also recalls he wasn't always a straight arrow. The two redheads had worked together a number of times on the road, besides her guesting on his *Ozark Jubilee* or *Jubilee USA* broadcasts from Springfield.

She recalled during a flight to Detroit that Red came up to her in the airport waiting room, asking if she had $10 he could borrow, as Sally (Mrs. Foley) wouldn't give him any money.

"By show time, he was so inebriated that he could barely sing," explains Martha. "He affected this laryngitis thing, saying he was sick. Therefore, he did go out to perform, in order to get paid, doing a sort of whispery vocals."

Another time, in Montana, he and the Cossés were riding in her new Fleetwood Cadillac - and Red had the backseat full of toilet tissue. When he told X he had to find a toilet because he had diahrrhea bad, Martha warned him, "Red, I'll kill you if you crap in my car..." He said, *"Well, I gotta go! Now! There was a toilet you passed up a'ways back there."*

"I told X, 'Make a u-turn and get him back to that crapper!' He drove back in that direction and Red jumped out, running down the hill towards an outhouse, toilet paper flying behind him! What a sight."

As her delivery day drew nearer, Martha was joyful on the one hand and heartbroken on the other, merely because she felt her husband didn't want their baby - after all, *hadn't he said as much several times already?*

"Keep in mind, I was 35 years old, having my first baby, so I had some concerns. I had taken X at his word that he wouldn't be there for me at the hospital, and I felt like somebody close to me should be there. I called my mother in Ohio, who rode a Greyhound bus down from Cincinnati, just to be with me.

"Well, he was very bitter about that, asking me 'What's she doing here? I had planned for one of my friends to go to the hospital.' But, he hadn't told me that. He literally run my mother off! She got her feelings hurt and my sister came and took her over to their house.

"Anyway, I spent 44 hours in labor. Women came in hours after me and had their babies. Dr. Pace was trying to keep from knocking me out, so I could be the first to see that baby born. Finally, he had to induce labor. I remember rolling past the nurses' station where the radio was blaring (the Ames Brothers') 'It Only Hurts For a Little While,'

Martha said she had prayed that their infant would have olive skin and black hair just like X: "Most of the babies in my family were fair skinned and either redheaded or cotton topped." She needn't have worried. René Paul had it all together when he made his appearance on July 11, 1956: "He was such a beautiful baby. René had so much black hair he had sideburns; the nurses were brushing his hair back in a duck-tail." No mother ever loved her "precious gift from God" more than Mrs. Xavier Cossé.

Motherhood came at a time when X was trying to promote his wife as a sophisticated singing star. Undaunted, RCA lined up further recording sessions in New York for their new signee, even penciling in a new recording of her signature song, "Satisfied," complete with big band accompaniment.

Martha recalls on one occasion, she met fellow RCA artist Perry Como, a crooner, whose voice she and her sisters had long admired: "Perry Como was on the same plane and he said he had *my* records. I couldn't believe it!...that anyone that special would want to hear me sing!"

(Como made movies and was one of the nation's all-time great singers, with such standards as "Till The End of Time," "If" and "Wanted" to his credit, as well as the country-flavored "Don't Let the Stars Get In Your Eyes." He was with RCA for more than 50 years, and would later record Jean's composition "Lonely Again.")

While Martha was recording for RCA, her sister, now rechristened Jean Chapel, was recording "rockabilly" songs for Elvis Presley's old label, Sun Records in Memphis.

Sun, of course, was moving along great guns having produced hits on country boys like Presley, Carl Perkins ("Blue Suede Shoes"), Johnny Cash ("I Walk the Line"), and Roy Orbison ("Ooby Dooby"). Sam Phillips was reasoning that it was time to find a female rocker - and like Martha, little sister could rip it up in concert. And she was willing to sing non-sacred songs.

Multi-talented Jean played banjo, fiddle, bass and guitar. She was a proven vocalist, who had recently scored as Mattie O'Neil with Salty Holmes on Al Gannaway's *Classic Country* filmed shows, sharing the loft with such tried-and-true talents as Ray Price, Ernest Tubb, Minnie Pearl, Carl Smith, Ferlin Husky, Goldie Hill, Red Sovine, Faron Young, Kitty Wells, Johnnie & Jack, June Carter, Rod Brasfield and the First Lady of Gospel, Martha Carson.

(These kicked off Nov. 26, 1954, at the Ryman with production being handled by Flamingo Films of New York City. Executive Producer was Gannaway, assisted by director Dick Kahn, scripter Noel Digby and chief cinematographer "Bake" Baker, utilizing both New York and Los Angeles film crews.

WSM's Louie Buck announced many of these shows, initially called "Stars of the Grand Ole Opry," until a later legal dispute between Gannaway and WSM prompted a change to "Classic Country.")

Salty & Mattie won new fans singing songs like "Cherokee Eyes," "Echoes Over the Smokies" and their popular comedy cut-up "The Hiccough Song." Her own magic pen produced songs that were recorded by such celebrated artists as Molly O'Day ("Don't Sell Daddy Anymore Whiskey"), Wilma Lee & Stoney Cooper ("Rachel's Guitar," about the 19th century First Lady Rachel Jackson), Milton Berle and Rosemary Clooney (each separately performing "I Found My Mama").

Not so surprisingly, Sun was labeling her "the female Elvis" in plugging her single "Welcome To The Club." There were additional cuts before Sun sold her contract and recordings to RCA, including "Ooo-ba-la" and "Don't Let Go" (which was finally issued by RCA in 1964). Incidentally, the latter song, "Don't Let Go," was a #2 R&B hit for Epic's Roy Hamilton (and in 1979 became a #11 R&B success again for Polydor's Isaac Hayes). Unlike Elvis, Jean Chapel's recording career failed to catch fire, despite a rousing appearance on Alan Freed's wildly popular rock-and-roll road show, performing "I Won't Be Rockin' Tonight."

In September 1956, Charlie Lamb's new *Music Reporter* scooped all other trade publications by headlining that "Jim Denny exits Opry." It came as a bombshell to the industry that the all-powerful Denny was ousted for owning outside music publishing companies.

WSM's Irving Waugh met with the executive board to discuss the potential for "conflict of interest" charges against officials like Denny and Jack Stapp (who was then running the new Tree Music publishing house). By then, Cedarwood had grown into a major force in Nashville.

Waugh reportedly instructed WSM President Jack DeWitt to offer Denny the option of selling his interest in the outside firms and staying on or resigning. DeWitt had other axes to grind, so he didn't give Denny the choice, he just dismissed Denny. His hand-picked replacement was Dee Kilpatrick, who stepped in Sept. 25, as both Artists Service Bureau chief and Opry manager. (Stapp eventually resigned.)

One of Denny's first steps was to contact Xavier Cossé and Webb Pierce. He had decided to form the Jim Denny Artists Bureau, Inc. (note similarity with the Opry's booking agency title) and wanted their support.

"Jim asked X to hold a meeting in our den to talk to the various *Grand Ole Opry* acts, whom he had been booking on behalf of the Opry," explains Martha. "He wanted to tell them that he would still be glad to represent them from his offices at Cedarwood."

The Opry and especially DeWitt and Kilpatrick were furious that the response was so great for Denny. He ended up with half of the Opry roster. Besides Pierce, he roped in Ray Price, Carl Smith, Minnie Pearl, Jimmy C. Newman, Hank Snow, Kitty Wells, Johnnie & Jack, Justin Tubb, Little Jimmy Dickens, Jean Shepard, Hawkshaw Hawkins, Porter Wagoner, Del Wood, Grandpa Jones, Bill Monroe, Whitey Ford, George Morgan and the Willis Brothers, plus non-Opry stars like Lefty Frizzell, Jimmy Dean, Carl Perkins, Claude Gray and Marvin Rainwater. It was unprecedented.

Naturally these artists and their managers were well aware of the booking contacts Denny had amassed across the country. Ex-Marine Kilpatrick was an unknown quantity, as far as bookings were concerned. In retrospect, however, Martha seems to have been a bit naive regarding the significance of *the Opry vs. Denny.*

Meanwhile, throughout the year, RCA continued to release singles on Carson, including "David and Goliath" (backed with "I Wanna Rest a Little While"), "Dixieland Roll" (and "Music Drives Me Crazy" as its B side) and "All These Things" (featuring "Faith Is In the Sky").

Christmas was an especially happy event for Martha now that she had her "little miracle baby," René Paul. She says he was a bright and happy child. Having grown up in a big family, more than once Martha thought about how nice it would be for her son to have a little sister or brother to share his childhood.

Obviously, she never broached the subject with her husband, whose greatest satisfaction seemed to come from his work: *"Oh, I think X was proud of me in his way, but he just wanted me all to himself."*

X, in the promotion end of the business, probably sought an identity as the breadwinner. When queried on this, Martha agrees: "He sometimes said he felt like he was *Mr. Carson,* but I know he liked what I did. I had one song, 'I'm Gonna Walk and Talk With My Lord,' that whenever I sang it, I saw tears well up in his eyes."

As 1956 drew to a close, RCA had one more single to put out: "Get That Golden Key," backed with "He Was There." Meanwhile, another album, "Rock-a My Soul," was being prepared for release with the promise of a more natural Martha Carson; that is, boasting more of a rockin' style than her debut LP.

"You know, lookin' back, I was really rockabilly before it came into being. I was rockin' with my songs before that ever happened with Elvis or Jerry Lee Lewis."

Her Christmas 1956 joy was short-lived. *Billboard's* Dec. 29 issue carried this news item: *"X. Cossé, personal manager of Moon Mullican, Cowboy Copas and the Louvin Brothers, has announced his resignation from these acts to move to New York City with his wife Martha Carson."*

CHAPTER 22

Music, Motherhood and Me...

The Opry's Martha Carson named
Most Programmed Gospel Singer,
Cash Box's National DJ Poll 1955

"She was on the (CBS-TV) *Ed Sullivan Show* and when she came out there in that tight dress," says picker George McCormick. "I said to myself, 'It's all over.' X got that pop stuff recorded on her at Capitol, but they wouldn't release it, so he goes over to RCA...It tore all of us up when she left the Opry."

Kid brother Don Chapel saw it from a different perspective: "I watched Martha on the (NBC-TV) *Steve Allen Sunday Show* and I'll never forget how proud I was of my sister. *I liked to have bust my buttons!* Steve Allen told his audience that she was just dynamite...I remember seeing her walk across that big stage in New York, coming off down the side, into the audience, and she just tore 'em up."

Carson felt very uncertain how she would be received on Allen's new Sunday show (Feb. 17, 1957). Unlike Sullivan, he was more than just a host. He was a sophisticated New York actor-comedian, author, jazz pianist, bandleader, arranger (and future Grammy Award-winning composer, whose credits include classics like "This Could Be the Start of Something Big" and "South Rampart Street Parade)."

Prior to her performance, Carson inquired of Allen, who in 1954 had first hosted the *Tonight Show,* if it would be alright if she walked out into the audience during her performance of "Let the Light Shine On Me"? (RCA had re-released "Let the Light Shine on Me" in 1957, with "Satisfied" as its flipside.)

"He told me, *'Why sure. It's the cameraman's job to follow you out there.'* When I got about half way, my arrangement had a modulation in it, which gave me an opportunity to go down into the audience area. The crowd just froze for a few seconds, then they started rockin' with me, and it was a wondrous experience. Unforgettable."

She needn't have worried about Allen. A week after her showstopping appearance, he ran a full page ad in the trade weekly *Billboard,* proclaiming: *"Martha Carson is not just a singer; she's an explosion!"*

Martha, who had signed with the General Artists Corporation, was suddenly the toast of the town. Her bookings reflected it, including New York's poshest niteries and supper clubs like the Latin Casino and the Chase Hotel and even farther afield at Chicago's *Chez Paree.*

A song she developed as a rousing finale for her club dates was "Saints and Chariot" (which Elvis Presley would also record). Although most U.S. viewers didn't have color sets enabling them to fully appreciate this redheaded musical evangelist's colorful appearances in that era, her movements ignited the sets on such TV shows as *Tennessee Ernie Ford's, Arlene Francis' Home, The Tonight Show* and the *Jimmy Dean Show.*

Homesick, she missed her family and friends while living in the New York area. It was a culture far removed from her Southern lifestyle, one that seemed to appeal more to her manager-husband. Thus the couple bought a home in nearby Stamford, Conn.

As if being a new mother wasn't enough, Martha had days and nights filled with recording sessions, receptions, interviews, personal appearances and club dates. Her latest single (following her RCA version of "Satisfied") released in late 1957, was "Now, Stop," backed with "Just Whistle or Call," *not typical Martha Carson fare.*

Back in the days before multiple tracks where they can "punch in" different parts or sounds here and there, Martha generally sang her songs all the way through, with whatever musical accompaniment was assigned.

"I took a jet from Jackson Hole to watch Martha Carson record, and it was more than just a recording session," said then-Wyoming DJ Bill Choates of station KSGT. "Believe me, she puts on a better show than most people do on stage."

More than a few influential producers were also championing the assets of this distinctive Kentucky lady, who confided she often felt like a square peg being forced to fit into a round hole.

"For my money, she was one of the forerunners of all spiritual singers, and in this field is in a class by herself," said Richard O. Linke, associate producer for *The Andy Griffith Show,* adding more pointedly, "She was a real pro on records, and worked most diligently with the sales organization in the field."

Throughout her busy New Yorker days, however, she still found time to write songs. One particular favorite "I Can't Stand Up Alone" was inspired by a very disappointing incident that occurred in her Manhattan performing period.

"I was scheduled to do a guest appearance on *Galaxy of Stars* (a variety program) and we had to be at the rehearsal hall at 8 o'clock. Others there included Tony Martin, Jaye P. Morgan and Georgia Gibbs, and they had me down for two songs.

"Pretty soon, around 9:30 a.m., they run through one of my songs. It got to be about 12:30 and X, who was usually very punctual about having lunch, asked, 'Why don't you go over and ask them when they're gonna run your next song?'

"I didn't want to bother the producer, Joe Cates. But, I'd been in the business long enough to sense when something's going on behind my back...and I could feel the knife working its way in."

At the time, Jaye P. Morgan seemed to be making a career out of guest stints on TV variety and game shows, thanks to two earlier Top 10 records, "That's All I Want From You" and "The Longest Walk" (and more recently did a cameo in the ill-advised "Gong Show" movie). *"Her Nibs, Miss Georgia Gibbs,"* as she had been introduced since her Garry Moore radio days, had the mega-hits "Kiss of Fire" and "Dance With Me, Henry" (a reworking of Hank Ballard's R&B sizzler "Work With Me, Annie"), also several seasons before. Like Martha, she was of the finger-snapping, upbeat, energetic school of singers and only a year older.

Carson continues, "I had seen Georgia Gibbs and Jaye P. Morgan in real close conversation with each other, very hush-hush on the other side, while eyeing me. All of a sudden, Mr. Cates starts striking some of the scenery and doing this and that. By now X is very hungry and growing more impatient. He snapped, *'Why don't you learn to stand up for yourself, and go over and ask when they're going to rehearse your next song.'* He kept bugging me so much, I finally walked over and said, 'Mr. Cates, do you think I'd have time enough to go have lunch before you're ready to run my next song?'"

Cates, an Emmy Award-winning TV executive, was one of the first to produce live television in 1947, via his *Wish Upon a Star* show with Bess Myerson. More recently, he'd produced Jackie Gleason's show (and would produce the hit 1978 TV show *Fame).*

"He looked at me and said, *'Oh my God, Miss Carson, I am so sorry.'* And then it came: *'We had to cut your second song.'*

"It wasn't not getting to do the second song that hurt…it was what I knew had been going on under the current between those two. I just said, 'Well, if I'm not doing but one song, we're going to lunch.'

"Walking down the streets of Broadway, I had a lump in my throat as big as my fist, wanting to cry. I thought to myself, 'If I can just cry, I'd get rid of this hurt feeling.' I never felt comfortable in New York in the first place. When we got to this restaurant, I figured if I could just get to the restroom, I could cry in private.

"I swear when I found that Ladies' Room, every woman on Broadway must have had to go pee that day, judging by the line. So, I went on to the table where X was, knowing if I say one word, I'm gonna bawl.

"The waitress showed a menu to me, but God was also working with me, so I scooted it away and put a paper napkin in front of me. I reached out - and X knew to put a pen in my hand - took the pen and started writing down lyrics...the song that came out of me was 'I Can't Stand Up Alone.'

"It was strange because Tony Martin had talked to me at the rehearsal hall, saying he would just love to find a song like 'I'm Gonna Walk and Talk With My Lord,' to close his act with, as Johnnie Ray was then doing. I told Tony I didn't think I had one, but I'd keep him in mind. 'I Can't Stand Up Alone' was really that kind of song."

Martin, divorced from film star Alice Faye, was married to dancer Cyd Charrise, and best known for such romantic ballads as "To Each His own," "There's No Tomorrow" and "I Get Ideas." (He had also just completed a color movie musical "Let's Be Happy" with Vera-Ellen.)

"I didn't see Tony again, but I didn't need to cry anymore. The song God gave me straightened me right out. When I went back into the rehearsal studio, I walked straight up to Mr. Cates and said, *'I want to thank you, because you just helped me write one of the best songs I'm ever gonna write.'* He just stared at me like I was out of it...

"I recorded the song a week or two later for RCA. Then Clyde McPhatter cut it and his 1958 single (boasting 'A Lover's Question') sold over a million records. (The record was #1 on the R&B charts and went #6 pop.)"

"I can't stand up all by myself/I can't stand up alone/I need the touch of a mighty hand/I can't stand up alone..."

"You know, I've made more clear money on that song, because I published it, than I did on 'Satisfied,'" calculates Martha.

Even before the big "I Can't Stand Up Alone" royalties could pour in, Martha and X decided to return to Nashville again. The Cossé clan was settled back in Nashville when André Michael arrived April 10, 1958, as his daddy was promoting the

Five O'Clock Hops musical program on local WSMV-TV, Channel 4.

"It was the oddest thing, but X never made a fuss about my being pregnant with André," ponders Martha, who had a difficult labor with baby number two. "In fact, when my last son was born, X came to the hospital. I remember thinking that I was nearly 37 years old and a new mother again.

"Then there was a girl who came in with him and who sang. She was just dynamite and my husband calls her 'a young Martha Carson.' I thought, *'Sure, throw the dirt on me now....'*"

While the boys were still little more than babies, Martha was able to balance motherhood with a performing career.

"Back when they made big money, she always had a maid and a nurse-sitter for the boys," discloses Minnie. "Did you know at one time, they owned nearly every house within their radius.... They derived good income from that, too."

True, both Martha and X then felt that real estate was a prime investment.

Thinking of what might have been, Martha tells it straight: "I think the most we ever had was seven private homes, two apartment buildings and two office buildings. But it was really prime property."

The phenomenal success of McPhatter's Atlantic recording of "A Lover's Question"/"I Can't Stand Up Alone" assured Martha of a generous royalty check that autumn: "I was wanting to buy a couple pieces of property over on 16th Avenue (in Nashville) with the money."

Fate, however, had other plans for the windfall: "X had sent Oscar Davis to promote a tour he'd booked on Hugh O'Brian (ABC-TV's *Wyatt Earp)* through Florida. When he set out, Oscar got a signed blank check from X to cover expenses, but Oscar took his wife Doris along and made it a vacation."

This turn-of-events subsequently scuttled Martha's investment plan. "Oscar Davis had overwritten our account by $30,000, and by the time I got a royalty check, it took every cent to pay the bank."

Apparently in the Cossé household, what was her's was also his. That should have had a familiar ring for Martha.

"Back when X was booking Hugh O'Brian around the country as Wyatt Earp," Carson recalls, "I was on the show they did in Columbus, Ohio, out in a ball park. There were more people on stage than in the audience.

"Right after that show, I had another over in West Virginia. I told the band to meet me over there. They called to say they were being delayed, due to car troubles, but were sure to be there for the evening performance. Grandpa Jones was on the bill with me, so I figured I'd be alright, because I could use his band to back me at the matinee.

"Well, when Grandpa drove up, there was just him and his banjo," continues Carson. "We were sitting in the back trying to figure out what we could do, so the folks wouldn't want their money refunded.

"The management was wondering when we were going to get the show started. So, Grandpa says, 'I'll tell you Marthie, I'll second you, if you'll second me.' Just the two of us went on - and we did real good. And we also sold out everything we had to sell."

Country & Western Jamboree magazine, meanwhile, was pleased to notify Miss Carson that for the third straight year, fans had voted her Best Female Gospel Singer. She agreed to accept the prestigious award in person. (Earlier, AMIA - Automatic Music Industry of America - had named her best gospel artist of 1955-'56.)

Sometime after the birth of André, however, Martha and X realized that the bloom had gone off their relationship with RCA. He began putting feelers out with other labels to see what sort of package he could come up with that would be more beneficial.

During late 1958, an item in *Variety,* the trade weekly, pointed out that Martha Carson had signed with Archie Bleyer's Cadence Records label in New York. One of Bleyer's first successes was his own band's Top 20 version of "The Naughty Lady From Shady Lane" (1954); however, in 1957, Bleyer had inked the harmonious duo Don and Phil Everly, proteges of Chet Atkins. They had made some previous cuts for Columbia, to no avail. After signing with Cadence and thanks in no small part to excellent Boudleaux Bryant compositions like "Bye, Bye Love" and "Wake Up Little Susie," they became super hot.

A subsequent Bleyer-Carson session produced four songs, only two of which would appear under the Cadence logo in '59: "Light of Love," paired with "That Ain't Right."

The vocalist adds, "I liked Archie fine, but like so many others, he just didn't really understand what I did." (Archie enjoyed a very successful association, as arranger and music director, with household name Arthur Godfrey.)

With only one single under their belt, the Carson-Bleyer arrangement was short-lived, despite a publicity blurb that had proclaimed, *"Martha Carson would be concentrating on the type of song material which has made her the number one singer in her field."*

That "field" had turned into a "concrete jungle" for her, as she continued to perform throughout the *Big Apple,* whenever and wherever X secured her bookings.

During 1959, Dee Kilpatrick departed the Opry and was replaced by Ottis Devine. (Dee went on to operate several fabric stores in Nashville, until 1966, when Hickory Records engaged him as manager of the label's merchandising and promotion.)

"Long after my leave of absence was up, I had called Ott Devine from New York and said, 'I'd like to get back on.' Ott said, *'Sure, we'll be happy to have our Martha back...We need you.'* So X and I decided it was time to leave New York behind. We put our Stamford home on the market, and I caught a plane to Nashville to look for a house.

"When I called the Opry back, however, Ott told me there had been a change. He said, *'Because you're married to X. Cossé, Jack DeWittt says you can never be booked on the Opry again.'"*

After a little detective work on her part, Martha found out, "Johnnie & Jack's manager Frankie More had gone back to the

Opry to tell them X was holding meetings at our house (in Green Hills), trying to break up the Opry."

More had indeed been at the 1956 meeting - when both his acts, Johnnie & Jack and Kitty Wells, had signed with Jim Denny. He also made sure he was in any publicity photos that ensued. Obviously, Cossé wasn't trying to split the Opry, his loyalty just naturally leaned towards a fellow promoter: "Jim Denny opened a lot of doors that no one else had opened for the Opry (which no doubt helped Denny land in the Hall of Fame posthumously in 1966, three years after his death)."

Actually, Cossé never regarded the Opry as all-important in the big picture, as his wife had. He envisioned national television exposure and major concert venues for his artists, and even saw the Opry as somewhat *old hat*.

"Well, I wasn't going to get a divorce or raise my babies without a father, just to be on the *Grand Ole Opry*. So that was that," adds Martha. "I didn't need the Opry name. I could stand on my own two feet. But, I'm proud of my days on the *Grand Ole Opry* and I think they should be proud of the ground I covered for them; why, I've put more mileage on me than on a used car lot, advertising the Opry."

Joe Edwards says performing on the road with Martha was a special joy to him.

Some other musicians he worked with while part of Carson's band included George McCormick, "one of the best rhythm players there is," Earl Acock on bass, and Rudy Lewis on accordion.

"It's interesting that at Mercury, Dee Kilpatrick had signed McCormick and Acock as a duet - George & Earl. They had some success; I think one of their singles was 'Sweet Little Miss Blue Eyes,' before Earl up and quit to take off for Texas," explains Edwards.

Joe recalls, too, what he terms "The New York Thing," when a made-over Martha performed at the swank niteries in New York City: "Rusty Goodman, who was part of the Happy

Goodman Family, and Millie and Doug Kirkham were with us for some of that period."

It wasn't all peaches-and-cream, like the time Martha was to rehearse for her guest shot on *The Tonight Show,* bandleader Skitch Henderson, peering down his nose at the singer, asked, *"Do you want this played hillbilly?"*

Handing him her musical arrangement, and without missing a beat, the redhead calmly replied, *"No! Just play it the way it's charted!"*

Other performance high points Joe Edwards remembers, included playing the old Union Hall in Detroit with Casey Clark ("I met Buddy Emmons there"), a package show in Denver, the Riverside Rancho (Sue Thompson and then-husband Hank Penny's California night club), and doing NBC-TV's *Tennessee Ernie Ford Show."*

At the time, Edwards was singing Carson's lead parts on some of the songs, which made him an essential part of her act: "Believe me, we were all excited about doing the show, which also featured Molly Bee. Well, Martha and X flew in to Los Angeles and stayed at the Knickerbocker Hotel. We came behind with the car and gear. But, as it turned out, they only used Martha and me. We were all so disappointed.

"However, along with the Ford network show, we appeared on Cliffie Stone's *Hometown Jamboree* TV program and did Speedy West & Jimmy Bryant's radio show," adds Edwards (whose fiddling opened the weekend *Grand Ole Opry* broadcasts for many years). "I guess one of the things I enjoyed most, during those two years with Martha, was the tour in California."

On their itinerary was the famed Palomino Club, also founded by her old WSB buddy, Hank Penny, who also furnished her stage name.

"Yeah, we played there," Martha adds, "But I also played a bunch of them little ol' clubs out there, too."

Effective Dec. 31, 1999, Edwards suffered a similar slight like the Opry showed Carson some 40 years earlier, when they dropped him from the staff band, along with Buddy Harman, ex-

Texas Troubadour steel player Leon Rhodes, rhythm picker Ralph Davis and a newcomer, drummer Jerry Ray Johnston. Opry manager Pete Fisher called it an economic move to reduce the band size, but hired new players to "revitalize" the show, those who could play several instruments.

That was hard to fathom, considering Edwards is adept on fiddle *or* guitars. Perhaps Opry superstar Vince Gill's response to newspaper reporter Jay Orr, regarding the firings, best puts it all in perspective: "Leon Rhodes can play circles around most guitar players, and Buddy Harman can play circles around most drummers...the sad thing is *younger ain't better*...the real crux of the problem for me, is in Garth and in Reba and in Alan and in Clint and on and on and on - the so-called big stars of today - that don't support the *Grand Ole Opry.*"

Walt Trott

CHAPTER 23

Go West, Young Gal...

'Martha, when are you gonna do those happy spirituals you do?'

Prior to relocating to Hollywood, Martha Carson worked Las Vegas' Dunes Hotel. When one conjures images of that fabled gambling mecca, reputedly founded by mobster Bugsy Siegel in the late '40s, it's something of a paradox to imagine spirited musical evangelist Martha Carson headlining at the Dunes.

Yet, there were no more appreciative audiences for her lively gospel fare than the high rollers who visited Vegas' plush casinos to view rock 'n rollers or so-called "rat packers" like Frank Sinatra or Sammy Davis Jr. It was also in a sense true, that the artist was bringing *The Word* to those, who might not otherwise frequent a house of worship.

On the down side, Martha's health was not at its best. The performances were becoming more of a task for the usually uninhibited entertainer, and that puzzled her.

"After my second baby, I couldn't seem to get back the stamina I was used to having. My strength just didn't return like it should have. To make matters worse, my hands were hurting from eczema - it's an allergy I inherited from my mother's side.

"The skin was broken and every knuckle on my hand was just split open, so that I couldn't play my guitar when I sang. I began wearing white gloves to cover it and still did five shows a day, requiring more energy than I could seem to muster.

"That's when I got real skinny and looked like Olive Oyl (Popeye's bony cartoon girlfriend)! I had to have all my gowns taken in and the workload got to be too much. I'd just get home from work and my babies were waking up...

"After my Dunes' contract ran out, I was being asked if I'd open the show at the Flamingo (a lucrative offer), but I knew I wouldn't be able to do it. It was all suddenly getting to me. The Dunes manager suggested I go to L.A. for a physical and to see this doctor (he recommended).

"Well, we went out there and I saw the doctor, who examined me and wrote on my insurance papers, *'Complete physical exhaustion and malnutrition.'* I did love the climate out there in California, so X decided we'd stay awhile."

With no commitment to the Opry or a record label, she was free to explore a new lifestyle. X opened his own booking agency in Hollywood, and rented quarters for them in North Hollywood, until the Cossés' found a more ideal home in the San Fernando Valley.

"That was a nice little place," says Martha. "Lordy, the backyard looked like it had been landscaped, but I did it all myself. We had banana trees, tropical plants and a patio with flowers all around it. It was really beautiful.

"Next thing I knew, a neighbor inquired about my hands, and suggested a specialist. The doctor put me in the hospital and kept me there about a week. After I learned he was trying to make a mental case out of it, I told him, *'There's nothing wrong with my head. It's my lack of strength that's got me down.'* He said he couldn't find anything wrong - and would discharge me in the morning.

"Well, I had this pediatrician, who had been tending to my babies, who came by. He said, 'Mrs. Cossé, I've been noticing how you look when you bring your boys in. I want one of the best doctors in the San Fernando Valley to see you.' So I agreed. The doctor came by and with the help of a nurse gave me an exam while I was still in the hospital bed.

"He asked, 'How old is your youngest baby?' I told him about a year-and-a-half. He said, 'I'm not a gynecologist, but you definitely have a pelvic disorder.' When my other doctor came in, he ignored what that doctor said, and signed me out of the hospital.

"My legs were too weak to even drive a car, so X drove me the next day to a gynecologist. One of the first things he asked was did they run a urinalysis on me? I said I wasn't sure. He said he was concerned and couldn't believe that doctor had released me from the hospital yesterday. So, he did a urinalysis…

"After the test, he came in and told me I was full of infection. He said he hadn't seen that much infection in urine, only once before, and that was in his early doctoring days. That was a nurse who was so bad, he had to take out her natural urinary tube and replace it with a plastic tube.

"He said, 'I don't mean to alarm you, but I want you to go across the street to the hospital and have a kidney X-ray, then come back to my office.' When he got the results, he asked me if I drank a lot of anything in particular. 'I just don't understand it,' he said. Well, my weakness is coffee, so I told him, 'I guess you're gonna scold me for drinking too much coffee. But I always seem to have a cup of coffee in my hand to keep me going.'

"The doctor stared at me and said, 'No, I'm not going to scold you. You better thank God that you drank that amount of coffee. You see, coffee is a kidney stimulant, and He must have been looking out for you. The coffee kept the poison moving and saved your kidney. I can find no damage to your kidney.'

"I was amazed. He said, 'We've got to get this infection out of your system and then we're going to have surgery to correct it. You should never have been allowed to deliver your second baby by natural childbirth.' In fact, André was born breached and the doctor had told me then when I went into labor, he had no hopes of delivering the baby alive!

"I guess I always have to have something different about me. I was told in most women, the uterus is oval shaped on top, but mine's heart-shaped, like a box of Valentine candy - so they couldn't turn the baby without wrapping the umbilical cord around his neck.

"The doctor in California told me the baby should have been taken by Caesarian. When he was delivered, it tore all the supports away from the uterus, and my uterus was just laying on the bladder or the large intestine. He said, 'Whether you know it or not, you have never been able to empty your bladder in its entirety since that baby's birth (a year-and-a-half earlier)! As a result, the urine's just remained in there and the resulting infection almost killed you!'

"I remember now I had been given a choice of three surgeries: take the uterus out; have a full hysterectomy; or go in and put everything back in order. Well, number three was my choice. I wanted at least two more babies, if I could; hopefully, girls to go with my boys.

"Of course, X and I had to sign if they found any need for specific surgery after they got in the operating room and needed our permission before they could proceed. I don't know who approved it *now*, but the doctor cut the cervix off the uterus, so I couldn't get pregnant again! But *I wasn't told that he did that.*"

After Martha's surgery, which had taken six hours, her doctor told her to take some time off and "to not lift anything heavier than a newspaper" for about six months.

"I even had to wear a catheter strapped to my side for three months," says Martha, who without bookings was experiencing a cash flow problem. "I wrote to my mother and told her I wasn't able to work and of my shortage in money. I had made my parents' house payments about 12 years and they did fine during that time.

"Well, I have five brothers and sisters, so I asked her to have them pitch in so she could make the payments. She wrote me back and said they refused to do it as long as I was married to X...

"It hurt to think my family didn't have any more feeling for me than that. I had never asked anything of them before that time...So I took the deed to a notary public and signed the property back over to her.

"I guess the old home place run down about 30 years ago, so they had a little house rebuilt on the same grounds. It troubled me though to think that when I needed my family the most, they weren't there for me."

It saddened her that both the Opry and her family were down on her husband, the father of her babies.

After convalescing, Martha was able to resume her career, slowly but surely. She became a regular on the syndicated *Town Hall Party* series emanating from Channel 11, Compton, Calif. - a show directed by Wesley Tuttle.

"That was a good Saturday night happening," says Martha. "Different ones would act as guest hosts. Some of the artists performing then, as I recall, were Tex Ritter, Johnny Bond, Freddie Hart, Gordon Terry, Merle Travis and Joe and Rose Lee Maphis."

[Others who guested on the C&W program, which kicked off in 1951, included Rex Allen, Eddie Dean, Lefty Frizzell, Slim Willett, Cousin Herb Henson, Billy Mize, Myrna Jory, Tommy Collins, Fiddlin' Kate, Tom Tall, the Collins Kids (Larry and Lorrie), and Marilyn and Wesley Tuttle. *Town Hall Party,* a long-time favorite for country fans in Southern California, signed off in the early '60s.]

One viewer, Ken Nelson, contacted Martha to see if she might be interested in recording for Capitol again, and she did do a session on May 30, 1960, that yielded one single: "High On the Hill," backed with "Everything's Alright," released Aug. 12, 1960. Carson wrote both songs, which brought her back to her favored rockin' country gospel numbers.

More importantly, the goodwill created, encouraged Capitol to release its first full-fledged album on Martha Carson in 1960, titled appropriately enough "Satisfied." Regarding all the Martha material in their vaults, Capitol followed it up with another Carson LP, "A Talk With the Lord" in 1961. This, of course, gave a slight boost to her sinking fortunes.

Martha was much in demand for personal appearances and, by then, Cossé was running his own booking agency in Hollywood. He had all the right contacts. He also mixed in a number of younger artists, including the popular brothers Burnette, Dorsey and Johnny, who hailed from Memphis. Each worked closely with X in pursuing separate careers for themselves, and Dorsey, in particular, was a fan of Martha Carson's energetic performing style.

A former Golden Gloves boxer, Dorsey Burnette helped organize the Johnny Burnette Rock & Roll Trio with Johnny and Paul Burlison, all of whose roots were rockabilly. They performed successfully on the *West Memphis Jamboree* (KWEM) and then competed and won a *Ted Mack Amateur Hour* talent show. The trio had recorded for Von Records, before disbanding in 1957.

Johnny and Dorsey co-wrote Ricky Nelson's 1958 million seller "Believe What You Say," and on his own Johnny wrote yet another million seller for Nelson, "Just a Little Too Much," released in 1959, both Top 10s. (Sadly, Johnny died in a boating accident in 1964, at age 30).

These were easy bookings for Cossé's company. Dorsey, who himself was quite a showman, had just switched to Dot Records. He suggested they record Martha Carson, as well. She did do one Dot session, which resulted in a single 1961 release, coupling "Right Now, Right Now" with "Things Happen For the Best." The A side credits Martha Carson and Dorsey Burnette as co-writers.

She explains, "While out there on the West Coast, Dorsey Burnette invited me over to his house, at a time when I was writing a bunch of secular songs. He was doing some writing, so I went off in a room by myself and wrote two songs that night. X took both of them, 'Can't You Love Me' and 'Right Now, Right Now,' and put them in a publishing company he had opened for Dorsey, putting his name on as co-writer. Well, he never did write a word of my songs. Later, when X discontinued his working relationship with Dorsey, he tried to put them in my publishing company, but the copyrights and everything already had Dorsey's name and company on them. I think Dorsey later put his stuff with Acuff/Rose."

A short while earlier, Martha's good friend Mac Wiseman had been Dot's A&R head. Theirs might have been a far more creative collaboration. Another Carson cut for Dot (though unreleased) was "He Is the Shepherd of My Soul," which she calls, *"One of the best songs I ever recorded."*

The songstress says that what soured the Dot deal for her was Wink Martindale, serving as A&R man: "I think he later found his right calling as a game show host, but he sure wasn't an A&R man. He kept asking if I knew how to sing like an R&B singer - that's the way he wanted me to sound."

When it was apparent that she and Wink couldn't see eye-to-eye on performance, their association ended amicably. [A Jackson, Tenn. native, Martindale produced a hit for Dot - on himself - reciting the old Tex Ritter chestnut "Deck of Cards" (#7, 1959).]

Meanwhile, for a child's eye-view of their Out-West days, André Cossé searches his memory bank: "I do remember when I let the brake off once on their car in Nevada and it almost rolled over a cliff! Fortunately, my father came running out and got the car stopped before it went over!

"My parents were quite busy in California," he affirms. "We had some nice neighbors that lived next to us, but there were some mean little Mexican boys, who lived behind us. One time they threw this great big ol' rock over our eight-foot fence. Luckily, I had my cowboy hat and my brother's on top of it, so when I got hit by this rock it helped cushion the blow. As it was, I had to have 40 or 50 stitches.

"One time, my brother and I rode our miniature fire engines, equipped with little pedals, through a plate glass window! It's amazing that neither one of us got a scratch. We were racing each other, I think. I was just little bitty. When my parents came in, we were still riding our little cars, but got in trouble over that, of course.

"Looking back, I remember we had this wagon wheel with lights all over it, hanging over the dining room table. Well, us boys decided we were going to swing on it, and pulled that wheel down until the wires were exposed! Daddy came in, took one look and went for a belt. He didn't know he'd grabbed one of those little cardboard cowboy gun belts. He got hold of my brother first, I suppose because he was older.

"When he hit him with this, my brother laughed, so my Daddy hit him harder - and he laughed again. Looking up at my father, he says, 'Daddy, it tickles.' Finally, my frustrated father started laughing too, and he gave up on punishing us.

"I don't think we got into too many scrapes. We were pretty good kids, who didn't get into a whole lot of trouble. When we stepped out of line, it was usually mischievous things, like taking a BB-gun and maybe shoot at a bird or cat, stuff like that.

"Our parents never hit us or anything. Of course, they would scold us, maybe send us to our room or take away a privilege. My mother, a few times, would scare us to death by telling us, *'Now your Daddy's gonna deal with you when he gets home!'* The thought of him coming in and getting on to us would worry us."

Martha and X had enjoyed a good run on the West Coast, but the thrill was gone.

"With my asthma and all, the smog finally got to me, so I told X it was time to head back East," confides Carson, who adds that he agreed and put their home on the market. "I flew back first, trying to find a place to live. He stayed on to see that the furniture was loaded right, and all."

Back in Nashville, Martha found a nice house in Belle Meade, where the Cossés resided for the next two years. Soon, she was also performing again, occasionally sharing the stage with Danny Dill, who had won new fans performing with dynamic partner Annie Lou, on numerous Opry appearances.

Dill, whose compositions include the "Long Black Veil" and "Detroit City," teamed with Annie Lou to perform a vocal and instrumental team in the early '60s. Their theme was "Chime Bells." He had his own MGM LP, "Folk Songs of the Wild West," released in 1960, to draw from. (At one stage, Dill was also wed to Skeeter Davis' sister.)

Another who performed in Martha's troupe for a time was a former Drifting Cowboy, Hank Williams' ace steel guitarist:

"Yes, Don Helms sang with me some, too." Helms, who also backed Ray Price, was a veteran studio session player. He was becoming more interested in behind-the-scenes efforts, such as booking and publishing, which eventually brought him into partnership with the Wilburn Brothers, hence the Wil-Helm Agency (and later worked with Smiley Wilson's booking firm).

Although no longer an Opry artist, Carson found herself on package shows with a lot of their WSM stars, among them Bill Anderson, Porter Wagoner and Roy Acuff. In addition, she toured with such non-Opry acts as Hank Thompson, Bob Wills, Mac Wiseman and the Boots Randolph combo. It was while doing a show with the Opry's Charlie Louvin in Houston, Texas, that Martha encountered a rather odd reaction from a club operator: "Al Ford was the owner and he met me as I was getting out of our car, after we drove up to his club. He said, 'You're not going to do spirituals tonight are you, Miss Carson?' I thought to myself *I don't know what he thought he hired me for*.... But out loud I replied 'Let me just say this: I'll do what I do and if I haven't pleased you and your crowd, you don't owe me a thing!'"

While the crowd was out on the dance floor, Charlie called Martha up on stage and she received a big hand from the people. "Well, I started off with Hank Williams' 'You Win Again,' and I knew what was gonna happen. This couple shouted up to me, *'Martha, when are you gonna do those happy spirituals you do?'* I called back to them, 'That's all I was waiting on. Howdy!'

"When they left that dance floor, you'd have thought there had been a Holy Roller meeting going on! They'd been clapping hands and just having a great time out there. When I went off into the wings, the owner, pleased as punch, asked, 'What did you do to those people?!?' I smiled and said, *'I just gave 'em a little something they weren't gonna get, because they sure ain't gonna go to church!"*

Walt Trott

CHAPTER 24

In The Name of Love...

"I always had a certain closeness with my mother, that I didn't have with my father."
- André Cossé

"A couple of years after we left California, my doctor said, 'I don't want to put you on birth control pills, I want you to use a diaphragm. The pill is too new and I don't want to run any risks with you.'

"During my usual check-ups, however, the doctors didn't detect that my uterus had been surgically worked on, so later they put me on birth control pills. After a couple years of taking the pills, I experienced real problems, because I had phlebitis (a blood clot in the leg) and I told the doctor I could hardly walk, I was in such pain.

"That next day, they put me in the hospital and found blood clots in both my legs and arms. They packed me down with those thermal heat things and gave me something that was supposed to dissolve the blood clot. Someone there told me it was supposedly made out of some sort of rat poison! Well, I joked about that. I said *I'd be the only artist who can go out on stage, do a song, squeek and run under the curtain."*

She wasn't laughing when she learned that there had been no need for those years of precautionary birth control methods, such as diaphragms or pills, because the surgeon in California had made sure *she wasn't ever going to become pregnant again.*

That wasn't the doctor's fault alone? Someone had to authorize such a procedure!

Two days before her ninth wedding anniversary - and her mother's birthday - a tragedy occurred that would forever haunt Martha and her family. Her father, Robert Humphrey Amburgey,

74, was killed in a two-car crash July 29, which also took the life of his grandson, Daniel Amburgey. That fateful 1962 day, in Ohio, marked the first deaths in Martha's immediate family.

Martha's nephew Kenneth Woodruff recalls that "Poppy" and the younger boys had gone to church earlier and were on their way home, when he and "Mommie" began their drive to church for a later service.

"We actually drove right by the accident, but there were so many cars and people milling around on the other side, we couldn't see who it was. They were 100 yards off the road. After we got to church, the highway patrol had to come and get my grandmother..."

On her mother's 61st birthday, they buried the bodies.

Martha, too, was devastated by the loss. Her boys, René, 6, and André, 4, were a tremendous comfort to the singer. She worried about the great sadness that her mother and brother Glenn had to cope with, and prayed that God would help them all through this trying time.

On Aug. 17, 1963, this item appeared in *Billboard* magazine: "Martha Carson signs to Sims Records." Work was always a fine form of therapy for the lady. Entrepreneur Russell Sims, who said he had long been a fan of Martha Carson's, was launching a new label. Sims, who called it by his surname, concluded a pact with the artist in 1963.

Sims also recorded five males, who managed to chart for the fledgling label, with the best showing being Autry Inman's "The Volunteer," peaking at #22 in 1963. The other contenders were Glenn Barber, "How Can I Forget You" (#48), Bobby Barnett's "Worst of Luck" (#47), Bob Jennings with both "The First Step Down" (#32) and "Leave a Little Play" (#34), and Joe Penny's "Frosty Window Pane" (#41), all in 1964.

Finally, Sims lucked out with burly Canadian Hal Willis, a French-speaking *basso profundo* from Quebec, who could have made it in Grand Opera. Instead, he chose to learn English from the love-of-his-life, singer Ginger Booth, then followed her into *Grand Ole Opry*-style music. In '64, Willis' "The Lumberjack" became a Top Five *Billboard* record for Sims, and even garnered pop play. Ginger and Hal co-wrote the number. After that hit, he enjoyed a Top 40 success, "Doggin' in the U.S. Mail." Willis has stated, however, he never saw much in the way of royalties from his Sims' singles.

The good and bad of it for Martha was that Sims agreed she could own all the recorded tracks cut for him, if their subsequent album didn't sell *in the black*. It wasn't because of a lack of quality that sales failed to register. Sims produced and Cliff Parman handled the arrangements on an excellent 1963 album, Carson's favorite.

Some of Nashville's finest session people were assembled for the 12 selections, including Harold Bradley, rhythm guitar; Buddy Harman, drums; Grady Martin, lead guitar; Bob Moore, bass; Pig Robbins, keyboards; and Chuck, Jim and Tompall Glaser as background vocalists, along with the Jordanaires' Ray Walker and Winnie Breast, Millie Kirkham and Priscilla Hubbard. (The latter, the wife of Jerry Reed - as Priscilla Mitchell - recorded the #1 "Yes, Mr. Peters" with Roy Drusky in 1965; and she co-wrote Connie Smith's Top Fiver "If I Talk To Him" that year.)

On the Sims' album cover, Carson wears a frilly blue street-length dress with white opera gloves and heels, while standing outdoors on the grass with a floral backdrop. The star spotlights sister Jean's superb song "(I Found It) Just Around the Bend," which features a striking modulation that makes a dramatic reading. The track also boasts some excellent pickin' by the legendary Grady Martin and a hair-raising vocal presentation that made little "Sunshine Sister" proud.

Martha's self-penned "It Takes a Lot of Livin' (To Learn How to Live)," also included, is one of those songs that sort of sums up life, much as Paul Anka's "My Way" did for Frank Sinatra.

Fine piano work by Robbins, enhances Martha's soulful delivery. It's as close to secular as she's come since her RCA version of "A Satisfied Mind," a song popularized originally in

1955, separately by Porter Wagoner, Jean Shepard and Red Foley's duet.

It also represents some of her most poetic writing: *"It takes a lot of living, to learn how to live/I started out in this big world/I thought I knew it all/I touched the blossom of success/Know how it hurts to fall/Know how it hurts to fall...*

"My Daddy said you gotta learn in life/You take and give/And it takes a lot of living, child, to learn how to live/To learn how to live...

"Well, I've been up, And I've been down/My child's heart still yearns/With each mistake/ I give and take/I'm living, just to learn/I'm living, just to learn...

"We learn to craw/Before we walk/Get hurt, but we forgive/It takes a lot of living/To learn how to live/To learn how to live...Oh yes, it takes a lot of living, child, to learn how to live."

In the same vein, her recitations, "That's Life" and "Real Life," are also poignant pieces of philosophy from Carson's poetic pen. Buddy Harman's sticks set a frenetic pace for her uptempo "Joy, Joy, Joy (In My Father's House)," with which there's no doubt, she's right at home.

There isn't a filler in the collection. There's terrific Martha Carson performances throughout, most notably on the ballad "Bells of the Chapel," the medium-tempoed "Walkin' in the Garden," and the listener can marvel at her impeccable phrasing throughout, particularly effective on "Move That Mountain For Me."

If we thought she put all her feelings into "It Takes a Lot of Livin'," then what a delight to hear there's lots left for "Good, Good Feelin'," wherein she's given superb vocal support from Kirkham, Walker and the Glasers. There's yet more of that infectious rhythm and stylized singing alloted to "Somebody Told Me" and "Everybody Needs Somebody."

The latter song, backed with her moving "It Takes a Lot of Living," was the sole single issued by Sims in 1963. Carson had never been in better voice than on the Sims' set, her best album to date. Sims was having financial problems, however, and couldn't get the distribution needed to promote the album, titled simply "Martha Carson."

In accordance with the terms of their contract, the masters reverted to Martha. She wrote 11 of the dozen songs chosen. The Cossés were disappointed that the album wasn't the comeback hoped for on the recording scene.

In 1964, another independent Christian label, Scripture Records, based in Newark, N.J., contacted Carson to sing another dozen selections, this time renditions of standard gospel numbers, including the album's title tune "This Old House," written (as "This Ole House") by Stuart Hamblen, "Do Lord," the tune that helped launch the so-called *religioso* movement in Hollywood a decade earlier, "Lonesome Valley," "He'll Understand and Say Well Done," "I'll Fly Away," "Just a Closer Walk With Thee," "Swing Low, Sweet Chariot," "That Lonesome Road," "Ezekiel Saw the Wheel," "We'll Understand It Better," "Crying Holy To The Lord" and "(I'll) Shout and Shine." The latter song she had recorded (in 1949) with James for Capitol: "This was the first time, however, that I sang lead on it."

Noticeably, despite her prolific songwriting, there were no new Carson tunes.

"These people didn't want any original songs because they didn't want to have to pay me royalties," explains Martha. "I recorded it for a flat fee, so I could use the money and buy out my partners in Marpat Music, Inc., which we established in New York. When we organized, there was my attorney, Wallace Magaziner, and Patricia Blum, wife of my then-manager Harry Blum. She thought she was a songwriter, but she couldn't write 'Yankee Doodle.' So I bought 'em out."

Backing her vocally on the Scripture session are old pals Kitty and Smiley Wilson, augmented by others, billed as The Rangers. She grins, noting, "It tickled me that Kitty and Smiley did the album with me. On the syncopated 'Ezekiel Saw the Wheel,' when Smiley and Kitty were singing backup, we had a little error. They were a little delayed in singing their part, that is they hesitated before singing the word 'air,' and they all wanted to do it over. But I listened to it and said, no, I like it like that."

At the time, the Wilsons were more involved in behind-the-scenes booking activities, such as the Wil-Helm Agency, where Smiley was president. But they also kept up with performing, most notably on Nashville WTVF-Channel 5, where they were featured for 11 years on *Country Junction.* They were particularly pleased to work again with Carson on the Scripture session.

Scripture produced it as an album and had no intention of releasing singles.

"Can you believe that I recorded it all in a three-hour session? Well, we did it at the Lonzo and Oscar (Sullivan's) studio, somewhere around Goodlettsville, in three hours," sighs Martha.

Kitty Wilson later recalled, "It was a joy to work with that woman. When you get on stage, she just picks you up, even when you're feeling down."

The Scripture LP's cover depicts a beautiful, now 43-year-old Martha, sitting and strumming her guitar on the steps of an old, run-down home, in keeping with the title "This Old House." In contrast, she looks exquisite in a more traditional high-necked, street-length dress with gold edging that perfectly matched the gold high heels worn.

Liner notes state, in part, *"Martha has a style and a way with a song that no one can emulate. When she swings into one of the spirituals for which she is famous, the listener quickly gets the message, and the joy of her message comes through."*

It would be a baker's dozen years before she would record again in the studio. (In 1965, however, RCA's budget label Camden issued a new album on the glorious redhead, titled "Martha Carson Sings," coordinated by A&R person Ethel Gabriel. Of the 10 previously-recorded selections, seven were included for the first time on an album.)

Meanwhile, X. Cossé relished his association with Martha's long-time friend Chet Atkins, who had become a major force at RCA Records. In 1963, the promoter saw great potential in teaming Atkins on guitar with pianist Floyd Cramer (who enjoyed a multi-million selling instrumental in 1961, with his pop and country favorite "Last Date," followed by pop Top 10s "On the Rebound," and "San Antonio Rose," also a country scorer) and saxophone-tooting Boots Randolph (a Top 40 favorite via his 1963 "Yakety Sax" instrumental, which Atkins cribbed to create his only Top 10 guitar solo "Yakety Axe" in 1963), to launch a series of concerts.

Called "The Masters Festival of Music," Cossé managed the trio under their joint ARC Company Enterprises, with offices in the RCA building, then on 17th Avenue South, Nashville (owned by the Bradley brothers).

Of course, the ARC title was derived from the players' last names. This unique assemblage of country instrumentalists proved to be a stroke of genius, for The Masters enjoyed *standing room only* crowds in cities throughout the country - and longevity, as well.

Due to their chartings on the R&B record lists, their audiences proved rather diverse for such Nashville-based musicians. After a decade standing in the shadow of his famous wife, Cossé welcomed an opportunity to become the chief bread-winner in their household, and appreciated Atkins putting him at the helm of the successful Masters tours.

Cramer (who died of cancer Dec. 31, 1997, at age 64) himself said, "We did those for about 14 years, often with guest artists like Ray Price, Homer & Jethro or Martha Carson. I was proud of our association."

A news brief in *Billboard* on Nov. 28, 1964, stated, "Martha Carson joined the Wil-Helm Agency." Of course, the talent firm was a partnership between Don Helms, former Hank Williams' Drifting Cowboy, and the Wilburn Brothers - Doyle, Teddy, Leslie and Lester - a family that had made its mark in numerous ways.

While it struck many as strange that the gospel singer was signing with a company promoting country queen lady-in-waiting Loretta Lynn, while wed to a prominent booker herself; the facts make it quite clear why. In order to secure the pact with ARC, Cossé had to agree to represent only the instrumentalists for the duration of their partnership.

Mrs. Cossé was not yet ready to abandon the spotlight. Helms had, of course, been doing some gigs with Carson and convinced her that his agency could add some lucrative dates to her calendar. After Williams' death, Helms had worked awhile with Ray Price's Cherokee Cowboys, taking a breather from that band for a brief sojourn with Ferlin Husky's Hush Puppies, then returned to Price in 1955. While working with the Wilburn Brothers in 1957, they hit upon forming a behind-the-scenes working relationship, which resulted in formation of both Wil-Helm and Sure-Fire Publishing.

Nonetheless, Helms' steel guitar stayed hot in the studios, and is heard on such classics as Bobby (no relation) Helms' "Fraulein," Patsy Cline's "Walkin' After Midnight" and Stonewall Jackson's "Waterloo." Incidentally, Helms' stock in both firms was bought out in 1968, and subsequently he worked with Hank Williams Jr., Cal Smith, Ernest Tubb and both the Shorty Lavender and Smiley Wilson talent agencies.

One thing that struck Martha Carson in November 1964, was the fact that women had certainly come into their own, both in country and the pop world. When she had first accepted membership into the Opry cast, the distaffers were at a premium on the music scene.

Shortly after Martha made her breakthrough, country stylist Wells got attention on the national scene, but it took a while for more than a handful of ladies to gain firm-enough footing on the success ladder to break the masculine stranglehold on charts.

One of Carson's more devoted fans, Connie Smith hit the top of the country chart Nov. 28, 1964, holding steady eight weeks with her signature song "Once a Day" (written by Bill

Anderson). Smith was the only country gal to hit number one that year.

Meanwhile, The Supremes, a female trio, had just ended a four week run on the pop chart at #1 with their soulful "Baby Love," replaced by another girl group The Shangri-Las, whose "Leader of the Pack" hit the pop top Nov. 28.

Despite her signings, Martha Carson's career was clearly in another valley. This low period, however, afforded her more time with her boys, who were growing up too fast, it seemed to her. For a woman who had prayed so long to be a mother, in the name of love, that situation wasn't hard to take.

"Our parents always made sure we were properly supervised whenever they were gone," notes André. "Today, there's little supervision and that's where a lot of children get into trouble. The nanny we had was like a second mother to us. But, when our parents came home, we were always excited, because we missed them so much.

"I remember we had this real sweet lady, about 60 or 70, named Miss Haywood. Sometimes we'd get a few switches when we started acting goofy, if you know what I mean. Miss Haywood would walk us out to the backyard and have us pick out the switch. That was more frightening than the actual whipping. We'd always pick the smallest limb and she'd say, *'No, that's not the one.'* Sometimes she'd just act like she was going to pop us with it, and that would straighten us out."

René says whenever it was school season, "we had to do our homework and also do chores. But in summer, we'd play from daylight to dark. I never felt cheated if our parents weren't with us."

André confides, "I always had a certain closeness with my mother, that I didn't have with my father. Sometimes me and Dad would butt heads. For years, we clashed...he used to ride my brother a lot, too. That bothered me.

"Dad worked all the time," René continues. "If he wasn't in the office, he was at a show or on the telephone. He stayed busy constantly. When he did have some extra time, he might pitch a ball to us. He loved sports and showed up at some of our games, when we were playing in the league. And, we never had to throw a tantrum for either of them to be there."

CHAPTER 25

To Get To You...

"The homeless found a home on Susan's floor..."

"I think she first started writing a lot after the trio broke up, but with Salty gone, she went on a writing spree that never quit. I remember that she had written one once for Salty's talking harmonica called 'Stuck With Love.'" It was a hoot, adds Martha.

For King, Jean (as Mattie O'Neil) had recorded with Salty on his self-penned "Shackles and Chains," backed with "Our Love Is Gone" (which she had written) in 1949. Holmes also wrote the popular "Ghost Song" and "I Found My Mama," among others. Other Mattie O'Neil-Salty Holmes collaborative recordings include "Divorces," "Echoes Over the Smokies," "My Little Son's Plea," "My Worst Mistake," "Wake Up Little Blue Boys" and "Long Time Gone."

Whenever there was a lull as a performer for the show business Amburgeys, they could always count on their songwriting efforts to keep them in the game.

Following her 1950s divorce from Holmes, Jean began writing up a storm, Indeed, Chapel achieved great success with her compositional efforts, landing cuts with a who's who of musical artists, among them Carl Belew, Jim Ed Brown, Patsy Cline, Skeeter Davis, Jimmy Dean, Frankie Dee, Red Foley, Connie Francis, Bob Gallion, Don Gibson, Bonnie Guitar, Goldie Hill, Engelbert Humperdinck, George Jones, Hank Locklin, Bob Luman, Bobby Mack, Al Martino, Charlie McCoy, George Morgan, Tommy Overstreet, Stu Phillips, Jeanne Pruett, Jim Reeves, Roy Rogers, Ray Sanders, Nancy Sinatra, Connie Smith, Hank Snow, Kitty Wells and, of course, Martha Carson.

In 1963, Sonny James' recording of Chapel's "Going Through the Motions Of Living," co-written with Bob Tubert, spent nine weeks on *Billboard's* country chart, peaking at #17 for Capitol. In 1964, her "Triangle" hit #16 for Columbia's Carl Smith, also hung in there nine weeks.

Jean found 1967 a *banner year,* when actor-singer Bobby Wright (ABC-TV's *McHale's Navy* series' sailor) first scored country (his first charting, that is), 12 weeks, starting April 29, via "Lay Some Happiness On Me," the song which Dean Martin took to #55 on the pop charts; and Eddy Arnold enjoyed a #1 record with her "Lonely Again." That song stayed in top spot April 15, and the week of April 22, during its 15-week run on the charts. No doubt it helped Arnold earn the very first CMA Entertainer of the Year trophy in 1967.

RCA revived "Lonely Again" to include in a two-CD set (1993) retrospective on Arnold titled "Last of the Love Song Singers: Then & Now." Arnold had this to say about Chapel's poetic number, *"Listen closely to this lyric, because it tells a story about someone who is really in love. Who knows! You might fall in love all over again, listening to 'Lonely Again'."*

Her song "To Get To You" was recorded by Jerry Wallace for MCA, charting 22 weeks, a near Top 10. It crossed over into the Pop Top 40 field, as well. Wallace invited Jean to record a duet with him on her romantic ballad "Until You," resulting in a dazzling rendition that is at once sweet and sexy.

In an attempt to turn country singer, Pittsburgh Stealers' ex-quarterback Terry Bradshaw recorded it for Benson Records in 1980. His version of "Until You" charted five weeks, topping out at #73. Today, the grid hero, who led the Stealers to four Super Bowl victories, is more familiar to viewers of *Fox NFL Sunday* for his snappy commentator quips.

Before ending her run as a Las Vegas attraction, golden girl Judy Lynn recorded Chapel's "Green Paper." The Western-styled artist, once managed by Nashville's Charlie Lamb, deserted the casino in favor of church, where she became an ordained minister. Chapel songs have also served as titles for artists' albums, including Eddy Arnold's "Lonely Again" RCA (LSP-3753), "Happiness Is...Dean Martin" Reprise (R6242), both in 1967; and Jerry Wallace's "To Get To You" MCA (S-50) in 1973. Of course, the "Happiness" in Martin's LP is derived from Chapel's award-winning "Lay Some Happiness On Me." (His daughter Deana recorded Chapel's "When He Remembers Me.")

Her compositions have earned Jean Chapel seven BMI Awards for both pop and country recordings, including two (pop and country) for the Martin (1967) and Wright (1968) versions; three for Arnold's "Lonely Again," pop and country 1967, and country 1968. In 1964, she received her first BMI Award for Smith's "Triangle," and in 1973 a country BMI Award for Wallace's "To Get To You."

Smith, incidentally, also recorded Chapel's "Till I Looked At You," "Little Crop of Cotton Tops," "The Morning After" and "To Get To You." But Eddy Arnold appears to have recorded the most of her songs: Besides "Lonely Again," he cut "There's This About You," "Baby, That's Living," "I Really Go For You," "No Matter Whose Baby You Are" and "Lay Some Happiness On Me."

Her most recorded songs are "To Get To You" (which gained her a Song of the Year CMA nomination in 1972), "Lonely Again," "I'm Your Woman," "Lay Some Happiness On Me," "Triangle" and "Another Way To Say Goodbye."

No doubt her shortest title is "A Ha," recorded in 1956 by Don Gibson, while the most novel has to be "Ain't Gonna Wash My Face For a Month ('Cause You Kissed It Last Night)." Other Chapel titles include "Crazy Dreams," "Always Missing You," "Another Way to Say Goodbye," "Circumstantial Evidence," "Gentle Rains Of Home," "Happiness Is My Belief," "Crashin' Rollin' Thunder in My Mind," "Walking Shadow, Talking Memory," "You Turn Me On," "The Flower, The Sunset, The Trees," "Have Mercy!" and "These Autumn Years."

According to son Kenneth, over 40-plus years, she has written over 2,000 titles, placed with 26 different publishing companies and has more than 175 different releases out there: "I'm very proud of her. She was so talented."

As an artist, she was heard briefly on Smash Records, a subsidiary of Mercury, also home to Norro Wilson, Jerry Lee Lewis and Roger Miller. Her main track for that label was her own composition "My Reasons For Leaving." When Acuff/Rose's Hickory Records signed the singer-songwriter, they billed her as Opal Jean, but again she failed to chart any of her records.

Joe Johnson cut a number of original tracks on Jean for his independent Challenge Records label, among them "Hungry Eyes," "Green Paper," "This Waltz Was Mine," "In Reach of Your Arms," "A Lonely Woman," "Contagious," "Lonely Again," "To Get To You," "Sunshine Every Day, Moonlight Every Night" and "I'm Your Woman."

Earlier, Johnson (fresh out of law school) was engaged to run Gene Autry's Four Star music publishing house (after Autry bought it from Bill McCall, who first recorded Patsy Cline). Johnson later took over Four Star from Autry and ended up bankrupting the company.

"That relationship (with Johnson) didn't work out very well for my mother. He seemed to have broken her spirit, because she stopped writing after that for a long while," says son Kenneth Woodruff, a travel agent.

Another recording pact in the late 1960s had Jean singing for the Kapp label, which produced such Chapel tracks as "Bluebird Ridge," "Always Missing You," "Love Is," "Will I Ever Stop Loving You" and the gospel standard "When the Roll Is Called Up Yonder, I'll Be There."

"Three or four years before we lost her, she resumed writing again," added a wistful Woodruff.

During the 1970s, while launching her nightclub act, she altered her last husband Jeff Calongne's name to bill herself as Opal Jean Cologne. On her song "I'm Your Woman," she gives a co-author's credit to Alda Calongne.

"She was that way. If anyone caught her in the right mood, bought her a cup of coffee, gave her an idea or a hook, their name went on her song," notes Kenneth. "My mother was very generous."

To date, her songs have been recorded as bluegrass, spirituals, country, pop, rock and blues. Even Hollywood's King of the Cowboys' Roy Rogers charted with Chapel's "These Are the Good Old Days" four weeks in 1972, and he later recorded a version of "Lay Some Happiness On Me" (1990). It's inspiring that a number of R&B artists had a special affinity for recording her white country soul songs, as well, including Louisiana native Joe Simon (who first scored a million seller via a redo of Waylon Jennings hit "The Chokin' Kind," written by Harlan Howard), singing both "In Reach Of Your Arms" and "To Get To You"; Roscoe Shelton, a Tennessee artist who once recorded for Sims Records, also cut a pair of Chapel songs, "I'm Trying To Quit" and "Love Is the Key"; while Herbie Hancock recorded "Triangle"; and Big Joe Turner sang Chapel's "My Reasons For Living."

In 1991, she moved to Florida with her husband, who played guitar, but was not a professional picker. Her daughter Lana, married to Mark Kolb, also lived there, to be by her mother and stepfather Jeffrey Calongne in Port Orange. Like her mother, Lana has a natural talent for songwriting, but she doesn't seem to have the connections to properly pitch her tunes, and living in Florida puts her out of the mainstream.

Jean and Martha's brother Lloyd (Don) Amburgey, also bitten by the entertainment bug, ventured from Ohio to Nashville to seek his own fortune.

"I had been down there as a young fellow sitting in the first or second row at the Ryman once, watching Webb Pierce singing 'There Stands the Glass' (1953) and my sister doing 'Satisfied.' But I never dreamed that I would one day be on that Opry stage. Well, in 1969, my daughter Donna Kaye and I were invited to guest on that same stage - *we done it!*"

Musically, Don's earliest influences weren't his sisters.

"Initially, it wasn't the girls because by the time I got big enough to pay any attention, they were gone. I grew up in Ohio and back then wouldn't think of picking up a guitar. I did listen a lot to WCKY-Cincinnati, so I started liking country music and before long the *Midwestern Hayride* was on TV, and I watched that."

In high school, Don participated in baseball, basketball and track - "I was an athlete first in my mind back then. But, I also played in the school band." As a youngster, he did get to visit WSB-Atlanta: "I went one time to see my sisters, and I met Lily May Ledford, who played guitar. She was just a doll! James Carson played potato bug mandolin. He'd have been a great bluegrass player today. Together, he and Martha kind of led the way as it were..."

Don says both of his brothers are musically-inclined, though neither elected to pursue a music career as he did: "We're all different. Glenn sang in a Fats Domino-style, while Conley, who served 17 years in the sheriff's department here, used to get up and sing once in a while at our shows.

"My earliest influences, however, were singers like Frank Sinatra and Dick Haymes. Cincinnati was strictly a pop town in those days. If you played country you got laughed at. In fact, we were living a couple houses down from an excellent singer named Jack Smith, who made it onto TV himself."

(A labelmate to James & Martha Carson at Capitol, the upbeat Smith, best known as radio's Smilin' Jack Smith, was a tenor who scored best with cover versions of "Civilization (Bongo, Bongo, Bongo)," and "Cruising Down the River," both pop Top 10s. Other Smith successes from 1947-1949, included "Baby Face," "You Call Everybody Darling" and "Sunflower." He also supported Doris Day, another Cincinnati native, in the 1951 Warner Bros. feature film "On Moonlight Bay.")

The middle son, Don attended Oxford University, just up the road in Lima, Ohio.

"Martha and Jean both helped me pay for my college. I don't ever want to forget that," Don acknowledges.

While there he joined the ROTC, and appeared in a musical comedy with the University players: "That was a great thrill.

There were three girls around me and I'm out there doing a Perry Como...it was great fun!"

Unfortunately, it was also the period that the Korean War broke out and Don found himself serving Uncle Sam in the Air Force. When he returned to Cincinnati, he got married for the first time and became a daddy to Donna and Mike.

Don was 19 and Kathleen was 17.

"I was in sales," says Don. "We sold and built homes for people. After nine years, when our marriage fell apart, I was devastated, so I left Ohio."

With the marriage over, Don decided it was time to try his luck in Nashville: "I got disgusted with the domestic stituation at home, more than anything else. I suppose another reason why I chose Nashville was because of Martha, and the music kept pulling me here. Now, I could easily have lived at Martha's or Minnie's. Instead of taking the easy way, I got a little place on 16th Avenue, on what is now Music Row. I think all that was there at the time was Decca Records, the Wilburns (Sure-Fire Music and the Wil-Helm Agency) and maybe two or three other music businesses."

Not one to name drop, he decided if something was going to happen good for him, it would be under his own steam. Possibly his most inspiring contact in town was Sue Brewer, now known for giving helping hands to beginning songwriters.

"The way I discovered her, it had to be fate," says Don. "I was feeling lonely and went out Eighth Avenue to a place called The Zodiac. I was just sitting there I guess, looking sad, because Sue came up to me and said, 'You gotta be a songwriter. Welcome to Nashville.' She had an ol' understanding eye and a big heart. Sue told me about a little efficiency apartment that would be available right behind her's. It was just what I wanted. She also said, *'Let me fix you a home-cooked meal.'* "

While waiting on his own place, he slept *on Susan's floor,* just as the song says.

"One night Harlan Howard walked in and Sue introduced us. He was a helpful guy, who drew me a skeleton of a song, saying,

'Here's what you do. You put it on paper verse, chorus, verse, tag, whatever... I'd go up to Sue's two or three nights a week and just sit around, trying to write."

(Of course, Howard is regarded as the dean of country writers today, thanks to five decades of hit songs, among them "Pick Me Up On Your Way Down," "Heartaches By the Numbers," "I Fall to Pieces," "Key's in the Mailbox," "A Tiger By the Tail," "Too Many Rivers," "No Charge," "Life Turned Her That Way," "Somebody Should Leave" and "Somewhere Tonight.")

Chapel remembers that Harlan had interesting advice for the newcomer: "If you write enough and get them down on paper, then your natural ability will get you a certain number of hits. If you get a certain number of hits, you get a home run. That sounds sort of cold, but it really is a percentage thing."

Sue Brewer, as hinted to earlier, was immortalized by writers Vince Matthews and Shel Silverstein in their 1971 ode "On Susan's Floor," which was first recorded by Mac Wiseman on RCA, and covered by Gordon Lightfoot. (Her special pal Waylon Jennings and another friend Roger Miller later paid homage via a CBS-TV documentary tribute about the songwriters' best friend, also featuring Wiseman warbling the title tune.)

Of course, the song tells the story, *"the homelss found a home on Susan's floor."* These included not only struggling songwriters, but transient artists and pickers. Sue, a bartender, got to know these guys who initially hung out at a late night restaurant to keep out of the cold, when she'd stop in at the eatery to get a snack after completing her shift.

Often they were hassled by police patrolling the area, who would inquire about their address, when really they didn't have one to offer. She was touched by their devotion to a dream of making it in Music City. After determining who were regular guys, she'd allow them to bunk out in an extra bedroom or just on the floor of her living room…

Sometimes she'd count as many as eight a night staying over. Besides Jennings, Miller and Dallas Frazier, there were such future hitmakers as Hank Cochran, Johnny Paycheck, Buddy Emmons, and Kris Kristofferson.

She said one night Cochran actually composed his hit "Don't You Ever Get Tired of Hurting Me" at her place (and which Ray Price cut in 1965). After such guys made it, they'd help her buy groceries to feed "my boys." Realizing the good she was doing, some who were already stars even donated to the cause, among them stalwarts, who had seen hard times earlier: George Jones, Faron Young and Webb Pierce.

Sue said, "Those guys used to give me $100 at a clip and I couldn't have helped the boys a lot of times if it hadn't been for those donations. Occasionally, they'd take some of the musicians out on the road to work, even if they didn't really need them, just to help out."

This benevolent lady would also slip the down-and-out troupers a loan herself from her modest income to tide them through a tough time: "Vince (Matthews) was one of the boys who slept on that floor. When I heard his song about me, I was in Seventh Heaven! It made me feel loved."

Before she began her downhill battle with cancer, which eventually claimed her life, George Jones had engaged her to run his Possum Holler Club.

Don Chapel recalls how he came to write his biggest success - and the part Sue Brewer and Jones played in it: "You see, I'm a family man and I missed my little children so much. I was just sitting in my apartment one night, feeling depressed and I wondered, 'When am I gonna get over this,' then it hit me, *when the grass grows over me…*

"I had played that song for Sue and she said, 'Give me a tape on that,' on which there was only me and my guitar. Then one day I came home and she had stuck a note on my door saying, *'George Jones' cutting your song, tonight at 6 o'clock!'* That was a thrill. Then he and Melba (Montgomery) recorded some of my songs."

At the time, Chapel placed his songs with Glad Music.

"When the Grass Grows Over Me," as recorded by George Jones, would become his biggest hit. "When the Grass..." was also recorded by Liz Anderson, Ernest Tubb, Conway Twitty, Jack Greene and Jerry Lee Lewis. Jones also cut Chapel's "From Here To the Door," and with Melba Montgomery did "Call Off the Party" and "Let's Get Together," which they used as an album title on Musicor.

Other Don Chapel songs recorded include "All Night Long," cut by Johnny Duncan, Jerry Lee Lewis, Peggy Sue (Loretta Lynn's sister), Randy Travis and Merle Haggard, and by Joe Walsh on the "Urban Cowboy" movie soundtrack; "United We Stand, Divided We Fall," recorded by Tammy Wynette and David Houston, also Anne Murray and Glen Campbell; "Misty Morning Rain" by Ray Price; the lesser known "My Heart is Soaking Wet" and "Joey's Song," both cut by Wynette.

"It's not easy getting songs to leading artists," recalls Chapel. "I guess in the long run, I was closer to sister Jean in Nashville. Martha was off to New York and L.A. when I first came here, so Jean and I had more time together. I watched her write and she absolutely helped influence me a lot."

In homage to his sister, he adopted the surname Chapel. One time in bringing him on stage to sing for the customers, she said, *"Let's hear a song from my brother Don."* Thus, he became Don Chapel, singer-songwriter.

The process of writing for him is a simple one, says Don: "I don't write every day. But when I write a song, the melody comes right along with the lyrics, like an 'instant' marriage."

An early part of Chapel's plan was to try his hand as a recording artist. He fronted the bands Nashville Image and High Chapparel, before linking up with the woman who became Tammy Wynette.

"I recorded on Musicor first. That's when I became a sort of running buddy of George Jones. I did two sessions for (Harold) Pappy Daily and then I re-signed. I left Musicor to go with CBS, as I wanted to record duets with Tammy, because then I wanted us to be together. I had two CBS singles, 'Hurtin' Time' and 'Summer Winds' (which later, in 1988, became a #2 record for the Desert Rose Band). "

At CBS, Don was first produced by Billy Sherrill. It also marked the first time Don had recorded on more than one track. He immediately liked Billy's style as a producer: "He produced my first session, after I left Musicor. After that, he said he was too busy and he had (Royce) Glenn Sutton take over A&R for me. He (Sutton) was the guy who married Lynn Anderson (and wrote 'You're My Man' and 'Keep Me in Mind' for her)."

Speaking of weddings, Chapel had married wannabe singer Wynette Byrd *nee* Tammy Wynette, as chronicled in *Music City News'* "Down South With Dixie (Deen)" column in September 1967: *"Who other than (booker) Hubert Long could manage to book a European honeymoon? Newlywed Tammy Wynette and Don Chapel are departing on a 26-day tour of England and Germany beginning Sept. 1. That's what you call a long one!"*

In 1967, Don also brought teen-aged daughter Donna Kaye to Nashville to tour with him and Tammy on his bus, which advertised the *Don Chapel Show featuring Tammy Wynette.*

Here's how it began for Don and Tammy: Early in 1966, the former Virginia Wynette Pugh arrived in Nashville in a beat-up car, with no contacts and a whole lot of hopes to become a country music star. She had completed beauty school in Birmingham, after breaking up with first husband Euple Byrd, and her main professional credit was singing on the WBRC-TV *Country Boy Eddie* (Burns) morning show in Birmingham.

In retrospect, she said her fascination with Don Chapel grew out of loneliness, but he was just getting a leg up on the music scene and was then recording with Musicor, under the aegis of veteran producer Pappy Daily. A Texan, Daily had promoted the careers of such promising artists as Arlie Duff, George Jones, Judy Lynn, Gene Pitney, Melba Montgomery and Roger Miller. Surely none of this was lost on the struggling Wynette Byrd.

She was born May 5, 1942, in Itawamba County, Mississippi, just across the Alabama state line. Her musician father William Hollis Pugh died at 26, when she was eight months old. Her mother left her with her parents, reportedly to work in a defense plant in Birmingham.

Much of little Virginia Wynette's youth was spent in the care of the maternal grandparents on a farm in Red Bay, Ala., where she picked cotton and sang the songs of Kitty Wells, most notably "How Far Is Heaven" - "Mother asked me to learn that. It was so close to home, you see, Daddy being dead." (Another song that caught her ear was Martha Carson's bombastic "Satisfied.") In keeping with her father's request, her mother had paid for five years of her daughter's music lessons, which served her well in years to come.

"I dreamed of being a singer, but I also wanted to be a housewife and mother like my girlfriends. When two of my best friends got married, during our senior year in high school, I mistook infatuation for love and did the same thing. I thought marriage would get me off the farm..."

As a wife, she found herself living in poverty. The couple had three daughters, Gwen, Jackie and Tina (who was born prematurely and suffered from spinal meningitis). Their mother worked briefly as a chiropractor's receptionist before studying cosmetology, and also worked in a lounge.

Following her graduation from beauty school, she made trips to Memphis and Music City seeking help with a singing career. Her tapes were left with representatives of Hickory, United Artists and Kapp, but to no avail.

According to Chapel, "I was working as a night desk clerk at the Anchor Inn Motel on West End Avenue. She had called for a reservation as she was supposedly coming up here to see Porter Wagoner about a job with his group. Well, when she got here, I found we hadn't marked her down, and I felt bad, so I put her in the Bridal Suite - and she loved that!

"Later, she called down to say her meeting with Porter had fallen through and could she come down and watch TV in the lobby. We talked and got to know each other a bit. When I walked her back upstairs to her suite, as a joke, I picked her up and carried her over the threshold, since it was the Bridal Suite! There was a guitar there, so I asked her to sing for me. And, as soon as I heard her, I thought, *'Wow! This gal can really sing!'*

"When I took her to George Jones' Possum Hollow Club on Broad Street, I got her up to sing for the crowd. I didn't know that George was her childhood idol. Anyway, we had a fling that night.

"When she came back up with her children, they moved into the motel with me. The management had allowed me to have a suite there to live in. But you should have seen her when she moved up here...

"She came in a '60 Chevrolet on four bald tires, no suitcases...she just threw the clothes into the car, and the kids were laying on top of the clothes. This gal, who would become a country queen, had dark roots showing through the blonde, and she had 32 cavities in her mouth (I learned later).

"When the management discovered her and the kids there in the motel with me, I was fired. We then moved into a two-bedroom apartment in East Nashville, where we stayed three weeks, before they put us out for not paying the rent. We really had some bad times at first...

"When I got married with her, we continued to have our problems. I think her children loved me then. I tried to treat them just like my own. Actually, I felt terribly sorry for them - the way she treated them so coldly. I told her that one day they would abandon her -- and I'd heard that they did for a time. All that mattered to her was a career. I had no children with Tammy, thank God!"

Chapel said he is the one who introduced her to Billy Sherrill, who at the time was looking for a female singer to work with. Sherrill had in mind Ruby Wright, but on advice from others, she didn't continue with him, though she was at Epic, if only briefly. Earlier, Chapel had taken Tammy to RCA and Imperial, neither of which were interested in signing her.

Don contends for publicity purposes, the star liked to say that she came to Sherrill's office one noon when his secretary was out to lunch and sashayed right on in and sang for him - and that's the story most scribes stuck to in writing about her. There's no mention of Chapel.

"Truth is, I had heard this fantastic record on David Houston, 'Almost Persuaded,' so I went down to the Ernest Tubb Record Shop to buy it. It was on Epic, a label I hadn't heard of, but discovered was part of Columbia. And (pianist) Billy Sherrill had produced it. So, I had her practice several songs before I went to his office - without an appointment. It was true his secretary was at lunch, so I barged on in, saw him sitting there at this old beat-up desk, knocked and called out, 'Anybody home?' He said, 'Yeah, in here.'

"Believe me, it wasn't a great looking place - I think they were in the process of relocating or something - but whoa! this guy had produced a terrific session on David Houston. So, I told him, *'I've got this great singer who will replace Loretta Lynn in a year.'*

"He had her sing - and I think he then figured I knew what I was talking about. At the time, I don't think they had anyone but Lois Johnson and Stan Hitchcock on the label.

"You know at first she wanted to use her real name, but I told her *Tammy Wynette* sounded better. I remembered that song 'Tammy' and thought it fit her. I had also bounced it off my sister Jean, who said, 'She looks like a Tammy to me.' Billy agreed: 'I like it.' So that's how she got her show name."

Shortly after her arrival, Don had hooked Tammy up with his sister Jean, who liked her vocals so much she engaged Tammy to cut demo tapes of Jean's compositions intended for "pitching" to other artists.

"I wrote two songs with Tammy to make her look more like a writer in the marketplace. One was titled 'I've Stayed Long Enough.' I still have the original demo with both of us singing the song. Yet, she took it to Al Gallico (publisher) and put only her name on it. There wasn't really anything I could do about it. You can point out the similarities between the song and 'When the Grass Grows Over Me.' Tammy wasn't really a writer. She says she co-wrote 'Stand By Your Man' with Billy (in 25 minutes), but to me, it's got Billy Sherrill all over it."

Walt Trott

CHAPTER 26

Run 'em Off...

*"I left CBS because I didn't want
any more affiliation with Tammy,
to have to go to the same social events
or to be with DJs in the same room..."*

Even back then, Don had great respect for Billy Norris Sherrill, who had produced a variety of acts, ranging from the R&B Staple Singers to country's Charlie Walker, and was then helping to redefine the *Nashville Sound*.

Born Nov. 5, 1936, in Alabama, Billy was the son of an itinerant Baptist preacher. He got his start playing piano and saxophone in blues and rock bands, before moving to Nashville, where he landed a job as engineer for (ex-Sun Records legend) Sam Phillips' new label Phillips International.

Besides "Stand By Your Man," he co-wrote the classics "Almost Persuaded" (which earned him a 1966 Grammy for best song), Charlie Rich's "The Most Beautiful Girl (in the World)" and Wynette's "I Don't Wanna Play House" and, in fact, is credited with a record 66 country BMI awards (not counting 16 that garnered BMI pop citations, as well).

Sherrill helped make stars of such struggling artists as David Houston, Jody Miller, Johnny Paycheck, Barbara Mandrell, Wynette, David Allan Coe and Tanya Tucker, while injecting new zip into the careers of George Jones, Bobby Vinton, Marty Robbins, Freddy Weller and Charlie Rich.

Don's daughter Donna sang backup with Wynette during their touring days together, and after Tammy had her first chart record "Apartment #9." Incidentally, Paycheck had written that song and it was initially recorded for Tally Records by Bobby Austin, a session fiddler (who had been in Wynn Stewart's band), but it had stalled on *Billboard's* country chart at #21 in the winter of '66.

"I had tried to buy the master from that little label it was on, but they wouldn't sell. Meanwhile, I thought it would be a great woman's song. I played the record for her (Tammy) and she thought it was great, too," explained Sherrill. "At that time, I had no female artists to produce, so we recorded it the next night...at the end of that track, (session leader) Jerry Kennedy turned and said, *'Do you realize what you've got there?'* And, we hadn't yet given her a new show name."

Although peaking at a disappointing #44, it started a long string of successes for the Sherrill-Wynette team. Their follow-up single, "Your Good Girl's Gonna Go Bad" (titled apparently on the mark in Don's mind), hit #3 on *Billboard,* first charting March 18, 1967.

The newcomer followed that with a duet featuring super-hot David Houston, "My Elusive Dreams," which became credit-wise her first chart-topper (while she and Don were then touring in Europe).

In a 1967 interview with writer Dixie Deen (now Mrs. Tom T. Hall) for *Music City News,* Tammy confided, *"Mother had always wanted me to sing, but she has never liked the idea of me working in clubs where there is drinking, and where I often have to perform. I personally don't - and neither does my husband (Don) - care a thing about drinking. I don't think social drinking is wrong, but neither do I believe that you have to be a drinker to work in clubs...believe me, Dixie, I love my husband and children more than anything else in this world, and I am doing what I believe in my heart is best. Mother does like my records though."*

Chapel began suspecting that there might be something developing between his wife and sometimes-touring partner-Jones during their gigs, and hired a detective to pursue the matter: "He (the private eye) caught up to her in Louisiana, shacked up with Jones..."

Meanwhile, Wynette's first solo number one record was "I Don't Wanna Play House," which hit top spot Oct. 14, 1967, and hung in there three weeks of its 20-week run on *Billboard.* Early in 1968, she was riding high with another number one, "Take Me To Your World," followed by yet another "D-I-V-O-R-C-E," which also proved prophetic for the Chapels.

Don says the scene in which he confronted them both with his evidence of infidelity was unlike the Hollywoodized version where Jones the actor thrust a chair through a window of the Chapels' 17-room Hendersonville home to "rescue" her from an unhappy situation: *"That was pure fabrication. There was no glass broken and I ran 'em both off, yelling, 'Get out of this house!' What husband wouldn't? I was totally true to her and her actions just blew me away!"*

He also had some show dates booked up in Maine, which, unprofessionally, she failed to keep. Apparently concerned that Chapel might go public with the detective's findings, he said Tammy told him to keep their Hendersonville house and their nine-room lake-front property, and she would make the payments on those.

Once he refused her offer, Don says she threatened to do everything she could to scuttle his career chances. Shortly after she ditched him for Jones, Chapel invited his ex-wife Kathleen down from Ohio to help look after sons Michael and Gary.

"Tammy called demanding to know why she was there," adds Chapel. "I explained I needed help with the children, but she screamed at me, *'Get that bitch out of my house, or I'm gonna burn it down!'* It was then 'MY' house not ours. She didn't care anything about the kids either.

"I had thought she and Donna got along OK. But after it was all over, Donna said sometimes she'd come back on the bus and chew her out for supposedly making mistakes on stage. That didn't exactly build her image. She just hated my son Michael because he looked like his mother. What a narrow vision she had…I was deeply hurt by her and Jones' affair. He had been my longtime friend, or so I thought.

"I left CBS because I didn't want any more affiliation with Tammy, to have to go to the same social events or to be with DJs in the same room. I didn't want to have to try and be sweet and pleasant," says Don Chapel. "It was not a good situation, and I'm sure it wasn't a good financial decision on my part, leaving a major label like that."

Another story he brands "untrue" that made the rounds - and which cut to the bone - was that he showed nude photos of his wife to other men. He feels that such an allegation by her - or anyone else - is beneath contempt, but suspects it was a way to hurt his credibility, if he spoke out about her extramarital affair.

Shortly after their split, Chapel had recorded a single titled "In a Phone Booth (On My Knees)" about a jilted lover trying to win his woman back. He had second thoughts about that track: "She just had 'D-I-V-O-R-C-E' out and I thought it over and didn't want that message to go out to the public. I didn't need any reminders, I just wanted to go on from that. By the way, *I divorced her* - and it's right on record at the Metro Courthouse. She had such a preposterous history of lies that I prayed God to help straighten her out."

Wynette had briefly traveled with *The Porter Wagoner Show,* which was then one of the hottest on the road. He had just lost Norma Jean (mother of his daughter Roma), who departed the still-married Wagoner's troupe to pursue a solo gig. A disappointed Wynette wasn't hired permanently, but another young blonde from Sevierville, Tenn., did fill the bill: Dolly Parton. Had she toured full-time with Wagoner, Tammy might never have teamed with Jones.

On Aug. 22, 1968, Tammy first announced she and George were wed (though the only official ceremony documented is Feb. 16, 1969). Tammy and George Jones' marriage produced a daughter, Tamala Georgette (Oct. 5, 1970) - and yet another divorce decree for Tammy, in 1975, allegedly due to his drinking problem. Of their marital differences, Tammy stated facetiously, "I always said he nipped and I nagged!"

"D-I-V-O-R-C-E" didn't spell the end of Don Chapel's life or career, it merely presented a slight detour. There were other factors that prompted his decision to back off and concentrate more on songwriting. Don's 15-year-old daughter Donna Kaye, who served her apprenticeship as backup vocalist with stepmother Tammy Wynette, had landed her own Columbia Records' contract. She needed Dad's help. Her debut single, "If I Were a Little Girl," was released Sept. 15, 1968, while her dad was still signed to Epic Records, a Columbia affiliate. At the time, Chapel's other children were Mike, 13, and Gary, 6.

Both Don and his daughter had signed with the Joe Taylor Agency for bookings. Donna's first performance professionally was at a National Guard Armory in Jacksonville, Fla., more than a year before her pact with Columbia. That was when Wynette was headlining the troupe. Donna sang Bobbie Gentry's then-current hit "Ode to Billie Joe," but was so stage shy, she ran right to the dressing room after completing the number. A rousing reception from the crowd prompted two encores, which did not delight her stepmother, insists Chapel.

With her dad's show, Donna performed in New York City's Nashville Room, Minneapolis' renowned Flame Club, and the Longhorn Ballroom and Panther Hall in Dallas-Fort Worth, among other notable venues. She also toured overseas in England and Germany. A news report in the December 1968 issue of *Country Music Life* magazine, published in Orange, Calif., explains what happened to Don and Donna Kaye later: *"Don Chapel and his daughter Donna have each signed a recording contract with Monument Records, and will each have a record released soon after the first of the year, according to Monument A&R Director and producer Fred Foster."*

Don had left Epic Records (by his own request) and then obtained the release of his daughter Donna from Columbia. She had been under contract only a few months, but Tammy was fast becoming the group's top female sales star. Thus the father and daughter team went into a closed session Nov. 12, to record singles by Don, and duets by Don and Donna. Foster was reportedly impressed enough with the session to immediately sign both to long-term recording contracts.

Despite such a promising beginning, the stars obviously weren't aligned just right in Donna Kaye's orbit, and perhaps she was overwhelmed personally by the well-publicized bad blood between her former stepmother and father; whatever the reason, she soon stepped out of the spotlight, turning her back on Music City for good.

Ironically, at the very time that Don Chapel was coping with his latest personal anguish, the composer's great musical breakthrough "When the Grass Grows Over Me" was bringing major success to George Jones, the man responsible for his grief. Chapel's song was Jones' Musicor solo follow-up to his 1968 hit "As Long As I Live" (co-written with Gene Pitney), a single that peaked at #3, while the vocalist was romancing the then-Mrs. Chapel.

On Nov. 23, 1968, "When the Grass Grows Over Me" made its *Billboard* debut, and would enjoy a healthy 17-week run on the country charts, peaking at #2 for two weeks. Oddly enough, while Tammy and George were exchanging holy vows, her recent husband's creation was riding high on the charts - as sung by her new bridegroom.

In response to Chapel's criticism about her career-oriented attitude when she hit town, Wynette admitted candidly, after the fact, "I put my career first before anything. I put my career before my children when I first came to Nashville. I defend myself on that because I had to. If I had put my children first, we would have starved to death. I had to put my children second and work on my career, so I could put food in their mouths and a roof over their heads, 'cause it was left up to me to do it. I did what I had to do, what I was forced to do. For example, when I got my first bus, I couldn't afford a driver. So I drove my own bus. I did things a lot of women wouldn't attempt to do, but when you're limited like that, you find alternatives."

Although those duets that Don had dreamed about making with wife Tammy were never-to-be, she joined voices with

Jones, and from 1971 through 1980, the team charted 13 tunes, ranging from "Take Me" (#9) to "A Pair of Old Sneakers" (#19) for Epic. Jones continues today as an important voice in country music, and was inducted into the Country Hall of Fame in 1992. He appears to have found a happier union with wife Nancy, a non-professional, who helped him turn away from drinking.

During their several stormy years together, George and Tammy became known affectionately by fans as *Mr. & Mrs. Country Music*. Many of them were irate when their female favorite didn't heed her own musical advice to "Stand By Your Man," and proceeded to divorce the *ol' possum* in 1975.

Subsequently, she was married briefly (44 days) to musician-realtor (John) Michael Tomlin, whom she accused of taking her to the cleaners for $15,000, though he denied it: "I have never said an unkind word about Tammy since our separation and I don't intend to start now. I lost more than money when we separated." It wasn't until late summer 1977, that they reached a compromise financially (Tomlin had reportedly asked $30,000 initially).

Less than a year later, she was taking vows with her fifth husband, producer-pianist-songwriter George (Richardson) Richey on July 6, 1978, a marriage that lasted until her death, April 6, 1998, allegedly from a blood clot to the lung. He also served as her manager and occasional co-writer.

No stranger to tragedy, Richey's ex-wife Sheila Hall Richardson was despondent and allegedly committed suicide at age 37; but, oddly enough, her beloved poodle was also found dead. George's children, Deidre and Kelly, were by his first wife, Dorothy Ann Tippitt, who also divorced him, citing abusive behavior.

Even before they wed, George Richey and Tammy had their ups and downs. Perhaps their most bizarre incident was the alleged 1978 abduction of Tammy from Nashville's Green Hills shopping center, during which she was supposedly beaten and abandoned on Interstate 65 (55 miles south of Nashville) near Pulaski. No one was ever arrested in that highly-publicized case.

Some hinted Jones was behind it, but Tammy's elder daughter Jackie Daly wrote in her recent biography that stepfather George Richey conceived it as a cover-up for bruises he may have inflicted on his wife.

Six months after Wynette's death, her daughters were telling Nashville Channel 5-WTVF television commentator Larry Brinton that it's their desire to have their mother's body exhumed for a full autopsy. Presumedly, Jackie Daly and siblings Tina Jones and Georgette Smith were upset amid reports of their then-62-year-old stepfather's alleged romance with ex-Dallas Cowboys' Cheerleader Sheila Slaughter, 32, so near to Wynette's passing.

They soon instigated a $50 million wrongful death lawsuit against Richey and Dr. Wallis Marsh of Pittsburgh, Pa. (Tammy's elder daughter Gwen Nicholas was not a participant initially, but soon climbed aboard the legal-wagon, as all the facts unfolded.)

Supposedly, TV producer Slaughter became close to the widower, while working on a program saluting the songstress (who was posthumously inducted into the Country Music Hall of Fame, Sept. 23, 1998, along with Elvis Presley and George Morgan).

Assuredly, the untimely April 6, 1998 death of Wynette, at age 55, left a lot of unanswered questions. Reportedly, Sunday (April 5) she told her husband she was suffering some pain after having problems with an intestinal blockage. Richey allegedly telephoned her primary physician, Dr. Marsh in Pittsburgh, saying his wife was showing symptoms of a blood clot. Reportedly, this prompted Marsh to say she should check into a hospital.

According to Richey's sister-in-law Sylvia Richey, the couple's administrative assistant, instead Tammy said a little later Sunday that she was feeling better and was not going to the hospital. On Monday, the star died at her home on Franklin Road - according to George Richey, at around 7 p.m. Her daughter Gwen arrived at 7:30 p.m.

Police were not notified until nearly 9 p.m. Tammy's daughter Jackie Daly said she visited her mother's house around noon and found her asleep on the sofa. Before departing, she asked her stepfather to let her mom know she had been by. After going out to dinner that night, Jackie returned to her home to find a message that her mother had died.

When the daughter arrived at the Richey house, she was surprised to find her mom's body still lying on the sofa, "in a fetal position." She was stunned to see people coming and going, staring at her mother's lifeless body. Police officer Doug Anderson also noted Sheila Slaughter arrived there "in her pajamas."

Wynette's hairdresser Jan Smith stated that someone had called as early as 5:30 p.m. Monday, informing her of the singer's death. A media inquiry regarding the entertainer's death came into police headquarters at 7 p.m. (from the *National Enquirer* magazine). Meanwhile, shortly after the Richeys' lawyer Ralph Gordon's arrival on the scene, he telephoned 911 (reportedly at 8:55 p.m.): "When I got there, I asked if anybody had called 911, and they said no..."

Sylvia Richey in a later press conference, stated that she and George felt 911 was for the living (who could be saved), and that's why they didn't dial it. Nonetheless, Richey called Dr. Marsh to charter a plane and fly down to sign her death certificate.

Marsh's brief examination of the dead woman, he stated, convinced him she had died from *a blood clot to the lungs,* which he cited as the cause, signing the document long hours after her death.

Later, Nashville Medical Examiner Bruce Levy would say that he might have performed an autopsy had he been informed by Marsh that the deceased was taking narcotics, antibiotics and a blood thinner prior to her death.

The physician's defense was that he had assumed home healthcare nurses tending Mrs. Richey had relayed such information to the appropriate authorities.

In June 1996, the veteran vocalist had signed a will that left her $1.008 million home and personal property to husband George Richey (plus a $1 million insurance policy), and named him and his brother Paul Richey as co-executors. She waived any requirement for an official inventory of the estate's assets, stipulating that the remainder of her estate would go in trust for the benefit of her four daughters, his two children, and their seven grandchildren. Further, songwriting and performance royalties would go into trust, but no distribution of these should be made until after Richey's death.

Three of Tammy's daughters banded together to file a $50 million lawsuit against Richey, who admittedly administered some of his wife's medications (through a catheter in her large vein), and Marsh, whom they claim gave her too many painkillers, and didn't monitor her medical condition close enough.

This prompted an autopsy on April 14, which did cast doubt on Marsh's "blood clot on the lung" death declaration. The artist's daughters feel she could have lived longer with proper medical care, and sadly had become "addicted" to her drugs.

On April 7, 1999, Dr. Marsh had issued a statement denying any such wrongdoing and insists he "provided extraordinary medical care to a person who suffered extraordinary medical problems," and implied the daughters' suit was without merit.

In turn, Richey petitioned April 22, 1999, for dismissal of his name from the lawsuit, which he contends wrongfully charges him with *medical malpractice.* His motion claims that's invalid as he is not a doctor. (A judge later ruled in his favor.)

That autopsy indeed prompted a change to cause of death being from "heart failure" prompted by "cardiac arrhythmia," whatever that means: *a heart attack?* Tammy's girls are still awaiting their day in court.

Shortly after Wynette's death, Opry veteran Jean Shepard confided that she admired the star's spunk earlier, and recalled that she first met the blonde singer when she was *Mrs. Don Chapel.* "They had a bus, and she was driving that bus! Later, she, George (Jones) and I worked together helping (Alabama) Gov. George Wallace (campaign). I was then very large with my baby, who's now 29 years old. She patted my tummy, looked at Jones and said, 'That's what I want.' She called me some time later and said, 'Guess what?' I said, *'You're pregnant.'* She said, 'How did you know?' I said, 'A lucky guess.' Tammy was Tammy. She never changed."

Don Chapel enjoyed another Top 40 success in late 1979, when Ray Price released his recording of "Misty Morning Rain," which charted nine weeks for Monument Records. Chapel continued with his writing and was married nearly 20 years to third wife Beth, mother of his two children: Robbie, now 16, and Allison, 10. He also got into studio production to help put bread on their table. Divorce also ended that liaison.

In 1995, never-say-die Don and his fourth wife, Gobie, were wed.

"I just love her. She's so precious," said Martha, at the time. "She's blonde and a very good Christian lady. I remember telling her, *God took our Jean, but sent you to us."*

The Amburgeys didn't shy away from second chances - or third and fourth chances - at marital happiness. After about five years of being a widow, Don's mother Gertrude had also married again, a widower named Edgar Ramsey.

"Minnie knew him in Ohio," says Martha. "He and his wife had been friends with my Daddy and Mother. After his wife passed away and Mama had lost Daddy, they got together through the church...I'm not sure it was what you'd call a real love match, but somehow they decided to marry...I guess he'd been dead about 15 years (before Gertrude's death)."

While Don and Jean were enjoying success with their writing, Martha's career was in a slump. A 1967 *Variety* item had reported Martha Carson "signed" with Decca Records. Despite discussions with the label's Owen Bradley, nothing had really developed. Her career was actually put "on hold" as she spent more time with her boys.

During the 1970s, Jesse Winchester, a Shreveport, La.-born pop singer, recorded Carson's "I Can't Stand Up Alone." He's the middle-of-the road artist who became a Canadian citizen in 1973 (protesting the war in Vietnam), and is probably best known for his 1981 hit "Say What."

Martha says her "Satisfied" has been recorded 136 different times, relying on a recent count. (The latest was a duet by Dolly Parton and gospel star Vestal Goodman.)

Off stage, Martha's joys have always been cooking, sewing and gardening. She has a taste for shrimp and liked it when X would take her to New Orleans, where they could indulge themselves at seafood restaurants and listening to Dixieland jazz.

"I remember going down once on a night train - a sleeper. I was just bushed, really worn out," Martha recalls. " I had lived all my life with a prayer to one day get down there to the home of Dixieland jazz. So I looked forward to that trip.

"Dixieland jazz had been one of my favorite music forms since I heard it as a child on the radio," she continues. "As a matter of fact, I loved Pete Fountain to death. He then had his Pete Fountain Sextet at the Roosevelt Hotel Ballroom in New Orleans. You remember I had worked with Pete at Grossinger's in New York. That had been a big thrill for me, because I had been one of his biggest fans."

Whether living in the constant shadow of the road or simply working at being a homemaker, whenever she received a request from one of her fans, Martha would generally respond with a personal note. She also relished family get-togethers when they would all "pick and sing," and looked forward to holiday dinners with her husband and sons, especially Thanksgiving and Christmas.

Martha adds fondly, *"My boys, though they're grown now, still come home for the holidays and I fix dinner with all the trimmings. Even when I was working so much, I usually always managed to be at home with them for the holidays."*

CHAPTER 27

Career Sunset...

*"Whenever I'm forbidden to do something,
I'm just hell-bound to do it."*

"The hardest thing I ever did in my life was to give up that audience," sighs Martha Carson. "That audience is the only time in my life that I ever experienced complete love that gave me confidence for what I have in my heart, and what I want to do - and it gives me the feeling I am able to do it, professionally.

"The audience gives that to me, I don't have it otherwise. Until I walk out on that stage, I am empty as an artist. I find I can do all things, once I get in front of that crowd," continues Carson. "They ignite something in me that nothing else can."

What wasn't easy for the artist in her was the fact that the man who should have been her knight in shining armor wasn't there for her careerwise by the mid-1960s.

Admittedly, he did turn to Martha when someone failed to show or whenever he felt a need for her talent.

"Sometimes he'd have me open a show, but he was very cold about it. He'd say something like, 'They wouldn't approve of you being on the bill, because you're my wife.' Then he'd schedule someone else. I heard that a lot of people had come up to him on the festival dates and inquired about me a lot. I don't think X liked that."

While she watched Kitty Wells' career continue in full swing - and she was two years older than Martha - X would tell his wife that she was too old to perform anymore and her place now was at home.

"Those years I didn't have my audience, there was an awful lot I missed," she stresses. "It took the heartbeat out of my professional life. I was simply a shell, walking around, not fully living. I was hungering so much to sing that I did write a lot more...If someone wanted me to do a benefit, I'd do it. Otherwise, I just erased myself from the scene."

Although her manager-husband seemed to have simply put the lid on Martha Carson, performer, she devoted herself to her sons: "I love to cook, so I concentrated on being a good mother - and a good wife."

On a local basis, however, she was being coaxed by Smilin' Eddie Hill to rejoin her traveling buddies Kitty and Smiley Wilson on his WLAC early morning show. Martha confides: "For two or three years, I did that TV show, until X became jealous of the man sponsoring the program. He was telling the audience that I was one of his favorites, and X thought the man had designs on me. That got kind of messy for me."

André recalls, "I was never into country music much. What I knew about my mother's music, I had only heard on TV. I remember she performed on the Eddie Hill show. At that time, while I was growing up, there were many influential music people coming to our house, artists like Chet Atkins and Tammy Wynette, but I really didn't know who they were.

"When my mother was doing the morning TV show, she'd get breakfast ready for us boys before we went to school. Between that time and when she traveled, we had a lady named Miss Haywood who looked after us."

Meanwhile, Nashville was developing into something other than a country capital, with pop music notables turning to studios in Music City, seeking a new sound for their albums. By late 1965, the list included Perry Como, Peter, Paul & Mary, Ray Charles, Dean Martin, Connie Francis, The Ventures, Vic Damone and the zany Spike Jones crew. In 1968, Bob Dylan had his "John Wesley Harding" Columbia LP out, and during February 1969, he returned to record his famed "Nashville Skyline" album, inviting country legend Johnny Cash in to record.

In *Record World* trade magazine's year-end balloting for 1965, Cossé's artists Chet Atkins and Floyd Cramer won #1 and

#2 Top Instrumentalists honors, attesting to the popularity these musicians enjoyed on record and road-show appearances. Ironically, Kitty Wells, 46, was still hanging in there popularity-wise, tying for top female vocalist with Loretta Lynn, while another newcomer Dottie West was in second place. Buck Owens was top male vocalist, and won best album, as well, with "I've Got a Tiger By the Tail," while Sonny James' "You're the Only World I Know" earned best single trophy. The Wilburns won as best vocal duo, after the Louvins had disbanded.

The nation was mired down in another police action in South Vietnam that soon escalated into a war that would help topple a President (LBJ) and fuel the comeback of controversial politico Richard M. Nixon.

When it came to politics, the Cossés' usually kept hands-off; however, Carson's feelings got the best of her on one occasion: "Mayor (Beverly) Briley was running for re-election, and Brenda Lee was doing TV commercials for Casey Jenkins...I felt as though he was spewing racial hatred, and I didn't approve of that.

"Well, X was fixin' to go to Canada on one of his tours with Chet, Boots and Floyd. I told him I ought to call the Mayor's office to see if I could do anything to help his campaign, but X said, 'No! Don't you dare get involved!'

"I'm a strong Democrat, and whenever I'm forbidden to do something, I'm just hell-bound to do it. I also believed that I could write a commercial, then go in and do something to help Mayor Briley. It kept eating on me after X left on his trip, so while sitting at the pool, I got me a piece of paper and wrote something, then called the Mayor's office, asking if they'd like me to do it.

"They said he'd be delighted if I'd do it! So they set me up at WSIX-TV, around the corner from where I lived at the time (Curry Road) on Murfreesboro Road. I remember a guy saying, 'Miss Carson, would you like a chair?' I said, 'No sir, just sit me up a fence there; I want to talk over the fence to the neighbors!' I finished the video and they used it. They said it was most effective.

"Anyway, the Mayor won and he personally brought me this Appreciation plaque to my house after the election was over - and I cherish it! It was dated Aug. 26, 1971. I know he had some problems, but he was a better Mayor drinking than most mayors are sober."

Unfortunately, drinking became a problem in Martha's household, as well. By the 1970s, her husband's indulgence was beginning to interfere with his work. Word was drifting back to her about X's neglecting his duties on the road.

"Sometimes show time would come and he wasn't able to get out of the hotel and over to the auditorium," explains Carson. "He'd have his secretary or a stagehand go over and 'open' the box office on his behalf. He'd say, 'Tell 'em I'll be over at intermission.' That irritated the artists, as it would have me. Ultimately, it affected his relationship with them. Once they decided they didn't want to work anymore with him…it really tore him up."

She began noticing that before she could prepare breakfast for him, he would have gotten up and mixed himself a drink. This despite the fact that he was experiencing heart problems.

During the early 1970s, X suffered prostate problems and in 1973 underwent open heart surgery.

"He was told not to drink anymore," recalls Martha. "But that didn't stop his drinking."

Besides hurting his own health, his drinking habit began hurting their family life, and was eating into their savings and eventually caused the Cossés to sell off all their properties, which had been their choice for investment in the future - and a nest egg for their retirement years. It also meant there was no inheritance for their sons.

As if all this wasn't enough, Martha suffered a fall that nearly took her life in '73.

"It was the time I went up to New York with X, for him to undergo acupuncture on his back, as he was in such pain. And I loved to go there to shop," she relates. "While we were gone, our cleaning lady had decided to change the breezeway furniture around. We had wrought iron tables with Plexiglas tops, so you could sit out there, relax and have some refreshments.

"There were some plastic coverings out there, and when we got home, I stepped on plastic and slipped, bumping over furniture, until the fall pitched me forward...I hit my head on a table! Well, it sliced my scalp open - and X nearly went crazy. But despite being stunned, I got up, walked across the breezeway and went inside, proceeding to wash the blood off, while he summoned an ambulance crew.

"They rushed me to the emergency room to be stitched up, and I was hospitalized for several weeks. I heard later that I was near death, and they had inserted a metal plate in my head..."

For the next 20 years, the singer suffered severe headaches, going back and forth to doctors, trying to determine why and how to treat her condition: "The first doctor thought it had to do with my vision. But you know, I think doctors take it for granted that all women just whine."

While Martha took comfort in teen-aged André's pride in his school work, a wholesome interest in athletics, and an apparent determination to make something of himself in life, she was beginning to worry about his younger brother: "Once René was 16, he took driving school and passed, but his father didn't seem to appreciate that; yet, when André turned 16, X took him right down to buy a car - and he hadn't really learned how to drive properly. So, he takes it out and wrecks it!"

Despite their father's seeming show of favoritism, the brothers' relationship remained warm and friendly for the most part, untainted by hostile rivalry as one might expect would occur between them.

"I remember the time we even played on the same baseball team," notes René, who pitched, played on third and sometimes caught in the outfield.

"Yeah, one year he got cut from the team and the next year he came back and made the team, so we played ball together," adds André. "I was a catcher in the outfield mostly. My brother was amazing! Playing on the same team together was real fun."

Martha's grateful her sons are friends, "They're very close and they even play golf together at times."

André admits his parents had their hands full with his rebellious ways: "I was a growing boy, who used to experiment around a little bit (with drugs). When I was 16, it was rampant in the schools; it was everywhere, until I learned it just wasn't for me."

In 1977, Moe Lytle contracted Martha to re-record some of her classic gospel tunes for the Gusto independent label. It also marked a comeback of sorts for the former Opry great. *Country Style* magazine headlined "Spirituals great Martha Carson returns," citing the new recordings, the growth of her strapping sons, and the resumed touring under the banner of Buddy Lee Attractions.

In a 1978 by-lined comeback story "Martha Carson is back," the *Nashville Banner's* Bob Battle wrote: "Martha Carson - the redheaded spiritual singer who traded stardom to be a mother to her two boys - is going to sing professionally again after 12 years. Once a household name...the singer has returned to music after a self-imposed exile to raise a family. And she admits that show business has always been in her blood. And now, with the comeback trail hot, Martha has a new album on the market - her first in all these years since retirement.

"On the Gusto label, 'Martha Carson's Greatest Hits' include 'Satisfied,' 'Jesus Said,' 'The Patience of Job,' 'Dip Your Fingers in Some Water' and 'I'm Gonna Walk and Talk With My Lord.'"

In turn, she told Battle, "I came off the road and dedicated my life to raising my sons. Now I feel I have completed my pledge to God. Today, they are men - beautiful men...With all the love God could put in this house - and in the hearts of everyone in it - there was still an emptiness in my heart for the audience. Once you have gotten the taste of a crowd loving you,

you can't rub it out like you do a mistake with a pencil eraser. You just can't."

Battle's report noted further, "She kept her voice in shape by appearing at Nashville-Middle Tennessee charity functions, including the PTA, her boys schools and her church. She laughs, 'Just about anytime anybody had anything a'goin', if they called Martha, she went. And, you know what? That put a flame on the candle that was already burning.' Mission accomplished. Martha Carson is searching for stardom the second time around."

Not quite what this realist had in mind. More aptly put, she was hoping to refill the family coffers which were dwindling down fast. Unfortunately, there seemed to be more command performances for charity than more-profitable bookings, but being big hearted, Martha seldom said no to a benefit.

Sister Minnie recalls that her brother-in-law was a good booking agent, but that he lacked vision as far as the talent he was married to was concerned: "Martha's had a rough life. He could have done more for her. With a little help, Martha could have gone places till she was 80 years old. Oh, he'd carry on at time, saying things lie, *'I'm gonna get the three of you girls together again. Oh my God, what a show that would be!'* You know, going on like that, then he'd be off five or six weeks with Chet, Floyd and Boots. Other times he'd say to her, 'I can't believe a woman your age, wanting to get out there and put on a show!' That was very destructive to her."

By 1981, Martha had her fill of the drinking and abusive language. She said she was also embarrassed publicly by his drinking: "Many times…I had to get away from him, I'd be so filled up with it. I hate saying it, but I just couldn't stand being around him anymore. I'd jump in the car and go over and stay at Minnie's for the night, sometimes I'd even stay two or three nights."

Prostate surgery some 20 years prior to his death, precluded any sexual activity for the veteran showman. Martha, not one to discuss personal business with others, did confide in her sister Minnie.

Martha said that in spite of her husband's profitable arrangement with ARC, a pact which required his being away from home, "I never felt X was unfaithful to me. He had also grown to love his boys - and was close to them, very much so, as they got bigger. Sure, he traveled a lot, but he would occasionally take them out in the yard and play ball with them. I appreciated that."

René recalls while youngsters, he and his little brother spent a lot of spare time at the Boy's Club, "It was a healthy place, with good supervision for us kids." He also remembers that his mother was one who would go to PTA meetings or attend their little league games whenever she was in town: "They were both there for us when we needed them."

Having never given much thought to the jobs his parents had, René reflects, "I remember that others would ask me about her and I'd come home and tell her, 'Mommie, people want to know why you're not singing anymore.' Oh sure, I saw her performing occasionally on the TV, but I never considered her being a star or being different than other kids' mothers."

A woman who enjoys shopping - and some husbands wonder if there are any that don't - Martha liked to buy her boys suits or sport coats and trousers that matched, often dressing them in white shirts and bow ties. An impulsive shopper, she found herself unable to stay out of the shoe department, often buying too many pairs for herself (which may have been the litle girl in her remembering how it took her so long to buy those little white patent leather shoes for $2.98 on layaway, that she'd outgrown by the time she made the final payment).

But she was also thrifty at times, even to the point of clipping out coupons to help cut down on the grocery tab. It was a good habit which would serve her well in the darker days of economic hardship ahead.

Being boys, René and André didn't dig the sartorial splendor their mom pressed upon them, preferring play clothes that were more fitting for tossing a ball or just getting *down and dirty*.

"Growing up, we boys couldn't wait to play sports," says André. "The Boys Club was like a home away from home for us. We'd go from the time they opened until they closed. I remember that we went to several different church Sunday schools. I went to Catholic school, but never did claim to be Catholic. To this day, I am non-denominational."

René's heart was more into sports than music. At about 7, André first tried playing piano ("I took lessons for about six months"), then developed an interest in the drums ("I went to hear my mother perform and I liked the drums"), pursuing it more aggressively than his big brother.

"Andre's very creative that way. He didn't have any designs on being a star attraction, he just loved playing those drums. He played for Sheb Wooley and Sheb just loved the way he played," says Mom, who also had her son back her on occasional gigs.

Remembering his start on the drums, André notes, "I began hounding my parents for a drum set when I was about 8. They finally got me a miniature set, one of them little bitty ones I played on for awhile. Mom and Dad were lucky because we had a little portable room where I'd go up and practice, so the noise didn't drive them crazy. But I'd stop beatin' on 'em when the other kids came over. Then we played baseball or football down in the field."

He recalls when he was 16, the late Motown studio drummer Larrie Londin, "taught me how to tune the drums. So, I got to know him. At that time, I was still involved in sports, but me and my friends put together a little combo. I'd invite them all over and we'd get up in our little shed and play around. A couple of the guys I was involved with then, I still know: Don Mooney and Mike Scinta."

The boys, who played a lot of Jimi Hendrix music, had rented a place in back of a black funeral parlor to rehearse: "They'd come back to tell us when a funeral was going on and we'd stop playing.

"One day we were playing and unaware that a funeral was going on. We were playing the blues and one of our musicians happened to glance out the window and the people were all dancing out there!"

Mom recalls that René was the more serious student in school, and was aiming at going to college: "He was determined to gain the knowledge he was looking for. I'd wake up and sometimes at 2 in the morning he'd be out in the other room studying."

René majored in, and earned his degree in, business administration at Aquinas College. His proud parent adds, "He holds the record of being the youngest bank president working at First Tennessee in Columbia (Tenn.). Now, he's into real estate in Knoxville."

André, who took a more circuitous route to a profession of selling insurance, did not graduate. Possessing movie star good looks, he wowed the girls as a drummer, however, but remains a bachelor in his 40s.

"My sons are as different as day and night," reflects Martha. "You know, when the boys were growing up, I felt as though X favored our youngest son. But André ended up breaking his father's heart by dropping out of school - and he got to running around with a drinking crowd. In the end, X turned around and just adored René."

René's romances took a more serious turn. He was wed first to Marie, who had a child when he married her, but wasn't intent on having anymore. Thus, they were divorced. After five years, René married a second time, to Benna, a secretary, who was already a mother, but willing to have another baby with her new husband. (Fortunately, during October 1994, Martha's only grandchild, Michelle Reneé, was born. Unfortunately, Michelle's parents went through a divorce in 1998.)

It was in March 1982, that Minnie had lost her husband Charles.

"We were married 40 years, until he died of cancer," notes Minnie, who had three children with Charlie: Sandra, Shirley and Mike.

Just before her brother-in-law Woodruff's death, Martha had left her husband.

"Yes, there came a time that I really felt like I couldn't take another day of it. I actually went up town and filed divorce papers," Martha confirms. "That shook him up a little. After they delivered the divorce papers to him, he started complaining about his heart hurting. Naturally, his heart was hurting, because he was doing so much drinking. Of course, he did have a heart problem. Our oldest son would go and beg his father not to abuse himself by drinking. I thought a lot about it and really he had nobody else. X had run up all those long-distance calls trying to book a lot of acts, based out there in California, such as Kay Starr. So, we were hurting financially, as well.

"After I backed down (withdrawing the divorce papers), I took him to the heart doctor. On the way there, I told him, 'If the doctor asks if you're drinking, you better tell him or he's liable to prescribe medication that might kill you.' He said sure, but when the doctor called X in, I marched right in with him, because I knew he would fib. And, sure enough, the doctor asked if he was drinking and he said about three drinks a day...

"I spoke right up and told the doctor it was more like *three quarts a day - of hard whiskey - and a half case of beer!* He had run up a huge liquor bill over there on Murfreesboro Road!"

Having been through the harrowing experience of two husbands turning to alcohol, and suffering the heartache of watching her youngest run with a drinking crowd, Martha says it cured her of even drinking socially: *"From what I'd seen it do, I didn't want to ever get hooked on that!"*

Walt Trott

CHAPTER 28

'Fame' - and misfortune

"That song has been good to me..."

"My father thought my mother should retire and raise us kids," says André. "Actually, I don't think she entirely gave up on her career because my father said those things...

"There would be times when he would get a bit mean. My brother and I were more-or-less confused and didn't know how to act. We'd see him and her go back and forth, and it was like you didn't want to side with one over the other, because you loved them both.

"There was some difficulty there. During this time he was having problems, my mother would come to comfort us. She said, 'Your Dad's under a lot of stress.' It wasn't real bad, but it wasn't fun either.

"Later, I found out a lot about the stress he was under, when I went out on the road with him. I saw how he might lose money on those shows. He could lose many thousands of dollars and indeed that was stressful.

"There were times when he'd make us cry, because it just hurt our feelings. It may be he was lashing out at us for his shortcomings. We would try and do something, and he would holler at us, if he didn't feel it was done right. He was never physically mean, but he could be mentally abusive without even saying much to us. One sentence could tear you up. It was during this time that he was being so rough on my brother. I guess my father was just real set in his ways, and a perfectionist, and when someone drinks, it's that much worse."

On tour with The Masters, young Cossé was 15: "I worked part time at places like Municipal Auditorium in Nashville or out on the road. As a stage-hand, I'd help unload the trucks and set up the musical equipment. I started getting involved with people that opened up and showed me what it was all about. I began seeing what the drums were all about from a professional level."

With his mother at home more, André encouraged her to perform with his fledgling musical pals: "My mother would come out to our old refrigerator to put something in and us guys would yell down to her, 'C'mon up and pick some with us.' She'd come on up and just floor us with her ability. We'd try to play along with her, but her music was so detailed, with so many chord changes, our young guitar players had it hard to pick up and play something that someone like Chet Atkins had put down for her.

"She must have liked it, jamming with us, because it got so that almost every night, she'd come up and play with us for a little while. I guess it took her getting 'back on the bike' to realize she could still ride. She had always kept on writing, then she made up her mind she wasn't through with performing, so we started doing a few little shows here and there.

"I thought I was beginning to learn it by playing 10 songs, but then she'd introduce 10 more songs that would just blow you away -- a lot of stuff she'd written before I was even born. Her music had a lot of rock and roll roots in it. Even some of her older stuff. I don't think she ever imagined young guys in the shed playing rock and roll to her 'Satisfied.'

"I played drums for her - and even the guys in our garage band she'd use on occasion. Then we started doing shows away in places like Georgia, New York and Missouri. Sometimes it would be a gospel-oriented concert or we'd be on a package show with legends like Kitty Wells and Johnny Wright, acts like that."

Initially, Cossé said he mainly knew how to keep a beat and to hit the skins as hard as he could: "When I did country and gospel, however, I found it's as much what you leave out as it is what you put into it that counts. A lot of times if you put too much into it, you're over playing. You have to lay back, do a lot of brush work...I learned a whole different meaning to music while working with Mom.

"After that (apprenticeship), I played a lot of clubs and performed in several good bands, until I got involved in insurance sales in the 1980s. Really, the shows we were doing didn't pay a lot of money, because of the number of musicians involved. And, because it's Nashville, other musicians would come in and play for free. They'd play for a $1 a head at the door, though some clubs would slip us a little extra because they thought we were good. But, it's so competitive with so many bands playing the circuit. That's why I got out."

In November 1983, NBC-TV aired a special segment of its popular youth program *Fame,* an episode that showcased Martha Carson's composition "I Can't Stand Up Alone."

"They paid me $4,000 for the right to release the song in episodes overseas," says Martha. "That song has been good to me..."

Her son André adds, "That episode of *Fame* where they used her song 'I Can't Stand Up Alone' hit me hard. Hearing it on TV, and even hearing it on the radio now makes me really listen to the words.

"I never understood the meaning behind 'Satisfied' all the times I played it," denotes André. "After a person had deceived me and taken things from me, I was really crushed. But, hearing the song, the words kind of put a calm over my body. You have to really have lived a little to understand the true meaning of those songs. From there, all the other songs she wrote started taking on new meaning for me.

"I no longer looked at them from a musicians' standpoint, but started realizing what went on in the songwriter's mind when she composed the song. You know all the things that had happened to her, what she's been through; yet, she still comes on strong and writes things that are positive. There's none of my mother's songs, that I've heard, that have any kind of a negative feeling. They're more triggered to no matter how wrong things get, there's a higher power you can relate to and gain happiness."

André recalls that his Dad didn't approve of him playing in bars.

"My father said if I was going to play music, to go and study it at Belmont College or join an orchestra and play big time. My mother was more lenient and understood me wanting to play with the guys. As I got older, we grew out of that. I'd go to my mother with a problem and she would often be the mediator between us. She understood me better. I know my brother always felt closer to my mother."

René says he and his brother became close to their mother's younger brother Conley Amburgey, who worked for the Davidson County Sheriff's department, in Nashville.

"He moved next door to us on Curry Road, so naturally we saw more of him than our other aunts and uncles. Uncle Conley was always a cut-up with us. Being boys, we were always tight with him. He wound up buying that house from my parents."

According to René's younger brother, "Every now and then when I'd go through Lebanon (Tenn.), I'd stop and see Aunt Jean, who lived out there in a trailer, where all she'd do is write. I knew Jean had written 'To Get To You,' which was a hit, but when I'd visit, I was shocked to see stacks of songs just sitting there. I didn't realize Jean had recorded for Sun Records...it's special when you have a family where everyone would play and sing something. You know Uncle Don writes, too, and Conley would get up and sing at family get-togethers. He has a good voice, too. I guess they were all musical on my mother's side.

"Sometimes they'd come down to a club where I was performing. My cousin Lana's a hoot. I first remember her back when there were flower children. She taught herself, but boy could she sing and play. We've got a little fellow in the family about 9, who plays bass guitar already."

André says he feels his parents handled it just right with him and his brother regarding their previous marriages: "It was understandable they didn't tell me when I was younger. I was older when I met my father's other children. It was at first kind of shocking to me. There were never any jealous feelings, however, it didn't bother me. We were never very close with that side of the family. Our parents had explained to us about life…

"It was so ironic later when I went to Knoxville to help paint my brother's house. Of course, I knew my mother had been married to James (Roberts) Carson in her younger days. While I was living there, I was only about a mile from WNOX.

"Naturally being in insurance and dealing with older people, I'd get inquisitive and asked if they had heard of Martha Carson. It was amazing how many people said yes.

"One guy told me, 'I used to live out in the country and I'd be there in the middle of the tobacco field and we'd all come in at noon just to hear the *Mid-Day Merry-Go-Round* and especially to hear your momma sing.' Some of the folks didn't know she'd been divorced and they asked me how ol' James was doing.

"I never did know James (Roberts), but I would hear things that she never did tell me, like how they used to play in school houses, churches and gymnasiums. They knew all the songs and these strangers were telling me about my mother's life earlier and the people that she had worked with.

"One time, I called her and asked her about this guy who said he'd played harmonica for her at this school house in Loudon. But she'd usually remember. It was astounding how many people knew of her."

In late summer 1986, Richard Weise of Bear Family Records near Hamburg, Germany, released a retrospective album "Martha Carson Explodes! Music Drives Me Crazy (Especially Rock 'n' Roll)!" (BFX-15215), utilizing tracks he leased from RCA Records in the states. A National Public Radio documentary, "From Neon to Nashville," produced by Appalshop, also garnered much attention of Martha Carson devotees.

Except for a few guest shots on Ralph Emery's TNN variety series *Nashville Now,* or an occasional benefit show like "The Legendary Ladies of Country Music," at the Station Inn, Martha Carson's appearances were few and far between.

At the latter gig with proceeds donated to the Reunion Of Professional Entertainers (ROPE), Carson stole the October 1989 show from her more subdued co-stars Jeannie Seely, Jean Shepard, Melba Montgomery, Norma Jean and Liz Anderson, all backed by Harry Pierce's Sons of the West group. As the closing act, she was joined on stage unexpectedly by good friend Kitty Wilson, who played stand-up bass -- much to the delight of the crowd.

Veteran music writers such as Ed Morris of *Billboard* and Arnold Rogers of *Country Music Parade* magazine praised Carson as the star-studded evening's most entertaining act.

Sadly, the night before the program, Opry artist Del Wood, who was scheduled to perform, had died. The Nashville native, best known for her ragtime piano, was 69. She had joined the Opry the year after Carson signed on, and was friends with Martha, Jean and Minnie.

Martha, meanwhile, had encouraged Minnie when she began dating a barber named Bob Garcia, who worked downtown at Reno's For Hair. According to the widowed sister: "I stayed single about seven years, until I met Bob. His daughter dated my son Mike, so our children really brought us together. His wife had also died of cancer...Bob's about six years younger than me."

Minnie and Bob Garcia were wed June 19, 1988, at the Church of Christ on Lebanon Road in Nashville. After 12 years, he and she are still devoted. "My mother told me I was fortunate, because I've had two good men."

That year Martha spent the summer opening for the Opry's Del Reeves and his vivacious blonde singer-daughter Kari, backed by his *Good Time Charlies* band, during a series of concerts coordinated by the Ramada Inn, Four Seasons and Gatlinburg Convention Center in the Great Smokies.

"You don't truly live to your fullest, if you don't get out there once in awhile in front of that audience," Carson told *The Tennessean* daily newspaper's then-music writer Bob Oermann.

Reeves, who came to Nashville in 1962 from the West Coast, originally hailed from Sparta, N.C., where he was born July 14, 1933. After a trio of moderately successful singles - "Be Quiet Mind," "He Stands Real Tall" and "The Only Girl I Can't Forget" - he switched labels (to United Artists) and struck gold with his 1965 charttopper "Girl On the Billboard," followed in rapid succession by "Belles of Southern Bell" and "Women Do Funny Things To Me." Reeves' later Top 10s include "Lookin' At the World Through a Windshield," "Good Time Charlie's" and "The Philadelphia Fillies."

Carson welcomed the opportunity and was pleased that it was only a short ride from Knoxville, where both her sons were then in residence. It provided tourists a lively double set, too, with the spirited Martha Carson and multi-talented Reeves, who also did right-on impersonations of stars like Roy Acuff, Johnny Cash, George Jones, Walter Brennan and James Stewart.

Meanwhile, the popular entertainer had lost none of her sparkle. Her sometimes-picker Bob Saxton asserts, "Martha works a crowd real good -- because she projects to the people, making them feel a part of what's happening. It's spiritual nourishment to be a part of a Martha Carson performance. She really ministers to the audience musically.

"Martha may be dressed more informally at home, but she's the same whether backstage or when you're visiting her at the house," continues Saxton. "She's sincere, a fine woman, whom I've been proud to be associated with."

That same fall, Xavier Cossé spent some much-needed bonding time with both sons in Knoxville. According to Martha, "A week before going on his little trip, X suffered severe pain while urinating. He had scar tissue that developed and they had cut it out. I remember René brought him home on a Saturday. X told me he had the most beautiful visit with our two sons. I said, 'I sure am glad.' He seemed to be alright.

"I fixed us all a good meal that night, and he went on to bed early. I stayed up, talking with René. When I started to go to bed, X got up to go to the bathroom. Being conscious of his trouble urinating, I kept listening for him, but didn't hear anything wrong.

"When he finally came back from the bathroom, he sit on the edge of the bed and said, sort of despondent, 'Mama, I wish I could just go on. I'm no good to anyone anymore.' I said, 'You don't need to talk like that.' So he laid down and then went off to sleep."

The next morning, Martha got up, fixed coffee and he cautioned her not to fix him a big breakfast. Next thing she knew, X was off in the car, drove to the store and bought some Danish pastry, then brought her in the Sunday newspaper.

He had said simply, "I just want a little of this pastry." Then he went into the den, just across the breezeway, and watched a ballgame on TV.

Meanwhile, Martha cleared off the breakfast dishes, and René whisked by her, saying he was going to the den, as he had a question for his father: "I heard him call out, 'Daddy, Daddy…' but didn't hear any answer. I started to run towards the den, because I was always concerned about his health. René came out and said, 'Mommy don't go in there! Daddy's dead!'

"I rushed on in anyway, thinking he might just be sleeping. I patted him on the cheek, saying, *'Daddy, wake up! René wants to ask you something.'* No response. I took both cheeks in my hands and kept talking to him, but already I could feel the chill of death on his face."

René, meanwhile, had called 911. The ambulance arrived and its attendants administered a shot and attempted to revive him, but there was no reaction: Xavier Benedict Cossé had died, apparently of a heart attack at his home, on Nov. 18, 1990. He was 73 years old.

A brief news obituary, Nov. 19, in *The Tennessean* made mention of his world tour promotion of the Masters Festival of Music with Atkins, Cramer and Randolph, and added, *"He also promoted such entertainers as Kenny Rogers, Perry Como and the Beatles."*

Martha had notified his other children and an estranged brother.

"His brother, Clayton, came in from Atlanta, and his daughter (Donna Walker, also of Atlanta) came, but his son, Trent, who lived in Arizona, didn't make it in. X and his brother hadn't spoken for several years (after he had married X's former wife). The Christmas prior to my husband's death, we went to Atlanta. His brother, who at one time was part owner of radio station WENO, was 17 years X's senior."

A sister, Margie Drury of Fort Lauderdale, Fla., and five grandchildren also survived Cossé. In accordance with the Catholic-raised X's wishes, Martha had him cremated: "I held a memorial service over at Woodlawn and had a minister come and say a few words. That was it…"

Walt Trott

CHAPTER 29

Family and Friends...

"As soon as they pour the love on me, it just pushes the pain away...."

"X was an alcoholic. For 20 years I thought I was gonna lose my mind. But I have never regretted staying with him, for no one else would ever do it. I've found that love outdoes hate unanimously. Something good lives on and creates more good."

Despite satisfaction at standing by her man, Carson suffered indignities of a financial nature, most of which surfaced after her husband's death. There was no insurance, for starters.

Martha lit up another cigarette.

"When he died, we were many thousands of dollars in debt. We ended up losing every one of those properties we had invested in, including the house we lived in when he died. At one time, we had our (Curry Road) home within $6,000 of being paid off. Then X took out a mortgage on it (followed by two more mortgages).

"We were not working anymore, so there wasn't that income," continues Carson. "There was nothing left in the bank. Then René stepped in...Yes, if it wasn't for that little baby he didn't want me to have, and that God gifted me with, I'd have been out on the street. With the help of that son, I got all the bills worked out, and got this house next door to Minnie. I don't think I could ever have made it without him."

There was very little royalties coming her way. Like Bear Family, other independent labels had leased Martha Carson recordings and issued albums on her, including ACM (Anthology of Country Music) Records' "Early Gospel Greats," the British Stetson label's "Satisfied" (utilizing her Capitol tracks), and Hollywood Records (a division of Highland Music of Dearborn, Mich.) which released "Martha Carson's Greatest

Gospel Hits." Yet none of these consisted of any new recordings by the artist.

While they served to keep her name and music before the public, she derived little, if any, actual royalties off the product: "In the early 1990s, (publisher) Harry Fox contacted me and said they couldn't get anything from the Hollywood Record Company, so they pulled their license."

Little wonder that she suffered headaches.

In the summer of 1992, Martha was invited to participate in a tribute to her old mentor Lowell Blanchard in Knoxville, and consented to appear for the festivities.

Backstage there was a buzz about James Carson, she says, "I heard he was out in the audience with his third wife, but that was no concern of mine."

Actually, both had been inducted earlier into the Atlanta Country Music Hall of Fame, though they were not required to appear together, which was the way James' redhaired-ex preferred it.

"I don't think about any of that anymore," bemuses James, now a bona fide preacher, complete with a Certificate from the Association of Independent Ministers (AIM), signed by Walter Bailes, the singer-songwriter of yore.

Since settling down, James had held day jobs such as piano tuning, and more recently conducted Bible classes in his adopted hometown of Lexington, where at the most he had 35 students meeting in a building his current wife owned next door to their Camden Avenue house.

Two of his recent cassette albums are "Tell Me Again, There is No God" and "Keep Your Hand On the Plow," which he'd financed himself. These do demonstrate, however, that the retiree is still in fine form vocally.

In 1993, Martha Carson was invited to Murfreesboro, Tenn., to participate in a CBS-TV special "The Women of Country Music," adapted from psychologist Mary Bufwack and her writer-hubby Bob Oermann's collaborative coffee table chronicle, "The Women of Country Music: Finding Her Voice."

While younger players like Mary Chapin Carpenter, Lorrie Morgan, Pam Tillis and Tanya Tucker were getting most of the attention (and beaming cameras), some "oldtimers" such as Patsy Montana, Jean Shepard and Kitty Wells were also included in the line-up to lend authenticity to the documentary-styled production. Mostly, the senior ladies sat silently in the audience while the younger *fillies* dominated stage center, performing their hits. Archival film footage of the pioneer ladies from earlier days was later interwoven, mostly utilizing mere snippets of their signature songs, as edited.

Still, it provided a nice opportunity to *smooze* with friends from yesteryear. Today, one of Martha's dearest friends is Marlene Sloan, whom she met through a mutual buddy, Ann Butts, a realtor. Martha calls Marlene, who's about 20 years younger: *"My little guardian angel."*

In turn, Marlene says, "We talk every day. We have a prayer and then we laugh. I call her 'Sunshine.' She just amazes me everyday, at her age, the way she gets around. I tell everybody who she is, because she won't. She won't toot her own horn."

Marlene also offered to administer Martha's B-12 shots which seemed to make the artist feel better:

"Ann said they bruised her (Martha) when they gave her a shot - and had charged her $45. I told Ann it costs about 45-cents and said, 'Bring your friend on over and I'll have it ready.' So, I gave her the shot and she said it didn't hurt a bit. *'There's something about you, girl. You've got it!'* (Martha exclaimed)...And I asked, 'What did you say?' and she replied, 'I'm sorry. That was rude and sounds so country.' I told her, 'Oh, no. It means so much to me.' Then we hugged."

The women first met in February 1992. Marlene had lost another good friend, singer Dottie West, who died Sept. 4, 1991, from injuries sustained in an automobile accident near Opryland.

"Dottie and I raised our children on the same street. She and I were both very strict with our kids...Dottie and her (then-)husband Bill had written 'Here Comes My Baby,' and she was so excited when Dean Martin recorded it."

That song also launched West's career, winning her a Grammy - the first for a country female artist (in 1964). Following her death, Marlene was honored when Dottie's son Dale invited her to TNN: "It was for Mother's Day and he took me to the television special 'I'm Still Missing You.' Dale started crying, then said, 'I'm so embarrassed!' I told him, 'You're a man, honey, but it's OK if you cry.'"

Marlene cited a time she attended a program featuring her new friend Martha Carson, along with other stars like Roni Stoneman of *Hee Haw* TV fame: "Well, I was sitting next to a young, handsome blond fellow, and I smiled at him and said, *'It's nice having a good-looking guy next to me.'*

"When I went outside, he also came out, and I noticed these flap-jawed women also following us around, for some reason I didn't understand. I mentioned it to him and he laughed. I punched him on the arm and said, *'Watch this! Martha's going to get a standing ovation!'* She did, and he said, 'I wonder who could follow Martha Carson!' Well, when Roni Stoneman introduced *John Schneider* I found out who my friend was - and just why those gals were following us around!"

Schneider, of course, was the hunky young star of TV's *Dukes of Hazzard* action-comedy series shown on TNN of late, and had later scored as a country crooner via the #1 ballads "I've Been Around Enough To Know" and "You're the Last Thing I Needed Tonight."

Another of Marlene's friends is producer-songwriter-guitarist Scotty Turner, who also received her *famous, non-painful B-12 shots.* Turner produced such artists as Slim Whitman and Roy Clark, and had co-written hits like "Shutters and Boards," "When the Wind Blows in Chicago" and "Hick Town," which incidentally was Tennessee Ernie Ford's last Top 10.

"I hadn't seen Scotty since 1980, and I knew his real name wasn't Turner, so I looked him up under Turnbull (the name he was born with in Canada) when I wanted to contact him," continued Sloan. "He had a leg injury from his hockey-playing days and I used to administer shots to him while working at this doctor's office. After I finally caught up to him, I told Scotty about Martha, and how fine a woman she is, and he said, *'Bring her out to the house.'*

"After we got there, within 60 seconds, he had her records on the machine. When you look inside her eyes, you just see love. Well, something obviously was happening to Scotty. He was like a smitten teen-ager. I thought, *'Oh, what's she going to think of me - and him? He's always been such a gentleman.'* Martha had already told me, she'd never date again...

"The next thing I knew they were standing, staring at each other. Scotty said, 'Martha, you're taller...' She kicked her shoes off, 'Now we're the same size.' He was so in awe of her, and then they started dancing. As the music ended, he dipped her - and then kissed her goodnight."

Marlene said it was a memorable evening: "I felt like it was love at first sight."

Martha had been having a real problem with the headaches, however, and it was Marlene who encouraged her to see a doctor.

"I would touch my forehead and I felt like a little wire sticking out of my scar from that fall I'd taken in the breezeway so long ago," says Martha, in recollection. "By this time, there was also a seeping of fluid which would run into my eye. I told the doctor there's something wrong with the plate in my head.

"He did a scan, got the results and called me, saying, 'You've been right all along. The screws from the metal have been working their way out because your body's been rejecting this plate. Get in here, soon.'"

Hospitalized, Martha was told that she would have to have her head shaved and the plate would have to be removed. "Then, in another six months, he said my head would have to be shaved to insert a plastic replacement...My little prayer partner (Marlene) was with me, and she was crying. I told him I'd just keep the metal plate in there. I noticed his eyes swelling with tears, then he said perhaps the one session would do it.

"So, it was decided that I'd undergo the surgery. He told me not to be surprised when I removed the bandages next day, to see a black eye. You know, the next morning when I looked at myself, there was no black eye. He was amazed, and he also told me that the damaged tissue had rebuilt itself so well (there was no need of a replacement)."

The doctor said Martha should be grateful the drainage hadn't gone backward (instead of forward) or it would have damaged her brain: "Indeed, God has been so good to me. There wasn't a day that passed in those 20 years that I didn't swallow a bunch of Tylenol, so I could stay on my feet. With the headaches gone, I felt as good as I did when I was 35!"

According to Marlene, "We were also told if it had been at the base of her skull or if she had waited another six weeks, it would have been too late!"

The result was another composition, Carson titled it "I Will Rise Above It All."

Carson was pleased in reading Peter Guralnick's 1994 biography "Last Train to Memphis: The Rise of Elvis Presley" to note the author's positive comments about her musical influence on his subject artist, now widely hailed as *Rock and Roll's King.*

There were two other men, besides Scotty Turner, who took an interest in *Martha Carson, performer,* during the '90s. The first, a Texan, was named Jamey Irby, who worked for the company that had made Chet Atkins' guitars. He had met Martha during a visit to Nashville and was determined to become her manager and promoter.

"He wouldn't take no for an answer. He kept calling me long distance and even sent roses. I did a benefit at Bell Cove (a club) in Hendersonville, and he came in. He was a smart young man, who had arranged some bookings for me.

"Then he got cancer of the prostate, which turned to bone marrow cancer. That boy really loved his mother, who had to nurse his father during a fatal illness. Well, he developed pneumonia, but was determined not to be an invalid on his mother, so, he shot himself!"

Another who admired Martha's talents greatly, was Dr. Douglas W. Parker, Jr., of Fort Smith, Ark. For a brief period, he had managed newcomer Billy Ray Cyrus, and handled business affairs for the Kentucky HeadHunters.

Parker saw that Martha was still driving around in an aged Cadillac that Cossé had left her, and decided to turn over one of his late-model cars for her personal use. Then, out of the blue, the orthopedic surgeon died from a heart attack, June 20, 1995. He was 46 years old.

The deceased's father, Parker Sr., moved quickly to recover the car from Martha, claiming it as part of his son's estate. Meanwhile, she was deeply saddened by Parker's death, and unconcerned about disposition of the automobile. Material things can always be replaced, but not the care and kindness of a friend...*Look for the silver lining.*

A more profound loss that year to her was the cancer death of her younger sister Opal, better known as Jean Chapel, on Aug. 12, 1995: "She was so spiritual, so precious to us. It's a terrible, terrible emptiness that's left. What hurts even more is knowing she never got a break all her life. A lot of people used her. She should have had a beautiful home with the money her songs earned...

"I remember she wore patches of morphine all over to keep the pain bearable," Martha recounts..."She had cancer in her lungs and liver, and finally it went to her stomach. She had discontinued radiation treatment in recent weeks. Her little heart's at peace now. *If He needed her more in Heaven, then that's the way it has to be.*"

Jean was 72. The whole family, including her mother Gertrude, was in Nashville paying their last respects at Woodlawn Funeral Home. She had left her mark on so many people. Daughter Lana Holmes Kolb was influenced by her mother to write country and gospel songs. Jean's son Kenneth Woodruff, who's so proud of her, began actively campaigning to have his mother named to the Songwriters Hall of Fame.

"My sister was the sunshine of the whole family, with such a glowing personality," a visably shaken Martha proclaimed at the time.

Looking back over the expanded family, Carson noted that their list includes Glenn's sons David and Denny (Danny had died in the 1962 car crash with his grand-dad) plus three daughters, Pamela, Patti and Paula; while younger brother Conley also has three daughters: Cindy, Connie and Sharon.

Matriarch of all these, Gertrude (Quillen) Amburgey Ramsey, died March 27, 1997, in Nashville. At the time, she was living with her daughter Minnie, next door to Martha.

"Mama didn't look to be 95 years old," said a heartbroken Martha. "She was buried in a pink suit that was originally bought for her to wear on Easter...I thank God for letting her go easy. I don't think she had any pain."

Of course, her talents inspired her children's love of music. She was also survived by sisters Mildred Fields, Georgia Ferrell, Gladys Yancey; 33 grandchildren; 22 great-grandchildren; and seven great-great-grandchildren. Her final services were conducted in Amelia, Ohio.

Death has reduced the number of those touching Martha's life, as she approaches her 80th year. Some have died young, like Elvis Presley, who was only 42 when he departed in August 1977, while others like Ernest Tubb, Minnie Pearl, Roy Acuff, Grandpa Jones, Bill Monroe, Stuart Hamblen and Floyd Cramer lived to become senior citizens. Today, she's hurting for her friend Kitty Wilson, who died on June 19, 2000, from cancer.

Still, Martha's thankful for all their good times together, throughout the years. She's had her own share of sick days, but faith and *something else* has kept her going.

"I remember when I could be hurtin' myself, like crazy, with heartache or bad health, and there's one thing that seemed to help me, *performing!* I've said to Minnie, 'This arthritis is killing me!' Then she says, 'You sure don't show it, when you're out there on stage!'

"Yes, I've gone on when the bursitis was so bad in my shoulder that I needed Minnie to help me get into my costume, but get me out there on stage with that audience, and *as soon as they pour the love on me, it just pushes the pain away.* I'm in another world altogether."

Another scare occurred at the funeral services for Kitty Wilson, June 22, when their mutual friend Bill Carlisle collapsed. Martha's brother Don was one of those who ran to his aid. Fortunately, the plucky 91-year-old entertainer recovered consciousness on the scene and began joking about his spell. Although hospitalized over the next few days, Bill was back on stage in the Opry House performing, the first weekend in July 2000.

Martha's friend's stamina may have influenced her through the years, as well.

While walking in her backyard one sunny day, hoping to trim some vines, Martha ran into a bush that injured her lower leg. She brushed aside son André's concern, until the leg began swelling to almost twice its size. First, she was taken to St. Thomas Hospital, where they administered antibiotics, then she was transferred to Summit Medical Center closer to home.

With time and good home health care, she was soon able to walk on it again, though one less-than-subtle physician had even suggested at one stage that it might have to be amputated.

On another occasion, Martha injured her pickin' finger and went through much of the same aggravation. The artist was subjected to several months of surgery and specialized treatment, yet the finger didn't seem to heal properly. Again, she heard a doctor suggest that maybe it would have to be amputated.

Her faith and resolve were strong enough that she survived even that later threat: "Every time I've gone through a trying time, God has given me the inspiration to carry on, and I guess until the day I die, that's the way it will be."

Walt Trott

CHAPTER 30

Light My Fire...

*"I've never been overseas...
I'd love to give it a try."*

"I've thought on this, and I'm sure Elvis Presley would want me to set the record straight...and it may be that God planned it this way. He knows best for all of us."

Martha Carson boasts a gentle soul and a good heart, but cross her, and one finds the lady can become fired-up rather fast. After watching a recent video advertisement on The Nashville Network for a Presley compilation of spirituals, she spotted her song "Swing Down, Sweet Chariot," among the tunes in the package.

Heartland Music was behind the telemarketing of "Gospel Treasures," featuring Elvis singing spiritual songs, then appearing on TNN. Upon closer inspection, it was a song Martha wrote and copyrighted in 1958. Martha's own recording of the disputed number appears on the RCA label, which was also Presley's starship.

"I wrote it! I published it! I should get a three-way royalty off its use!" fumed Carson, who learned Elvis' name appears as writer, with Blackhawk Music cited as its publisher. "He never wrote a song in his life, but I know Elvis wouldn't want to take away my creation."

The veteran entertainer contacted Music Row attorney Ralph S. Gordon, who successfully negotiated an earlier settlement for Del and Ellen Reeves with Billy Ray Cyrus (and was Tammy Wynette's lawyer, as well). In the Reeves case, the couple had recorded the unknown Cyrus at their expense, and were instrumental in bringing him to the attention of Mercury Records and his former manager Jack McFadden.

Unfortunately, Cyrus chose to turn his back on the couple, after scoring such a phenomenal success with "Achy Breaky Heart," prompting them to turn the matter over to the courts.

In pursuing her copyright problem, Carson concluded that Elvis Presley's "Bosum of Abraham," which he recorded on June 9, 1971, was also previously a Carson composition she'd titled "Rock-A-My Soul."

"They utilized a portion of my song - 'Rock-A-My Soul' (in the bosum of Abraham) - as the title, which I would guess was a way of concealing it, and put four names on it as writers, including Elvis Presley's."

Presley first recorded "Swing Down, Sweet Chariot" for RCA on Oct. 31, 1960, and later re-recorded it on Oct. 15, 1968, perhaps in an effort to upgrade his performance. Presley, his own worst critic, was always a perfectionist in the studio.

During his lifetime, Presley never won a Grammy for his secular songs, but was awarded three for gospel recordings: "How Great Thou Art" (1967); "He Touched Me" (1972) and "How Great Thou Art" (track, 1974). Among his more successful gospel-styled singles are: "Peace in the Valley" (1957), "Crying in the Chapel" (1965) and "Where Did They Go, Lord" (1971).

It isn't the first time that Carson discovered an alleged infringement of her copyright concerning "Swing Down, Sweet Chariot." She says country superstar Barbara Mandrell had recorded the number and copyrighted it in her name in 1980.

At the time, Carson contacted entertainment attorney Dick Frank, informing him of the situation, but he declined to take her case, noting a conflict of interest as he then represented Mandrell. Then she got sidetracked by other more pressing problems.

It's ironic that Presley and Mandrell, both country-pop oriented at the time, won their Grammy trophies for gospel efforts. Mandrell first won the award in 1982, for her Songbird/MCA album "He Put the Music in Me." Incidentally, Presley's track on Carson's song appears on the RCA album

"His Hand In Mine" (LPM-2328), featuring the Jordanaires. On the actual vinyl, it's printed that "Swing Down, Sweet Chariot" (as registered with BMI) was "arranged and adapted by Elvis Presley."

Of course, through the years, there have been many lawsuits charging copyright infringement. On the country scene, however, two of the more celebrated cases involved Buck Owens and the Boudleaux Bryants: Buck Owens lost his case on melody for his ballad "Cryin' Time" (a 1966 hit for Ray Charles), which a court ruled was the same as the pop standard "Vaya Con Dios" (a 1953 million seller by Les Paul & Mary Ford).

On the other hand, Boudleaux and Felice Bryant were successful in a legal determination that their "Rocky Top" (copyright in 1967, and a 1968 single for the Osborne Brothers) is the source for the 1981 Shelly West-David Frizzell charttopper "You're the Reason God Made Oklahoma."

Unlike the Bryants, Martha Carson never has cared for co-writing and though she's been forced to share writer credits on a couple of her songs, insists she's the true author. There is an exception though, and it came in the person of Tony Graham, an Englishman, and via long distance.

"Tony writes some beautiful songs, but never finishes doing the verses. Through Scotty (Turner), he sent over a tape and they then talked to me about it. I admired the song in question and sat down and wrote a few verses. I sent it back to him, and he just loved it. He said it blended well with the idea he'd started with."

According to Martha, she and Scotty are best friends, and occasionally he may dine at her home. With their show business backgrounds, however, they do have a lot in common.

In May 1997, Scotty enticed Martha into recording again (at the Lawrence Welk Champagne Studio on Music Row), utilizing some of the Union's finest session players, including Harold Bradley, rhythm guitar; Billy Linneman, bass; Buddy Harman, drums; Thom Bresh, guitar; Jack Daniels, guitar; and Michael Behymer, keyboards. Besides duets and harmony supplied by

Tony Graham, there were some female harmony vocalists, notably two female R&B specialists.

"I couldn't have asked for any better backup," says Carson, who was in fine fettle for the occasion. "I couldn't pick a favorite of the songs recorded. Scotty did a magnificent job. He sure knows his way around a studio. Despite all he has accomplished, he remains one of the most humble, deserving people I've ever known in my life. He can't accept a compliment, it just kills him. But he is so creative and talented."

Scotty Turner, a native of Nova Scotia, was once an All-Canadian hockey player and a track team member in the British Empire Games. After earning a degree in Music Theory at Stanstead College in Quebec, he attended the University of Dubuque, Iowa, and did postgraduate work at Texas Tech University.

While at Texas Tech, he became friends with a fellow guitarist, a then-unknown Buddy Holly in Lubbock. The two jammed together and eventually co-wrote the songs "I'm Gonna Love You," "September Hearts" and "Am I Ever Gonna Find It?"

As the music world knows, Holly did find it - fame - as leader of The Crickets, renowned for such pop classics as "That'll Be The Day," "Peggy Sue" and "Oh, Boy!" (Tragically, Holly died at age 22 in a plane crash at Clear Lake, Iowa, Feb. 3, 1959.)

Professionally, Turner and ex-linebacker Hal Goodson of the Texas Tech Red Raiders team, formed a group they tagged (yup!) The Raiders, and first recorded in Clovis, N.M., in 1956. That session produced their first single "Later, Baby" (backed with "Who's Gonna Be the Next One, Honey"), which even got airplay in England!

Turner and company (minus Goodson, who returned to football) lit out for the West Coast, where one of their first assignments was as support band for then-teen idol Tommy Sands (who segued from TV's "Singin' Idol" to the big screen's

"Sing, Boy, Sing," showcasing Carson's "I'm Gonna Walk and Talk With My Lord").

Three years later, Turner found himself both lead picker and music director for another singer-screen actor Guy Mitchell (who scored with pop versions of the country classics "Singin' the Blues" and "Heartaches By the Numbers"), a star of Paramount movie musicals "Those Redheads From Seattle" and "Red Garters." He and Turner also did a bit of co-writing together, including "My Lonesome Room."

After two years with Mitchell, Turner hit the road with pop crooner Eddie Fisher, then married to film star Debbie Reynolds. Fisher, of course, had made his name via such ballads as "Any Time" (a pop cover of Eddy Arnold's hit), "Wish You Were Here" and "Oh, My Papa." According to Turner, the star of the movie "Bundle of Joy" (with Debbie) was about to switch to Liz Taylor, which sort of upset Fisher's musical applecart, but set him up to co-star in Taylor's flick "Butterfield 8" - and created one of the major Hollywood scandals of the era.

Thus Turner turned his attentions to assisting Cliffie Stone in managing Central Songs for Ken Nelson (Martha's former producer), alternating those chores with a role as arranger for Herb Alpert and Jerry Moss' A&M Records label. That led to a job as executive producer for Liberty/Imperial's country division, then he progressed to chief of United Artists' country label in Nashville. Among artists he produced were Del Reeves, Penny (Starr) DeHaven, Bill Phillips, Slim Whitman, Oliver, Vikki Carr, Dale Robertson, Rosemary Clooney and Waylon Jennings.

It was through his association with Guy Mitchell that Turner met Audie Murphy in 1961. Mitchell had landed a role in the short-lived Murphy TV series "Whispering Smith," based on an Alan Ladd Paramount feature (rather ironic because Murphy's screen debut was a 1948 Alan Ladd feature "Beyond Glory").

Shortly after returning to the States amidst his own glory, the heroic soldier's face had been seen on the cover of *Life* magazine, and spotted by legendary actor James Cagney. He put

Murphy under personal contract, and saw that he received drama lessons. When Paramount asked for Murphy's services, Cagney consented, but declined any portion of the war hero's loan-out money for his firm.

The young Texan had earned 24 decorations for action in the face of the enemy, reportedly killing 240 throughout his service in Europe and capturing single-handedly just as many. He received the nation's highest award, the Congressional Medal of Honor (usually presented posthumously), along with such other achievements as the Distinguished Service Cross, Silver Star With Oak Leaf Cluster (seven battle stars), Legion of Merit, Bronze Star, French Legion of Honor Chevalier, Belgian Croix de Guerre and three Purple Hearts for his wounds.

Among Murphy's later movies were "Red Badge of Courage," "To Hell and Back" (in which he played himself in a screen adaptation of his biography), "Destry," "The Quiet American" and "The Unforgiven." The wiry, youthful-looking thespian usually put himself down, grinning, "As an actor, I'd make a very good stuntman."

Turner, several years younger, says Murphy always insisted to him that the real heroes of the war were those who died in battle. When Scotty and Audie met, Murphy was a frustrated poet, and he valued their collaborative efforts which turned his words into lyrics.

"Please, Mr. Music Man" was their first song together. It was recorded in 1962 by co-writer Harry Nilsson (although not released until 1975). Meanwhile, the duo's first major hit was "Shutters and Boards," as recorded by Jerry Wallace (who later enjoyed a hit on "To Get To You" by Jean Chapel), a Top 20 pop entry in 1963.

Another success for the unlikely songwriting team was "When the Wind Blows in Chicago," an early click for Roy Clark. Country vocalist Bonnie Guitar had a good cut on the Murphy-Turner tune "Leave the Weeping Willow To the Willow Tree" and the Baja Marimba Band did well with "Maria's First Rose." Artists who recorded their efforts include Eddy Arnold,

Bobby Bare, Brook Benton, Teresa Brewer, Dean Martin, Jody Miller, Charley Pride, Slim Whitman, Jimmy Dean and Mitchell.

In composing, Turner says Murphy was more adept at rhyming and had an innate sense of rhythm: "He was stronger on lyrics and ideas. And Audie knew instinctively where the music should go."

Like Turner's earlier pal Buddy Holly, Murphy died in a fiery plane crash, on Brushy Mountain near Roanoke, Va., May 28, 1971. He was 46 years old. This self-penned poem made a fitting epitaph to America's beloved Audie Murphy: *"Freedom flies in your heart like an eagle/Let it soar with the winds high above/Among the spirits of soldiers now sleeping/Guard it with care, and with love..."*

In guiding Martha Carson through her paces for her first album in two decades, Turner was very considerate of her concerns at recording again, and realized there had been many technical innovations made in the interim, all unfamiliar to her.

Although still a smoker, Carson's voice was in amazingly good shape for the session. Turner encouraged her to help select the numbers to be recorded, including her signature song "Satisfied."

She was especially amazed at the results achieved with "Dip Your Fingers in the Water," which she had recorded a number of time before: "I think this is the best rendition I've ever got on that song."

Tony Graham's high-pitched vocals enhanced Carson's performance on the touching hymn "Bells of the Chapel," and he matched her phrasing precisely during their haunting duet on his composition "Show Me the Way," resulting in some hair-raising harmony by this dynamic new twosome. Other numbers include "I Feel It In My Soul," "Higher Power," "Amazing Grace," "Swing Down, Sweet Chariot" and "Let Your Light Shine On Me."

Having worked previously with A-Team musicians (who helped create the *Nashville Sound)* Bradley and Harman, Martha was well-aware of their reputation as two of the most-recorded musicians in the world, but was pleasantly surprised by Thom Bresh's amazing dexterity on the strings. Acknowledged now as the son of the late Hall of Famer Merle Travis, Bresh in his own right had scored a Top 10 single with "Home Made Love" in 1976, and his 1982 duet, "When It Comes to Love," with Lane Brody (she of the #1 duet "Yellow Rose" with Johnny Lee) received critical kudos.

Jack Daniels, of course, was a member of the hit-making group Highway 101 (which also featured Cliffie Stone's son Curtis), acclaimed for "The Bed You Made For Me," "Somewhere Tonight" and "Walkin', Talkin', Cryin', Barely Beatin' Broken Heart" (co-written by Carson pal Justin Tubb and Roger Miller) singles.

The Turner-produced collection represents one of Carson's finest efforts and would qualify as a great valedictory album for gospel music's pioneering artist.

"It was a great birthday present," beams Martha, referring to the time the session was held, near her's, to be precise. " I love it! I'll say a little prayer that maybe someday people will get to hear it."

Word must have gotten out about Carson recording again, because she was invited to sing a number for a Christmas CD, featuring other veteran artists such as Bobby Bare, Stu Phillips and her former touring buddy, Bill Carlisle. Carson found herself at the session recording a seasonal hymn she wrote, "Peace On Earth (At Christmas Time)," for Greg Hudgins, a Hendersonville, Tenn. producer, in Oak Ridge Studios, Sept. 11, 1997.

"I was told they're going to sell the album on the gospel network," she says, smiling.

The following year - September 1998 - Martha did a favor for Del Reeves by performing at his annual Hometown Reunion Benefit in Sparta, N.C. "It was fun..."

A short time later, her one-time sister-in-law Tammy Wynette was posthumously inducted into the Country Music

Hall of Fame, during the annual fall CMA awards telecast. (By then, her death, five months earlier at age 55, was already sparking controversy in the national news media.)

Martha's continued to accept invitations to perform here and there. Early in 1999, Reverend Larry Black, a former WSM DJ, invited Martha to appear on camera (Jan. 27) for a gospel-country *Homecoming* video, being hosted by the Opry's Bill Anderson.

There was no scripting, no cue cards and no general plan, it was just a "spontaneous" reunion of veteran artists, with Anderson as sort of a Ringmaster. For this telemarketing project, Black's idea was to document the songs and stories of 29 all-time greats from the Golden era of country in an informal setting for posterity's sake.

"They deserve to be honored," insists the very congenial Black, who worked long and hard to bring his video venture to fruitation, just the way he envisioned it, natural and aglow with spontaneity, not unlike the popular Bill Gaither-produced Gospel Reunion series in which he had assisted earlier. "When I talked to each of the artists, who agreed to participate, I said, 'I want you to be prepared to sing your signature song and a gospel classic,' that was all."

Looking around at familiar faces, Carson was pleased to see such survivors as Bill Carlisle, Kitty Wells, Hank Locklin, Charlie Louvin, Jim Ed Brown, Wanda Jackson, Billy Walker, Jimmy C. Newman, Margo Smith, Jack Greene, Stu Phillips, Charlie Walker and Bobby Lord. After she sang her signature song "Satisfied," her peers stood as one to give Martha a rousing standing ovation, acknowledging she still had the touch. "Believe me, it was a thrill!"

Then the following month, on Feb. 14, 1999, she hosted the St. Valentine's segment of WSM's long-running *Midnight Jamboree* at the Ernest Tubb Troubadour Theatre, utilizing Del Reeve's Goodtime Charlies band, and sharing the mic with another friend Johnny Russell, who hustled over from the Opry. It felt good to be back in the circle.

(Turnabout's fair play. When Del hosted the July 30, 2000 edition of *Midnight Jamboree*, Martha agreed to guest star, backed again by his Goodtime Charlies, but this time also accompanied by talented pianist Ronnie Dale, heard almost nightly playing in the fabled Nashville Palace on Music Valley Drive.)

Mention of Johnny Russell reminds Martha she appeared in a 1966 low-budget Ron Ormond movie, filmed in Nashville, with him, Ralph Emery, Gordon Terry, Kitty and Smiley Wilson, daughter Rita Faye, her husband Earl (Snake) Richards, Walter Haynes, Rachel Roman and Tim Ormond, titled "Girl From Tobacco Row."

"It was completed, but I don't think it had much distribution," says Martha, who notes, "I sung one song in it. That was all I did. There was one other movie I did here later, with *('Bonanza's')* Lorne Greene, who sure was a nice person. I remember he was in character and I did a scene with him on a riverboat, which was docked at the lower end of Broad. But I can't recall the film's title. I didn't sing in it though."

While she doesn't live in a time warp - like some from bygone days - Martha Carson watches how she dresses, when stepping across her threshold, aware that out there, even at a department store, she might run across a die-hard fan, who's paid hard-earned money for a record or to attend a concert she's headlined. Not wanting to disillusion them, she carries herself like a star, while remaining approachable.

She has a new CD and cassette album "The Gospel Truth" ready for fans, boasting a collection of songs such as "It Takes a Lot of Livin'," "Joy, Joy, Joy," "That's Life" and "Bells of the Chapel." This 2000 MC indie release is available through her new web-site: www.marthacarson.tripod.com.

Yes, Martha Carson still has her dreams -- one of which is to perform abroad.

"I've never been overseas. X used to book Chet, Boots and Floyd over there, but he never would put me on (the bill). At one time, Scotty (Turner) had talked about a tour (in England)...I know George Hamilton (IV) and Billie Jo Spears appear a lot over there. This I would still like to do. I have a tape, recorded 'live' of Johnnie Ray, performing at the Palladium in London, and the people just loved it when he sang 'I'm Gonna Walk and Talk With My Lord.' If they enjoyed him singing my song, why wouldn't they enjoy hearing me sing it? I'd love to give it a try!"

Martha's a long-standing member of the Nashville Association of Musicians, AFM's Local 257, the Union headquartered in Nashville.

Current 257 President Harold R. Bradley, who is also Vice President for the American Federation of Musicians' (AFM) International headquarters, has a great deal of respect for Martha's musical talents. The younger brother of the late Hall of Famer Owen Bradley, is himself the most recorded studio guitarist in the world.

Bradley sums up her talents: "Martha Carson is not only a great vocal stylist, she is a wonderful songwriter. All her records are on fire with her energy. Martha Carson's flamboyant, hard-driving style of performing upbeat gospel, combined with spirited vocals and rhythmic playing of riffs and simple chords, pre-dated the rockabilly hybrid sound that set the stage for rock 'n' roll. Without a doubt, she was an influential and innovative artist in any field, and Martha is my favorite country gospel artist!!"

Walt Trott

Walt Trott

• DISCOGRAPHY •

James & Martha Roberts - White Church Records
He Will Set Your Fields On Fire/I Ain't Got Time, 1947
Budded On Earth (ToBloom in Heaven)/The Man of Galilee, 1947
The Sweetest Gift (A Mother's Smile)/ When He Heard My Plea, 1947
Got a Little Light/There's An Open Door Waiting For Me, 1947

James & Martha Carson - Capitol Records
I Ain't Got Time/When God Dips His Pen, March 1949
I'll Shout and Shine/Budded On Earth, March 1949
Living in the Promised Land/Don't Sell Him Another Drink, March 1949
Looking For a City/King Jesus (Spoke To Me), August 1949
When Mother Read the Bible/Where Could I Go, August 1949 (Unissued)
Crossing Over Jordan/When I Reach That City, December 1949
Filled With Glory Devine/Heaven's Jubilee, December 1949
I Feel Like Shouting, June 1950 (Unissued)
Got a Little Light, June 1950 (Issued Sept. 17, 1951, with Salvation Has Been Brought Down)
He Will Set Your Fields On Fire/Man of Galilee, June 1950
We Will Rise and Shine/I'll Fly Away, June 1950
I Ain't Gonna Sin No More/Lay Your Burdens At His Feet, September 1951
Shining City/I'm Gonna Sing, Sing, Sing, September 1951
Old Country Church, September 1951 (Unissued)

Amber Sisters - Capitol Records
Lonesome Road/When I Want Lovin' Baby, November 1952
I've Waited Too Long/One More Time, February 1953
Cherokee Eyes/Useless, July 1953

Look What Followed Me Home/Tired of Your Runnin' Around, November 1953

Minnie, Marthie & Mattie - King Records
You Can Dish It Out (But You Can't Take It) - November 1951 (Unissued)
You Can't Live With 'Em/Tennessee Memories, November 1951

• Solo Artist •

RICH'R TONE Records, Champs Studio, Johnson City, Tenn.
I Want To Rest/Lookin' This Way, #1031-A & B, September 1951
(Note: The A side featured only Martha Carson's vocals; while the B side, written by Bill Carlisle, was a duet featuring Carlisle and Carson on vocals.)

Martha Carson - Capitol Records
Satisfied/Hide Me Rock of Ages, December 1951
You Sure Do Need Him Now/Weighed in the Balance, February 1952
I Wanna Rest/Old Blind Barnabus, May 1952
I'm Gonna Walk and Talk With My Lord/Beyond the Shadow, July 1952
Cryin' Holy Unto the Lord/Fear Not, October 1952
There's a Higher Power/Inspiration From Above, January 1953
I Feel It In My Soul/Ask, You Shall Receive, May 1953
Singin' On the Other Side/I've Got a Better Place To Go, October 1953
Lazarus/Bye and Bye, February 1954
I Bowed Down/He'll Part the Water, May 1954
Peace On Earth/Christmas Time is Here, November 1954
Counting My Blessings/It's Alright, December 1954

Martha Carson - RCA Records
I've Got So Many Million Years/Lord I Can't Come Now (w/Stuart Hamblen), 1955
Laugh a Little More/Let the Light Shine On Me, 1955
David and Goliath/I Wanna Rest a Little While, 1956
Dixieland Roll/Music Drives Me Crazy, 1956
All These Things/Faith Is In the Sky, 1956
Get That Golden Key/He Was There, 1956
Satisfied/Let the Light Shine On Me, 1957
Now, Stop/Just Whistle or Call, 1957
Get On Board Little Children
Let's Talk About That Old Time Religion
Rock-A My Soul
Be Not Discouraged
I'm Gonna Walk and Talk With My Lord
This Old House
Saints and Chariots
OK, Amen/Battle Hymn of The Republic
The Heavenly Road
He'll Understand and Say Well Done
I'm a Pilgrim
A Satisfied Mind
Swing Down, Sweet Chariot

Martha Carson - Cadence Records
Light of Love/That Ain't Right, 1959

Martha Carson - Capitol Records
High On the Hill/Everything's Alright, September 1960

Martha Carson - Dot Records
Right Now, Right Now/Things Happen For the Best, 1961

Martha Carson - Sims Records
Everybody Needs Somebody/It Takes a Lot of Livin' - Single released in 1963
Great Big Mountain
Good, Good Feeling
Somebody Told Me
Just Around the Bend

I've Got a Friend
That's Life
Joy, Joy, Joy
Bells of the Chapel
Walkin' in the Garden
Real Life

Martha Carson - Scripture Records
This Old House
Swing Lo, Sweet Chariot
Lonesome Valley
We'll Understand It Better
Ezekiel Saw the Wheel
Crying Holy to the Lord
Do Lord
He'll Understand and Say Well Done
That Lonesome Road
Just a Closer Walk With Thee
Shout and Shine
I'll Fly Away - 1964

Martha Carson - Starday/Gusto Records
Satisfied
Jesus Said
The Patience of Job
Dip Your Fingers in Some Water
I'm Gonna Walk and Talk With My Lord
Old Blind Barnabus
God's Unchanging Hand
On Top of the Mountain
Two White Wings
Singing On the Other Side
Faith
Valley of Prayer 1978

• Albums •

EPs
    Journey to the Sky, RCA EPA-674, 1955
    Journey to the Sky, RCA EPB-1145 (double EP), 1955

Albums
    Journey to the Sky, RCA LPM-1145, 1956
    Rock-A My Soul, RCA LPM-1490, 1957
    Satisfied, Capitol T-1507, 1960
    A Talk With the Lord, Capitol ST-1607, 1962
    Martha Carson, Sims LP-109, 1963
    This Old House, Scripture M-111, 1964
    Martha Carson Sings, Camden CAL-906e, 1965
    Country Girls (multiple artists), RCA (CAS 2403) 1970 (A Satisfied Mind)
    Martha Carson's Greatest Gospel Hits, Starday SD-997, 1978
    Martha Carson Explodes…, Bear Family Records BFX-15215, 1986
    Martha Carson's Greatest Gospel Hits, Hollywood HT-231, 1988
    The Gospel Truth, MC Records (a reprise of the Sims album), 2000

Walt Trott

Walt Trott

CHAPTER INDEX

P.S. The following appear in this Martha Carson biography, for whatever reasons. Due to deadline pressure, we didn't produce the usual index; however, we're showing you who appears in each chapter:

Abner, Buford , 8
Acock, Earl, 22
Acuff, Roy, 2, 9, 12, 13, 14, 16, 23, 28, 29
Acuff, Mildred, 12
Adams, Matt (Ky. String-Ticklers), 6
Adams, Nick, 14
Akeman, David (Stringbean), 6
Alexander, Van (Orchestra), 19
Allen, Rex, 2, 7, 20, 23
Allen, Rosalie, 2, 12
Allen, Steve, 22
Alpert, Herb, 30
Amber Sisters (Martha, Mattie & Minnie), 13, 15, 17
Amburgey, Alfred, 4
Amburgey, Allison, 26
Amburgey, Bertha (Minnie Woodruff Garcia), 1,4,5,6,8,10,11,12,15, -17,18,21,25-29
Amburgey, Beth, 26
Amburgey, Cindy, 29
Amburgey, Conley, 4, 25, 28, 29
Amburgey, Connie, 29
Amburgey, Daniel, 5, 24
Amburgey, David, 5, 29
Amburgey, Denny, 29
Amburgey, Diana, 4
Amburgey, Donna Kaye (Chapel), 25, 26
Amburgey, Elizabeth (Grandma Betty), 4
Amburgey, Gary, 26

Amburgey, Gertrude (Quillen, Ramsey), 3,4,5,9,10,26,29
Amburgey, Glenn, 4, 24, 25, 29
Amburgey, Gobie, 26
Amburgey, Irene (Martha Carson , Roberts, Cosse) 1-30
Amburgey, John, 4
Amburgey, Kathleen, 25,26
Amburgey, Lawrence, 4
Amburgey, Lloyd (Don Chapel), 4,10,22,25,26,28
Amburgey, Marguerite, 4
Amburgey, Mike, 26
Amburgey, Minnie, 4
Amburgey, Opal (Mattie O'Neal, Jean Chapel, Holmes, Calongne), 1,4,5,6,8,10-15,20,21,24,25,26, 28,29
Amburgey, Pamela, 29
Amburgey, Patti, 29
Amburgey, Paula, 29
Amburgey, Riley, 4
Amburgey, Robbie, 26
Amburgey, Robert H., 4, 5, 6,10,24
Amburgey, Sharon, 29
Amburgey, Vina, 4
Amburgey, Wiley, 4
Ames Brothers, 21
Amos 'n Andy, 5
Anderson, Bill, 7,17,23,24
Anderson, Doug, 26
Anderson, Liz, 25,28
Anderson, Lynn, 25
Anderson, Marian, 7
Anglin, Jack, 8
Anglin, Jim, 7
Anka, Paul, 24
Arkie the Ark. Woodchopper, 7
Armstrong, Louis, 3,21
Arnold, Eddy, 2,14,20,25,30
Art Van Damme Quintet, 19

Astaire, Fred, 20
Atchison, Tex (Prairie Ramblers), 11
Atkins, Chet, 9,12,13,15,16,17,19,20,22,25,27,28-30
Atkins, Leona (Johnson), 13,15
Atkins, Merle, 13
Austin, Bobby, 26
Austin, Gene, 6,19
Autry, Gene, 5,7,11,12,14,16
Bailes Brothers, 2
Bailes, Walter, 29
Bailey Brothers (Charlie & Danny), 9,12
Baja Marimba Band, 30
Baker, Bake, 21
Balchar, Bill, 21
Ball, Wilbur, 11
Ballard, Hank, 22
Bamford, A. V., 16
Bamford, Maxine, 16
Barber, Glenn, 24
Bare, Bobby, 30
Barnes, George, 20
Barnett, Bobby, 24
Bashful Brother Oswald (Pete Kirby), 1
Bate, Alcyon, 5, 7
Bate, Dr. Humphrey, 7
Battle, Bob, 27
Beatles, The, 28
Bee, Molly, 22
Behymer, Michael, 30
Belew, Carl, 25
Bennett, Blackie, 16, 18
Bentley, Mabel, 5
Benton, Brook, 30
Berle, Milton, 21
Bernie, Ben, 3
Bess, Big Jeff (Radio Cowboys), 17

Betsy the Bass Fiddler, 6
Beverly Hill-Billies, 20
Binyon, Claude, 14
Black, Bill, 14
Black, Clint, 17,22
Black, Larry (Reverend), 30
Blackwood Brothers, 20
Blackwood, R. W., 20
Blake, Dick, 20
Blake, Eubie, 3
Blakeman, Guy, 7
Blanchard, Lowell, 10-13,29
Bleyer, Archie, 22
Blom, Eric, 2
Blue Sky Boys (Bill & Earl Bolick), 8, 9
Blum, Harry, 24
Blum, Patricia, 24
Bolger, Ray, 21
Bond, Johnny, 16,23
Boone, Pat, 2,11
Boone, Debbie (Ferrer), 11
Boone, Shirley (Foley), 11
Bowen, Jimmy, 2,19
Bowman, Becky, 18
Bradley, Harold, 13,24,30
Bradley, Owen, 17,26,30
Bradshaw, Terry, 25
Brasfield, Rod, 14,21
Bratcher, Dwight, 8
Breast, Winifred (Winnie), 24
Brennan, Walter, 11,28
Bresh, Thom, 30
Brewer, Sue, 25
Brewer, Teresa, 30
Britt, Elton, 2,12
Brock, Blanche Kerr, 2

Brock, Virgil, 2
Brody, Lane, 30
Brooks, Garth, 2,17,19,22
Brown, Jim Ed, 1,20,25,30
Brown, Joe E., 5
Brown, Milton & The Brownies, 2
Browning, Gov. Gordon, 15
Browns, The (Bonnie, Jim Ed & Maxine), 1, 20
Brumley, Albert, 2,10
Bryant, Boudleaux, 7,8,22,30
Bryant, Felice, 8,30
Bryant, Jimmy, 22
Buck, Louie, 21
Buckle Busters, 11
Buetel, Jack, 19
Bufwack, Mary (Oermann), 29
Burlison, Paul, 23
Burnette, Dorsey, 23
Burnette, Johnny, 23
Burnette, Smiley, 7
Burns, Country Boy Eddie, 25
Burns, Jerry, 7
Burns, Jethro (Homer & Jethro), 13,20,24
Burns, Lois (Johnson), 13
Burr, Henry, 12
Buttram, Pat, 7
Butts, Ann, 29
Briley, Mayor Beverly, 27
Brinton, Larry, 26
Byrd, Billy, 20
Byrd, Euple, 25
Byrd, Gwen (Nicholas), 25,26
Byrd, Jackie (Daly), 1, 25,26
Byrd, Jerry, 13,15
Byrd, Tina (Jones), 25,26
Cagney, James, 30

Callahan Brothers, 2
Calloway, W. R., 11
Calongne, Alda, 25
Calongne, Jeffrey, 25
Campbell, Archie, 11-13
Campbell, Glen, 25
Campus Kids (Ken Nelson & Lee Gillette), 19
Cantor, Eddie, 4
Carlisle, Bill, 8-13,15,17,21,29,30
Carlisle, Bill Jr., 11
Carlisle, Cliff, 11,12
Carlisle, Shelia, 11
Carman, 2
Carpenter, Mary Chapin, 2,29
Carr, Vikki, 30
Carrier, Joseph (Cotton), 8,11
Carroll, Diahann, 21
Carroll Family Singers, 9
Carroll, Ronnie, 9
Carson, Fiddlin' John, 8
Carson, James (Roberts), 1,6-9,11,12,15,17,19,25,28,29
Carson, Jenny Lou (Lucille Overstake), 7,11,12,14,15
Carson, Martha (Marthie, Amburgey, Roberts, Cosse), 1-30
Carson, Rosa Lee (Moonshine Kate), 8
Carter Family, 2,8
Carter, June, 13,21
Carter, Mother Maybelle, 16
Carter Sisters, 13,16
Carter, Tom, 1
Carver, Cousin Emmy, 6
Carver, Will, 11
Cash, Johnny, 14,20,21,27,28
Cassell, Pete, 8
Cates, Joe, 22
Chance, Lightnin', 13,17,18
Chapel, Don (see Amburgey, Lloyd)

Chapel, Jean (see Opal Amburgey)
Chaplin, Charlie, 3
Chapman, Ceil, 21
Chapman, Steven Curtis, 2
Charles, Ray, 27,30
Charrise, Cyd, 22
Choate, Bessie, 12
Choates, Bill, 22
Circle 3 Ranch Gang, 15
Clark, Casey, 22
Clark, Old Joe, 7
Clark, Roy, 29,30
Clark, Terry, 7
Clement, Rep. Bob, 1,14
Clement, Gov. Frank G., 14
Clinch Mountain Clan, 11
Cline, Cousin Ezra (Lonesome Pine Fiddlers), 17
Cline, Patsy, 14,17,18,24,25
Clooney, Betty, 11
Clooney, George, 11
Clooney, Nick, 11
Clooney, Rosemary (Ferrer), 11,20,21,30
Clower, Jerry, 7
Coats, James, 2,9
Cobb, Gene, 7
Cochran, Hank, 25
Cody, Betty, 17
Coe, David Allan, 26
Cole, Nat (King), 2,19
Collie, Biff, 14
Collins (Kids), Larry & Lorrie, 23
Collins, Tommy, 19,23
Como, Perry, 21,25,27,28
Cooke, Sam, 2
Cooley, Spade, 8
Coon Creek Girls, 7,8

Cooper, George, 18
Cooper, Wilma Lee & Stoney, 2,11,12,13,15,17,21
Copas, Cowboy, 2,6,10,18,21
Cosse, Andre Michael, 22-24,27-29
Cosse, Benna, 27
Cosse, Clayton, 28
Cosse, Marie, 27
Cosse, Michelle Renee, 27
Cosse, Rene Paul, 1,21,23,24,27-29
Cosse, Xavier (X), 1,6,16-24, 27-30
Cosse, Donna (Walker), 16,28
Cosse, Sara, 16
Cosse, Trent, 16,28
Cramer, Floyd, 24,27-30
Craven, Vonetta, 16
Crickets, The, 30
Croce, Jim, 18
Crook Brothers, 5
Crosby, Bing, 3
Crosby, Bob, 19
Cumberland Mountain Folk, 15
Cutrer, T. Tommy, 1
Cy & Fannie, 7
Cyrus, Billy Ray, 29,30
Dailey, Dan, 14
Daily, Harold (Pappy), 25
Dale, Ronnie, 30
Dalhart, Vernon, 2,6
Damone, Vic, 27
Daniels, Jack, 30
D'Arezzo, Guido, 7
Davis, Chester, 11
Davis, Gov. Jimmie, 14,20
Davis Sisters (Skeeter & Betty Jack), 14,17,19
Davis, Beryl, 19
Davis, Betty Jack, 18,19

Davis, Doris, 22
Davis, Georgia, 17
Davis, Lynn, 6,10,15
Davis, Oscar, 16,22
Davis, Ralph, 22
Davis, Jr., Sammy, 23
Davis, Skeeter, 1,19,23,25
Day, Doris, 14,25
Dean, Eddie, 7,19,23
Dean, Jimmy, 2,11,21,22,25,30
Deason, Ellen Muriel (Kitty Wells), 12
Dee, Frankie, 25
Deen, Dixie (Hall), 17,26
DeHaven, Penny (Starr), 30
Delmore Brothers (Alton & Rabon), 5,8
Dempsey, Jack, 3
Denny, Jim, 13,15,16,19-21
Denver, John, 18
Desert Rose Band, 25
DeSylva, B.G. (Buddy), 9,19
Devine, Ottis, 12
DeWitt, Jack, 21,22
Dexter, Al, 14
DeZurik Sisters (Mary Jane & Carolyn), 7
Diamond, Neil, 14
Dickens, Jimmy, 8,15-18,21
Dietrich, Marlene, 11
Digby, Noel, 21
Dill, Danny & Annie Lou, 23
Dinning Sisters (Ginger, Lou & Jean), 15,19
Domino, Fats, 25
Dominoes, The, 2
Donohoe, Sam, 19
Dorsey, Thomas A., 2
Dressler, Marie, 5
Drifters. The, 2

Drifting Cowboys, 23
Drury, Margie Cosse, 28
Drusky, Roy, 2,24
Duff, Arlie, 25
Dunn, Holly, 17
Duncan, Johnny, 25
Durham, Buddy, 7
Dyer, Delbert, 9
Dylan, Bob, 27
Eckler Pop & His Young'uns, 8
Edwards, Joe, 1,20,22
Edwards, Olive, 20
Edwards, Ralph, 20
Elizabeth (Queen), 7
Emery, Ralph, 28,30
Emmons, Buddy, 22,25
Ephron, Henry, 14
Ephron, Nora, 14
Etting, Ruth, 3,12
Everly Brothers (Don & Phil), 8,17,22
Exile (J.P. Pennington), 7
Fairbanks, Douglas, 3
Fairchild, Barbara, 2
Faye, Alice, 22
Ferguson, Bob, 2
Ferrer, Gabriel, 11
Ferrer, Jose,11
Fiddlin' Kate, 23
Fiddlin' Linvilles (Charlie & Mrs.), 6
Fisher, Eddie, 30
Fisher, Pete, 22
Fitzgerald, Ella, 19
Fitzgerald, F. Scott, 3
Flatt, Lester (& Earl Scruggs & Foggy Mtn. Boys), 12
Fleming, Rhonda, 19
Florida Boys, 20

Foggy Mountain Boys, 8
Foley, Red, 1,7,11,13,16,19-21,24,25
Foley, Vern (Cotton), 7,16
Foley, Sally, 21
Ford, Al, 23
Ford, Mary (& Les Paul), 13,19,30
Ford, Tennessee Ernie, 2,16,17,19,20,22,29
Ford, Whitey (Duke of Paducah), 7,16,21
Foree, Mel, 12
Forrester, Howdy, 5
Foster, Fred, 19,26
Foster, Stephen, 2
Fotine, Larry, 2
Fountain, Pete, 21,26
Fowler, Wally, 16,18,20
Fox, Curly (& Texas Ruby), 6
Fox, Harry, 29
Francis, Arlene, 22
Francis, Connie, 25,27
Frank, Dick, 30
Frank, J. L., 10,16
Franklin, Aretha, 2
Frazier, Dallas, 25
Freberg, Stan, 19
Fredericks, Mildred, 9
Freed, Alan, 21
Freeman, Stan, 11
Freud, Sigmund, 3
Frizzell, David, 30
Frizzell, Lefty, 7,14,19,21,23
Fruit Jar Drinkers, 5
Fry, Theodore, 2
Gabbard, Ralph, 7
Gabriel, Ethel, 24
Gaines, Roland, 7
Gaither, Bill, 2,30

Gaither, Danny, 2
Gaither, Gloria, 2
Gallico, Al, 25
Gallion, Bob, 25
Gannaway, Al, 1,21
Garcia, Bob, 28
Garcia, Minnie (see Bertha Amburgey)
Garner, Mrs. John Nance, 7
Gaynor, Mitzi, 14
Gentry, Bobbie, 26
George VI (King), 7
Gibbs, Georgia, 22
Gibson, Don, 7,10,12,25
Gilbert, John, 3
Gill, Vince, 22
Gillette, Lee, 9,19
Gilmore, Voyal, 19
Girls of the Golden West (Dolly & Milly Good), 7
Gish, Lillian, 3
Glaser Brothers (Chuck, Tompall & Jim), 24
Gleason, Jackie, 22
Gobel, George, 7
Godfrey, Arthur, 20,21
Goodtime Charlies, 28,30
Goodman, Benny, 3,19
Goodman, Happy, 22
Goodman, Rusty, 22
Goodman, Vestal, 26
Goodson, Hal, 30
Gordon, Ralph, 26,30
Gore, Al Jr. (Vice President), 1
Graham, Billy, 13
Graham, Tony, 30
Grant, Amy, 2
Gray, Billy, 13
Gray, Claude, 2,21

Gray, Otto (Okla. Cowboys), 16
Greene, Jack, 17,25,30
Greene, Lorne, 30
Griffith, Andy, 22
Griffith, Rex, 8
Grizzard, Ted, 6
Guitar, Bonnie, 25,30
Guralnick, Peter, 29
Haggard, Merle, 19,25
Haines, Connie, 19
Hale, Georgia, 6
Hall, Tom T., 6, 26
Hamblen, Stuart, 1,2,11,19,20,24,29
Hamblen, Suzy, 20
Hamilton IV, George, 30
Hamilton, Roy, 21
Hancock, Herbie, 25
Handy, W. C., 2
Hardy, Uncle Bob, 20
Harman, Buddy, 17,22,24,30
Harper, Granny, 7,8
Harris, Emmylou, 9
Harris, Marion, 3.12
Hart, Freddie, 1,23
Hawkins, Hawkshaw, 18,21
Hawkins, Willard, 4
Hay, George D., 7
Haymes, Dick, 25
Haynes, Homer (& Jethro), 7,12,20,24
Haynes, Walter, 30
Haywood, Miss (Cosse children's Nanny), 24,27
Hefti, Neal, 20
Heidt, Horace, 11
Held, John Jr., 3
Helmer, Margaret, 17
Helms, Bobby, 20,24

Helms, Don, 23,24
Henderson, Skitch, 22
Hendricks, Scott, 19
Hendrix, Jimi, 27
Henson, Cousin Herb, 23
Herring, Fiddlin' Red, 10
Highway 101, 30
Hill, Faith, 14
Hill, Goldie, 14,17,21,25
Hill, Smilin' Eddy, 27
Hines, Stuart K., 2
Hitchcock, Stan, 25
Hobbes, Charlie, 7
Holly, Buddy, 18,30
Holmes, Salty (Floyd, Prairie Ramblers), 1,7,11-13,15,20,21,25
Hoosier Hotshots, 7
Hoosier Kids, 20
Hoot Owl Holler Girls (Marthie,Mattie, Minnie), 1, 8
Hoover, Herbert (President), 4
Hopgood, Helen Neal, 19
Horton, Johnny, 18
Houser, Hazel, 2
Houston, David, 25,26
Howard, Harlan, 7,25
Howard, Jan, 17
Hudgins, Greg, 30
Hughes, Glenn & Jean, 8
Hughes, Howard, 19
Hughes, Marvin, 13
Hughes, Ricca (Aunt Hattie), 7,8
Humperdinck, Engelbert, 25
Hurt, Chick (Prairie Ramblers), 11
Hutton, Betty, 19,20
Huskey, Junior, 17
Husky, Ferlin, 1,4,16-21,24
Huston, Walter, 19

Hutchinson, Josephine, 14
Hyatt, Walter, 18
Ingle, Red & The Natural Seven, 19
Inman, Autry, 16,24
Irby, James, 29
Isbell, Joe, 6
Jackson, Alan, 1,17,22
Jackson, George Pullen, 2
Jackson, Mahalia, 2,20
Jackson, Rachel (Mrs. Andrew Jackson), 21
Jackson, Stonewall, 17,24
Jackson, Tommy (and Mrs.), 13,15
Jackson, Wanda , 13,19,30
James, Sonny, 17,19,27
Jamup & Honey, 10
Jarrett, Ted, 20
Jean, Norma (Roma), 26,28
Jenkins, Casey, 27
Jenkins Family, 8
Jenkins, Floyd (Fred Rose), 12
Jenkins, Ray, 10
Jennings, Bob, 24
Jennings, Waylon, 25,30
Johnnie & Jack, 1,9,12,14,16,20-22
Johnson, Joe, 25
Johnson, Lois, 25
Johnson, Luther (Cousin), 5
Johnson, Lyndon B. (President), 27
Johnson, Timothy (Uncle), 4,5
Johnson, William, 7
Johnston, Jerry Ray, 17,22
Jolson, Al, 3,14
Jones, George, 25,26,28
Jones, Georgette (Smith), 26
Jones, Grandpa, 1,11,17,21,22,29
Jones, Isham, 3

Jones Sisters (Julie & Judy), 9
Jones, Spike, 27
Jordanaires, The, 7,13,19,24,30
Jory, Myrna, 23
Judds, The 9
Kahn, Dick, 21
Karl & Harty, 7,8
Kennedy, Jerry, 26
Kenton, Stan, 19
Kentucky HeadHunters, 29
Kern, Jerome, 3
Kerr, Anita (Singers), 2,19
Kessel, Sid, 5
Kidwell, Harpo, 8
Kilgallen, Dorothy, 14
Killen, Buddy, 7
Kilpatrick, Dee (Walter), 9-12,15,17,1921,22
Kimball, Harrison (Chick), 8,9,10
Kincaid, Bradley, 7
King, Pee Wee, 10,12,14,16,19
King, W. L. MacKenzie, 7
Kirby, Fred, 11
Kirkham, Doug, 22
Kirkham, Millie, 22,24
Knapp, Roy (Percussion School), 17
Knight, Jack, 3
Kohler, Esther (Violet), 7
Kolb, Lana (Holmes), 11,12,25,28,29
Kolb, Mark, 25
Krise, Speedy, 10
Kristofferson, Kris, 2,7,25
Krupa, Gene, 17
Ladd, Alan, 30
Lair, Isabelle Coffey, 7
Lair, John (Cumberland Ridge Runners), 7-10,16
Lair, Thomas Burke, 7

Lamb, Charlie, 10,19,21,25
Lane, Cristy, 2
Lange, Evelyn (Daisy, 7
LaRosa, Julius, 21
Lavender, Shorty, 24
Ledford, Coy, 7
Ledford, Custer, 7
Ledford, Daw, 7
Ledford, Lily May (Pennington), 7,8,25
Ledford, Minnie (Black-Eyed Susan), 7
Ledford, Rose, 7
Lee, Buddy, 27
Lee, Brenda, 1,17,27
Lee County Boys, 6
Lee, Johnny, 30
Lee, Peggy, 19
LeFevres, The, 20
Levy, Bruce, 26
Lewis, Jerry Lee, 14,21,25
Lewis, Rudy, 22
Lewis, Ted, 3
Lightfoot, Gordon, 25
Lillie, Margaret (Aunt Ida), 7,8
Lilly Brothers (Burt & Everett), 2
Linke, Richard O., 22
Linneman, Billy, 30
Linville, Charlie sse Fiddlin' Linvilles
Little Clifford, 7
Little Ella, 7
Little Richard, 14
Locklin, Hank, 25,30
Logan, Betty, 10
Logan, Jane, 8
Lombardo, Guy, 3,19
Londin, Larrie, 27
Long, Hubert, 25

Long, Jimmie, 12
Lonzo & Oscar, 1, 16,19, 24
Lord, Bobby, 30
Lou, Bonnie, 17
Loudermilk, John, 7
Louvin Brothers (Charlie & Ira), 2,10,12,19,21,27
Louvin, Charlie, 23,30
Louvin, Ira, 18
Lucas, B., 7
Luman, Bob, 25
Lum 'n Abner, 5
Lunn, Robert, 5
Luther, Martin, 2
Lyles, Bill, 20
Lynn, Judy, 25
Lynn, Loretta, 2,4,6,14,17,24,27
Lynyrd Skynyrd, 18
Lytle, Moe, 27
Mac & Bob, 8
Mack, Bobby, 25
Mack, Ted, 23
Macon, Dave (Uncle), 5-7
Macon, Dorris, 5
MacRae, Gordon, 19
Maddox Bros. & Rose, 2,16
Maddox, Rose, 19
Magaziner, Wallace, 24
Main, Marjorie, 8
Maphis, Joe & Rose Lee, 16
Mainer, J. E. (Mountaineers), 8
Mandrell, Barbara, 1,26,30
Maple City Four, 7
Marcum, Ralph, 7
Marlin, Sleepy, 7
Marsh, Dr. Wallis, 26
Martin, Asa, 6,8

Martin, Benny, 11
Martin, Bob, 16
Martin, Dean, 19,20,25,27,29,30
Martin, Deana, 25
Martin, Eliza, 6
Martin, Geneva, 6
Martin, Grady, 24
Martin, Tony, 22
Martin, Troy, 19
Martino, Al, 25
Martindale, Wink, 23
Mason, Rep. Paul (Ky.), 1
Massey, Guy, 2
Massey, Louise, 7
Masters Family (Johnny, Lucille, Owen), 10
Matthews, Vince, 25
McCall, Bill,25
McCormick, George, 17,18,22
McCoy, Charlie, 25
McCrea, Joel, 11
McEuen, Brad, 20
McFadden, Jack, 30
McGee, Sam & Kirk, 5
McEntire, Reba, 18,22
McIntire, John, 14
McMichen, Clayton, 6,7
McPhatter, Clyde, 1,2,22
Mercer, Johnny, 9,19
Merck, Rev. Brother, 9
Merman, Ethel, 14
Meyers, Paul (Country Harmonica Boys), 11
Millar, Bunny, 21
Miller, Bob, 11
Miller, Glenn (Orchestra), 19
Miller, Jody, 26,30
Miller, Marilyn, 3

Miller, Mitch, 20
Miller, Roger, 25,30
Miller, Scott, 1
Mitchell, Guy, 30
Mitchell, Priscilla (Hubbard), 24
Mitchell, Thomas, 19
Mize, Billy, 23
Mobley, Pleaz, 7
Monash, Paul, 14
Monroe, Bill, 9,16,17,21,29
Monroe Brothers (Charlie & Bill), 8
Monroe, Marilyn, 14
Monroe, Vaughn, 21
Montana, Patsy (& Prairie Ramblers), 7,11,14,20,29
Montgomery, Melba, 25,28
Mooney, Don, 27
Moonlight Ramblers, 15
Moore, Bob, 24
Moore, Garry, 22
Moore, Lee & Juanita, 15
Moore, Scotty, 14,19
More, Frankie, 22
Morgan, George, 14,16,21,25,26
Morgan, Jaye P., 22
Morgan, Lorrie, 29
Morris, Ed, 28
Morrison, Marilyn, 14
Morse, Ella Mae, 19
Moss, Jerry, 30
Mullican, Moon, 17,21
Murphy, Audie, 30
Murray, Anne, 17,25
Murray, Lyn (Orchestra), 19
Muse, Ownie, 6
Myerson, Bess, 22
Nathan, Syd, 11,15

Neal, Bob, 19,20
Nelson, Ken, 9,13,15-17,19,23,30
Nelson, Ricky, 18,23
Newman, Jimmy C., 21,30
Newton, Ernie, 13
Newton, John, 2
Nichols, Red, 3
Nilsson, Harry, 30
Nixon, Richard (President), 27
Norwood Hoedowners, 7
Null, Cecil, 17
Nunn, Gilmore, 6
Oak Ridge Boys, 2
O'Brian, Hugh, 22
O'Brien, Edmond, 14
O'Connell, Helen, 19
O'Connor, Donald, 14
O'Day, Molly (Mountain Fern, LaVerne Williamson), 2,6,8,10,12,15,21
Oermann, Bob, 28,29
Oliver, 30
Oliver, King, 3
O'Neal, Mattie, see Opal Amburgey
Orbison, Roy, 21
Ormond, Ron, 30
Ormond, Tim, 30
Orr, Jay, 22
Osborne Brothers (Bobby & Sonny), 7,12,30
Oscar see Lonzo & Oscar
Oswald, Brother (Pete Kirby), 1
Outler, Johnny, 10
Overstake, Eva (3 Little Maids), 11
Overstake, Evelyn (3 Little Maids), 11
Overstake, Lucille, see Jenny Lou Carson
Overstreet, Paul, 2
Overstreet, Tommy, 25

Owens, Buck, 19,27,30
Oxford, Vernon, 12
Page, Patti, 19
Panhandle Punchers, 11
Parker, Dr. Douglas, Jr., 29
Parker, Douglas Sr., 29
Parker, Linda, 7,8
Parker, Col. Tom, 14,16,20
Parman, Cliff, 24
Parton, Dolly, 12,17,26
Patti, Sandy, 2
Paul, Les & Mary Ford, 13,19,30
Paycheck, Johnny, 25,26
Payne, Leon, 2
Pearl, Minnie, 13,14,16,21,29
Pellettieri, Vito, 16
Pennington, Glenn, 7
Pennington, J. P., 7
Penny, Hank, 8,10,22
Penny, Joe, 24
Perkins, Carl, 14,21
Perkins, Ma, 5
Peter, Paul & Mary, 27
Peters, Brock, 20
Phillips, Bill, 30
Phillips, Sam, 1,14,21,26
Phillips, Stu, 25,30
Pickford, Mary, 3
Pied Pipers, 19
Pierce, Harry, 28
Pierce, Webb, 13,15-17,19-21,25
Pitney, Gene, 25,26
Possum Hunters, see Humphrey Bate
Prairie Ramblers see Salty Holmes, Chick Hurt, Tex Atchison, Jack Taylor
Pratt, Talmadge (& Nora), 5

Presley, Elvis, 1,2,14,17,19-22,26,29,30
Price, Ray, 14,16,21,23,24-26
Pride, Charley, 30
Pruett, Jeanne, 25
Pugh, William H., 25
Quigley, Pat, 19
Quillen, Bertha, 4
Quillen, Carrie (Vinters), 4
Quillen, Conley, 4
Quillen, Cosby (Johnson), 4
Quillen, Georgia (Ferrell), 4,29
Quillen, Gertrude see Amburgey
Quillen, Gladys (Yancey), 4,29
Quillen, Herbert, 4,6
Quillen, James (Uncle Jim), 4,16
Quillen, Mildred (Fields), 4,29
Quillen, Nora (Pratt), 4,5
Quillen Quartet, 4,6,7
Quillen, Richard, 4
Quillen, Victor, 4
Rager, Mose, 2
Raiders, The, 30
Rainwater, Marvin, 21
Ramsey, Edgar, 26
Ramsey, Gertrude see Amburgey
Rangers, The, 7,24
Rainey, Ma, 2
Rand, Sally, 6
Randolph, Boots, 24,27,28,30
Ray, Johnnie,1,14,17,19,22,30
Ray, Wade, 11
Rector, Red, 10
Reed, Jerry, 24
Reeves, Del, 1,17,28,30
Reeves, Ellen, 30
Reeves, Jim, 13,17,20,25

Reeves, Kari, 28
Reisman, Joe (Orchestra), 20
Reno, Don (& Red Smiley), 2
Rensch, J. Leonard, 8
Rey, Alvino (Orchestra), 11
Reynolds, Debbie, 30
Rhodes, Leon, 22
Rhodes, Speck, 1
Rhubard Red (Les Paul), 19
Rich, Charlie, 26
Richards, Jody (Ky. Speaker), 1
Richardson, Deidre (Richey), 26
Richardson, Dorothy (Tippitt), 26
Richardson, Kelly (Richey), 26
Richardson, George (Richey), 26
Richardson, Paul (Richey), 26
Richardson, Sheila (Hall), 26
Richardson, Sylvia (Richey), 26
Riddle, George, 11
Ritter, Tex, 1,9,11,14,16,19,23
Roark, Short-Buckle, 6
Robbins, Hargus (Pig), 24
Robbins, Marty, 16,17,26
Roberts, Anna F. (Risk), 6, 9
Roberts, Anna Mae, 6
Roberts, Anna Marie, 15
Roberts, Clevie, 6
Roberts, Curaleen, 6
Roberts, Doc Fiddlin' (Philip), 6,8
Roberts, Donald, 6
Roberts, Doris, 6
Roberts, James see James Carson
Roberts, Rosella, 6
Roberts, Sally (Fitzpatrick), 15
Roberts, Kenneth, 6
Roberts, Margaret Lucille, 6

Roberts, Martha see Carson
Roberts, Pearl (Arman), 11,15
Roberts, Philip Jr., 6
Roberts, Philip, 15
Roberts, Thomas, 6
Robertson, A. C. (Eck), 3
Robertson, Dale, 30
Robertson, Texas Jim, 11,12
Rockefeller, John D., 4
Rodgers, Jimmie C., 2,6,11
Rogers, Arnold, 7,28
Rogers County Cowboys, 15
Rogers, Roy, 14,25
Rogers, Kenny, 17,28
Rogers, Will, 5
Roman, Rachel, 30
Ronstadt, Linda, 9
Roosevelt, Eleanor (First Lady), 7
Roosevelt, Franklin D. (President), 4,7
Rose, Andrew & Annie, 12
Rose, Arthur, 6
Rose, Fred, 7,8,11-15,19,20
Rose, Wesley, 15
Rosenthal, Warren, 7
Russell, Andy, 19
Russell, Bill, 7
Russell, Della, 19
Russell, Jane, 15,19
Russell, Johnny, 30
Ruth, Babe, 3
Ryman, Capt. Tom, 13
Sanders, Ray, 25
Sands, Benny, 14
Sands, Tommy, 1,14,30
Sandusky, Sandy, 9,11
Sarie & Sally (Edna Wilson & Margaret Waters), 5

Satherley, Art (Uncle), 7
Savage, Mr., 6
Saxton, Bob, 28
Schlemmer, Paul, 18
Schneider, John, 29
Scinta, Mike, 27
Scruggs, Earl (& Lester Flatt), 6,12
Seely, Jeannie, 28
Seldom Scene, 9
Sellars, Marilyn, 2
Selvin, Ben, 3
Shangri-Las, The, 24
Shea, George Beverly, 2
Shelton Brothers, 8
Shelton, Ricky Van, 7
Shelton, Roscoe, 25
Shepard, Jean, 1,13,14,19,21,24,26,28,29
Sherrill, Billy, 25,26
Shilkret, Nat, 3
Sholes, Steve, 17,19,20
Shook, Jack (& His Mountaineers), 5
Shubert, Lee, 3
Siegel, Bugsy, 23
Silverstein, Shel, 25
Siman, Si, 15,21
Simmons, Vickie, 7
Simon, Joe, 25
Sims, Russell, 24
Sinatra, Frank, 23, 24,25
Sinatra, Nancy, 14,25
Sinks, Earl (Richards), 15,30
Sinks, Rita Faye (Wilson), 15,30
Skaggs, Ricky, 6
Skidmore, Morgan, 7
Skinner, Jimmy, 12
Slack, Freddie, 19

Slatts, Pappy, 8
Slaughter, Sheila, 26
Sloan, Marlene, 29
Smiley, Red (& Don Reno), 2
Smith, Bessie, 3
Smith, Carl, 12,14,16,17,19,20,21,25
Smith, Cal, 24
Smith, Connie, 1,2,7,24,25
Smith, Fred, 10
Smith, (Reverend) Guy, 2
Smith, Hal, 7
Smith, Jan, 26
Smith, Jack (Smilin'), 19,25
Smith, Kate, 5,20
Smith, Michael W., 2
Smith Sacred Singers, 8
Smith, Velma (Williams), 7
Snow, Hank, 11,15,16,19,20,25
Soul Stirrers, 2
Sovine, Red, 16,21
Spears, Billie Jo, 30
Stafford, Jo, 19
Stamper, Pete, 7
Stamphill, Ira, 2
Stanley Brothers (Carter & Ralph), 11,12
Stanton, Jim, 12
Stanwyck, Barbara, 11
Staple Singers, 26
Stapp, Jack, 13,17,21
Starr, Kay, 19,20,27
Starrett, Charles (Durango Kid), 11
Statesmen Quartet, 11
Statler Brothers, 2
Stewart, Eleanor, 11
Stewart, James, 26
Stewart, Redd, 14,15,19

Stewart, Wynn, 26
Stone, Cliffie, 22,30
Stone, Curtis, 30
Stone, Harry, 13
Stoneman, Roni, 29
Storer, Lester (Natchee the Indian), 6
Story, Carl, 10,11
Stowe, Harriet Beecher, 2
Strength, Texas Bill,20
Stripling, Chick, 8
Stuart, Marty, 1
Sue, Peggy, 25
Sullivan, Ed, 22
Sullivan, Oscar see Lonzo & Oscar)
Sunshine Boys (Doug & Marvin), 8,20
Sunshine Sisters (Bertha, Irene & Opal) see Amburgeys
Supremes, The, 24
Sutton, Glenn, 25
Swanee River Boys, 8
Swanson, Gloria, 3
Sweet Violet Boys (Prairie Ramblers), 11
Tall, Tom, 23
Tanner, Georgie, 9
Tanner, Gid (& The Skillet Lickers), 6,8
Tarleton & Darby, 8
Taylor, Dennis (Ky. Boys), 6
Taylor, Elizabeth, 30
Taylor, Jack (Prairie Rambler), 11
Taylor, Joe, 26
Texas Daisey , 13
Texas Ruby (& Curly Fox), 13
Texas Troubadours, 20
Temple, Shirley, 5
Terry, Gordon, 23,30
Tharp, Sister Rosetta, 20
Thawl, Willie, 11

Thomas, Danny, 14
Thompson, Hank, 11,14,16,19,20
Thompson, Uncle Jimmy, 7
Thompson, Sue, 8,11,22
Tillis, Pam, 29
Tillman, Floyd, 14,19
Tilton, Martha, 19
Tipton, Carl, 17
Tomlin, John Michael, 26
Torme, Mel, 19
Trader, Bill, 19
Travis, Merle, 2,13,16,19-21,23,30
Travis, Randy, 25
Tubert, Bob, 25
Tubb, Ernest, 11-14,16,20,24,25,29,30
Tubb, Justin, 21,30
Tucker, Sophie, 3,12
Tucker, Tanya, 26,29
Tunesmiths, The, 17
Tunzi, Joseph, 14
Turner, Big Joe, 25
Turner, Lana, 11
Turner, Scott (Turnbull), 1,14,29,30
Turner, Zeb, 12
Tuttle, Marilyn, 23
Tuttle, Wesley, 23
Twitty, Conway, 25
Tyler, T. Texas, 11
Uncle Henry's Ky. Mountaineers, 19
Upchurch, Mom, 20
Vallee, Rudy, 3
Van, Bobby, 16
Ventures, The, 27
Venuti, Joe, 19
Vera-Ellen, 22
Vincent, Gene, 19

Vinton, Bobby, 26
Wadsworth, Gladys, 17
Wagoner, Porter, 1,15,17,20,21,23-26
Wakely, Jimmy, 2,7,14,16,19
Walker, Billy, 15,30
Walker, Cas,12
Walker, Charlie, 26,30
Walker, Cindy, 14
Walker, Donna, see Cosse
Walker, Ray (Jordanaires), 24
Walker, William, 2
Wallace, Gov. George, 26
Wallace, Jerry, 25,30
Wallace, Sheila, 14
Waller, Fats, 20
Wallich, Glenn, 9,19
Walsh, Joe, 25
Ward, Billy, 2
Waterford, Bob, 15
Waugh, Irving, 21
Weavers, The, 11
Webb, Chick (Orchestra), 19
Weise, Richard, 28
Welk, Lawrence, 2,30
Weller, Freddie, 26
Wells, Kitty, 1,2,8,12,13,16,17,19,20,22,25,27-30
Wendell, E. W. (Bud), 2
Wesley, John, 2
West, Bill, 29
West, Dale, 29
West, Dottie, 18,27,29
West, Shelly, 30
West, Speedy, 22
Westergaard, Mr. (WNOX Manager), 12
Weston, Paul (Orchestra), 19
Whiteman, Paul (Orchestra), 3

Whitley, Ray, 12
Whiting, Margaret, 2,19
Whiting, Richard, 19
Whitman, Slim, 29,30
Wilburn Brothers (Doyle & Teddy), 20,23,24,27
Wilburn, Leslie, 24
Wilburn, Lester, 24
Willett, Slim, 23
Williams, Audrey, 15,17
Williams, Hank, 2,6,8,11-13,15-17,19,23,24
Williams, Hank Jr., 24
Williams, Leona, 1
Williams, Lillian (Stone), 15
Williams, Tex, 16,19
Willis Brothers (Guy, Skeeter & Vic), 21
Willis, Ginger, 23
Willis, Hal, 23
Wills, Bob, 2,14
Wilson, Edith (First Lady), 7
Wilson, Edna (Sarie & Sally), 8
Wilson, Floyd, 17
Wilson, Grace, 7
Wilson, Kitty, 15-17,24,27-30
Wilson, Norro, 25
Wilson, Smiley, 15-17,23,24,27,30
Wilson, Woodrow (President), 7
Winans, CeCe, 2
Winchester, Jesse, 26
Wiseman, Lulu Belle & Scotty, 7,8,14
Wiseman, Mac, 6-9,15,23
Wood, Del, 14,21,28
Woodall, Boots (& The Wranglers), 11
Woodruff, Bruce, 8
Woodruff, Charles (Ducky), 8,17,18,27
Woodruff, Kenneth, 5,8,24,25,29
Woodruff, Mike, 17,18,27,28

Woodruff, Sandra, 8,27
Woodruff, Shirley, 27
Woodruff, Wilbur (Curly), 10
Woods, Joe, 7
Wooley, Sheb, 27
Wright, Bobby, 25
Wright, J.B.F., 2
Wright, Johnny, 12,13,28
Wright, Ruby, 25
Wynette, Tammy ,1,25,26,30
Yates, Bucky, 6
Ybarra,Thomas Russell, 8
Young, Faron, 1,14,15,17,19,20,21,25
Zanuck, Dick, 14
Zanuck, Lili Gentle, 14
Ziegfeld, Florenz, 3,8,16

About The Author

Walt Trott, a Nashville-based journalist-historian, previously authored the ARSC award-winning "Johnnie & Jack Story," Bear Family, Hamburg, 1992; "Honky Tonk Angels," Nova/Nashville, 1993; and wrote 50 Who's Who entries for the Country Music foundation "Encyclopedia of Country Music," Oxford University Press, NY, 1998. A graduate of Westbrook University in Maine, he was a Marine Corps correspondent in the Vietnam War; and later, under the GI Bill, attended Tennessee State University, majoring in Communication Arts. Trott was a music writer for the *Portland Press Herald* in Maine; *The Capital Times*, Madison, WI; daily *European Stars & Stripes*, Darmstadt, Germany; New York's *Variety* weekly; and served as Editor of *Country Scene, Entertainment Express* and currently *The Nashville Musician*. Since 1990, he has contributed monthly news and columns to *Country Music News*, Ottawa, Canada; and *Country Music People* magazine in London, England.

Printed in the United States
2543